Southeast Asia and the Civil Society Gaze

As developing countries with recent histories of isolation and extreme poverty, followed by restoration and reform, both Cambodia and Vietnam have seen new opportunities and demands for non-state actors to engage in and manage the effects of rapid socio-economic transformation.

This book examines how in both countries, civil society actors and the state manage their relationship to one another in an environment that is continuously shaped and (re)constructed by changing legislation, collaboration and negotiation, advocacy and protest, and social control. Further, it explores the countries' divergent experiences whilst also uncovering the underlying basis and drivers of civil society activity that are shared by Cambodia and Vietnam. Crucially, this book engages with the contested nature of civil society and how it is socially constructed through research and development activities, by looking at contemporary discourses and manifestations of civil society in the two countries, including national and community-level organizations, associations, and networks that operate in a variety of sectors, such as gender, the environment and health.

Drawing on extensive fieldwork conducted in Cambodia and Vietnam, this book will be of huge interest to students and scholars of Southeast Asian studies, Southeast Asian politics, development studies and civil society.

Gabi Waibel, **Judith Ehlert** and **Hart N. Feuer** are all senior researchers at the Centre for Development Research (ZEF) at the University of Bonn, Germany.

Routledge studies on civil society in Asia
Series Editor: Mark Sidel
University of Wisconsin, USA

Routledge studies on civil society in Asia address the role of civil society, non-profit, philanthropic, NGO, religious and other organizations in their social context both in individual countries and in comparative perspective across East, Southeast and South Asia. Themes include defining the role and scope of civil society; relations between civil society and the state; NGOs in regional and country contexts; governance and accountability in civil society; civil society and religion; the political role of civil society; the role of foundations, religious philanthropy and other philanthropic organizations; business, philanthropy and civil society; ethnography of particular civil society, NGO, community-based or other organizations; transnational civil society organizations in Asia; the legal regulation of civil society; self-regulation and accountability; Asian diasporas and civil society; and resources and fundraising for civil society.

The series is edited by Mark Sidel, Professor of Law, University of Wisconsin, USA, who has served in program positions with the Ford Foundation in Beijing, Hanoi, Bangkok and New Delhi working on strengthening the nonprofit sector, philanthropy and civil society and has consulted widely in the region.

Southeast Asia and the Civil Society Gaze

Scoping a contested concept in Cambodia and Vietnam

Edited by Gabi Waibel, Judith Ehlert and Hart N. Feuer

Routledge
Taylor & Francis Group

LONDON AND NEW YORK

First published 2014 by Routledge

2 Park Square, Milton Park, Abingdon, Oxfordshire OX14 4RN
711 Third Avenue, New York, NY 10017

Routledge is an imprint of the Taylor & Francis Group, an informa business

First issued in paperback 2017

British Library Cataloguing in Publication Data
A catalogue record for this book is available from the British Library

Library of Congress Cataloging in Publication Data
Southeast Asia and the civil society gaze: scoping a contested concept in Cambodia and Vietnam/[edited by] Gabi Waibel, Judith Ehlert and Hart Feuer.
 pages cm. – (Routledge studies on civil society in Asia; 3)
 Includes bibliographical references and index.
 1. Civil society–Cambodia. 2. Civil society–Vietnam. 3. Non-governmental organizations–Cambodia. 4. Non-governmental organizations–Vietnam. 5. Social change–Cambodia. 6. Social change–Vietnam. I. Waibel, Gabi, editor of compilation. II. Ehlert, Judith, editor of compilation. III. Feuer, Hart, 1983– editor of compilation.
 HN700.3.A8S68 2013
 303.409596–dc23
                                                                    2013015797

ISBN: 978-0-415-70966-8 (hbk)
ISBN: 978-1-318-57921-7 (pbk)

Typeset in Times New Roman
by Wearset Ltd, Boldon, Tyne and Wear

Contents

15 Conclusion: the civil society gaze 253

HART N. FEUER, PHUONG LE TRONG AND JUDITH EHLERT

Figures

Tables

Contributors

Bach Tan Sinh is the Director of the Department of 'Science and Technology Human Resources Policy and Organization' of the National Institute for Science and Technology Policy and Strategy Studies (NISTPASS), Ministry of Science and Technology, Vietnam. He has more than 20 years of experience in policy analysis and governance, focusing on science, technology and the environment, as well as civil society development in Vietnam. Dr Sinh completed his PhD in Environmental Social Science at Aalborg University, Denmark, in 1998. Afterwards, he was awarded a Fulbright post-doctoral visiting scholarship at the University of California, Berkeley (1999–2000) and is currently a visiting lecturer at the Heller School for Social Policy and Management, Brandeis University (USA).

Benedikter, Simon is a senior researcher at the Center for Development Research (Zentrum für Entwicklungsforschung, ZEF), University of Bonn, Germany. Being permanently based in Can Tho City, Vietnam, since 2007, Simon has been engaged in a wide range of social science research on water resources management and governance. Simon holds an MA in Southeast Asian Studies, Economics and Vietnamese Language Studies from the University of Bonn (2006). His MA thesis critically explored tendencies of decentralization, grassroots participation and the role of civil society in post-renovation Vietnam. In 2013 he completed his PhD, which investigates the nexus of hydraulic engineering, environmental change and bureaucratic power in the Mekong Delta.

Bourdier, Frédéric is an anthropologist from the University of Bordeaux and currently works for the Research Institute for Development in France (IRD). He has lived in southern India, where he worked on medical anthropology. Between 1999–2003, he conducted research in the Brazilian Amazon on migration- and health-related issues while affiliated with the Museum Emilio Goeldi in Belém, Pará, Brazil. Since 2004 he has been in charge of two French-Cambodian programmes dealing with the policies and challenges of the extension of antiretroviral drugs in Cambodia. Currently he is in charge of an interdisciplinary research project on malaria in Southeast Asia.

Ehlert, Judith is a sociologist by training and holds a postdoc position at the Department of Development Studies (Institut für Internationale Entwicklung, IE), University of Vienna. Between 2011–2013 she was Senior Researcher at the Center for Development Research (Zentrum für Entwicklungsforschung, ZEF), University of Bonn, where she received her PhD in Development Research in 2011. Her thesis focused on flooding, environmental knowledge and agrarian change in the Mekong Delta, Vietnam. She wrote her MA thesis on decentralization and civil society in rural Cambodia (2007), and also conducted field research on this topic in Senegal (2004). Her current research focuses on socio-cultural food dynamics in Vietnam.

Feuer, Hart N. is a senior researcher at the Center for Development Research (Zentrum für Entwicklungsforschung, ZEF), focusing on ecological modernization, agrarian change and the development of higher education in post-conflict societies. He received a PhD in Agricultural Sociology from the University of Bonn, Germany (2012) and an MPhil in Development Studies at Oxford University (2008). As a Fulbright recipient, he conducted research on arid agriculture in Jordan while based at the Arava Institute for Environmental Studies (Israel, 2006). He has been a student of diverse topics in Cambodia, Germany and the Middle East since 2003.

Hiwasa, Ayako is an independent researcher and consultant working in various development sectors. She is committed to ethnographic praxis as the starting point for systemic change to overcome structural inequity. She has spent over four years working in Cambodia in various fields. She holds a masters' degree in international health (Erasmus Mundi) and an MSc in international cooperation policy from Ritsumeikan Asia Pacific University, Japan. She previously worked as a consultant for the World Bank, conducting social research in rural areas to improve household energy services, and worked to set up an office and launch a pilot project for a Japanese non-profit organization in Phnom Penh. Currently, she lives between Japan, the US and Cambodia.

Kim, Sedara has been a senior research fellow for over ten years at the Cambodia Development Resource Institute (CDRI) in Phnom Penh. He holds a PhD in Political Science/Development Studies from Gothenburg University, Sweden, entitled *Democracy in Action: Decentralization in Post-conflict Cambodia*. He received his MA in Socio-cultural Anthropology from Northern Illinois University, USA. He has published extensively on local politics, elections, decentralization and civil society in Cambodia, including 'Korob, Kaud, Klach: In Search of Agency in Rural Cambodia', in the *Journal of Southeast Asian Studies* (2006).

Le Thi Quy is Professor of Sociology and History, and Director of the Research Center for Gender and Development (RCGAD) at the Hanoi University for Social Science and Humanities. She obtained her Bachelor of History at Hanoi University, and her PhD, also in History, at the Academy of Sciences in the USSR. She has more than 30 years of experience working with research institutes, ministries, networks and development agencies all over the globe. Currently she is the President of the Network Empowering Women (NEW), and consultant of the National Committee on Social Issues. Her research interests centre around ethnic minority groups, trafficking in women and children, and violence against women and children. She was one of 1,000 Peace Women from around the world who were nominated for the Nobel Peace Prize in 2005.

Le Trong, Phuong is a sociologist working as a lecturer at the Department of Southeast Asian Studies, University of Bonn, Germany. His fields of study include cross-cultural communication, civil society, development issues in Southeast Asia, with a focus on modern Vietnam including society, culture, literature and language. He holds an MA in Sociology and Philosophy. Besides providing training courses for development experts working in Vietnam, he also has been publisher of a culture magazine in Vietnamese. Currently, he is working on the transition process in Myanmar.

Thim, Ly is a social science specialist at the Mekong River Commission Secretariat in Laos. He holds a masters' degree in Regional Development Planning from the joint University of Dortmund (Germany) and University of Philippines (2002), and a PhD in Development Studies from the University of Bonn, Germany (2010). His PhD research focused mainly on water resources planning in the Mekong Basin with an emphasis on conflict management along the Se San River in Vietnam and Cambodia.

Öjendal, Joakim is Professor in Peace and Development Research, with his primary institutional affiliation at the School of Global Studies, Gothenburg University, Sweden. He has extensive research experience in, and publications on, East and Southeast Asia, in particular Cambodia, spanning more than two decades. His research includes, inter alia, the fields of conflict management, democratization, decentralization, good governance and civil society. Recently he co-edited *Beyond Democracy in Cambodia* (NIAS Press, 2009) which reflects on the post-conflict reconstruction process in Cambodia. He is the author/editor of ten volumes and some 40 journal articles. Currently he is leading a research project on the long-term effects of peace building (see further www.joakimojendal.se).

Ou, Sivhuoch was a research fellow for six years (2008–13) at the Cambodia Development Resource Institute (CDRI), Phnom Penh. He holds an MA in International Relations from Waseda University, Tokyo, Japan. Currently he is a PhD student of Political Science at the University of Guelph, Ontario, Canada. He is the author and co-author of seven papers and book chapters on NGOs, civil society, state capacity, peace-building and local politics in Cambodia.

Pistor, Nora is a PhD student at the Center for Development Research (Zentrum für Entwicklungsforschung, ZEF) at the University of Bonn, Germany focusing on women and politics in Myanmar. She works as an independent consultant specializing in gender issues and development. She holds an MA in Political Sciences, focusing on development policy, international law, criminology and gender, from the faculties of Political Sciences and Law at the University of Freiburg (Germany). Her thesis analysed the impact of integrating gender issues in an IWRM (integrated water resources management) project in the central highlands of Mexico. Through work, consultancy assignments and research related to gender equality, women's rights and women's health in various development projects on four continents (Africa, Asia, Europe and America), she has gained significant practical experiences from the grassroots to the macro-political levels. Her fields of interest include interdisciplinary topics and cross-cutting development issues such as gender-based violence, the economics of human trafficking and gender in climate change.

Reis, Nadine is a researcher at the Institute for Social and Development Studies, Munich School of Philosophy (Germany). She is a specialist in development theory and politics, and the political and institutional dimensions of water management. She holds a PhD in Development Sociology from the University of Bonn, and a diploma in Geography, Sociology and Political Science from the Free University Berlin. Her doctoral thesis investigated policy practices in the domestic water supply sector in the Mekong Delta, Vietnam. In her diploma thesis she dealt with the political ecology of water resources management in Mexico. She is currently working on the nexus between water bureaucracies, organizational theory and the cultural dimensions of globalization.

Waibel, Gabi is a senior researcher at the Center for Development Research (Zentrum für Entwicklungsforschung, ZEF) at the University of Bonn, Germany. She holds a PhD in Social Sciences from the University of Bielefeld (Germany), a diploma in Sociology from the same university, as well as an MA in Human Resource Management (University of Kaiserslautern, Germany). Gabi has worked in academic, policy-making and development aid organizations, with a thematic focus on gender, civil society, natural resources management and organizational development. She has more than ten years research and work experience in sub-Saharan Africa. Since 2007 she has coordinated the ZEF's social science research in the Mekong Delta of Vietnam (www.wisdom.eoc.dlr.de).

Wells-Dang, Andrew is a researcher and practitioner on civil society, networks and governance, currently working as Team Leader for the Vietnam Advocacy Coalitions Support Program implemented by Oxfam. He holds a PhD in Political Science from the University of Birmingham (UK) and is a visiting scholar in Southeast Asian Studies at the Johns Hopkins University School of Advanced International Studies in Washington DC (USA). The author of *Civil Society Networks in China and Vietnam: Informal Pathbreakers in Health and the Environment* (Palgrave Macmillan, 2012), Andrew has lived in Vietnam since 1997. He has made over two dozen trips to Cambodia since 1994, including serving as an election observer in 1998 and 2003.

Preface

This volume represents the findings of a year-long process of writing and discussion amongst Vietnam and Cambodia scholars from many parts of the world. The process started at the University of Bonn, Germany, where a group of researchers began questioning how to make light of the growing organizational pluralism and the steady increase of so-called non-governmental organizations in these two countries. Reviewing the empirical and conceptual literature, they found it lacking many facets and ongoing dynamics of civil society development; furthermore, much of the available research findings were outdated, or overlooked Cambodia and Vietnam. Additionally, there was an observable inclination to frame civil society in the context of democratization processes (notably in the development aid literature), which tended to produce a reductionist view and otherwise limited understanding of what actually happens on the ground. Against the background of these broad-base observations, 17 academics and development experts with experience and knowledge of the local scene were invited for a three-day 'writeshop,' which took place 18–20 January 2012, at the Center for Development Research (ZEF) in Bonn.

During this intensive workshop, participants critically reflected on their work and discussed the conceptual approach and outline of a book we would author together. The heterogeneity of the participants, which included practitioners as well as scholars from various disciplinary backgrounds, age groups, nationalities and professional histories (see contributor profiles), made for an inspiring and thought provoking exchange. Furthermore, the workshop was designed as a forum where junior and senior academics had an opportunity to meet and lay the groundwork for the growth in different academic fields and regional studies. The combination of working sessions, social activities and a public forum provided an ideal ground for relationship-building and networking, which has been essential for a productive and forward-looking process, and aimed at lasting beyond a joint publication.

During the writeshop, several sessions were dedicated to elaborating on old and new insights as well as key lessons from the case and country studies. Most of the papers introduced research topics that have hardly been investigated in any of the two countries (e.g. civil society networks, community-based organizations, gender and mobilization, and discourse analysis, among others), and are primarily empirically-based. Lively discussions revolved around 'politics of civil society' and the question of autonomy, local expressions of civil society, as well as the distinctive narratives and forms of civil society in Vietnam and Cambodia. These discussions and other results emerging equally from individual chapters and from the overall book, are presented in a summary chapter at the conclusion of this volume.

Due to the interdisciplinary and transdisciplinary range in authorship, as well as the practical relevance of the subjects covered in the book, the editors wish to bring this book to a diverse audience, both within and beyond academia, including students, civil society actors and development practitioners. The larger goal is to share new insights and methodologies, encourage debate, and broaden as well as challenge some of the current understandings of civil society. To that end, contact information for the editors and authors is available; we would enjoy hearing from readers with questions, challenges and ideas for moving forward.

Acknowledgements

The book is first and foremost a product of its authors, who conducted fieldwork in the context of various research projects and assignments and made an additional effort to contribute the respective chapters. The Fritz Thyssen Foundation generously granted funding for the writeshop and some editorial work. The Center for Development Research (University of Bonn) graciously organized and hosted the writeshop. Special thanks also go to Adam Fforde and Jörg Wischermann, who participated in the writeshop and provided valuable feedback. Finally, our regards to Michaela Doutch, an intern at ZEF, and Sebastian Eckert, ZEF's public relations assistant, who both were a source of great support throughout the whole project and helped to bring the final manuscript into a proper shape.

Abbreviations

3SPN	3 S Rivers Protection Network (Cambodia)
ACLEDA	Association of Cambodian Local Economic Development Agencies
ACWF	All-China Women's Federation
ADB	Asian Development Bank
ADHOC	Cambodian Human Rights and Development Organization
AEC	Agriculture Extension Club (Vietnam)
AFTA	ASEAN Free Trade Area
AMRC	Australia Mekong Resource Center
ANU	Australian National University
ART	antiretroviral treatment
ASEAN	Association of South East Asian Nations
AUA	Antiretroviral Users' Association
AusAID	Australian Agency for International Development
BDSA	Buddhism and Society Development Association (Cambodia)
BFD	Buddhism for Development (Cambodia)
BSDA	Buddhism for Social Development Action (Cambodia)
CAG	Commune Action Group (Cambodia)
CAMBOW	Cambodian Committee of Women
CARDI	Cambodian Agriculture Research and Development Institute
CBD	Centre for Biodiversity and Development (Vietnam)
CBO	Community-based Organization
CCC	Cooperation Committee for Cambodia
CCD	Community Capacities for Development (Cambodia)
CDRI	Cambodia Development Resource Institute
CEDAC	Centre d'Etude et de Developpement Agricole Cambodgien (Cambodian Centre for Study and Development in Agriculture)
CEDAW	International Convention on the Elimination of All Forms of Violence against Women
CERWASS	Centre for Rural Water Supply and Environmental Sanitation (Vietnam)

CIAP	Cambodia-IRRI-Australia Project
CIDIN	Center for International Development Issues Nijmegen
CMC	Commune Monitoring Committee (Cambodia)
CNCW	Cambodia National Council for Women
CNMC	Cambodia National Mekong Committee
Come N'GOs	Come-and-go NGOs
CPN	Community Peacebuilding Network (Cambodia)
CPP	Cambodian People's Party
CPRGS	Comprehensive Poverty Reduction and Growth Strategy (Vietnam)
CPV	Communist Party of Vietnam
CSO	Civil Society Organization
DAALI	Department of Agronomy and Agriculture Land Improvement (Cambodia)
DARD	Department of Agriculture and Rural Development (Vietnam)
DoWA	Department of Women's Affairs (Cambodia)
DRV	Democratic Republic of Vietnam
D&D	Decentralization and Deconcentration Reform
EIA	Environmental Impact Assessment
EWMI	East–West Management Institute
FAO	Food and Agriculture Organization of the United Nations
FiBL	Forschungsinstitut für biologischen Landbau (Research Institute of Organic Agriculture)
FNN	Farmer and Nature Network (Cambodia)
Forwet	Forest and Wetlands Research Centre (Vietnam)
GAD	Gender and Development
GAP	Gender Action Partnership (Vietnam)
GAPE	Global Alliance for the Preservation of the Environment
GCOP	Government Committee on Organization and Personnel (Vietnam)
GIZ	Gesellschaft für Internationale Zusammenarbeit (German Agency for International Cooperation)
GNP	Gross National Product
GONGO	Governmental Non-Governmental Organization
GoV	Government of Vietnam
HUSTA	Hanoi Union of Science and Technology Associations (Vietnam)
HYVs	High Yielding Varieties
IDS	Institute of Development Studies
IFAD	International Fund of Agriculture Development
IFOAM	International Federation of Organic Agriculture Movements
ILLSA	Institute of Labour Science and Social Affairs (Vietnam)
ILO	International Labour Organization
INGO	International Non-Governmental Organization

IRRI	International Rice Research Institute
ISEE	Institute of Social Studies, Economics and Environment
IUCN	International Union for the Conservation of Nature
JICA	Japan International Cooperation Agency
LGBTI	Lesbian, Gay, Bisexual, Transgender and Intersexual
LNGO	Local Non-Governmental Organization
MAFF	Ministry of Agriculture, Forestry and Fisheries (Cambodia)
MARD	Ministry of Agriculture and Rural Development (Vietnam)
MDM	Médecins du Monde
MoC	Ministry of Commerce (Cambodia)
MOLISA	Ministry of Labour, Invalids and Social Affairs (Vietnam)
MONRE	Ministry of Natural Resources and Environment (Vietnam)
MOSTE	Ministry of Science, Technology and Environment (Vietnam)
MoWA	Ministry of Women's Affairs (Cambodia)
MOWRAM	Ministry of Water Resources and Meteorology (Cambodia)
MRC	Mekong River Commission
MW	Mekong Watch
NCFAW	National Committee For the Advancement of Women (Vietnam)
NEW	Network for the Empowerment of Women (Vietnam)
NGO	Non-Governmental Organization
NGO – CEDAW	Cambodian NGO Committee on CEDAW
NGOF	NGO Forum on Cambodia
NIPH	National Institute of Public Health (Cambodia)
NIS	National Institute of Statistics (Cambodia)
NORAD	Norwegian Agency for Development Cooperation
NPA	Norwegian People's Aid
NSDP	National Strategic Development Plan
NTFP	Non-Timber Forest Products
NWFN	National Women Farmers' Network (Cambodia)
ODA	Official Development Assistance
OECD	Organization for Economic Co-operation and Development
PAVN	Peoples Army of Vietnam
PLWHIV	People living with HIV/AIDS
PPWG	People's Participation Working Group (Vietnam)
RCC	Rivers Coalition in Cambodia
RCGAD	Research Center for Gender and Development (Vietnam)
RSWG	Ratanakiri province Se San Working Group (Cambodia)
RUDECO	Vocational Training in Rural Development and Ecology (EU Project)
SAT	Sida Advisory Team
SCN	Se San Community Network (Cambodia)
SEDP	Socioeconomic Development Plan
Sida	Swedish International Development Cooperation Agency

SOE	State-owned Enterprise
SPM	a Swedish consultancy
SPN	Se San Protection Network (Cambodia)
SRI	System of Rice Intensification
SRP	Sam Rainsy Party (Cambodia)
SWECO	Swedish consulting firm
SWG	Se San Working Group (Cambodia)
TAF	The Asia Foundation
TERRA	Towards Ecological Recovery and Regional Alliance
UN Women	United Nations Entity for Gender Equality and the Empowerment of Women
UNAIDS	Joint United Nations Programme on HIV/AIDS
UNCDF	United Nations Capital Development Fund
UNCED	United Nations Conference on Environment and Development
UNDP	United Nations Development Programme
UNEP	United Nations Environment Programme
UNESCAP	United Nations Economic and Social Commission for Asia and the Pacific
UNIFEM	United Nations Development Fund for Women
UNTAC	United Nations Transitional Administration in Cambodia
USAID	United States Agency for International Development
USSR	Union of Soviet Socialist Republics
VACVINA	Vietnam Gardening Association
VASW	Vietnam Association for Social Work
VCP	Vietnamese Communist Party
VEO	Voluntary Economic Organization (Vietnam)
VFF	Vietnam Fatherland Front
VFEJ	Vietnam Federation of Environmental Journalists
VGCL	Vietnam General Confederation of Labour
VIDS	Vietnam Institute of Development Studies
VND	Viet Nam Dong (currency)
VNGO	Vietnamese NGO
VNMC	Vietnam National Mekong Committee
VRN	Vietnam Rivers Network
VUFO	Vietnam Union of Friendship Organizations
VULAA	Vietnam Union of Literature and Arts Associations
VUSTA	Vietnam Union of Science and Technology Associations
VWU	Vietnam Women's Union
WARECOD	Centre for Water Resources Conservation and Development (Vietnam)
WB	World Bank
WCFP	Women and Children Focal Point
WHO	World Health Organization
WID	Women in Development

WTO	World Trade Organization
WU	see VWU
WUG	Water User Group
ZEF	Zentrum für Entwicklungsforschung (Center for Development Research)

1 Grasping discourses, researching practices
Investigating civil society in Vietnam and Cambodia

Gabi Waibel

Introduction

Writing on civil society has gone in and out of fashion since the eighteenth century, but clearly re-emerged as a political rallying call, development initiative, and academic fixation with the political changes occurring in Eastern Europe during the 1980s. The wealth of issues covered by these writings has continued to increase since then, and portrayals of civil society now routinely capture the stories of local communities, countries, global movements and even certain periods in (regional) history. Despite, or perhaps because of the growth of this concept, corresponding conceptual frameworks have not only escaped consolidation, they continue to diverge. While civil society is broadly understood as a realm of social action and civic engagement outside the state, the context and inherent flux of every case tends to defy a unitary (or at least universally agreed upon) definition.

This book embraces the idea that forms of civil society are in continual change and that 'tracking', as opposed to 'pinning down', civil society should be the long-term goal of academic inquiry. In this respect, civil society remains, contrary to recent claims, under-researched, with its value in contemporary studies derived less by generalizations and more by situating the functioning of civil society in certain contexts. This is particularly true for developing countries like Cambodia and Vietnam, where a recent history of war, isolation and extreme poverty, followed by restoration and reform, have altered the opportunities and the demand for non-state actors to engage in, and more often than not, manage the effects of, rapid socio-economic transformation. This is most visible in the recent and substantial growth of civil society actors and organizations in the two countries. Vietnam, for instance, has a broad range of organizations which are affiliated with the party-state and officially classified as civil society organizations (CSOs) (Bach Tan Sinh, in this volume) and, at 51 per cent of eligible women, has the highest membership in women's groups worldwide (primarily because of its high level of formal participation in the Vietnam Women's Union, which is discussed more extensively in this volume) (World Values Survey Database 1999–2004, cited in: UNIFEM (2008: 19)). In the same vein, Cambodia has, since the 1990s, witnessed a huge expansion of non-governmental organizations (NGOs) as well as community-based organizations (CBOs) (Öjendal, in this volume). The terminology and meaning of civil society, nevertheless, remain contested even as the concept is used and instrumentalized in these countries. This book examines this contestation openly, looking at (1) contemporary discourses and manifestations of civil society in the two countries, including indigenous and nascent local groups (Ehlert, Hiwasa, Waibel and Benedikter); (2) national-level NGOs and agencies (Bourdier, Feuer, Pistor and Le Thi Quy), as well as; (3) translocal networks (Thim Ly, Wells-Dang) that operate in a variety of sectors, such as gender, environmental and health. A crucial dimension emerging in the contributions to this volume lies in understanding the politics of civil society (which is particularly interesting in the Vietnamese one-party system and Cambodia's external donor-driven environment). As suggested by Foley and Edwards (1996: 7 (3), 38–52: 47):

> this 'political variable' must include both the political associations that play important roles in any society and the work of political compromise, restraint, and accommodation necessary for reconciling competing interests in a peaceful and more or less orderly way.

In Vietnam and Cambodia both, civil society actors and the state seek out and develop strategic responses for managing their relationship to one another in an environment that is continuously shaped and (re)constructed by changing legislation, collaboration and negotiation, advocacy and protest, and the restrictions placed by measures for social control (Bach Tan Sinh, Öjendal, Wells-Dang in this volume; Thayer (2009)).

The authors of this volume do not confine themselves to one particular definition of civil society, but aim at expanding the largely European-oriented conceptual and empirical understandings of the concept. Before discussing the contemporary content, however, the following section traces the origins and ideological evolution of civil society as an idea and as a development objective. Subsequently, trends in civil society research are taken up, paying particular attention to two sticking points; first, (the influence of) the dominant research questions in this field of study and, second, the normative conceptions underlying much research, which often shape the way civil society is actually investigated. Finally, key approaches and findings from the civil society literature on Southeast Asia will be summarized in order to erect a regional frame for the studies of the two countries. This introductory chapter concludes by outlining the main strands of discussion in this book.

Civil society: a brief history of original ideas[1]

The idea of 'civil society' first emerged with the work of Aristotle and Cicero more than two millennia ago, and most of the subsequent works are conceptually derived from Western political thought. In the original writings of Roman philosophers, 'civil society' was understood 'as [being] synonymous with the state' and basically described a 'social order of citizenship' (Kumar 1993: 376f.). More than a millennium later, Thomas Hobbes (1588–1679) defined civil society as, in the words of Ehrenberg (2011: 19), 'the arena in which interest-bearing individuals pursued their private goals', and argued that it was the sovereign state which was tasked with controlling this segment of society. Different ideas about civic virtues, social structures, state power and the role and rights of the individual were further developed thereafter, but it was only during the Age of Enlightenment in the eighteenth century that civil society was written of as a realm distinct from the state. Drawing on the pioneering writings of economic theory, Adam Ferguson (1723–1816), Georg W. F. Hegel (1770–1831) and later Karl Marx (1818–83) provided some of the most influential, but also controversial interpretations and visions of civil society. Two of the core themes of their studies looked at the role of the (capitalist) economy (in constituting civil society) and how 'civilization' – as contrasted with the uncivilized, 'barbarian' world – could be engendered and maintained. Differing understandings of civil society contributed to an intellectual divide that, later on, would fundamentally shape world history: liberalism vs. socialism. 'Liberalism developed a theory of civil society because it wanted to democratize the state. Marxism developed a theory of the state because it wanted to democratize civil society' (Ehrenberg 2011: 23). Indeed, Marx's vision was to overcome the 'alienation and exploitation' of the bourgeois civil society by dissolving it into the state (Alagappa 2004b: 29).

Alexis de Tocqueville (1805–59), in the mid-nineteenth century, went into greater detail about civil society. He argued that, in addition to the state and the economic sphere (described by Kumar (1993: 381) as an 'arena of private interests and economic activity'), a third dimension, namely 'the art of association', existed. The latter can be understood as 'a largely autonomous sphere of freedom and liberty encompassing an organizational culture that fosters democracy, both political and economic' and thus constitutes 'a positive force … between the individual and the state' (McIllwaine 2009: 137). It was this three-dimensional model which became constitutive of many of the modern appraisals of 'civil society'.

However, de Tocqueville's framework also generated fundamental critique. It was assessed as being highly idealistic, overlooking inequality and power imbalances – in both democratic and authoritarian regimes. An important strand of theory developed by Antonio Gramsci (1891–1937), a Marxist and oppositionist of Mussolini's fascist regime, took these critiques into account. He called the assumed distinction between civil society (which included the market) and the state into question, and argued that in reality the two realms tend to overlap. Gramsci's theory points out that the state establishes its hegemony through force *and* consent. In this light, he perceived civil society as the realm of consent where 'the exploited classes [are persuaded] to accept the way society developed under capitalism as natural and legitimate' (Howell and Pearce 2001c: 34).[2] He nevertheless recognized that 'the state's hegemony over civil society is never complete' and therefore acknowledged the latter's 'potential for radical social transformation' (Landau 2008: 246). Gramsci's conceptual approach influenced not only ensuing theory building, but also inspired many political activists in Latin America, Eastern Europe and beyond.[3]

Despite the prominent theoretical writings mentioned above, the interest in the concept of civil society remained rather low during the end of the nineteenth and first half of the twentieth century (Hann 2004: 44). Other concepts emerging from social theory building, however, became constitutive for the civil society debate, which re-emerged later on. An influential piece of work reflecting this period is Habermas' (1991) book on the historical evolution of a 'bourgeois public sphere' in eighteenth century Europe. The idea of a public sphere that provides space for citizens to debate and influence politics is one aspect of civil society discourse that has been widely adopted. Reis, in this volume, applies this conceptual framework in her critical examination of the contextual factors and relevance of civil society in contemporary Vietnam.

The political transformation in Eastern Europe, led by a heretofore unknown segment of the population, eventually led to a revival of the concept of civil society, which can be explained as follows:

> The failure in Eastern Europe of revolution (Hungary 1956) and reform from above (Czechoslovakia 1968) led in the 1970s to the idea of a third way: reform from below, by the construction or reconstruction of civil society.
>
> (Kumar 1993: 388)

In the aftermath of 1989, civil society was thus conceptualized as a counterweight to oppressive and authoritarian regimes. In this same period, scholars such as Ernest Gellner and Robert Putnam contributed to the advancement of theories that were to eventually play an important role in debates about civil society (Edwards 2004: 7). Gellner (1994) ascribed civil society the ability to counterbalance the state, while Putnam (1993) identified the linkages between civil society and social capital. Putnam's empirical research in present-day Italy and the United States provided evidence that a high level of associational activity fosters solidarity that contributes to society's collective ability to counterbalance the state.[4] This concept of social capital had great influence on the civil society debate at the time (Edwards 2004: 7) and spawned numerous studies on the role, political and otherwise, of social relations in different cultures and societies.

Coming into fashion: civil society as a (development) objective

Against this background, policy makers and development aid agencies around the globe 'discovered' civil society (as well as the related concepts of social capital and participation), and, deeming it worthy of sponsorship and promotion, from the 1990s onwards started to channel huge funds to parties that they viewed as representative of civil society.

During the same time, the discourse on NGOs began to appear on the inter-national political scenes, and newly emboldened organizations began clamoring to be heard, respected and funded. The first Earth Summit in Rio de Janeiro, in 1992, witnessed unprecedented NGO participation and is considered a key event in this regard, while the influential NGO forum, organized in parallel to the Beijing UN Women's conference in 1995, confirmed this new trend (Hulme and Edwards 1997: 5). As a result, a new global discourse on civil society was born and thereafter nurtured by a slew of conferences, research activities and media portrayals. The general, if uncritical, understanding during this period of (re) awakening was that civil society was 'doing good'.[5]

As the strengthening of civil society became 'big business' (Hulme and Edwards 1997: 6), civil society organizations mushroomed. Typically, this involved capacity building programmes for new NGOS as well as the provision of project funds aimed at promoting non-state actors, particularly in the service delivery and social welfare sectors. Concurrently, indicators for assessing, moni-toring and evaluating civil society, as well as 'giving it legitimate substance and rendering it amenable to planning', were being developed (Howell and Pearce 2001a: 81). Emerging definitions of civil society became instrumental in justi-fying development interventions, a prominent example of which is the following definition from the World Bank (2012):

> [Civil society refers to] the wide array of non-governmental and not-for-profit organizations that have a presence in public life, expressing the inter-ests and values of their members or others, based on ethical, cultural, political, scientific, religious or philanthropic considerations.

The definition employed above presents several artificial dichotomies – govern-mental versus non-governmental, profit-making versus non-for-profit and public versus private sphere – all of which are meant to invoke an idealized notion of civil society. In practice, all these boundaries are blurred (Alagappa 2004a; Howell and Pearce 2001b). For instance, there are numerous NGOs which engage in business (e.g. consultancy work) and depend (to some extent) on gov-ernment funding; members and staff switch from NGO work to state employ-ment or vice versa, and some 'groups' are 'the virtual creation of a single individual' (Sidel 1995: 299).

Moreover, because the relevant national laws actually determine the criteria for formal registration and operational space, 'very different kinds of groups may count as NGOs in different countries' (Weller 2005: 3). Although donor agencies generally advocate globally for recognition of civil society through legislations or various types of reforms, they often have to adapt to, and operate within, the legitimate space available for non-state actors in a given country (which can range from being fairly open to strictly controlled). Salemink (2006), drawing on his experience in Vietnam during the 1990s, argued that donors tended to re-interpret the encountered concepts in ways that matched their inter-ests. Primarily through the sponsorship of development aid programmes, several new types of organization came into being.[6] Among those are, for example, the GONGOs (governmental non-governmental organizations) (Hann 2004: 46) – a creation which clearly illustrates the interdependence of civil society organizations, the state, and, sometimes, donor funding. Civil society country portrayals, statistical reports, and similar documents, however, tend to disguise this lack of clarity and require very critical reading.

In many aid-receiving countries, including Cambodia and Vietnam, formal NGO (or associational) legislation is highly controversial. However, potential beneficiaries of development aid, in spite of their heterogeneity, have proven that they can adapt dynamically to funding criteria and national restrictions (see Ou and Kim, this volume). Some of these mechanisms created various unexpected and negative impacts (Hann 2004: 45ff.; see also Ou and Kim in this volume), leading some observers to start questioning the idea of civil society as a panacea.

Critical responses and theoretical debates

One of the fundamental critiques challenged the idea that there is something like 'one' or 'the' civil society; divisions within civil society in terms of diversity, fragmentation, rivalry, unequal power relations and also direct conflicts are increasingly recognized. Research (and aid) agendas, as a result, have shifted gradually to looking at the 'quality' of civil society, including issues of exclusion and 'barriers to entry' into civil society (Howell and Pearce 2001a: 86). Similarly, concerns have been raised about the new elites managing the NGO sector for their own benefit, and the lack of participation of the poor (stimulated by the work of Chambers (1983; 1997) and others). This critique of civil society dynamics emerged in the context of increasing inequality in other social spheres.

The emergent heterogeneity of civil society has also raised questions about the assumed state–civil society divide. Gramsci's critical perspective has regained prominence in contemporary civil society studies, because it

> does not proceed from the distinction between the state and civil society ... [and] also challenges the assumption that civil society is the site of democratic and egalitarian relationships; ... it therefore rejects the thesis that the state is the primary source of oppression and exploitation.
> (Quadir and Jayant 2004: 7, 10)

Moreover, in communist regimes, such as China and Vietnam, such a divide is officially non-existent. In contrast, 'the space of ... civil society may, in one sense, be encompassed within space claimed by the state' (Hann and Dunn 1996: 19), which, in the case of Vietnam, is to a great extent filled by mass organizations and their many affiliates (see Bach Tan Sinh, this volume). Regardless of the legally sanctioned space, people are, as the title of an edited volume by Kerkvliet suggests, 'getting organized'. He argues that within the given sociopolitical context it would be more insightful 'to think of arenas in which boundaries, rights, jurisdictions, and power distribution between the state and societal agencies are debated, contested, and resolved (at least temporarily)' (Kerkvliet 2001: 240).

For a number of reasons, diverging views on how to analyse, interpret and support civil society continue to exist. The so-called liberal-democratic approach, which refers to Tocqueville's work, is, for example, still in use – especially in the donor community. Nevertheless, and as Alagappa (2004d: 457) argues for contemporary Asia, '[which] frame dominates and how different features combine are largely a function of the legitimacy of the state and its policies'.[7] As recent history shows, the latter are by no means fixed but rather continuously re-shaped and negotiated.

Another even more fundamental critique about the leading frameworks emerged in the new millennium, questioning their 'fitness' in the social, cultural and political contexts of non-Western societies. The collected edition of Hann and Dunn (1996), entitled *Civil Society – Challenging Western Models*, was an important piece of work in this school. The authors (1996: 7) emphasized the necessity of anthropological research in order to grasp the local meanings and practices of civic engagement and social cohesion, arguing:

> An awareness of the shifts in European intellectual debate, and of the common rootedness of the dominant modern strands in a specifically western theory of autonomous individuals, should alert us to the errors and dangers of exporting models of civil society to non-western societies.

This argument became prominent in some of the earlier as well as contemporary writings on Southeast Asia, which will be discussed below. However, frustrated with the evolution of writing on civil society, Hann (2004: 45ff.) later on rejected that the concept of civil society had any analytical value and, according to him, should be sent 'back to the conceptual graveyard'. Yet, and despite a prevailing unease and intellectual struggle with the civil society concept, a vast body of literature, both theoretical and empirical, as well as countless consultancy reports, were being produced – although, more recently, a decline can be observed. In addition, a wealth of studies on social capital, social movements, participation and public space have investigated similar phenomena. Perhaps unsurprisingly, there seems to be more confusion than understanding about what civil society actually is or should be.

The various criticisms suggest that a critical reading and judicious use of the conceptual frameworks is imperative; they also show that more empirical research is needed to uncover the hybrid understandings and practices of civil society in a given context. In this regard, scholars have to take the complex cultural and political dimensions into account, as well as the multiple interactions, objectives and room to manoeuvre of different actors in order to go beyond the unrefined 'search for civil society'.[8] A preconceived understanding of civil society, particularly when it engenders normative categories of civil society actors, constrains the needed openness to local perceptions and manifestations, which, from our understanding in the editing of this volume, should be the guiding object of research.

Civil society research: operationalizing a highly contested concept

Broadly speaking, research on civil society encompasses the study of a whole range of actors and organizations argued as being part of civil society, dealing with different issues at different scales (varying from the local to the global), and including both historical and contemporary developments.

Donor agencies, as mentioned earlier, have had one of the strongest influences on the contemporary research agenda. The instrumentalization of various definitions, such as the one promulgated by the World Bank (see above), is one area that this book aims to elucidate. First, the delimitation of civil society actors to organizations not only overlooks the plurality of forms of engagement, it often constrains research perspectives and outcomes. As a result, some individuals, informal groups, networks and other not registered entities, including those which lack legal provisions, were (and oftentimes still are) disregarded in assessments of civil society. Furthermore, locally specific manifestations risk to be ignored, if the employed definitions of civil society (e.g. organizations) are too narrow (Weller 2005: 4). This often includes 'earlier ties of religion, community, and kinship – [which] are important to developing civil societies' (see also Ehlert, this volume). Second, this definition makes no mention of contestation that arises as the respective political environments determine which groups and associations qualify as civil society organizations. Third, the use of externally developed indicators for interpreting and measuring civil society activities tends to exclude local perspectives and conceptions. Indeed, the reception, translation and adaptation of the concept in different languages, cultures and political systems often results in different understandings (Alagappa 2004c: 15), which may overlap with or contradict international formulations.

Some of the more recent conceptualizations of civil society constitute attempts to overcome some of these shortcomings. For example, the London School of Economics' Centre for Civil Society uses the definition: an 'arena ... [which] embraces a diversity of spaces, actors and institutional forms, varying in their degree of formality' (The Change Institute 2008). Yet, apparent difficulties in operationalizing the concept still lead to a preoccupation with formally registered organizations, notably in quantitative surveys. To date, and this is very evident in the cases of both Cambodia and Vietnam, many spaces of civil society action remain under-researched. Responding to this, the contributions to this book fall in line with Hannah (2007: 92, 94), who suggests:

> I prefer to look at actions and activities – the processes – that embody and promote civil society interests, rather than predetermining which groups or organizations are to be included in and excluded from civil society.
>
> [...]
>
> Research methods, therefore, need to shift ... to looking at who within a society/state constellation is undertaking which civil society activities and

who is accomplishing which civil society objectives.... [This] would neces-
sitate that the social actors themselves define which state–society relationships and activities are important, rather than have such normative
categories imposed on them by (us) outside researchers.

It is obvious that the so-called Western view continues to shape our knowledge
and understanding of civil society (development). A 'reality check' therefore
often leads to a picture where civil society has 'failed' to meet the corresponding
(ethical) values (Alagappa 2004c: 11); Ou and Kim, this volume). In contrast, a
critical reflection of one's own epistemological background as well as an examination of the local discourses might serve to open our minds and engage with
multiple perspectives. The chapters of Bach Tan Sinh and Phuong Le Trong (this
volume), which argue that there is a 'Vietnamese way' of conceptualizing civil
society, are illustrative in this regard.

A last set of points should be made here about various biases that commonly
emerge in the civil society literature. First, although research interests have certainly evolved over time, much emphasis has been (and still is) placed on
studying the role of civil society in democratic change processes, or – more
generally – on 'understanding politics' (Alagappa 2004c: 16). Many of the contributing authors in this volume also intensively discuss this dimension, as politics unavoidably shapes the understanding and practice of civil society in
Cambodia and Vietnam. Yet, as emerges in the contributions to this book, civil
society actors do not necessarily confine themselves to the ultimate goal of political change; the objectives and rationales for associational activity, as well as the
consequent state–society responses, have to be investigated from a broader perspective. A second source of bias is derived from disciplinary boundaries since
the disciplines are typically preoccupied with investigating certain types of
social, economic or political structures (Hann and Dunn 1996: 14). Interdisciplinary research, which might alleviate this problem, tends to be rare. Third, biases
often exist with regard to either urban or rural, regional foci as well as certain
subjects (in particular, the environment, women, and human rights tend to domi-
nate the literature). The orientation of many research topics can be attributed to
priorities set by development policies. The preoccupation with service delivery
functions (Hulme and Edwards 1997: 9), for which the notion of the 'third
sector' has been widely used, is a good example in this regard. The picture of a
country's (or a region's) civil society landscape is therefore always socially constructed and consequently non-comprehensive. The following section elaborates
more specifically on academic and non-academic studies of civil society in Asia/
Southeast Asia and situates the focus of this book in this broader field of study.

Civil society in Southeast Asia: body of knowledge/ knowledge gaps

During the past two decades a host of publications on civil society in Southeast
Asia/Asia emerged, of which a few employed a regional perspective similar to

that of this book. Among those, a survey initiated by the Japan Center for International Exchange provided the first overview on civil society organizations in Asia-Pacific countries (Yamamoto 1995b: 2). The report, which is more practically than conceptually oriented, contends that the 'indigenous development of the nonprofit sector is a very recent phenomenon in most of the countries' and found that it closely relates to the 'negative consequences of rapid economic growth' (Yamamoto 1995b: 3, 11). The study also emphasized that the response of the state to the newly established, mostly community service and welfare oriented organizations, varied greatly; in some countries leading to significant changes (Yamamoto 1995a).

Following the first insights into the 'new' phenomena presented in this report were a series of donor-funded workshops aimed at exploring the specific meanings and practices of civil society in the region (Heinrich Böll Foundation 2005; Lee Hock Guan 2004a). During these sessions, scholars provided evidence for the longstanding existence and tradition of 'civil society-like' institutions in Southeast Asia and emphasized that significant disruptions in associational life occurred during colonial rule. With the struggle for independence and the emergence of trade unions in the 1950s and 1960s, the picture changed again. The dominance of authoritarian regimes in the early post-colonial era restricted the formation and operation of groups. At least for a period, communist regimes in Vietnam, Cambodia and Laos even banned most types of organization outside the party-state. Later on, social movements played a significant role in the overthrow of the regimes in the Philippines, Thailand and Indonesia, where, in the aftermath, NGOs virtually mushroomed (Lee Hock Guan 2004b: 10ff.). Although some common historical threads and traces were identified in these workshops, the discussants concluded that something as concrete as *a* Southeast Asian civil society can hardly be said to exist (Heinrich Böll Foundation 2005). In contrast, they rather highlighted a regional plurality of civil societies and expressed their unease with the Western conceptual frame. Hudson (2003: 4) summarized this general unease concisely, noting that,

> In many Asian societies it is not clear that civil society is a distinct sphere – that is non-governmental – or that its institutions are voluntary. Equally, not all groups organized for collective purposes outside the economy and the state may be civil society groups.

Still, from a regional perspective, several conferences and publications during the late 1990s initiated a debate about how civil society in Southeast Asia relates to religion, in particular Islam. As Mitsuo (2001: 11–14) suggests, the Muslim obligation to volunteer seems to be highly conducive for the development of civil society. These scholars also argued that the constitutional linkages between religious and state affairs shape the conditions of religious freedom and association and that, on the one hand, political Islam flourished with democratization processes (Bajunid 2001: 189). On the other hand, whether the strengthening of Muslim civil society might 'lead to democratic civility' remains a contested

issue (Mitsuo 2001: 14). In the same vein, the role of Buddhist values and institutions for civil society (development) (Queen and King 1996) has also been
explored, revealing a long tradition of community work in many Southeast Asian
countries, including Cambodia and Vietnam. Buddhist engagement has been
especially prominent in environmental protection (Palmer and Finlay 2003) and,
more recently, in political protest against Myanmar's military rule supported by
monks. Similarly, the (Catholic) church is a significant player in the Philippines
and South Korea, and, to a lesser extent, in a few other countries, including
Vietnam (where 8 per cent of the population is Catholic). Faith-based civic
engagement, which is also present outside of the mentioned religions, can have,
among others, traditional, indigenous and local dimensions. There is also a
global dimension that describes the funding mechanisms and support systems of
larger, often international or translocal organizations or networks that help local
religious groups. As a subject of research, the interest in religious institutions
and their relationship with civil society has shown recent signs of growth (James
2007: 2).

The early debate on Islam and civil society also critically examined the idea
of 'Asian values' (Bajunid 2001: 192), which became prominent during the
1990s, by suggesting that Asian countries share common characteristics and
values which were different from those of the West. Advocates of the 'Asian
value' theory, who often represented ruling elites, highlighted values such as
order and discipline, defended authoritarian regimes as being suitable in the
given context, and contested the notion of universal human rights, which, they
argued, was rooted in Western liberal thought (De Bary 2000; Sen 1997). This
culturalist strand of argumentation was rejected by many activists and scholars,
who, for example, argued that comparative studies in the region should be
limited to analyses of the similarities of economic and political features (Weller
2005: 16f.). Moreover,

> the so-called Asian values ... are not especially Asian in any significant
> sense.... The thesis of a grand dichotomy between Asian values and Euro-
> pean values [in contrast] adds little to our comprehension, and much to the
> confusion about the normative basis of freedom and democracy.
>
> (Sen 1997: 30f.)

Considering the substantial amount of studies examining the diversity of roles
played by civil society with regard to democratic change, the idea of universally
applicable norms and values for (for example) 'good governance', remains a
controversial issue. Alagappa (2004a), who produced one of the most comprehensive (and perhaps most quoted) volumes on civil society and political change
in Asia, comprising 12 country studies (though notably not including Vietnam
and Cambodia), framed this issue by investigating the 'nature of civil societies'
and the role of civil society organizations in 'fostering or inhibiting political
change in the direction of open, participatory, and accountable political systems
and institutions' (Alagappa 2004c: 8). Alagappa's overview confirms a dramatic

increase in civil society organizations since the mid-1980s, despite uncertainties about legal status in various countries. According to him, key drivers for these developments include rapid economic transition, political liberalization, the strengthening of religious and ethnic engagements (often as a response to discriminatory practices), as well as the intensification of regional and international integration.

The scale and scope of activity of these early civil society organizations broadened and, sometimes expanded into social movements, while coalitions at both domestic and transnational levels, including diaspora communities, emerged (Alagappa 2004d: 458ff.). Two chapters in this volume provide empirical case studies of such linkages: Thim investigates how a community initiative in rural Cambodia managed to grow into a major national initiative by successfully liaising with other affected villages, national NGOs and international players, while Feuer analyses how local Cambodian ecological initiatives render parts of the global environmental movements viable for local political institutions.

With regard to state–society relations in view of democratization, Alagappa (2004d: 469) concluded that, in Asia, 'by and large, civil society organizations do not fundamentally challenge the state or the political order'. Instead, they try to achieve their individual objectives by utilizing the room to manoeuvre provided by the political system in place (an illustrative empirical account of such strategies is provided by Wells-Dang, this volume). This is important because, generally speaking, limitations and sanctions on civil society remain widespread throughout the region.

Other studies on Asia come to similar conclusions. A collection of papers, edited by Quadir and Jayant (2004: 8), frankly suggest that, 'the democratic potential of civil society in the region is more limited than is widely assumed'. Similarly, Weller *et al.* (2005) found that, in most of their eight-country case studies (including one on Vietnam), the relationships between civil society agents and governments are rather 'symbiotic than antagonistic', being characterized more by 'corporatist arrangements' (Weller 2005: 7, 9). Many contributions in this book take on this criticism by viewing government engagements – or the lack thereof – as an aspect of engendering and envisioning civil society rather than as a linear oppositional force.

Vietnam and Cambodia

In the above-mentioned edited volumes on Southeast Asia, studies on so-called vibrant civil societies tend to be overrepresented. Among those, Japan, Malaysia and Indonesia attracted most attention, while South Korea, Thailand, Singapore, Taiwan and the Philippines are also well captured. China and Vietnam appear in a few (although not in Alagappa's (2004a) work). In contrast, studies on Laos and Cambodia are, with little exception, basically absent (although country-specific monographs dealing with civil society in Cambodia do exist, see, e.g. the references in Ou and Kim, this volume).

This book concentrates on Cambodia and Vietnam, where earliest publications on civil society came out in the 1990s. The two countries offer many interesting starting points for research and reflection, and we find that analysis of common threads and differences in the evolution and discourses of civil society is of scientific value. More specifically, the distinct political systems and question of donor influence, as well as the reception and adaptation of (the concept of) civil society are worthy of critical, comparative investigation. The existing literature is also demonstrative of the plurality of ways that civil society is approached and researched (what we call the 'civil society gaze'). Both countries also exhibit a variety of local practices for making use of existing civil society space, and gaining more of it.

In Cambodia, the civil society sphere expanded rapidly during restoration and, to date, NGOs fulfil a large part of typically state functions and operate at all societal and geographical scales. Moreover, democratization and also decentralization policies have built upon the (re)establishment of the indigenous associational realm, which was assumed to be non-existent or formerly destroyed – a perspective which is only preliminarily challenged in this book. With a gradual decline in foreign aid occurring, newer cleavages, such as the competitive nature of civil society and local support structures for civic engagement, are starting to emerge.

In Vietnam, the civil society debate similarly emerged during the 1990s but research access has remained limited for some time. To date, the topic is considered politically sensitive, although *Đổi mới* reforms and the effects of globalization have opened opportunities for organizational pluralism. The various chapters on Vietnam demonstrate that state–society relationships are particularly blurry and therefore challenge many of the Western conceptions of civil society.

The book

This book is structured in three parts. The first one, *Framing the Contemporary Civil Society in Cambodia and Vietnam*, provides country-specific overview chapters on the historical and present context of civil society, and critically examines the respective concepts, discourses and thematic boundaries in both countries. These, as well as the political and social systems, are crucial to understanding how local actors, organizations, governments, and even scholars act and interact to create, reproduce, and define civil society. Different conceptions of civil society and their issues are becoming particularly exciting in their relevance for development, civic engagement and political action.

The second part, *Advocacy and Political Space*, concentrates on the political dimension of the civil society debate. It subsumes six chapters that – in one way or another – describe and analyse the relations between state and society. In this regard, the political space denotes a space of *contestation*, in which the state and various groups in society negotiate their (development) agendas, their mutual obligations and rights, and create room to manoeuvre. The individual chapters cover various aspects and forms of advocacy work and its impact at different scales in either Cambodia or Vietnam, while Wells-Dang's study engages in a comparative analysis of advocacy strategies in the two countries.

The third part of the book, which is headed *Traces and Tendencies*, holistically focuses on the interface of locally grown and externally mandated organizations and norms of social engagement. Beneath the broader tendencies observed in the evolving institutional forms and practices of contemporary civil society are traces left by history and culture. On the surface, the 'imprint' of the state and international organizations circumscribes the form, functioning, and identity, as well as understanding, of the emerging civil society. The analysis of Cambodia's NGO sector by Ou and Kim, for instance, provides an overt example of such processes. However, more subtle factors, such as local norms, collective practices, and cultural/religious institutions also leave smaller, but in no way less important, traces on the patterns of social engagement that contribute to, or restrict, civil society.

The final chapter, 'the civil society gaze', concludes by critically reflecting on the contributors' selection of themes, theoretical and methodological approaches, as well as empirical findings. This includes a review of the making and evolution of this book, and comments on the range of issues and shortcomings found in contemporary civil society research that was outlined in this chapter. The authors, in summary, argue that research on civil society, because it serves to legitimize or delegitimize based on the lens used by the observer, is, far from being a distant analysis, itself a political act.

Notes

1 This section largely draws on secondary literature, but references to the original texts are also included. The epistemological history of civil society is extensive and complex. Comprehensive overviews are provided by Cohen and Arato (1992), Edwards (2004) and Keane (1998).
2 Landau (2008: 245) points out that 'Gramsci's conception of civil society is rather unclear as he failed to provide a precise definition of the term'. Indeed, his ideas are literally presented in fragments, noted down in his 'Prison Notebooks', written between 1929 and 1935 (Hoare and Nowell Smith 1971).
3 More recently, analysts of international relations and the contemporary world order developed the so-called neo-Gramscian perspective (see, e.g. the work of Robert Cox), which focuses on the constitutive elements of the capitalist, transnational hegemony. Gramsci's critical thoughts therefore continue to foster intellectual debates and political theory building (Keucheyan 2012).
4 The concept of social capital has been explored from various disciplines and perspectives. In the context of the civil society debate, the following suggestion is illustrative:

> Social capital is usually defined as assets accruing from social relations upon which people, including poor people, can call to help accomplish either individual or collective goals as they navigate through life's complex landscapes. These assets can be mined for both individual and collective benefits, including obtaining work, participating in political activities or implementing community projects.
> (Daniere and Hy V. Luong 2012: 3)

After Putnam published his findings, the concept entered the donor platform in the 1990s. For a critical review see for example Howell and Pierce (2001b).

5 This refers to the title of one of the various critical reviews by Fisher (1997): 'Doing Good?: The Politics and Anti-politics of NGO Practices'.
6 Lewis and Kanji (2009: 9), for instance, list 46 different NGO acronyms in the English language. These include constellations like LINGOs (Little International NGOs) or RONGOs (Royal non-governmental organizations). Another interesting form is the BRONGO, which stands for Briefcase NGO (e.g. in Ghana).
7 Several Southeast Asian scholars actually discuss the relevance of Gramsci's and Tocqueville's theoretical frameworks for present-day civil society analysis (e.g. Alagappa 2004, Landau 2008, Tasnim 2007).
8 This expression is picked from the following research paper: White, G., Howell, J. A., and Shang Xiaoyuan (1996) 'In Search of Civil Society: Market Reform and Social Change in Contemporary China', Oxford: Oxford University Press.

References

Alagappa, M. (2004a) *Civil Society and Political Change in Asia: Expanding and Contracting Democratic Space*, Stanford: Stanford University Press.

Alagappa, M. (2004b) 'Civil Society and Political Change: An Analytical Framework', in M. Alagappa (ed.), *Civil Society and Political Change in Asia: Expanding and Contracting Democratic Space*, Stanford: Stanford University Press: 25–57.

Alagappa, M. (2004c) 'Introduction', in M. Alagappa (ed.), *Civil Society and Political Change in Asia: Expanding and Contracting Democratic Space*, Stanford: Stanford University Press: 1–21.

Alagappa, M. (2004d) 'The Nonstate Public Sphere in Asia: Dynamic Growth, Industrialization Lag' in M. Alagappa (ed.), *Civil Society and Political Change in Asia: Expanding and Contracting Democratic Space*, Stanford: Stanford University Press: 455–77.

Bajunid, O. F. (2001) 'Islam and Civil Society in Southeast Asia: A Review' in N. Mitsuo, S. Siddique and O. F. Bajunid (eds), *Islam and Civil Society in Southeast Asia*, Pasir Panjang: Institute of Southeast Asian Studies: 177–202.

Chambers, R. (1983) *Rural Development: Putting The Last First*, Essex and New York: Longmans Scientific and Technical Publishers & John Wiley.

Chambers, R. (1997) *Whose Reality Counts: Putting the First Last*, London: Intermediate Technology Publications.

Cohen, J. L. and Arato, A. (1992) *Civil Society and Political Theory*, London/Cambridge (Mass.): MIT Press.

Daniere, A. and Hy V. Luong (2012) 'Vibrant Societies and Social Capital in Asia' in A. Daniere and Hy V. Luong (eds), *The Dynamics of Social Capital and Civic Engagement in Asia*, New York: Routledge: 1–23.

De Bary, W. T. (2000) *Asian Values and Human Rights: A Confucian Communitarian Perspective, Second Edition*, Cambridge: Harvard University Press.

Edwards, M. (2004) *Civil Society*, Cambridge: Polity.

Ehrenberg, J. (2011) 'The History of Civil Society Ideas' in M. Edwards (ed.), *The Oxford Handbook of Civil Society*, Oxford: Oxford University Press: 15–25.

Foley, M. W. and Edwards, B. (1996) 'The Paradox of Civil Society' in *Journal of Democracy*, 7 (3): 38–52.

Fisher, William (1997) 'Doing Good? The Politics and Anti-politics of NGO Practices' in *American Review of Anthropology*, 26: 439–64.

Gellner, E. (1994) *Conditions of Liberty: Civil Society and its Rivals*, New York: Penguin Press.

Habermas, J. (1991) *The Structural Transformation of the Public Sphere*, (first published in German in 1962) London/Cambridge (Mass.): The MIT Press.

Hann, C. (2004) 'In the Church of Civil Society' in M. Glasius, D. Lewis and H. Seckinelgin (eds), *Exploring Civil Society: Political and Cultural Contexts*, London: Routledge: 44–50.

Hann, C. and Dunn, E. (1996) 'Introduction: Political Society and Civil Anthropology' in C. Hann and E. Dunn (eds), *Civil Society: Challenging Western Models*, London and New York: Routledge: 1–26.

Hannah, J. (2007) *Local Non-Government Organizations in Vietnam: Development, Civil Society and State-society Relations*, Seattle: University of Washington.

Heinrich Böll Foundation (ed.) (2005) *Towards Good Society: Civil Society Actors, the State, and the Business Class in Southeast Asia – Facilitators of or Impediments to a Strong, Democratic, and Fair Society?* Berlin: Heinrich Böll Foundation.

Hoare, Q. and Nowell Smith, G. (1971) *Selections from the Prison Notebooks of Antonio Gramsci*, London: Lawrence and Wishart.

Howell, J. and Pearce, J. (2001a) 'Civil Society, the State, and the Market: A Triadic Development Model for the Twenty-first Century?' in J. Howell and J. Pearce, *Civil Society and Development*, Colorado: Lynne Rienner: 63–88.

Howell, J. and Pearce, J. (2001b) *Civil Society and Development*, Colorado: Lynne Rienner.

Howell, J. and Pearce, J. (2001c) 'Civil Society and Development: Genealogies of the Conceptual Encounter' in J. Howell and J. Pearce, *Civil Society and Development*, Colorado: Lynne Rienner: 13–38.

Hudson, W. (2003) 'Problematizing European Theories on Civil Society' in D. C. Schak and W. Hudson (eds), *Civil Society in Asia*, Hampshire: Ashgate Publishing: 9–19.

Hulme, D. and Edwards, M. (1997) 'NGOs, States and Donors: An Overview' in D. Hulme and M. Edwards (eds), *NGOs, States and Donors: Too Close for Comfort?* London: Save the Children Fund, Macmillan Press Ltd: 3–22.

James, H. (2007) 'Introduction: civil society, religion and global governance – the power and persuasiveness of civil society' in H. James (ed.), *Civil Society, Religion and Global Governance. Paradigms of power and persuasion*, New York: Routledge: 1–10.

Keane, J. (1998) *Democracy and the State: New European Perspectives*, London: Verso.

Kerkvliet, B. J. T. (2001) 'An Approach for Analysing State-Society Relations in Vietnam' in *Journal of Social Issues in Southeast Asia (SOJOURN)*, 16 (2): 238–78.

Keucheyan, R. (2012) 'Die guten Fragen des Antonio Gramsci' in *Le Monde diplomatique, German edition*, Berlin, 10 August.

Kumar, K. (1993) 'Civil Society: an inquiry into the usefulness of an historical term' in *The British Journal of Sociology*, 44 (3): 375–95.

Landau, I. (2008) 'Law and Civil Society in Cambodia and Vietnam: A Gramscian Perspective' in *Journal of Contemporary Asia*, 38 (2): 244–58.

Lee Hock Guan (2004a) *Civil Society in Southeast Asia*, Singapore: Institute of Southeast Asian Studies.

Lee Hock Guan (2004b) 'Introduction: Civil Society in Southeast Asia' in Lee Hock Guan (ed.), *Civil Society in Southeast Asia*, Singapore: Institute of Southeast Asian Studies: 1–26.

Lewis, D. and Kanji, N. (2009) *Non-Governmental Organizations and Development*, New York: Routledge Perspectives on Development.

McIllwaine, C. (2009) 'Development: Civil Society' in R. Kitchin and N. Thrift (eds), *International Encyclopedia of Human Geography*, London: Elsevier: 136–41.

Mitsuo, N. (2001) 'Introduction' in N. Mitsuo, S. Siddique and O. F. Bajunid (eds), *Islam and Civil Society in Southeast Asia*, Pasir Panjang: Institute of Southeast Asian Studies: 1–30.

Palmer, M. and Finlay, V. (2003) *Faith in Conservation*, Washington, DC: World Bank.

Putnam, R. (1993) *Making Democracy Work: Civic Traditions in Modern Italy*, Princeton: Princeton University Press.

Quadir, F. and Jayant, L. (2004) 'Introduction: Globalization, Democracy and Civil Society after the Financial Crisis of the 1990s' in F. Quadir and L. Jayant (eds), *Democracy and Civil Society in Asia: Volume 1, Globalization, Democracy and Civil Society in Asia*, New York: Palgrave Macmillan: 1–12.

Queen, C. S. and King, S. B. (1996) *Engaged Buddhism, Buddhist liberation movements in Asia*, Albany: State University of New York Press.

Salemink, O. (2006) 'Translating, Interpreting, and Practicing Civil Society in Vietnam: A Tale of Calculated Misunderstandings' in D. Lewis and D. Mosse (eds), *Development Brokers and Translators: The Ethnography of Aid and Agencies*, Bloomfield: Kumarian Press, Inc.: 101–26.

Sen, A. (1997) *Human Rights and Asian values: Sixteenth Morgentau Memorial Lecture on Ethics and Foreign Policy*, New York: Carnegie Council on Ethics and International Affairs.

Sidel, M. (1995) 'The Emergence of a Nonprofit Sector and Philanthropy in the Socialist Republic of Vietnam' in T. Yamamoto (ed.), *Emerging Civil Society in the Asia Pacific Community*, Singapore: Institute of Southeast Asian Studies: 293–304.

Tasnim, F. (2007) 'Civil Society in Bangladesh: Vibrant but not vigilant. PhD thesis in Political Science', unpublished thesis: University of Tsukuba.

Thayer, C. A. (2009) 'Vietnam and the Challenge of Political Civil Society' in *Contemporary Southeast Asia*, 31 (1): 1–27.

The Change Institute (2008) *Study on the best practices in cooperation between authorities and civil society with a view to the prevention and response to violent radicalisation*, London: The Change Institute.

UNIFEM (2008) *Who answers to women? Gender & Accountability*, New York: United Nations Development Fund for Women.

Weller, R. P. (2005) 'Introduction: Civil Institutions and the State' in R. P. Weller (ed.), *Civil Life, Globalization, and Political Change in Asia. Organizing between Family and State*, London and New York: Routledge: 1–19.

White, G., Howell, J. A. and Shang Xiaoyuan (1996) *In Search of Civil Society: Market Reform and Social Change in Contemporary China*, Oxford: Oxford University Press.

World Bank (2012) *Defining Civil Society*. Online. Available at: http://web.worldbank.org/ WBSITE/EXTERNAL/TOPICS/CSO/0,,contentMDK:20101499~menuPK:244752~ pagePK:220503~piPK:220476~theSitePK:228717,00.html (accessed 31 October 2012).

Yamamoto, T. (1995a) *Emerging Civil Society in the Asia Pacific Community*, Singapore: Institute of Southeast Asian Studies.

Yamamoto, T. (1995b) 'Integrative Report' in T. Yamamoto (ed.), *Emerging Civil Society in the Asia Pacific Community*, Singapore: Institute of Southeast Asian Studies: 1–40.

Part I

Framing the contemporary civil society in Cambodia and Vietnam

2   In search of a civil society
Re-negotiating state–society relations in Cambodia

Joakim Öjendal

Framing the study

The term 'civil society' does not sit easily in Cambodian culture and history, being marked by the presence of an autonomous elite, steep hierarchies, and a massive gap between the ruler and the ruled (Mabbet and Chandler 1995). Or maybe the modern conception of the term – formed by various understandings of European history, from revolutionary Gramsci to the totalitarian Eastern Bloc, from hegemonic neoliberalism to aggressive alternativism, from enlightenment to contemporary development practice (Edwards 2011) – is a non-starter for understanding the state–society nexus in Cambodia? Either way, the misfit of fashionable conceptualizations formed from the European experience and a lived reality in Cambodia is stark, or so it seems.

In the process of recovering from three decades of war, auto-genocide, renewed civil war, and a repressive socialist/centralist regime, it is obvious that the re-negotiation of state–society relations is a cornerstone for post-conflict reconstruction efforts. Moreover, the historically and culturally crafted civil society in Cambodia – further twisted through state-led violence and crude repression – does neither tally well with the ideas cultivated in a neo-liberal development community, deeply intervening in the emerging Cambodian state through bi- and multi-lateral donor engagement, nor with requirements for a deepening democracy in a liberal society. Rather, the historical civil society is to be found in the religious realm, as vertical patronage structures or in kinship-based relations (Ebihara 1968; Ledgerwood 2002; cf. Ovesen *et al.* 1996). These are, however, typically seen as archaic and pre-modern (and therefore counter-productive) in the prevailing development discourse.

Having said that – and remembering James Clifford's insight that 'cultures' do not hold still for their portraits (referenced in Hughes and Öjendal 2006: 417) – civil society in Cambodia is undergoing rapid transformation (World Bank 2009: 7; Öjendal and Kim 2006; cf. Hughes and Un 2012; Öjendal and Kim 2012). Reasonably, the process and outcome of this 'shifting portrait' – i.e. how historical and cultural images as well as practices of civil society are mutually adapting – is central for the long-term success of post-conflict reconstruction as well as for continuous democratization. Hence, fundamental macro-structural change hinges on a 'successful' re-negotiation of state–society relations in which the organized civil society plays a key role (cf. Paffenholz and Spurk 2006). The nature of the state–society nexus negotiated through the civil society is therefore not only an intellectual reflection, but a key challenge in the contemporary nation-state-building process in Cambodia. If one of the key problems is that there has always been a 'gap' between the state and its people, the current phase of state-building needs to see a social contract between the two form. This would include a mutual dependency of a positive nature, where the state does not operate autonomously and irrespective of the needs and wants of its citizens, and where the citizens have needs from the state that they are able to articulate. In such a process the civil society is the only 'actor' able to initiate such a dialogue or overcoming the 'gap' in state–society relations.

In a Tocquevillian sense, the 'gap' is seen as detrimental to effective, democratic, and sustainable state-building. An active civil society would fill that void and provide the intermediary structures not previously present in Cambodia. So far, arguably, the electoral democracy has not independently been able to shrink that gap. Following Tocqueville, civil society is believed to play a vital role in reconstruction and the stabilization of the emerging state. Which role and how it is played out largely remains to be seen and will be discussed below. To date, our systematic knowledge on this is remarkably thin; as Un (2008) points out, this field has neither been well understood nor properly researched, since the bulk of attention has gone to analyses of elite rationales. In this chapter, I will discuss Cambodian civil society from an historical perspective, focusing on dilemmas that emerged from a post-conflict reconstruction phase permeated by liberalism and donor involvement, and their impacts on the form of civil society that has emerged.

As a point of reference I will use a classic definition by White, understanding civil society as 'an intermediate associational realm between state and family populated by organizations which are separate from the state, enjoy autonomy in relation to the state and are formed voluntarily by members of society to protect or extend their interests or values' (White 1994: 337–8). While this definition emphasizes voluntarism and separation from the state, it does neither explicitly define how civil society is positioned in relation to the state, nor how it is organized. Furthermore, due to the special nature of the civil society in Cambodia, admittedly stretching this definition somewhat, phenomena of a slightly different character (e.g. societal institutions such as patron–client structures) will also be addressed and juxtaposed with the emerging contemporary situation.[1]

Below, I will present a brief historical background of the conception of Cambodian civil society (or rather, of its absence) and the pressure for change arising from the arrival of the neo-liberal international order in 1993. In particular, I will juxtapose two differing paradigms that go toward explaining the contradictions and uncertainties in emerging in civil society. One the one hand are the historically and culturally defined perceptions of civil society, and on the other hand are the normatively laden and imported modern/liberal conceptions of civil society. I then review a series of evolutionary phases the civil society has undergone in contemporary Cambodia, before I turn to three cases illuminating the variety at hand.

The historical role of civil society in Cambodia

The historical literature on Khmer civilization emphasizes two aspects of state–civil society relations. First, it is ripe with statements on the crude, distant, and violent nature of the ancient 'state'. The great Angkor was a slave society with extremely steep hierarchies, distance between rulers and ruled, and a nobility completely sheltered from the life of regular people (Vickery 1986; Mabbet and Chandler 1995; cf. Chou 1967). People were consumables – a means for achieving the higher, religiously created, purpose of honouring the rulers and serving them in different ways. Ozay Mehmet (1997: 676) expresses and explains this elegantly:

> [T]he Khmer-Sanskrit idea of devaraja [God-king] legitimizes a tradition of cult worship, or 'legitimacy by divine royalty', which, by putting emphasis on form rather than substance, and ritual rather than accountability, places a huge social distance between the ruled and the ruler, elevates the patron–client relationship to the divine order and ends up sheltering injustice and exploitation.

While these are ancient traits, the contemporary Khmer cosmology is to a remarkably high degree defined by its origin both in cultural terms (Martin 1994; cf. Ledgerwood and Vijghen 2002) and in political terms (e.g. Roberts 2009; Un 2009; Pak *et al.* 2007). For instance, the Khmer Rouge regime and its atrocities have been explained in these terms (Ovesen 2004). The extreme top-down approach, the total insignificance of regular people, and the inherited propensity for violence (Seanglim 1991), in combination with particular political circumstances, create a 'vacuum' and a state–society distance where society can only be governed through fear and violence. A related feature is the culture of *patronage* permeating all spheres of Cambodian society (Pak *et al.* 2007; Hughes and Un 2007), which amounts to a tangible societal institution of major significance.

Second, Khmer society is historically shaped by the fact that people do not (historically) bury their dead and have little attachment to their place of birth (in contrast to, for example, neighbouring Vietnam), and therefore easily clear new land and change location (Thion 1993). Thereby, regular people avoid being 'caught' by the state, creating a certain 'anarchic' society that is basically mobile, fluid, and loosely organized in very small units. Villages in ethnic Khmer Cambodia (in contrast to, for instance, many minority villages) are neither defined by social coherence nor geographically centred (Ovesen *et al.* 1996; cf. Ebihara 1968). 'Community' does not historically carry an intelligible meaning beyond extended families and neighbours (cf. Thion 1999), and although there are traditional cooperative measures at the village level, participation, solidarity, and collective action does not come easily (e.g. Chou 2011;

Ros 2011; cf. Öjendal 2000). Projected up to the national level, this rural dynamic has influenced the evolution of contemporary, donor-driven initiatives. As the World Bank (2009: 1–2) puts it:

> Civil society in Cambodia is also a product of the country's unique political and social history. Most professional NGOs in Cambodia today owe their existence more to the influence and financial support of international donors than to the gradual opening up of democratic space, the natural scaling up of grassroots organizations, the emergence of a culture of volunteerism/social activism or the organized charity of an established middle class.

Current attempts at 'inventing' more stable and productive state–society relations are struggling with both the historical 'gap' between the ruler and the ruled, and the fact that there is little or no 'natural' inclination for people to fill that gap with any distinct organizational form, especially when the burden of initiating and organizing falls on the community itself. One recent study (Kim 2012) holds up the lack of 'intermediate institutions', which has also been emphasized by Chandler (1991) as one of the key dilemmas for developing a sustainable democratization as well as for the prospect of exercising 'good governance'. In terms of formal political reforms, democratization and decentralization have aimed to (partly) close this gap by inventing a localized state authority. However, broadly speaking, there is still a lack of 'intermediary' agencies/institutions/organizations in society. While this is a historical pattern, the situation is evolving and the 'vacuum' is being filled up, albeit in unexpected and unpredictable ways.

Cambodia enters neo-liberal globalism

> Cambodian society is certainly not unique in incorporating what appears to be incompatible contradictions within its culture. But seldom has such a culture's divergent themes been played out in a more dramatic fashion on the contemporary world stage or with the concomitant tragic loss of life and human resources.
>
> (Seanglim 1991: xv)

There are distinct and unreconciled contradictions between historical trends and the emerging civil society. But Cambodia could be expected to breed contradictions. After two decades of isolation and authoritarian rule, and following the UN peacebuilding operation (cf. Doyle 1995), the country opened up in the early 1990s, almost literally overnight, and introduced a liberal constitution. Attempts at creating an authoritarian and centralized command economy throughout the 1980s (Gottesman 2004) gave way to an anarchic society with a crude liberalism (Curtis 1998; Lizee 2000) steeped in traditional social norms which themselves are negotiated and unstable. As Kent (2010: 128) more eloquently put it: 'The problem of sharing "real" power and responsibility remains trapped in the nexus of old and new norms, in a deep anxiety about the loss of tradition and the dissolution of moral order.' Breakneck social and political change (Hughes 2003) was wrestling with inherited conservatism (Martin 1994), the shadows (and fear) of an authoritarian state (Chandler 1998), 'random' hyper-violence (Luco 2002; Hinton 2004), and existential reluctance to open public debate (Seanglim 1991; cf. Mabbet and Chandler 1995).

A number of conditions can be added to the historical sketch above describing the 'opening up' of Cambodia after almost three decades of misery and isolation. First, a massive amount of resources became available for reconstruction and development. Second, the state was weak, divided, and (in part) dominated by international actors and their financial resources (Lizee 2000). Third, there was an emerging liberal order – bordering on anarchic (cf. Hughes 2003). Finally, the needs were endless, ranging from poverty alleviation to infrastructure rehabilita-tion, from agricultural services to rights education (cf. Curtis 1998).

What started as a centralized and foreign-dominated process, the proliferation of NGO/CSOs eventually expanded far beyond international NGOs based in Phnom Penh. Many Cambodian NGO/CSOs emerged, often financed by the international community, but occasionally also in a more home-grown fashion. This unfolded further into localized community-based organizations (CBOs), which are currently to be found in almost every village (Kim and Öjendal 2012; cf. World Bank 2009: 8–9). However, after an initial 'free-for-all' in the 1990s, the influence of international aid became increasingly more constrained and limited in scope. The period of international aid money chasing NGO/CSOs in an almost unregulated society with huge needs subsequently led to a period of increased political control, culminating in a much-debated and harshly drafted 'NGO law', which would appear to restrict the activities of the NGOs further. At the same time, international aid money for the sector began to dry up, altering the political dynamics in the sector (Ou and Kim, this volume). The World Bank (2009: 27–8) estimates that there are more than 8,000 CBOs, close to 2,000 NGOs, around 400 labour unions, and lots of 'other' organizations, including an unknown number of village-based 'traditional associations' (with minimal organizational structures). The World Bank also notices (as do Ou and Kim, this volume) that these numbers are masking a rather low activity level overall, and an uncertain degree of sustainability. These figures nevertheless represent a huge expansion of the sector since the early 1990s, but it is still far below what can be found in other development contexts in places such as India or the Philippines.

What is briefly highlighted in the paragraphs above outlines a powerful and intriguing mix of civil society elements, including an emerging local government that is assumedly democratic, development-oriented, and approachable, in com-bination with a vibrant NGO sector with a wide gap to fill that is seeking a viable role in the state–civil society matrix. Currently, the fanning out of the activity of NGO/CSOs and their increasing local presence, on the one hand, and the demo-cratic decentralization, on the other hand, provide a complex web of, and a promising platform for, experimentation and innovation. In particular, the civil society–local authority relations are under negotiation, with both sides searching for new roles and new relations in a sincere and interesting way (Öjendal & Kim 2012). Below, I will develop some of the key themes introduced above, and at the same time elaborate a chronology of this field, taking as a point of departure the year 1993 and the opening up of the Cambodian society.

The emerging civil society in Cambodia – from international NGO-ism to CBOs aplenty

In this section, I will review the historical emergence of organized civil society in Cambodia under five related themes; these themes are essentially ordered chronologically, but occasionally they overlap in time.

Development NGO-ism enters Cambodia

Throughout the 1990s, in a 'post-conflict' period, there were considerably more resources available than there were implementers to be found (cf. Ou and Kim, this volume). In addition, there were virtually no Cambodian CSOs available to receive and capably manage any major sums of money and undertake any significant projects under the conditions the international development community demanded. The few that were emerging (see, for instance, AMARA below) were tentatively exploring the space, developing their working methods, and slowly building trust. As a result, international NGOs found themselves with unprecedented space in which to manoeuvre, with massive resources accessible, and generally confronting a *tabula rasa*. They were, however, also working largely without counterparts directly implementing programmes and projects (e.g. SPM 2003a, 2003b). The slowly emerging Cambodian NGOs were hampered by the lack of historical/cultural tradition discussed above, and often resembled consultancy companies, complete with 'business ideas', 'entrepreneurialism', and 'funding plans', but lacking in popular constituency, bottom-up dynamics, and internally participatory practices (ibid.). It was not rare that they had political agendas and directly or indirectly engaged in politics (ibid.).

At the same time, at the local level, civil society – according to the definition above – hardly existed. Organized kinship relations were to a large extent broken, as a result of genocide and prolonged civil war, and the little 'community' to be found in the 1960s (cf. Ebihara, 1968, Hughes and Conway, 2004; cf. Öjendal 2000) had largely degenerated, leaving the society fragmented and weakened. The *Sangha*, the Buddhist order, and its local system of pagodas, monks, and laypersons, traditionally important in the local society, was also fragmented as a result of violence and the Khmer Rouge's explicit attempt at dismantling it. Finally, the historical patronage system was also undermined and was changing in nature (although not really 'organized' civil society, patronage remained a key social structure in society, cf. Ovesen *et al.* 1996; Ledgerwood 2002). None of these internal variations of civil society fit the new political-economic order, and did not receive any initial resources in the externally led reconstruction period.[2]

Hence, the early phase of emerging civil society was marked by external interventions, resources, and preferences, and with very few references to Cambodian society as we had known it up to this point.

From advocacy to development

Although elections of acceptable quality were held in 1993, a constitution written, and a government formed, 'normality' did not return instantly. In hindsight it is hard to view the latter half of the 1990s as a 'post-conflict' phase at all. Nonetheless, there was a gradual process of balancing and maturity taking place in the civil society realm. Two structural shifts tentatively emerged in the formation of civil society from the end of the 1990s onwards.

First, over time, international NGOs had been able to partly transfer responsibilities to Cambodian NGOs and, in the process, also transferred the 'civil society discourse' found in the development sphere. Initially, Cambodian CSOs were often not well organized internally as regards statutes and participation, largely replicating Cambodian cosmology with steep hierarchies and weak downward accountability (also reflecting their sometimes business-like nature). At the turn of the century there were a number of spectacular financial corruption scandals, demonstrating the immature nature of these CSOs and the insufficient financial control mechanisms in place at the time. In time, many Cambodian NGOs improved their internal structures and aimed at getting formally registered with the Ministry of Interior (see e.g. the case of Amara below).

Second, international NGOs (and later, their Cambodian counterparts) started to fan out of Phnom Penh, putting considerable efforts into establishing themselves in rural areas and acquiring a broader foundation among the Cambodian population. International NGOs also channelled resources – often through the local NGOs/CSOs – to more development-oriented activities outside the capital (SPM 2003a), such as to issues related to land, fisheries, and forest areas. This process was primarily possible by targeting particular areas with particular issues. For instance: fishery issues around the Tonle Sap by FACT, rice production in the lowlands by CEDAC (see Feuer, this volume), and anti-dambuilding advocacy in the northeast (see Thim, this volume). Occasionally, fully Cambodian CSOs emerged through this process (see the case of Buddhism for Social Development Action below), working with somewhat different methods to those that were integrated in the international development community.

Communities emerging, but remaining thin and weak

The next phase of the growing Cambodian civil society was the emergence on a broad scale of community-based organizations (CBOs) in the early 2000s. While they have roots in traditional Cambodia, many of these CSOs are not a 'natural' part of local mobilization. Nevertheless, by the mid-2000s they were mushrooming in virtually every village (cf. World Bank 2009). A combination of a basic recovery process in rural areas, the acceptance of participatory political pluralism, a decade of role-modelling by NGOs, and even the impacts of some government-run projects (e.g. 'Seila') had served to introduce basic organizational skills and some participatory ambitions, providing the groundwork for the capability of self-mobilization. This increasingly rendered localized and functional CBOs fit to fill a space where no civil society actors had previously operated (Öjendal and Kim 2006).

The opportunities and contexts for local mobilization were also expanding. Basic state services were (re)instated (although they were woefully incomplete and needed support); there was a national policy promoting irrigation (but little in the way of technical services was made available); primary education was systematically organized (yet local teachers needed extra income to make them appear in classrooms regularly); elderly people without family of their own needed support (but no such service was offered); fisheries became legally regulated (but illegal fishing was rampant). Hence, water utilization committees, school and parent committees, elderly committees, and fishery communities rose in relation to a need, thrived as a result of external organizational and financial support, and enjoyed formal state recognition (cf. Kim and Öjendal 2012; Öjendal and Kim 2012).

Having said that, it should be mentioned that the tasks these CBOs engaged in (water, education, elderly care, etc.) were hardly new. Historically, there have been local embryos of 'CBOs', albeit in considerably less organized forms and usually materializing unevenly and incompletely. Sometimes labelled 'Traditional Associations' (World Bank 2009: 8), these precursors to modern CBOs were led by anyone with engagement and some capacity. Thus, these are neither entirely new phenomena, which simply replicate self-help systems from the early post-Khmer Rouge era or even from the *Sangkum* era in the 1960s, nor are they as professional and 'organized' as they may appear. While there is no doubt these CBOs exist as a result of community initiative (see below for a case of a fishery organization), they have some unexpected features. First, although they serve the community by providing a much-needed service, and occasionally have broad popular legitimacy, they are typically pursued by a few individuals who define the nature of their work. Second, they often include local officials who are often acknowledged (and even registered and trained) by local state authorities (throwing their 'autonomous' nature in doubt). Third, they are often set up and initially financed by a foreign NGO or Cambodian CSO with foreign support, rendering their local legitimacy (in the eyes of both local authorities and local citizens) somewhat tarnished (Kim and Öjendal 2012).[3] To be financed from (and therefore accountable to) outside interests, *and* be accepted and cooperating with local authorities, *and* remain broadly legitimate/popular is a great balancing act for CBOs and local CSOs. This entails trade-offs that are imperfect. Therefore, these 'community-based' organizations are very much a hybrid phenomenon, where local, state, and foreign development interests co-exist.

Decentralization creating local space for civil society

Since 1993 Cambodia has had four consecutive national elections and three commune-based ones, has mostly enjoyed freedom of speech and freedom to organize, and has enjoyed a stable constitution; yet it is commonly considered a democracy with severe deficiencies (cf. Un 2009). While this debate is beyond the scope of this chapter (cf. Öjendal and Lilja 2009), there seems to be little doubt that the funding and space for NGOs – and especially for those working with advocacy issues – has diminished (Öjendal and Kim 2012). The state has reduced the liberties of NGOs, tightened regulation, and raised demands for various forms of registration. This is felt most acutely by NGOs working in sensitive sectors, while other sectors (see Feuer, this volume) renegotiate a plural relationship with the state. The year 2005, in which several human rights advocates were arrested, could be seen as the year in which political space for NGOs started to shrink (cf. Heder 2005; McCargo 2005), while around the same time democratic decentralization started to sink in and open for political pluralism locally (Öjendal and Kim 2011).

The paradox is that although central authorities are putting more pressure on major NGOs working with advocacy, decentralized authorities (commune councils) are more open to working with local NGOs on most issues, and certainly on service delivery and poverty alleviation. In recent studies the decentralized – and fairly democratic – local authorities have been seen as part of the reason for increased gender equality in politics (Kim and Öjendal 2011; cf. Hiwasa, this volume), and increased space for NGOs to work locally (Öjendal and Kim 2012). In a survey for the latter study it was found that commune councillors regard NGOs as crucial for local development, and that the commune authorities perceived themselves as more dependent on the NGOs than vice versa (ibid.), demonstrating that NGOs appear more threatening to central than to local powers. It was also overwhelmingly clear in that study that the commune councils wanted the NGOs to be active in their respective communes. Feuer (this volume) highlights a similar duality, with the state embracing and distancing NGOs while, at the same time, being locked into a relationship of mutual dependency.

Revival of the historical civil society

For more than a decade and a half (at least) there has been a sustainable regrowth of historical societal institutions. This is true for Buddhism and its institutional organization, driven by a local need for spiritual and moral guidance and various elites' (both from the diaspora and Phnom Penh) desire to gain merit through financing the building of pagodas (Marston 2009: 240). This is a highly uneven process with sometimes randomly distributed resources, creating pockets of strong presence and major local significance but also leaving some areas with institutions that are financially, organizationally, and morally weak. One possibility is that Buddhism has more significance as a localized institution, providing a moral model and guiding people in everyday life, than as a strictly religious institution or as a development agent (cf. Ehlert, this volume).

As was noted above with regard to the post-genocide period, family and kinship networks were broken, which added to the historically anarchic structure of Cambodian society, producing a rather extreme situation (cf. Ovesen *et al.* 1996). This was further emphasized by the absence of generalized trust following the extreme violence of the 1970s and the civil war of the 1980s (cf. Luco 2002). However, gender equality, family ties, and generalized trust are far more widely entrenched now, and wider kinship structures are emerging (albeit still in a comparatively modest fashion). A modernized version of patronage is also emerging, although not so much based on local landholdings and the typical dynamics of the rural areas, as on money, business, and political connections (cf. Pak *et al.* 2007; Hughes and Un 2007; Roberts 2009). Moreover, the highly mobile nature of contemporary Cambodian society, driven by partial urbanization, labour migration, and the overall pragmatic/loose family structure, often keeps families separated – furthening the fragmentation of social institutions.

An example of other organizations occupying a space between the family and the state are youth organizations; up to 70 per cent of the population is under 30 and this group is becoming increasingly educated. Youth organizations are steadily increasing their membership, although many remain local and issue-oriented. Trade unions also attract a major following; 40 per cent of the workforce is estimated to belong to one of the 370 registered unions (Makin 2006: 25; cf. World Bank 2009: 9). Both unions and youth organizations were recognized during the socialist era and, because both are now possible power-houses, they are subject to intense co-option attempts by state interests.

For better or worse there is a 'normalization' of sorts taking place, in which historical civil society reconstitutes itself (in new forms), functional organizational entities slowly emerge, and the development-oriented, externally funded, civil society is shrinking and searching for new ways forward. As one NGO worker told us during the fieldwork for this chapter: before it was 'money chasing NGOs', but now it is 'NGOs chasing money'. NGOs adapt economically in different ways, one way being through commercialization and private sector engagement. This path is most notably exhibited by ACLEDA, followed by CEDAC (cf. Feuer, this volume). Furthermore, many knowledge-based organizations are now increasingly pursuing private consultancy, while many others are simply scaling down. Adaptation to political pressure occasionally forces rights/advocacy NGOs to open a 'development window' in order to justify their presence and enhance their legitimacy (in the eyes of the state). For the moment the state seems to quite satisfied to co-opt or reduce the 'threatening' (i.e. the politicized and rights-based) spread of organized civil society, a venture that is inadvertently facilitated by the financial withdrawal from Cambodia of the international donor and NGO community.

The growing associational civil society[4]

Currently, there are many different creatures filling the 'intermediate associational realm', and doing so in different ways. A crude categorization[5] based on scale suggests three varieties of intermediate associations. First, we have the professional and (reasonably) well-funded NGOs working with formal statutes, internal organization, work plans, and educated staff (e.g. AMARA, ADHOC). These are typically supported by international counterparts, which also influence them quite a lot (albeit indirectly) in terms of ideology and practice. They rarely have a defined constituency or broad membership registration.[6] Second, there are the more home-grown CSOs, working 'less professionally', often with a limited geographical spread and a limited budget but operating from a more culturally adapted point of departure (e.g. BSDA, see below) and in close cooperation with local authorities. Third, we have CBOs, which arise from a functional need of a localized nature, with limited organization and no professional skills. This third category differs wildly in significance and success, in scope and engagement, but shares a typically para-statal characteristic, in that they are set up under directives from the local state machinery and often include village and/or commune officials (in a non-official role). In spite of their localized nature, they often also have outside patrons financing their activities and supporting their organizational structure. Below, I will provide a glimpse into the nature of these organizations by presenting three different cases.

AMARA, the first case, represents the large-scale, increasingly professional, and maturing NGO that is invented in Cambodia, by Cambodians, but deeply ingrained in international NGO-ism. BSDA ('Buddhism and Society Development Association') represents the home-grown and self-reliant NGO, working with culturally adapted methods. Finally, the fishery CBO represents a common form – albeit unusually successful here – of village-based community organizations arising from sheer need. Since other categories and other cases can be found, these should be seen as illuminative rather than representative in a strict sense.

AMARA – professional but 'domestic'

AMARA was established in Banteay Meanchey in 1994 and was immediately successful. It focused primarily on gender-based violence, which was highly relevant as the civil war had just ended, and was therefore extremely 'fundable'. The sources of funding have varied but include international NGOs and bilateral donors. In 1997, AMARA applied, and was approved, for registration with the Ministry of Interior as a local NGO. Back then, a representative recalls, the organization was blamed for being politically biased against the ruling party (the Cambodian People's Party or CPP), but, as we were also told, it was ironically also blamed for being too close to the CPP because of its strategy of engaging with the government. No hard evidence for either allegation has surfaced. As time went on, people in the government got used to the work of AMARA and acknowledged the results of its work. Looking back, representatives from

AMARA claim that, in the 1990s, it was really difficult to work with the government or to get its approval for working on women's rights and democracy. They were not allowed to train women in local leadership/rights at the commune level, but could do so at the district office – closely watched by the government. The organization was warned a few times by the provincial governor of Banteay Meanchey about the nature of its work. By 2005, the organization started to openly discuss women in politics and carry out other advocacy work, such as training men and women in community development (for a similar situation in a different context, see Hiwasa, this volume).

AMARA is shaped by the hierarchy and top-down perspectives of Cambodian society and applies a respectful attitude vis-à-vis government officials. At the local level, NGO work is less formal. Government, however, demands different things than do AMARA's donors, which makes it important to explain the organization's reasons and work plan to both parties. Issues of rural development and service delivery are easier to receive acceptance for from the side of the local authorities than issues of local governance or leadership, which do not provide material outputs. In AMARA's experience, in order to maintain good relations with the government, close engagement and participation are very important. The overall trend, one interviewee stated, is that local authorities are now easier to work with than before, as decentralization reforms bed in. The government also seems more straightforward than before, and the organization can even work on, and discuss with authorities, the issue of anti-corruption. Since late 2011, however, AMARA has faced a serious funding challenge; many international donors are pulling out of Cambodia and no obvious alternative funding is forthcoming.

Buddhism for Social Development Action (BSDA) – a home-grown CSO with close relations to local authorities and communities

The founding ideas of BSDA came from the venerable Thorn Vandong in 2001, but the organization was not registered as a CSO until 2005. The group was started informally by 40 members who worked without payment for three years and was financed by minor membership fees and contributions collected at Buddhist ceremonies. BSDA is currently operating in five major areas:

- Education and Buddhist leadership initiative: teaching street children, gangs, and other vulnerable young people about morals and social values, as well as how to behave properly and help society;
- Improvement of basic social morality in society: through a radio talk show, improving multi-cultural life skills and awareness about health issues, such as HIV and drug addiction;
- Orphanage program: BSDA works through scholarships, providing poor children, such as scavengers and street children, with skills to survive;
- Agriculture and livelihood: helping single-headed households (i.e. widows) and the most destitute families;

• Good governance and advocacy: helping to build the capacity of commune councillors and local authorities.

A BSDA interviewee said there is a need to have good internal management, including accountability, transparency, personal commitment, and care and concern for the public, rather than for individual interests. This helps, we were told, to build internal trust while making the organization a role model for behaviour. In line with Buddhist thinking, the personal behaviour of BSDA leaders is important for its popular appeal and its relationship with the authorities. As a leader of an organization, 'one needs to be humble, show respect and get everybody involved in the decision-making process'. This is important, as BSDA is dependent on membership fees from people that are voluntarily contributing.

CSO activities, it is often assumed, should also be adapted to, and understood in, the local context of culture, norms, and values. Since the Cambodian society was seriously wounded in the past, BSDA argues that it is extremely difficult to get people to engage with the authorities. Therefore, CSO activities must not imply further confrontation but should rather be geared towards healing the wounds. Overall, in the engagement with the commune, district, and province, it is very important not to be seen to be 'teaching' officials how to act. Instead, CSOs should, it is said, cooperate and work in partnership on the basis of mutual respect/trust; for example by being clear about what the organization can and cannot do. In return, in the experience of BDSA interviewees, the authorities tend to be supportive and helpful.

A successful community-based organization managing fishing

In the mid-1990s, fishing areas were awarded to private companies by the Fishery Department, while villagers were disallowed from fishing in these blocs even for subsistence. By 1995, three villages in this area had experienced tremendous hardships and suffered from harsh crackdowns by military and police officers hired by private fishing lot owners to protect their fishing zones. Any fishing by villagers was considered illegal and could lead to arrest and punishment. The key problem was that the private companies claimed fishing rights as far as the water went, which, during some wet seasons, was all the way up to the village houses.

With the assistance of an outside CSO, villagers sought to formally establish a community fishery,[7] and they organized workshops, conferences, and meetings with local authorities and line ministries to achieve this goal. In 2000, there was a new policy from the government implying that less fishing lots would be awarded to private companies and that some areas were allocated for community management/fishing. This suited the local community and they subsequently set up a fishery community, which was officially recognized by the government in 2001. They then set up a committee spanning three villages, established internal rules and regulations, mobilized members, and prepared working strategies.

The fishery community is headed by one chairman and three deputies, one from each of the three villages. These four are elected by the village populations in elections organized by the CSO and monitored by the commune council, the police, the military police, the district governor, and officials from the Fishery Department. The community committee, consisting of nine members from the three villages, has a lot of work but no formal mandate since the work is on a voluntary basis. It is funded by multilateral donors through domestic CSOs.[8]

Working with the local authorities and the Fishery Department, the fishery community carefully follows rules and laws as defined by the government, and encourages others to do so, especially people in the community. When fishing rights are violated, the fishery community members call upon and inform the commune councillors. The fishery community can then intervene by confiscating the illegal fishing equipment on the spot and by reporting the violation to the Fishery Department at district level. Due to this informal channel, crimes can be more quickly and effectively prevented than if they had to wait for approval from the Fishery Department and other authorities.

Before the fishery community was established, villagers were, as they recall, frustrated with the local authorities, the police, guards, and the Fishery Department, considering them their enemy and not communicating with them at all. Although the overall problem of illegal fishing is not completely solved, the situation is reportedly different now. The Fishery Department provides technical support, such as a legal framework, and helps to stop illegal activities. Meanwhile, commune and district authorities provide security through policing efforts and grant legal authorization for interventions.

Conclusions – growth, change, and contradictions

The emergence of the civil society in Cambodia is fed from a variety of interests and is in flux (cf. World Bank 2009). The flux is occurring during the process of change from historically and culturally defined positions and practices towards internationalized and development-oriented ones. There is potentially a swing back taking place, and even a hybridization of sorts. Another aspect of this flux is within the internationalized civil society realm, with links to various cultures and ideologies. We are forced to think of not one civil society, but of civil societies, occupying different spaces with different hallmarks, functions, and appearances.

In terms of plurality, we can juxtapose two extreme poles framing the nature of the organized civil society; one extreme is the confrontational position drawing on a Gramscian perspective, and the other extreme is a liberal Tocquevillian one. From having had an alien and oppositional/confrontational character – i.e. defined from the outside, inhering political opposition, focusing on advocacy for creating new societal norms, operating in the centre – civil society has now moved towards a more adapted character, aligning with the state, pursuing a problem-solving role inside the system. In other terms, the pattern of the civil society's (ies') progression is such that it has been moving away from a Gramscian position toward a Tocquevillian one.

In terms of interests, various forces drive the change described above. The balance between outside interests and those of domestic Cambodian ones has, during the last decade, shifted dramatically to the benefit of the latter. In a parallel movement, the state, previously overwhelmed by the shifts, is now attempting to control and co-opt this realm more systematically. Ironically, to some extent, the 'missionary' approach of international civil society has succeeded in triggering local capacity and a will to organize, which has invariably caused an amalgamation of sorts where local traits now are permeating a fair share of the civil society realm.

What seems to be beyond doubt is that the significance of the civil society has increased drastically during the last two decades, and that civil society serves many important functions. To some extent it has risen to populate the 'intermediary' sphere that has, historically, been an empty space. Having said that, this intermediary sphere is occasionally subject to processes of intense co-option attempts by the state, which harbours a reflex to close this space (cf. Ou and Kim, this volume), and which is generally repulsed by collective engagement and organization by the population at large. Actors and agents in this sphere may have space to refrain or accept various pressures and interests, but they must inevitably relate to government engagement. In this sense, civil society positions are in constant transition, mirroring a broader political economy and the possible space it allows for 'an intermediate associational realm'.

The civil society is growing, yet being co-opted; it is consolidating itself as a force to be reckoned with, yet adapting itself to the realm of the (politically) possible; and, in this growth, it is simultaneously under increasing pressure. In contemporary Cambodia, this process remains dynamic, multifaceted, and contradictory. More than anything, it is undecided, important, and interesting, the details of which are further explored in other chapters of this volume.

Notes

1 These societal institutions are hardly 'associational', but they have at times an overwhelming presence, and they may act as if they were associational.
2 Subsequently, rural pagodas received 'donations' from the Khmer diaspora and Phnom Penh-based politicians and tycoons, while family networks were mended and patronage returned to force with a more business-like character (contrasting to the historically localized landowning strongman patron).
3 Admittedly, some of these transform into self-financing operations (cf. Wells-Dang, this volume; Öjendal and Kim 2012).
4 The cases are based on an extensive qualitative fieldwork financed by The Asia Foundation, to which we are grateful. Ten qualitative case studies were reviewed, which are drawn upon here. The cases review NGO/CSO members' perceptions about their roles, their evolutions, and the conditions they work under. These case studies were researched by Kim Sedara and Duong Viriroth.
5 The World Bank suggests a different typology, namely: (1) Traditional associations; (2) 'Modern' community-based organizations (CBOs); (3) Non-governmental organizations (NGOs); (4) Trade unions; (5) Youth organizations; (6) Other categories (World Bank 2009: 8–9).
6 Un (2004: 272) states that the Cambodian NGO sector is a 'civil movement without citizens'.

7 Community Fishery is the term for the phenomenon of governing local fisheries locally. 'The fishery community' is the name of the actual community in our case.
8 The fishery community does not receive any funding from the commune councils' budgets, but they are very supportive in terms of liaising and networking with higher authorities and assisting with security issues. The fishery community gets good technical support from the Fishery Department, and support in terms of administration, security, and mobilization from the commune council and district authorities.

References

Chandler, D. (ed.) (1991) *The Tragedy of Cambodian History: Politics, War and Revolution since 1945*, New Haven, CT: Yale University Press.
Chandler, D. (1998) 'The Burden of Cambodia's Past' in Brown, F. Z. and D. G. Timberman (eds), *Cambodia and the International Community: The quest for peace, development, and democracy*, New York: Asia Society: 33–48.
Chou, C. (2010) 'The Local Governance of Common Pool Resources: The Case of Irrigation Water in Cambodia', Working Paper Series No. 47, Phnom Penh: Cambodian Development Resource Institute.
Chou, Ta-Kouan, (1967 [1297]) *Notes on the Customs of Cambodia*, trans. by Paul, J. G. d'A., Bangkok: Social Science Association Press.
Curtis, G. (1998) *Cambodia Reborn?: The Transition to Democracy and Development*, Geneva: United Nations Research Institute for Social Development.
Doyle, M. W. (1995) *UN Peacekeeping in Cambodia: UNTAC's Civil Mandate*, Boulder: Lynne Rienner.
Ebihara, M. (1968) 'Svay, a Cambodian Village in Cambodia', unpublished thesis, Columbia University.
Edwards, M. (2011) *The Oxford Handbook of Civil Society*, Oxford: Oxford University Press.
Gottesman, E. (2004) *Cambodia after the Khmer Rouge: Inside the Politics of Nation Building*, New Haven: Yale University Press.
Heder, S. (2005) 'Hun Sen's Consolidation: Death or Beginning of Reform?' in *Southeast Asian Affairs*, Singapore: Institute of Southeast Asian Studies: 111–13.
Hinton, A. L. (2004) *Why Did They Kill? Cambodia in the Shadow of Genocide*, Berkeley: University of California Press.
Hughes, C. (2003) *The Political of Cambodia's Transition, 1999–2001*, London/New York: Routledge Curzon.
Hughes, C. and Conway, T. (2004) *Understanding Pro-Poor Political Change: The policy process*, London: Overseas Development Institute.
Hughes, C. and Un, K. (2007) *Cambodia Country Governance Analysis*, Phnom Penh: Department for International Development (United Kingdom).
Hughes, C. and Öjendal, J. (2006) 'Reassessing Tradition in Times of Political Change: Post-War Cambodia Reconsidered' in *Journal of South East Asian Studies*, 37 (3): 415–20.
Hughes, C. and Un, K. (eds), (2012) *Cambodia's Economic Transformation*, Copenhagen: NIAS Press.
Kent, A. (2010) *Reconfiguring Security: Buddhism and Moral Legitimacy in Cambodia*, Copenhagen: Nordic Institute of Asian Studies.
Kim, S. (2012) 'Democracy in Action: Decentralisation Reform in Post-Conflict Cambodia', unpublished thesis, University of Gothenburg, Sweden.

Kim, S. and Öjendal, J. (2012) 'Accountability and Local Politics in Natural Resource Management' in C. Hughes and K. Un (eds), *Cambodia's Economic Transformation*, Copenhagen: NIAS Press: 266–87.

Ledgerwood, J. (2002) *Cambodia Emerges from the Past: Eight essays*, Dekalb, IL: Southeast Asia Publications, Centre for Southeast Asian Studies, Northern Illinois University.

Ledgerwood, J. and Vijghen, J. (2002) *Decision Making in Rural Khmer Villages*, Dekalb, IL: Centre for Southeast Asian Studies, Northern Illinois University.

Lizee, P. (2000) *Peace, Power, and Resistance in Cambodia: Global Governance and the Failure of International Conflict Resolution*, Basingstoke: Macmillan.

Luco, F. (2002) *Between a Tiger and a Crocodile: Management of Local Conflicts in Cambodia. An Anthropological Approach to Traditional and New Practices*, Phnom Penh: United Nations Educational, Scientific and Cultural Organization.

Mabbet, I. and Chandler, D. (1995) *The Khmers*, Oxford/Cambridge: Blackwell.

Makin, J. (2006) *Cambodia: Women and Work in the Garment Industry*, Phnom Penh: ILO's Better Factory Cambodia and the World Bank's Justice for the Poor.

Malena C. and Chhim, K. (2009) *Linking Citizens and the State – An Assessment of Civil Society Contributions to Good Governance in Cambodia*, Washington, DC: World Bank.

Marston, J. (2009) 'Cambodian Religion since 1989' in Öjendal, J. and Lilja, M. (eds), *Beyond Democracy in Cambodia: Political Reconstruction in a Post-Conflict Society*, Copenhagen: NIAS Press: 224–49.

Martin, M. A. (1994) *Cambodia: A shattered society*, Berkeley: University of California Press.

McCargo, D. (2005) 'Cambodia: Getting Away with Authoritarianism?' in *Journal of Democracy*, 16 (4): 98–112.

Mehmet, O. (1997) 'Development in a Wartorn Society: What Next in Cambodia?' in *Third World Quarterly*, 18 (4): 673–86.

Öjendal, J. (2000) 'Sharing the Good – Modes of Managing Water Resources in the Lower Mekong River Basin', unpublished thesis, University of Gothenburg, Sweden.

Öjendal, J. and Kim, S. (2006) '"Korob Kaud Klach": In Search of Agency in Rural Cambodia' in *Journal of Southeast Asian Studies*, 37 (3): 507–26.

Öjendal, J. and Kim S. (2011) *Real Democratization in Cambodia? An Empirical Review of the Potential of a Decentralization Reform*, Working Paper No. 9, Visby: Swedish International Center for Local Democracy (ICLD).

Öjendal J. and Kim S. (2012) *Is your Ground as Common as mine? A Critical Review of the Role of Civil Society in Local Governance in Cambodia*, The Asia Foundation, Mimeo, Phnom Penh.

Ovesen, J. (2004) 'Political Violence in Cambodia and the Khmer Rouge "Genocide"' in Richards, P. (ed.), *No Peace, No War: An Anthropology of Contemporary Armed Conflicts*, Athens, Ohio and Oxford: Ohio University Press and James Currey: 22–39.

Öjendal, J. and Lilja, M. (eds), (2009) *Beyond Democracy in Cambodia: Political reconstruction in a post-conflict society*, Copenhagen: NIAS Press.

Ovesen, J., Trankell, I.-B. and Öjendal, J. (1996) 'When Every Household is an Island: Social Organization and Power Structures in Rural Cambodia' in *Uppsala Research Reports in Cultural Anthropology 15*, Uppsala, Sweden: Department of Cultural Anthropology, Uppsala University.

Paffenholz, T. and Spurk, C. (2006) *Civil Society, Civic Engagement and Peacebuilding*, Social Development Papers, Conflict Prevention and Reconstruction Paper No. 36, Washington, DC: World Bank.

Pak K., Vuthy, H., Netra, E., Sovatha, A., Kim, S., Knowles, J. and Craig, D. (2007) 'Accountability and Neo-patrimonialism in Cambodia: A critical literature review' in *Working Paper 34*, Phnom Penh: Cambodian Development Resource Institute.

Roberts, D. (2009) 'The Superficiality of State Building in Cambodia: Patronage and Clientelism as Enduring Forms of Politics' in R. Paris and T.D. Sisk (eds), *The Dilemmas of Statebuilding: Confronting the Contradictions of Postwar Peace Operations*, New York: Routledge: 149–69.

Ros B., Ly, T. and Thompson, A. (2011) 'Catchment Governance and Cooperation Dilemmas: A Case Study from Cambodia' in *Working Paper 61*, Phnom Penh: Cambodian Development Resource Institute.

Seanglim, B. (1991) *The Warrior Heritage: A Psychological Perspective of Cambodian Trauma*, California: El Cerrito.

SPM Consultant (2003a) 'Civil Society and Democracy in Cambodia: Changing roles and trends', the Fifth Report of the Sida Advisory Team on Democratic Governance in Cambodia, Stockholm and Phnom Penh: SPM Consultants.

SPM (2003b) 'Leveling the Playing Field for Democratic Governance – Technical Review of the DESA Project Portfolio in Cambodia', the Sixth Report of the Sida Advisory Team (SAT) on Democratic Governance in Cambodia, Phnom Penh: Mimeo.

Thion, S. (1993) *Watching Cambodia: Ten Paths to Enter the Cambodian Tangle*, Bangkok, Cheney: White Lotus.

Thion, S. (1999) 'What is the Meaning of Community?' in *Cambodia Development Review*, 3 (3): 12–13.

Un, K. (2004) 'Democratisation Without Consolidation: The Case of Cambodia', unpublished thesis, Dekalb, IL: Northern Illinois University.

Un, K. (2008) *Civil Society, Public Space, and Democratization in Cambodia*, Dekalb, IL: Northern Illinois University.

Un, K. (2009) 'The Judicial System and Democratization in Post-Conflict Cambodia' in Öjendal, J. and Lilja M. (eds), *Beyond Democracy in Cambodia: Political Reconstruction in a Post-Conflict Society*, Copenhagen: NIAS Press: 70–100.

Vickery, M. (1986) *Kampuchea: Economics, Politics and Society*, Pinter/Rienner: London.

White, G. (1994) 'Civil Society, Democratization and Development: Clearing the Analytical Ground' in *Democratization*, 1 (3): 375–90.

3 Bringing past models into the present

Identifying civil society in contemporary Vietnam

Bach Tan Sinh

With a long history of decentralized state–society relations and formally recognized associational activity, the Vietnamese experience of civil society is not easily captured by current definitions. The one-party political system building off a base of historical local groups and colonial structures presents a model of civil society that must be explained from the ground up. Building from a platform of historically active parts of society, *Đổi mới*, or market reforms, in the mid-1980s, have resulted in a fundamental transformation of Vietnam's economic and social structure, especially in its civil society. Major changes in economic opportunities have provided the society with an impetus for the development of new mediating groups such as non-governmental organizations (NGOs), community-based organizations (CBOs), and civil society networks. These new groups not only need to situate themselves in a civic realm dominated currently by state-sponsored mass organizations, but they are also challenged to reinvent the idea of Vietnamese civil society in general. The interpretation of the civil society concept in the context of Vietnamese society inevitably needs to take into account the fact that this concept was initially developed in the West (see Reis and also Waibel, both in this volume). This is partly illustrated by the fact that it has been difficult to translate the concept into Vietnamese. The term most commonly used seems to be '*xã hội dân sự*' (roughly translated as 'society of citizens'), which has appeared recently but is still only sporadically used. If civil society can be defined as a separate public sphere (*công*), 'it is a well understood term going back centuries in Vietnam, representing the space in which people conduct affairs beyond family or private sector (*tư*), but not specifically under the jurisdiction of government officials (*quan*)' (Marr 1994). However, it is increasingly clear that contemporary definitions of civil society and their embeddedness in the Vietnamese language are becoming more differentiated as they come into jargon and practice; for a more detailed account of this, please read Phuong Le Trong's contribution in this volume.

As the concept of civil society takes shape in response to outside influences, economic trends and political changes, the civic space it constitutes invariably needs to reshape itself and grow. Strictly speaking, the Constitution of Vietnam provides a principal basis for the development of civil organizations that are established by citizens and independent from the government. Article 69 clearly states that, 'the citizen shall enjoy freedom of opinion and speech, freedom of the press, the right to be informed, and the right to assemble, form associations and hold demonstrations in accordance with the provisions of the law'. Although this is under the current circumstances something of an ideal rather than a practical framework for civic engagement, Article 69 does provide a foundation for various changes. For example, this article has come to play a more prominent role in a context of limited and declining subsidies for the bureaucracy as well as the increasing demand of the economy, which has created openings for other actors and renegotiating the roles of existing actors. Indeed, the government of Vietnam has come to acknowledge that many functions which used to be performed by government institutions can now be carried out by self-established organizations and individuals (Kerkvliet *et al.* 2008; Norlund *et al.* 2008; Wischermann 2010). This is particularly so in the field of research and application of science and technology, and of economic, governance and social development policies (Sinh 2011; Centre for Cooperation Human Resource Development 2010). Indirectly, this has also encouraged the growth and differentiation of civil society in many other realms (Norlund *et al.* 2008).

In this overview chapter I will illuminate the evolving landscape of civil society in Vietnam, paying close attention to the organizational forms that have emerged or been renegotiated over time. To understand the unique case of Vietnamese civil society, I first call into question the various definitions of civil society that may apply, or have been applied, to Vietnam. Following this, I describe the historical precedents of Vietnamese social organization, which plays a significant role in bracketing the development of civil society. Thereafter, I lay out the contemporary institutional sphere set up by the state, and elaborate the many organizational forms that both align with, and operate outside of, the state apparatus. Before concluding, I discuss how civil society has adapted itself to Vietnam and how Vietnam is adapting to the evolution of civil society.

Defining civil society in Vietnam

The concept of civil society proposed by Kaldor can be seen as a classic reference point for Vietnam. She defines civil society as intermediate-level association, which manifests as 'self organisations outside the formal political circles' and which expand the 'space in which individual citizens can influence the condition in which they live both directly through self organisation' and by '[providing] a substitute for many of the functions performed by the state ... which the state can no longer afford to perform' (Kaldor 2000: 4). Definitions applied to Vietnam, however, have typically not remained stable for very long. In 1994, during the first conference which explicitly dealt with the topic of civil society in Vietnam, David Marr suggested that the definition developed by Larry Diamond (1994: 5) most closely defined the political context in the country. In this formulation, civil society is the realm of organized social life that is voluntary, self-generating, (largely) self-supporting, autonomous from the state, and bound by a legal order or set of shared rules. It is distinct from society in general in that it involves citizens acting collectively in a public sphere to express their interests, passions, and ideas, exchange information, achieve mutual goals, make demands on the state, and hold the state officials accountable.

Diamond (ibid.) also argued that, 'actors in civil society need the protection of an institutionalized legal order to guard their autonomy and freedom of action'.

Over time, it has become clear that this definition, and indeed any definition not penned with Vietnam in mind, does not adequately define the evolving position and understanding of civil society. At the very least, the definition should be different from the international concepts. The condition of separation from the government should be exempted to some degree, since all organizations, in principle, fall under the aegis of the Communist Party and the state. Even without the presence of a specific law on non-governmental organization, all NGOs which were listed in the Vietnam NGOs Directory (Tran Tuan and Le Quoc Hung, 2002), are formally established and registered with government agencies and mass organizations. For example, many of them were registered with the former Ministry of Science, Technology and Environment (MOSTE),[1] particularly as research centres under the Vietnam Union of Science and Technology Associations (VUSTA). Party directives and government decisions not only often legally create these associations but also provide a framework for their development and activities. Moreover, people who run the so-called NGOs may also be state and Party officials.

In this context, the definition of Vietnamese civil society organization (CSO) should be based on the actual operations and activities of the organizations, which one finds in the works of Kerkvliet (1995; 2003) and Hannah (2005). In general, an associational unit should be termed CSO if it has indeed operated on behalf of, and contributed to, socio-economic development by virtue of its institutional features of autonomy, self-sufficiency in resources, and independence in managerial decision from the government. That said, these conditions need to be understood within the framework of Vietnamese society, history, and the evolving framework guided by the state and Party.

Interpreting civil society in the context of the Vietnamese history of social organization

Research on the traditional organization of Vietnamese society points to the cooperative relationship between state and villages, whereby the state would not intrude deeply into village affairs and thereby grant some degree of local autonomy. In this narrative, however, geographical differences and the impacts, cultural and structural, of Chinese domination (over the course of 1,000 years) play an important role. Villages, particularly in the north, sustained a form of organization that emphasized independence from the state as well as internal 'solidarity'. To some extent, these Vietnamese traditional villages could be viewed as heterogeneous civil society organizations.

This organization of these villages, in a broad sense, was defined by the traditional economic system of flooded rice cultivation, which necessitated a strong sense of community cohesion (to manage flood and natural disasters, to alternate labour, etc.). In addition, numerous wars taking place during the entire historical time span further enhanced the tradition of local solidarity intersecting with national engagement. There were also several dimensions which formed a basis for the existence of the villager's 'civic engagement' in the countryside: (1) mutual dependence in agricultural production among families stimulated reciprocal respect, equality and egalitarianism; (2) craft guilds (*phường*) and associations (*hội*) added to this interdependence and mutual respect; (3) age groups/ cohorts (*giáp*), egalitarian themselves, enabled a hierarchy with age roughly corresponding to rank; (4) the administrative organization of the village was based on the triangle of advisory (*kỳ lão*), legislative committee (*kỳ mục*), and executive council (*kỳ dịch*) that interfaced with '*giáp*' to form a very stable volunteer form of association. In addition, each village had its own laws (*huong ước*) and decentralized governance (*hội đồng kỳ mục*). To some extent, the idiom, 'The King's rule stops at the village gate' reflects a sort of democratic interdependence between state and village sector.

In urban centres in the past, social groupings called *phường* (ward) and *hội* (association), also existed. The old Ha Noi, the capital of Vietnam since 1010, was formed by an assembly of 36 *phường*. These *phường* produced and traded goods of high quality, such as silk, jewellery, leather, metal goods, and other different types of handicrafts. Internally, members of the *phường* were bound to help each other in the production of goods by, for example, providing technical assistance or loans to one another. In an expression of solidarity, they also committed themselves to protecting their trade secrets, maintaining a common price for products, and other similar activities. The names of these *phường* live on in modern times in the names of various streets in Hanoi, for example Paper Street.

During the French colonization, from the late 1930s up to 1940s, there was a significant emergence of civil society in Vietnam with the formation of many self-established associations that played counterpoint to the colonial government. The most prominent one was the Reform Association founded in 1904 by Phan Boi Chau,[2] who, among other things, sought to train young Vietnamese reformers in Japan and China. He called for general reforms, including the dissemination of the Romanized script, the development of industry and commerce, as well as the establishment of charities and farmers' associations. Phan Chu Trinh,[3] another reformist, organized campaigns against outdated customs and encouraged charitable activities. Most members of the Reform Association were intellectuals or social activists and mainly from urban areas. The financial resources were derived mainly from contributions by members and from wealthy families who opposed the colonialist government. Beyond the reform movement there existed many other forms of associations in economic, social, political, and cultural arenas. The trend among them was to favour overarching social reforms, of which many had anti-feudal, anti-colonialist, and revolutionary elements.

With the introduction of socialist construction in the north of the country since the mid-1950s, a new socio-economic and political space was established. It was defined by a highly centralized system with three pillars: the Party, the government, and the mass organizations. Within this scheme, the Party plays the leading role and exerts an encompassing power. The mass organizations, which are joined under the umbrella of the Vietnam Fatherland Front (VFF), although being broad-based and including participation of individuals from a wide spectrum of social groups, are also organized by the state with a mandate to mobilize people to achieve nationally defined goals. Despite the national orientation, the presence of these mass organizations indicates recognition of the need for local participation. In this respect, the government counts on the mass organizations. Thus, although organized and funded by the government, and therefore not non-governmental in a conventional sense, mass organizations play an important role in voicing local interests and needs to the government. With the market reforms initiated in the mid-1980s, a new socio-economic environment emerged that was more conducive to the development of civil society organizations and to the renegotiation of existing associational ties.

Legal and institutional framework for civil society in Vietnam

Vietnam went through a long period as a centrally planned economy and civil society was structured from the 1950s onwards – as mentioned earlier – by the establishment of government-led mass organizations, which aimed to penetrate every level of society (see Table 3.1).

Civil society, as a consequence of the formal structures emerging during this period, is defined to be uni-dimensional and socially homogenous. Although this definition has become less strict, particularly with the advancement of *Đổi mới*, the broader civil society apparatus is at odds with the expectations of international observers of civil society. Indeed, the sceptics insist that in Vietnam there is no non-governmental organization because all organizations are placed under the leadership of the Party and under the management of the state (Vasavakul 2003: 25ff.). While this type of categorical dismissal of Vietnamese civil society is not without its basis, it fails to consider the deviation from formal structures and the pre-existing diversity in associational forms.

While there is little precise agreement as to which associational forms should be included within civil society in Vietnam, particularly in terms of political and economic associations, they generally refer to the following classification:

1 the mass organizations (*đoàn thể*)
2 popular associations (*hội quần chúng*), including the professional associations
3 funds, charities, and supporting centres, often set up by government decree

Table 3.1 Political structure in Vietnam

Level	Communist Party	Legislative body	Executive body	Mass organizations
Central level	Central Committee of Communist Party	National Assembly	Government	Central Committees of Fatherland Front, Ho Chi Minh Youth Union, Women's Union, Trade Union, Farmers' Association, and other mass organizations
Provinces	Provincial Committee of Communist Party	Provincial People's Council	Provincial People's Committee	Provincial Committees of mass organizations
Districts	District Committee of Communist Party	District People's Council	People's Committee Services	District-level mass organizations
Communes	Party cell	Commune People's Council	Commune People's Committee	Commune mass organizations

4   professional centres or research/education centres (Vietnamese NGOs (VNGOs) – (*tổ chức phi chính phủ*), such as the ones listed in the VNGOs Directory[4] (Tran Tuan and Le Quoc Hung 2002)
5   community-based organizations (CBOs).

In addition to these, there are also civil society forms which do not fit a particular category. In general, however, all of these five categories of actors have managed to reach the provincial, district and even commune level, the extent of which depending naturally upon the nature of their work and their available resources. Therefore, it is very interesting to have a look at the hierarchy found amongst these actors, as well as the ways in which these actors communicate with each other and orient their systems of power within the landscape of civil society. Below, I will illuminate this broader landscape by exploring each category of group as well as discussing groups that are not easily sorted.

The landscape of civil society organizations in Vietnam

Group 1 – mass organizations

Article 9 of Vietnam's Constitution of 1992 (revised in 2001) states that:

the Vietnam Fatherland Front and its member organizations constitute the political base of people's power. The Front promotes the tradition of national solidarity, strengthens the people's unity of mind in political and spiritual matters, participates in the building and consolidation of people's power, works together with the State for the care and protection of the people's legitimate interests, encourages the people to exercise their right to mastery, ensures the strict observance of the Constitution and the law, and supervises the activity of State organs, elected representatives, State officials and employees. The State shall create favourable conditions for an effective functioning of the Fatherland Front and its component mass organizations.

Currently there are about 30 mass organizations under the umbrella of the VFF. The major ones are the Vietnam Women's Union (VWU), the Farmers' Association, the Federation of Labour, and the Ho Chi Minh Communist Youth Union, which involve millions of citizens. For example, the VWU has 12 million members across the country with a very well organized structure linking its central, provincial, district and commune levels. The Youth Union has 5.1 million members (Taylor *et al.* 2012: 6). The mass organizations generally aim at securing the people's active participation in the implementation of the Party's policies.

As mentioned earlier, mass organizations in accordance with the legal framework constitute a pillar of the state structure of Vietnam and thus may not be considered as components of civil society in a strict sense. However, if we are considering their recent transformation and ongoing activities, then increasingly mass organizations are playing an important role in civil society. Indeed, the contemporary role of mass organizations has shifted remarkably. From being overtly political organizations with the mandate to promulgate the policies of the Party and the government to all groups of society, and to convince and mobilize support from citizens for implementation of policy, mass organizations have shifted more towards to a position in which they represent and protect the interests of their members in various decision-making processes (see, for example, Pistor and Le Thi Quy, this volume). With the economy moving to market-based and the services of public agencies unable to expand fast enough to meet growing demand, mass organizations have often diversified their positions as economic service providers for their members. The advancement of the market economy also brings changing incentives for member participation in the sorts of economic activities of the mass organizations. The continued willingness of so many members to remain with mass organizations in this rapidly changing period suggests that the shift towards service and welfare provision is serving to maintain the relevance of mass organizations beyond their political alliance with the state.

In general, the central unions (the leadership committees) of the mass organizations are dominated by the state. The close integration of mass organizations with the government and Party ensures that the activities of the state and citizens are interwoven from the top to the bottom of the government chain. At the same time it should be noted that mass organizations are well placed to influence the government process, and therefore constitute an important entry point for informing policy-makers with respect to rural development and natural resources management. A few examples of the diversified social and economic activities

46 Bach Tan Sinh

organized by mass organizations in the shifting political and economic landscape will be presented below.

Vietnam Union of Science and Technology Associations (VUSTA)

VUSTA is one of the most prominent mass organizations under the VFF. VUSTA is an umbrella organization comprising four elements: the central organization, member professional associations, province-level unions, as well as research centres and institutes (often referred to by donors as NGOs) registered under VUSTA. It has about 650,000 members, or about half of the total number of Vietnamese intellectuals (defined as those graduating from university). Its periodicals are 'khoa học và tổ quốc' (Science and Fatherland) and khoa học và đời sống' (Science and Life). VUSTA's budget, which is indicative of its relative autonomy, comes not only from government subsidies, but also from the returns from various scientific and technological activities and enterprises, as well as donations from individuals, institutions and members.

Vietnam Women's Union (VWU)

Broadly organized throughout the country, the Union's activities include HIV/AIDS prevention programmes, revolving micro-credit schemes (see Waibel and Benedikter, this volume), support for small-scale private enterprises, and running campaigns such as 'Women help each other develop their household economy'. A fuller account of the Union, written by Pistor and Le Thi Quy, can be found in this volume.

Vietnam General Confederation of Labour (VGCL)

The VGCL is a labour-oriented mass organization in Vietnam. In 2005 it had 76,678 grassroots trade unions with about 5,250,000 members.[5] Article 10 of the Constitution defines the functions of the VGCL as a political and social organization under the leadership of the Communist Party, with a mandate to participate in state administration and 'social management'. The VGCL plays a dual role, expected to both protect the rights and interests of workers as well as to promote production and create jobs. In this capacity, the President of the VGCL is allowed to attend cabinet meetings as well as to attend meetings of government agencies and organizations when discussing matters relating to 'the rights, obligations and interests of workers'. The Trade Union Law of 1990 also gives the VGCL the right to submit 'draft laws and ordinances to the National Assembly and the State' in matters of concern for workers.

Vietnam Union of Literature and Arts Associations (VULAA)

VULAA is a cultural-oriented mass organization under the VFF. The statute of VULAA, revised at its Sixth National Congress in 2000, states that the Union is a political, social and professional organization *(tổ chức chính trị xã hội, chuyên nghiệp)*. VULAA's structure consists of the central union structure, ten central professional associations, and 61 provincial and municipal unions. The central union structure *(liên hiệp)* serves to coordinate activities of professional associations and provincial and municipal unions. Its periodical is called *'Diễn đàn văn nghệ'* (Literature and Arts Forum). The central Union's financial resources come from the government, income generated from its activities, and contributions from individuals or domestic organizations.

Group 2 – popular and professional associations

Popular or professional associations are established at a 'secondary' level under the structure of mass organizations. According to the Vietnamese government's statistics, as of July 2001 there were about 240 nationwide professional associations and 1,400 local professional associations. Since then, the number has been on the rise and, in 2010, the former Vice Minister of Home Affairs estimated that, 'there were nearly 15,000 associations across Vietnam' (quoted in Taylor *et al.* 2012: 6). These include, for example, professional associations in natural sciences, social sciences, applied sciences and technology, which constitute the second element of VUSTA's structure. Within this category we also find such groups as the Association of Vietnamese Writers, and Association of Vietnamese Folklorists, which fall under the umbrella of VULAA, and the Vietnam Association of Mathematics, and Vietnam Gardening Association (VACVINA), which fall under VUSTA. The number of professional associations registered with VUSTA alone increased from 15 in 1983 to 34 in 1992, to 49 in 2001, and to 114 more recently. VUSTA is comprised of 60 provincial unions of science and technology associations as well as of 73 national scientific and technological associations; an additional 300 organizations are affiliated. VUSTA members run 197 newspapers, magazines and websites.[6]

Popular and professional member associations report to the central unions of their respective mass organization biannually. Member associations take responsibility for their own finances. To set up a popular or professional association, for example under VUSTA, Vietnamese scientists in a particular professional branch will have to hold discussions with the central union to see whether a new association is needed. The central union will then seek approval from the Ministry of Home Affairs. The new association has to submit a draft statute, document its operational procedures, and furnish a list of full-time administrative staff. To receive preliminary approval from VUSTA, the applicant will have to show that there are at least 1,000 members interested in joining and that the new association will have sufficient financial resources.

In turn, the professional associations often sponsor smaller clubs or associations. For example, the Hanoi Union of Science and Technology Associations (HUSTA), which reports to VUSTA, has developed 34 popular professional associations, such as the Hanoi Gardener's Association and Hanoi Lawyer's Association.[7] Some of these member associations have complex organizational features, such as operating their own research centres or even private schools and universities. For example, the Association of Economics, under former Deputy Prime Minister Tran Phuong, administers a private university named the Hanoi University of Business Management. The Association of Physics runs a private university named Dong Do, and the Union of Technology and Science Associations of Hanoi runs a private university named Phuong Dong. VULAA has ten central professional associations such as the Associations for Vietnamese Writers, Musicians, Artists, Film Makers, Photographers, Dancers, Architects, Folklorists, and for themes such as Fine Arts or Minorities' Arts and Literature.

Formally, professional and popular associations are independent from the central unions of the mass organizations. They run their own organization, recruit their own personnel, and make their own decisions on how and to whom they grant membership. All of them publish their own newspapers and period-icals and some run their own publishing houses and clubs. The Association for Vietnamese Writers, for example, runs six newspapers and periodicals and its publishing house produced around 200 titles in 1999, while the Association of Vietnamese Architects issues two periodicals.

The main task of professional member associations is to assist their members in professional matters. In addition they advise the state on policies related to science, as well as to the arts and culture, and contribute to state projects when requested. The Association of Vietnamese Musicians, for example, proposed that music be taught in kindergartens and primary schools, while the Association for Vietnamese Architects assisted the government with urban planning and legal issues related to construction. The Association for Vietnamese Writers also assisted the Ministry of Education with the reform of literature textbooks, while the Association for Minorities' Literature and Arts helped with textbooks for ethnic minority primary schools.

Vietnam Gardening Association (VACVINA)

Set up in 1986 under VUSTA, VACVINA is a typical example of a popular association. VACVINA promotes sustainable agriculture through the develop-ment of the VAC ecosystem model. VAC is an acronym of three Vietnamese words: *vườn* which means garden or orchard, *ao*, fish pond, and *chuồng*, animal shed. The main strategies adopted by the VAC system are to recycle solar energy through spatial arrangements of crops, and to use residue from one farming sphere as material for another. The VAC model developed a systematic coher-ence over time and was adopted as an economic model (*kinh tế VAC*). Later it was expanded and applied to ecosystems of the delta, mountains, coast, and forest. Because it has been used to increase the income of rural households, it became a poverty reduction mechanism and, due to its ecological orientation, it has been used to promote sustainable development. By the mid-1990s, the VAC model had been adopted and applied nationwide by various groups. Colleges of Agriculture typically have a department focusing on the VAC model. During the third phase of its development, which began roughly in the mid-1990s, it has become the baseline for advice and assessment of other rural models of development.

VACVINA is organized from the central to the local level with branches in most provinces. In addition to the nationwide network of gardeners, VACVINA also runs five centres and three companies that support the promotion of the VAC ecosystem. The five centres are the Centre for Rural Communities Research and Development, the Centre for Marine Products, two centres responsible for the transfer of technology, and one centre responsible for consultancy work.[8] VACVINA communicates through newspapers and conferences with the Ministry of Labour or the cabinet. Beyond its connection through VUSTA, VACVINA has separately established relationships with the state structure, especially with the Ministries of Agriculture and Rural Development, Education, Finance, Planning and Investment, and Science, Technology, and Environment. VACVINA also has direct relations with the Party structure. Their horizontal linkages include other popular associations such as the Association of Fertilizer Producers and the Association for Vietnamese Planters.

Group 3 – funds, charities, and supporting centres

Funds and charities came into operation with Decree 177/ND-CP in 1999. According to these regulations, funds and charities should be non-governmental, not-for-profit organizations. By the year 2001, about 200 funds had been established in Vietnam. A small number of funds and charities were established by individuals; for example, a charity organization called 'Away from Mother' in Hanoi was independently established with the purpose of helping street children by organizing them into a newspaper-selling groups. Funds, in comparison, are typically set up by various organizations. There are funds formed by government organizations, such as the Fund for Protection and Support of Children, established by the Vietnam Committee of Protection and Care of Children (a ministerial level government body in charge of children's issues, which was, in 1991, transformed into the Committee for Protection and Care of Children (CPCC). Funds are also formed under mass organizations, like the Compassion Fund of the Vietnam Women's Union. Finally, there are funds under local governments; for example, the Fund for Housing Development of Hanoi under the Hanoi People's Committee.

Supporting centres, which were legalized through Decree 25/ND-CP in 2001, have since mushroomed. The main function of these centres is to provide care and support to vulnerable people, such as orphans, disabled people, and isolated elderly people. For example, a number of centres for orphans were formed under the Association for Protection and Support of Disabled People and Orphan Children. These centres register their operations either with local government agencies or through their umbrella organizations. Individuals rarely set up such centres.

Group 4 – research/training professional centres

Within the current institutional framework, mass organizations such as VUSTA or VULAA, as well as some government agencies such as the institutes and universities, have set up many professional research/training centres. These organizations have the highest degree of autonomy from the government and therefore are often referred to as 'local NGOs' or VNGOs. The activities of these NGOs are primarily in research and consultancy, covering a wide range of economic, social and cultural dimensions of development. Most of these research/training centres are listed in the VNGO directory, published in 2002 (Tran Tuan and Le Quoc Hung, 2002). A more recent survey of the Asia Foundation indicates a total number of 607 VNGOs in Hanoi and another 223 in Ho Chi Minh City (Taylor *et al.* 2012: 35). Since a new law on associations has not been issued by the government, all these NGOs have to be affiliated with government agencies or science, technology, education, training or environmental institutions. To set up a centre or a research institute is easier than to set up an association. Those interested in setting up a centre or institute will submit a proposal directly to the central union. Once the central union agrees to sponsor the centre or institute, it has to register its activities through the Department of Organization and Human Resource in MOST as outlined in Decree No. 35. In 2000 there were 52 centres and institutes registered directly under VUSTA, while in 2006 the number had increased to 56 (Taylor *et al.* 2012: 6). The centres and institutes concentrate mainly in the areas of business management, urban and rural development, poverty reduction, community development, gender equality, environmental issues and training.

A recent survey (Taylor *et al.* 2012) summarizes the main characteristics of the research centres and institutes based in Hanoi and Ho Chi Minh City. The vast majority of these organizations operate in more than one field and sometimes shift their focus, as they adapt to new policies and emerging development paradigms and fashions (such as climate change). They traditionally engage in service delivery and, more recently, capacity building, research and advocacy activities. The process of registration and other legal procedures are complex and contribute to regulating the institutes' opportunities for accessing donor funding. In general, the economic situation of the centres and institutes is often precarious, which might be one reason that they also face challenges with regard to their human resources. However, despite the weaknesses mentioned here, as professional organizations, occasionally their voices have created considerable pressure to deal with economic and social misconduct of state ministries or local authorities (see Wells-Dang, this volume).

Nevertheless, there are also critical voices concerning the research centres and institutes. There have been claims that a few of these civil society organizations carry out unregistered activities and therefore operate outside the legal framework. As a response to these suspicions, national unions like VUSTA have started reviewing the licences for some of these associations.

Group 5 – community-based organizations (CBOs)

CBOs in Vietnam are numerous and are on the rise. Thousands have been established by people in rural or urban areas, or by foreign intervention, to collectively provide many kinds of services. Typical examples are Water User Groups (WUGs), Credit Groups, Aquaculture/Agriculture Extension Clubs, and Farmer Groups (see Waibel and Benedikter, this volume). There are two types of CBO. The first is externally established through projects and development programmes. The second is self-established for the provision of services for communities and members.

Externally established groups and projects

With beginning of *Đổi Mới* in the 1990s, Vietnam has received significant amounts of overseas development aid to support national programmes for macroeconomic reform and social development. The National Programme for Hunger Eradication and Poverty Reduction has received the most support from donors. Since 1995 the UN Development Programme (UNDP), in collaboration with the International Fund for Agricultural Development (IFAD), the UN Capital Development Fund (UNCDF), and many international NGOs working at the grassroots level, implemented poverty reduction projects at the provincial level. The World Bank and Asian Development Bank have also started large-scale poverty reduction projects in many provinces. A main aspect of many of these poverty reduction projects is to promote the bottom-up participatory approach in rural development planning. The process of participation in most of the projects starts with the participatory identification of interests of the rural community, with particular emphasis on the needs of the poor, women, and ethnic minority groups. These projects thus promote the development of social capital through the establishment of grassroots or community-based organizations. These smaller groups become responsible for the overall management of local development projects and/or mobilization of community participation and contribution to these projects.

There are many examples of grassroots development groups that exist under donor-funded poverty reduction projects in Vietnam. These CBOs can thus play the role of mediating institutions, in which representatives from community work for the interests of local people rather than strictly following the directives of the local government. The Commune/Village Development Boards (CDB/VDB) or the Project Management Committees at the commune and village levels are one example. Typically, members of these groups are selected from grassroots elected bodies and representatives from local communities. In Tuyen Quang province, for instance, under the IFAD-funded Participatory Resources Management Project, VDBs were established with leadership directly voted on by the members. Similarly, in Quang Nam province, the UNCDF/UNDP Rural Infrastructure Development Fund channelled funds for small-scale infrastructure construction through the established CDBs, which consisted of representatives from the commune authority, mass organizations and local people. In the poorest districts of the northern mountainous provinces of Son La, Lai Chau and Hoa Binh, the UNDP-funded project on aquaculture for poverty reduction established Commune Action Groups in each of its target communes, which was composed of the best aquaculture farmers in the commune together with representatives from mass organizations. One criticism often levelled at these types of organizations, however, is that they tend to exist only during the life of the donor-funded projects.

Self-established groups, projects and committees

The second type of grassroots community organization comes much closer to the ideal of civic groups that anyone can voluntarily join if they have a shared interest. This second group includes those CBOs that directly provide services to their members and to the community. These organizations often do work that would normally be under the charge of local state agencies. Typical examples of these organizations include agriculture/aquaculture extension groups, WUGs, and credit savings groups. Those groups are usually formed in response to a specific need in a community (see Waibel and Benedikter, this volume).

CBOs of this type have developed rapidly, particularly in the rural areas, because the services of government agencies have not met the demands of the fast developing rural market. One example of self-established CBOs is the agricultural extension clubs (currently regulated by Decree No. 151 on cooperative groups from 2007), which developed extensively in the south of Vietnam. Farmers voluntarily join these clubs to share their experience and information on the markets of agricultural inputs and outputs. Another prominent example are WUGs, which are established by farmer households which share a common water supply system for their cultivation and consumption (see an example in Reis, this volume; also Bach Tan Sinh 2002). WUGs in many provinces are facilitated by the local authorities and are entitled to levy irrigation fees from farmers for their self-maintenance – a task that would normally be the responsibility of the local government's irrigation service company. WUGs are now widely found in Vietnam, having largely replaced the bureaucratic irrigation service provided by state companies that charged high irrigation fees while providing poor maintenance due to constraints in government allocation.

Group 6 – organizations of other forms

There are many organizations that cannot be classified within the categories above. Most of these organizations are informal or unregistered. These include self-help clubs, associations of schoolmates, chess player associations, informal credit groups, cultural/religious/'ethnic' organizations, etc. Some of these organizations can be very large and, like professional organizations, can have an impact on local authorities and state departments. For example, self-established advocacy groups in some localities voice critical views against various agencies or businesses; for example requesting them to pay attention to environmental concerns. As a result of such activities one factory was forced to install air filters to improve the quality of discharged air, while other factories were relocated (O'Rourke 2000).

It should be emphasized that in the past, once an association was allowed to be formed, its operations would be subsidized and closely supervised by the state apparatus. Nowadays the government still partly funds administrative work and coordination of the large unions and associations, but most associations and organizations are self-financed. As a result the government has less influence on the orientation and activities of these organizations (as long as they do not violate the law).

Adapting civil society to the Vietnamese context

Given the inter-linked and increasingly differentiated roles of state-sponsored organizations and their subsidiaries, Vietnam has a unique landscape of civil society. In order to give credit to the good works of groups (nominally) linked to the state, CSOs in Vietnam should refer to any organization or group that people are entitled to join to accomplish collective objectives that are practical and/or expand political space. Among these is the exchange of information, achievement of mutual goals, and levying demands on the state. Although activities may not be part of the process of government, they can take place 'under' the framework of the government. In general terms CSOs can act as a facilitator by assembling and articulating individual interests and helping these interests win consideration during the decision-making processes of government. Additionally, CSOs in various forms can not only help the government in monitoring socio-economic development issues, they also provide a substitute for many of the functions performed by the state, such as agricultural extension, credit management, irrigation maintenance, information exchange, etc. (see Waibel and Benedikter, as well as Reis, both in this volume).

By this definition, CSOs should also include the mass organizations and the popular associations that are formally under the Party or state control, particularly as these are undergoing a gradual functional transformation towards activities that are commonly associated with CSOs. Indeed, mass organizations (and their subsidiaries), in addition to NGOs and other civic associations, have proven their complementary roles in government service provision, especially in the areas of social welfare and poverty reduction. In no particular order, these activities now include: (1) organizing activities that aim at increasing the income, either directly or indirectly, of people (mass organizations, CBOs, credit groups, funds); (2) representing people in forming links and negotiating with local government authorities (mass organizations, NGOs, CBOs, cultural/religious groups); (3) spreading knowledge and exchange of experience (professional organizations, NGOs); and (4) providing feedback between government and communities (mass organizations, NGOs, advocacy groups, CBOs, cultural/religious groups).

Although there are advantages to working within the current legal, socio-economic and political framework, these organizations commonly face constraints and challenges that include: (1) lack of a clear legal framework for their operation; (2) poor transparency of the state administration concerning access to public resources, particularly in bidding and selection of sub-contractors; (3) limited access to available information held by state agencies; (4) no, or limited, support from authorities at all levels in terms of infrastructure, incentives and other logistical assistance; and (5) very limited participation, if any, in policy formulation.

To allay the government's reluctance to provide widespread legitimacy to CSOs, the development community can facilitate by demonstrating to policy-makers, in both theory and practice, that autonomous CSOs are effective and efficient for socio-economic development in Vietnam, and that the transformation of mass organizations is necessary in the market economy. The areas of poverty reduction through sustainable natural resources management would be amongst the most visible and measurable socio-economic dimensions. At the same time, the conditions for entry for CSOs must be prioritized in some way, as there are already many existing models from CBOs, NGOs and professional associations in poverty reduction and natural resource management that are available for research, evaluation, demonstration, replication and finally institutionalization.

Conclusions – key opportunities and challenges

With the partial retreat of the state from the provision of subsidized and organized welfare, existing (planned) social safety nets have increasingly been in decline. In addition to this, the relative decline in the capacity of family networks or informal mechanisms to provide alternatives have been mounting pressure on individuals to seek a way to access economic and social services, which has been an incentive for CSOs of varies types. At the same time, current government policies for grassroots democracy have increasingly opened opportunities for individuals and communities to actively participate in economic, social and political affairs.[9] Increasingly, the government has come to recognize its changing role and the importance of developing a strong civil sector to provide complementary services, which used to be the government's sole responsibility.

As the result of all the fundamental changes described above, the past few years have witnessed the mushrooming of thousands of CSOs in Vietnam. The recent issuing of relevant legal documents, notably Decrees 29, 35,[10] 177[11] and 151, has provided a necessary, though still insufficient legal framework for the establishment and operations of these CSOs. Decentralization and grassroots democratization policies have contributed to an enabling environment that has significantly increased CSOs' involvement in various economic, social, and political affairs at different levels. The government's need to develop a state with a rule of law, social equality, wide participation, and sound governance, has clearly required a supporting contribution from the civil and private sector in order to keep pace with these challenges. In addition, the challenge of establishing regional and international integration (e.g. to participate in the Association of Southeast Asian Nations (ASEAN), ASEAN Free Trade Area, World Trade Organization, etc.) has also reinforced the necessity of this third sector. Finally, growing involvement of international organizations and donors has given more impetus for the growth of this sector.

In any case, the present trend is irreversible as these CSOs continue to demonstrate their indispensability to the socio-economic and political development of the country. Against a backdrop of various macro processes, and with growing recognition from the government, these quasi civil society organizations are firmly on their way to becoming civil and professional.

Notes

1 The MOSTE was then reorganized to become the Ministry of Science and Technology (MOST) in 2005.
2 Phan Boi Chau (1867–1940) was a pioneer of Vietnamese twentieth century nationalism. In 1903 he formed a revolutionary organization called the 'Reformation Society' (*Duy Tân hội*). From 1905–8 he lived in Japan where he wrote political tracts calling for the liberation of Vietnam from the French colonial regime. After being forced to leave Japan he moved to China where he was influenced by Sun Yat-Sen. He formed a new group called the 'Vietnamese Restoration League' (*Việt Nam Quang Phục Hội*), modelled after Sun Yat-Sen's Republican Party. In 1925 French agents seized him in Shanghai. He was convicted of treason and spent the rest of his life under house arrest in Huế. See http://en.wikipedia.org/wiki/Phan_Boi_Chau (accessed 1 October 2012).
3 Phan Chu Trinh, also known as Phan Châu Trinh (1872–1926) was a famous early twentieth century Vietnamese nationalist. He also used the alias, Tây Hồ. He sought to end France's brutal occupation of Vietnam. He opposed both violence and turning to other countries for support, and instead believed in attaining Vietnamese liberation by educating the population and by appealing to French democratic principles. Though he failed in this project, Vietnam was later liberated via an armed uprising led by Hồ Chí Minh. Hồ started his political activism working with Phan Chu Trinh and other activists in France. See http://en.wikipedia.org/wiki/Phan_Chu_Trinh (accessed 1 October 2012).
4 This Directory of Vietnamese NGOs has been prepared and published by the Research and Training Center for Community Development and supported by the World Bank in 2002.
5 See: www.congdoanvn.org.vn/details.asp?l=1&c=23&c2=23&m=580 (retrieved 25 November 2012).
6 See: www.vusta.vn/home3/news/?42624/Gioi-thieu-chung-ve-Lien-hiep-cac-Hoi-Khoa-hoc-va-Ky-thuat-Viet-Nam.htm (accessed 25 November 2012).
7 See: http://husta.org.vn/Husta.aspx?Module=News&Id=2 (accessed 1 December 2012).
8 The three companies run by VACVINA are VAC Co., VACVINA Co., and RUDECO. VAC Co. buys and sells fruit; VACVINA Co. sells fertilizer and rice wine; and RUDECO supplies agricultural implements for those applying the VAC concept.
9 The Grassroots Democracy Decree is defined by Decree 29/1998/ND-CP of 11 May 1998 (later amended by Decree 79/2003/ND). The decree is part of the state's decentralization efforts. It aims at enhancing the participation of the people, and strengthening the accountability of government agencies.

10 Decree 35 issued by the Council of Ministers on the management of scientific and technological activities, Decree No. 35/HDBT of 28 January 1992.
11 Decree 177 on the Organisation and Operation of Social Funds and Charity Funds, Decree No. 177/1999/ND-CP of 22 December 1999.

References

Bach Tan Sinh (2002) 'Government and NGO partnership in managing community-based water resources in Vietnam: a case study of Thai Long Dam Project' in *Business Strategy and the Environment*, 11 (2): 119–29.

Bach Tan Sinh (2011) 'Civil Society in Vietnam' in S. Elies and T. Chong (eds), *An ASEAN Community for All: Exploring the Scope of Civil Society Engagement*, Singapore: Friedrich-Ebert-Foundation: 138–47.

Budinan, A. (1990) *State and Civil Society in Indonesia.* Clayton, Australia: CSEAS, Monash University.

Centre for Cooperation Human Resource Development (2010) *Civil society and successful models in poverty alleviation with the participation and monitoring of the people*, Hanoi: Center for Cooperation Human Resource Development.

Diamond, L. J. (1994) 'Rethinking Civil Society: Toward Democratic Consolidation' in *Journal of Democracy*, 5 (3): 4–17.

Gray, M. L. (1999) 'Creating Civil Society? The Emergence of NGOs in Viet Nam' in *Development and Change*, 30 (4): 693–713.

Hannah, J. (2005) 'Civil Society Actors and Action in Vietnam: Preliminary Empirical Results and Sketches from an Evolving Debate' in Heinrich Böll Foundation (ed.), *Towards Good Society: Civil Society Actors, the State, and the Business Class in Southeast Asia – Facilitators or Impediments to a Strong, Democratic, and Fair Society?* Berlin: Heinrich Böll Foundation: 101–10.

Hyden, G. (1997) 'Civil Society, Social Capital and Development: Dissection of A Complex Discourse' in *Studies in Comparative International Development*, 32 (1): 3–30.

Kaldor, M. (2000) 'A note on concepts', Paper for the Global Civil Society Almanac Brainstorming session, London, February 4–5.

Kerkvliet, B. J. T. (1995) 'Politics of Society in Vietnam in the Mid-1990s' in B. J. T. Kerkvliet (ed.), *Dilemmas of Development: Vietnam Update 1994*, Canberra, Australia: Department of Political and Social Change, Research School of Pacific and Asian Studies, Australian National University: 5–43.

Kerkvliet, B. J. T., Heng, R. H.-K., and Koh, D. W. H. (eds) (2003), *Getting Organized in Vietnam: Moving in and around the Socialist State*, Singapore: Institute of Southeast Asian Studies.

Kerkvliet, B. J. T., Nguyen Quang A., and Bach Tan Sinh (2008) *Forms of Engagement between State Agencies and Civil Society Organizations in Vietnam*, Hanoi: VUFO NGO Resource Center.

Marr, D. (1994) 'The Vietnam Communist Party and Civil Society', paper presented at the Vietnam Update Conference Doi Moi, the State and Civil Society at the Australia National University, Canberra, Australia, 10–11 November.

Nguyen Kim Ha (2001) *Lessons Learned from a Decade of Experience. A Strategic of INGO Methods and Activities in Vietnam, 1990–1999*, Hanoi: VUFO NGO Resource Centre.

Nguyen Huu Tho (2002) Theo bước chân đổi mới, (Vietnamese publication, Following Footsteps of Doi Moi).

Nguyen Ngoc Lam (2007) 'Legal regulations on organization, Management of Association, and Measures of refinement', presentation for a workshop organized by the Legal Reform Assistance Project, Hanoi, January.

Nguyen Tran Bat (2001) 'Vietnam's Business and Professional Associations and their Role in State', presented at the Vietnam Update 2001, Singapore: Institute of Southeast Asian Studies.

Nguyễn Vặn Sáu, Hỗ Vặn Thộng (2001) *Cong Dong Lang Xa o Viet Nam Hien Nay* (People's Communities in Villages and Communes of Vietnam), Hanoi: Political Publishing House.

Norlund, I., Dang Ngoc Dinh, Bach Tan Sinh, Chu Dung, Dang Ngoc Quang, Do Bich Diem, Nguyen Manh Cuong, Tang The Cuong and Vu Chi Mai (2006) *The Emerging Civil Society: An Initial Assessment of Civil Society in Vietnam*, Hanoi: Vietnam Institute of Development Studies (VIDS), UNDP Vietnam, SNV Vietnam and CIVICUS Civil Society Index.

O'Rourke, D. (2000) 'Community-Driven Regulation in Vietnam', unpublished thesis, University of California, Berkeley.

Pedersen, K. R. (2001) *Civil Society in the Context of Development Aid – The Case of Vietnam*, CBS/IKL', Working Paper, Copenhagen: Copenhagen Business School.

Taylor, William, Nguyen Thu Hang, Pham Quang Tu and Huynh Thi Ngoc Tuyet (2012), *Civil Society in Vietnam: A comparative study of Civil Society Organizations in Hanoi and Ho Chi Minh City*, The Asia Foundation: Hanoi

The Government of Viet Nam (1957) 'Decree on the Establishment of Association', Decree No. 102/SL/L004 of 5 May 1957.

The Government of Viet Nam (1957) Decree 258/Ttg dated 14 June 1957.

The Government of Viet Nam (1992) Decree No. 35/HDBT dated 28 January 1992.

The Government of Viet Nam (1992) Constitution.

The Government of Viet Nam (1998) 'Grassroots Democracy Decree', Decree No. 29/1998/ND-CP dated 15 May 1998.

The Government of Viet Nam (1999), Decree No. 177/1999/ND-CP on Organisation and Operation of Social Funds and Charity Funds dated 22 December 1999.

The Government of Viet Nam (2000), Socio-economic Development Strategy 2000–2010.

The Government of Viet Nam (2000) Socio-economic Development Action Plan 2000–2005.

The Government of Viet Nam, (1995) Civil Code, National Political Publishing House.

The Government of Viet Nam (2000), Law on Science and Technology No. 21/2000/QH10 of 9 June 2000.

Tran Tuan and Le Quoc Hung (2002) *Danh Bạ Các Tổ Chức Viêt Nam Mang Đặc Trưng Tổ Chức Phi Chính Phủ* (Directory of Vietnamese Organizations that have Characteristics of Non-governmental Organizations), Hanoi: Research and Training Center for Rural Development.

Vasavakul, Thaveeporn (2003) 'From Fence Breaking to Networking: Popular Organisations and Policy Influence in Post-Socialist Vietnam' in Kerkvliet, B. J. T., Koh, D. W. H., and Heng, R. H.-k. (eds), *Getting Organized in Vietnam: Moving in and around the Socialist State*, Singapore: Institute of Southeast Asian Studies.

Weimer, D. L., Vining, Aidan R. (1999) *Policy Analysis, Concepts and Practice*, Third Edition, Engelwood Cliffs, New Jersey: Prentice-Hall.

Wischermann J. (2010) 'Civil Society Action and Governance in Vietnam: Selected Findings from an Empirical Survey' in *Journal of Current Southeast Asian Affairs*, 29 (2): 3–40.

Part II

Advocacy and political space

4 Civil society networks in Cambodia and Vietnam

A comparative analysis

Andrew Wells-Dang

In Cambodia and Vietnam, networks of non-governmental organizations (NGOs), individual activists and local communities have formed in the past two decades to advocate collectively for the common concerns of their members. Responding to challenges of rapid, unequal development and to shifting political opportunities, networks bring actors together across geographic, sectoral and social boundaries and have engaged on a range of issues including health care, education, poverty reduction and environmental protection.[1]

The emergence of networks has created new spaces for social action in both countries and contributed to existing civil society structures. In Vietnam, networks share a space previously occupied by Communist Party-sponsored mass organizations and state-owned media; in Cambodia, they are partially replacing competing political parties and professionalized NGOs. Most networks are unregistered entities. Neither Cambodian nor Vietnamese law contains the category of networks, although some networks register as NGOs or businesses. Cambodian networks have developed autonomously from the state, as 'three-sector' theories of civil society would predict. Vietnamese networks, by contrast, straddle the boundaries between society and the state, including members both within and outside state institutions (Read and Pekkanen 2009; Wells-Dang 2012).

Following an introduction to network approaches to civil society, this chapter presents empirical case studies of networks in Cambodia and Vietnam – with a focus on environmental controversies over dams and forests that link the two countries – and illustrates divergent network structures and advocacy strategies. Although Cambodian and Vietnamese networks struggle with similar social and developmental issues, the outcomes of their advocacy efforts have been distinctly different.

Civil society as networks

Recent scholarship on civil society has moved away from the question of 'who is in civil society?' to asking 'what does civil society do?' Drawing in part on Gramscian roots, many analysts of Vietnam have theorized civil society as an arena of struggle and contestation clustering around a range of possible advocacy activities and forms of engagement with the state (Hannah 2007; Kerkvliet *et al.* 2008; Thayer 2009). Regarding Cambodia, critical political economy theorists have shown how NGOs' independence is limited by donor funding and manipulation by the authorities (Öjendal and Lilja 2009; Hughes 2009).

The extent of civil society in Cambodia and Vietnam may be evaluated differently depending on the selected criteria. A conceptualization of civil society as made up of voluntary, non-profit associations autonomous from the state (Cohen and Arato 1992; Anheier *et al.* 2003) applies more closely to Cambodia, with its large, diverse NGO sector. Local and international NGOs in Cambodia have organized themselves, without involvement of state authorities, into two membership networks, the Cooperation Committee for Cambodia and the NGO Forum on Cambodia. In Vietnam, the concept of autonomy is problematic, since no registered organization is completely independent from the state. The majority of Vietnamese NGOs participating in networks are registered through VUSTA, the Vietnam Union of Science and Technology Associations (*Liên hiệp các Hội Khoa học và Kỹ thuật Việt Nam*). Founded by a revolutionary scientist and former Minister of Defence, VUSTA is a 'socio-political organization' with special status to 'advise, give feedback, and act as a check on society' (*tư vấn, phản biện, giám định xã hội*) from within the Party-state system (Government of Vietnam 2002, 2010). Corporatist in structure and intent (Vasavakul 2003: 34–45), VUSTA has effectively used its quasi-state 'umbrella' status to register and supervise Vietnamese NGOs, while also offering links to Communist Party and state authorities (Pistor and Le Thi Quy, this volume).[2]

Thus, if civil society is theorized as an intermediate sphere of activity between individuals, families and the state (Habermas 1992; Öjendal, this volume), Vietnamese civil society appears more robust. Vietnamese participate in many local associations, such as farmer groups, that may or may not be voluntary, non-profit and autonomous (Waibel and Benedikter, this volume). A focus on NGOs alone misses much that is taking place in Vietnam, while making Cambodian civil society seem more dynamic than it actually is, at least at the village level. In comparison, if one includes Party-sponsored mass organizations in the Vietnamese intermediary sphere, it overstates the level of advocacy and deliberation that actually takes place in these associations.

A network perspective offers a locally relevant path through the definitional pitfalls of civil society. Without overlooking the importance of NGOs, a focus on networks as the component parts of civil society presents a broader and more balanced view of contemporary dynamics in Cambodia and Vietnam. Networks have been described as 'the new social morphology of our societies' (Castells 1996: 469), extending from personal social ties to business connections and international relations. Network analysis stresses the importance of personal ties among members in building social capital, understood as 'trust, norms, and networks' (Putnam 1993: 167). These social associations are most clearly expressed in informal associations, especially in rural areas, that often 'have most value for citizens' (Krishna 2002: 5). 'Civil society networks' are a subset of networks that engage in advocacy, which is defined as a range of forms of engagement with various state authorities, corporations, and other elites on behalf of a collective interest (Wells-Dang 2012).

Networks may be *formal*, with fixed structures, organizational or individual membership, meeting schedules, and budgets, among other features. By contrast, *informal* networks are based on personal ties among individuals and unregistered groups, ranging from community volunteer groups to virtual networks. In either case, the makeup of civil society is not limited to legally registered 'civil society organizations'. Networks may have individual, organizational, or community membership, or a mixture of these, but they are not reducible to organizational or personal interests alone. Despite close connections to NGOs and outward similarities in functioning, networks are presented here as a distinct form of civil society action.

Networks perform many functions: they train and support their members, build civic identities, share information, link with international partners, and conduct advocacy.[3] The existing network advocacy strategies in Vietnam and Cambodia can be summarized as embedded, media, and community-based (Wells-Dang 2012). Embedded advocacy consists of working within the system and making direct contact with elites using personal and institutional ties (Ho 2008). Networks employing media strategies work through state-owned newspapers, online media, blogs and international media to reach advocacy objects indirectly. Finally, community advocacy is used to put public pressure on advocacy objects by involving more people and building links between local residents and elites.

Within a particular advocacy strategy, networks choose among multiple tactics (or methods), such as personal lobbying and blogging, to reach an objective. A network may have more than one strategy and use multiple tactics within these strategies, constituting an advocacy repertoire. After forming strategies and tactics, networks conduct specific advocacy activities or events, such as meeting a particular official over tea or posting an open letter online. As networks seek appropriate frames and audiences for their advocacy messages, their repertoires often take shape organically through trial and error or 'venue shopping' (Keck and Sikkink 1998: 18). The prevailing strategies and tactics vary to some extent among networks in different sectors in Cambodia and Vietnam, depending on the perceived sensitivity of an issue and the openness of elite allies.

The following case studies present the history, structure, mission, and advocacy activities of issue-based advocacy networks in both countries, as well as their relations with government and donor agencies. The selected cases in the areas of natural resources and land management may be characterized as moderately contentious – generally more than gender equity or health policy, but less than human rights or labour organizing – although individual cases vary. Although environmental issues link Cambodian and Vietnamese networks through transnational impacts on water resources, forests and livelihoods, distinct advocacy repertoires have been adopted in the two countries, with embedded and media strategies generally favoured in Vietnam and community strategies predominant in Cambodia.

Advocacy within the system: the Vietnam Rivers Network

Advocacy networks in Vietnam have developed through relationships between scientists, media, local NGOs and state officials. The Vietnam Rivers Network (*Mạng lưới Sông ngòi Việt Nam*) is an illustrative example of such cross-sectoral networking. VRN began in 2005 as a discussion group among scientists and local government officials concerned about dams and flooding. It has since expanded to 150 individual and 20 organizational members,[4] with three regional nodes (or sub-groups) based in Hanoi, Hue and Ho Chi Minh City. Initially focused on information sharing, VRN has developed a greater advocacy orientation over time, for instance by submitting comments and revisions to the Law on Water Resources. Its advocacy efforts sharply increased in 2011 through participation in a high-profile regional campaign against construction of dams on the mainstream of the Mekong River in Laos and Cambodia. Advocacy makes up one of VRN's four objectives, the others being information exchange, capacity building of members, and domestic and international network-building (VRN 2011a).

VRN has no separate legal status. It is officially a project of a local NGO, the Centre for Water Resources Conservation and Development (WARECOD) in Hanoi. WARECOD hosts the secretariat of VRN, consisting of a coordinator and two support staff. Funding for VRN activities passes through WARECOD from international donors in the Netherlands and USA. According to VRN members, this system has largely functioned smoothly but has resulted in some overlap and confusion between the roles and responsibilities of WARECOD and VRN. WARECOD is registered with VUSTA, which serves as a theoretical political check on VRN's activities but does not interfere in day-to-day operations. In fact, VUSTA has proven a useful advocacy channel and ally on several occasions. Through such arrangements, Vietnamese networks have considerably more space to operate in practice than restrictive regulations on associational activities, such as Decree 45 (Government of Vietnam 2010), appear to indicate.

Many of VRN's individual members are local government officials, staff of government research institutes, journalists employed by Vietnam's state-owned media, or university lecturers. The regional core groups in the north, centre, and south are each coordinated by a local NGO. The southern group has been the most active, including a Mekong Delta-based node of scientists, professors and supportive provincial officials. Some advocacy activities, such as sign-on letters, are circulated through the whole network's e-mail list. Direct communications with government leaders, for instance at the Ministry of Natural Resources and Environment (MONRE) and the Government Office, are mostly conducted privately by an informal working group within VRN's membership. The Ho Chi Minh City-based NGOs Centre for Biodiversity and Development (CBD) and Forest and Wetlands Research Centre (Forwet), both VRN members, have spoken out in the media about the ecology of the Mekong Delta (Nguyen Huu Thien 2011). One Vietnam-based international observer terms this activism 'still mostly undercover, but with legitimacy since they know what provincial governments are thinking'. While advocacy is included in VRN's public profile, a significant portion of advocacy efforts are kept separate from open, official network activities.

In 2011, VRN's primary advocacy focus was the proposed Xayaburi Dam on the Mekong River. Xayaburi is the first of 11 dams proposed on the Lao and Cambodian sections of the river; Vietnamese corporations are the lead investors for two of the dams: Luang Prabang in Laos and Stung Treng in Cambodia (Hirsch 2010). As the plans were publicized, Vietnamese officials and civil society realized that if constructed, mainstream dams could be more damaging to the ecology of the Mekong Delta than the effects of climate change (IUCN 2011).

VRN members tailored their advocacy messages to the primary concern of Vietnamese officials: the potentially devastating livelihood and economic impacts of upstream dams on the Mekong Delta. In April 2011, leading up to the Mekong River Commission's (MRC) annual meeting in Vientiane, VRN held a press conference with VUSTA repeating their concerns about the Xayaburi Dam. Their interventions appear to have tipped the balance. The Vietnamese government representative took the lead in pressuring Laos to postpone dam construction for ten years until further study on its environmental impacts, which was eventually endorsed by the full MRC in December.

VRN's advocacy includes engagement with domestic, in addition to transnational, environmental controversies. In 2011 the VRN secretariat and southern core group members joined with a Vietnamese NGO, PanNature, to oppose construction of the Dong Nai 6 and 6A Dams in southeastern Vietnam. A cascade of seven 'run of the river' hydroelectric power projects on the Dong Nai River had been under development since 2003 (Brown 2011). Two of these dams lie within protected land in Cat Tien National Park and a forest buffer zone, but this did not appear to pose a threat to approval of the projects until the director of Cat Tien, with support from members of VRN's southern core group, issued a statement to journalists criticizing the dams. On a visit to the park, scientists and activists then discovered that the environmental impact assessment for the dams had been falsified (Thanh Nien 2011). In August, VRN, VUSTA and Cat Tien National Park held a joint workshop to examine environmental and social impacts of the project and recommended its suspension (VRN 2011b). In November a provincial workshop in Dong Nai reinforced this conclusion. The combined testimony of scientists, journalists and NGOs resonated sufficiently with local officials to halt the encroachment of dam projects on protected land.

In both the Xayaburi and Dong Nai cases, the recommendations of advocates were presented in nuanced scientific language, far from criticism of the government or appeals to nationalism. But their heterodox implications were clear, and officials listened: a sign both of the power of embedded and media advocacy, and of a 'general broadening of public discourse in the last decade' (Brown 2011: 15). VRN members conducted embedded advocacy through circulation of a petition against the Xayaburi project, open letters, workshops, and personal communication with Vietnamese leaders, both at the national level and with provincial government officials in the southeast and Mekong Delta. VRN joined with VUSTA on several of these activities, in part to provide political cover, but also since many of VRN's organizational members are registered there, and individual members are frequently part of other VUSTA-linked scientific and technical associations. Rather than VUSTA controlling VRN activists, the activists effectively used VUSTA's quasi-state umbrella status to legitimize their campaigns and organize policy dialogues between experts and relevant branches of the state.

The Vietnamese media has also been heavily involved in advocacy, both as a channel for communication and as direct participants in VRN activities. Network members have written their own articles for publication in print and online media, and others have been interviewed by journalists of key newspapers, such as *Thanh Niên*, *Tuổi Trẻ*, and *Lao Động*, and online news sites such as VNN and VNExpress. Some journalists are individual members of VRN and/or the Vietnam Federation of Environmental Journalists (VFEJ), a loose network with over 100 members who specialize in writing about environmental issues (Bass *et al.* 2010: 30). Through platforms such as VFEJ, certain journalists have become civil society actors in their own right.

Both VRN and PanNature are part of the regional Save the Mekong campaign, a civil society network that has co-organized workshops in Vietnam and gathered over 23,000 individual signatures on a petition to the Prime Ministers of Cambodia, Laos, Thailand and Vietnam, calling for a moratorium on dam construction. Through Save the Mekong, VRN is connected to the NGO Forum on Cambodia and to other transnational networks in Thailand, Laos and beyond.

The rise of community advocacy in Cambodia

Advocacy around water resources in Cambodia has proceeded without significant involvement of national or local government agencies. The NGO Forum on Cambodia has selected river protection as one of its priority issues and is a member of the Rivers Coalition in Cambodia (RCC), 'an alliance of civil society organizations working to protect and restore river ecosystems and river-based livelihoods in Cambodia' (Baird 2009). The six members of the RCC are local NGOs and networks with overlapping membership and mandates.[5] The RCC, in turn, engages with the NGO Forum's working group on river protection and the regional Save the Mekong campaign. This convoluted network structure may appear redundant, but is actually a source of strength, as members are connected to each other through multiple channels.[6] Unlike VRN, the RCC includes no government participants or individual members, but several of its member organizations represent local community interests and voices in a way that has not yet occurred in Vietnam.

The most active RCC member is the 3SPN Network, named after the three rivers (Sesan, Srepok and Sekong) that flow through northeastern Cambodia's Ratanakiri province (Ly, this volume). While 3SPN organizes communities, the RCC structure provides channels to engage with donors and the Cambodian government. This division of roles has led to some tension, as communities and local networks take a more principled, radical stance against dams while Phnom Penh-based NGOs urge dialogue. In the words of an NGO Forum leader, 'we understand why communities are against dams. They have no information: the companies tell them nothing. From the NGO side, we can see lessons learned from other countries and take a broader view'. Like VRN, the NGO Forum and RCC engage in tactical advocacy, recommending a delay and full environmental impact assessment, since they sense that a strong anti-dam position would be perceived as anti-government.

To some 3SPN members, this tactical approach is self-defeating: 'The government will listen to communities, not to NGOs!' In their view, authorities are able to dismiss the concerns of urban-based NGOs, and therefore allow them apparent freedom to speak out with lower risk of suppression. Rural community organizing, by contrast, has a stronger potential political impact, hence attracts more government attention. Both Khmer and international activists express criticism of 'so-called engagement' by well-funded, professional NGOs who avoid challenging the system, while local residents are prepared to go to jail to protect natural resources in their communities.

Cambodia has traditionally been a decentralized society with substantial autonomy for village chiefs. However, village structures have re-formed over the past 30 years under the influence of a growing state apparatus as well as new right-based conceptions of citizenship. The first community networks self-organized in the early 2000s around fisheries and forest concession issues, at a time when authorities initiated privatization of what had been common resources (Öjendal, this volume). Community voices at that time were successful in forcing elites to back down. Over time, these efforts led to the formation of cooperative structures between professional NGOs and networks based in the capital city and grassroots community groups in the provinces. One of these efforts became the Community Peacebuilding Network (CPN), a 'national grassroots advocacy project' consisting of a group of advocates in each province of Cambodia who work with communities on land rights and community forestry issues (CCD Cambodia, undated). As an unregistered entity, CPN does not serve an 'umbrella' function; it is more like a loose federation of representatives of other local networks.

Initially, CPN was funded by the US Agency for International Development (USAID) through the Asia Foundation. Funding was channelled through one of the five coordinating members, whose power in the network was strengthened as a result. According to participants, CPN has made many disparate efforts at organizing, yielding few cohesive results and often raising questions of accountability and internal governance, in addition to creating tension among NGOs and between NGO hosts and community activists. The network re-formed itself at a 2010 assembly, selecting a new grassroots-based steering committee of 24 members, one per province. One international NGO partner, Bridges across Borders, trained grassroots facilitators from across community networks and conducted local legal education. Some community networks have also received small grants from the East–West Management Institute's (EWMI) Program on Rights and Justice, funded by USAID.

In 2011, an innovative example of community networking emerged around the Prey Lang Forest, which stretches across four northern Cambodian provinces. A CPN affiliate, the Prey Lang network had been meeting since 2000 or 2001 when the forest was first threatened by commercial logging. With a direct democratic form of community representation, villages in Prey Lang have formed what one of its coordinators terms a 'natural network'. The structure consists of a core leadership group of 20 plus an assembly of over 100 village representatives, many from the Kuy ethnic group. In all, more than 70 villages in the forest area participate fully in the network, with an additional 70 villages having some active members. Network members conduct outreach to the remaining 150 villages in the forest. Most communication is by direct contact and mobile phone, with few written materials. The Prey Lang network is unregistered, which makes engagement with higher levels of government difficult, but it has support from some local commune councillors. Village-level activities, such as forest patrols, are funded through contributions from villagers of 500 riel (US$0.12) per month. External events are funded through CPN and other donors, and network members also benefit from meetings and other events organized by CPN, EWMI and others.

In early 2011, as forest clearance in Prey Lang by Vietnamese and Cambodian rubber companies accelerated, the network ventured into national and international advocacy for the first time, using images linked to the movie *Avatar* (with villagers and supporters painting their faces blue for a public rally) and a national day of prayer in Buddhist wats, dubbed 'Pray long for Prey Lang' (Prey Lang Community Network 2011). Unable to attract coverage in Khmer language newspapers, network members turned to radio programmes of Voice of America and Radio Free Asia's Khmer service. The *Avatar* campaign attracted the attention of international cable television channels, and finally the Cambodian public. Thanks to CPN's nationwide membership, the prayer day activities in August 2011 attracted participants in every province, making the government sit up and take notice. The network has since made efforts to communicate via the internet and social media, but mainly for the purpose of gaining international contacts; few Khmer, outside a small urban elite, have access to these technologies. The Prey Lang network's website, blog and printed materials are mainly in English, although training and community education materials have been developed in Khmer.

According to Prey Lang network members, they do not aim to convince government leaders through personal contact, but rather to create public pressure by creating local power bases that the government will have to respect in order to maintain its authority. The main network activities continue to be constituency- and community-based, i.e. direct organizing of villagers and linkages with other local networks. At the same time, the Prey Lang campaign has fostered a network of grassroots and international supporters ('Friends of the Forest') in Phnom Penh. One significant secondary effect of greater public and international attention has been an increase in Kuy ethnic identity and pride, and a positive shift in Khmer public attitudes towards indigenous people.

Cambodian community network members engage with government officials when possible, but frequently reach the conclusion that engagement produces limited results. 'We tried cooperation with government first', says one network coordinator, 'but this got us nowhere'. Local network leaders say they keep some contact with local authorities at the commune level, who may be receptive but have no power to change the situation. Anyone above this level cannot cooperate with networks because there is 'too much pressure from the top'. Members of the Prey Lang network, as well as the Boeung Kak campaign profiled below, have been arrested and spent time in jail. 3SPN facilitators have also been harassed and threatened. Yet network members insist that their efforts are not anti-government and are not connected with any political movement:

> Working with political parties is pointless. Opposition parties can't get anything done, and [if networks try to link with them] then the ruling party will just label you as part of the opposition and start a crackdown. Opposition politicians may try to latch on to networks' agendas, but this is for their own purposes. It's better not to register and keep on operating as a community network!
>
> (interview with network coordinator, Phnom Penh, October 2011)

Both the 3SPN and Prey Lang networks emerged from community leadership capacities that developed organically in response to perceived external threats. The local activists attempted to use embedded advocacy strategies first, but seeing no positive response from authorities they moved on to media and community strategies, seeking to reach a wider audience of NGOs, urban Cambodians and international supporters. Prey Lang's advocacy has drawn effectively on unassailable Buddhist religious and cultural images, as well as Hollywood movies: a powerful combination of mobilizing frames that aim not only at short-term policy victories, but ultimately the transformation and democratization of Cambodian society.

To this end, Cambodian networks have employed what is known in human rights advocacy as the 'boomerang strategy': faced with a blockage or weak connections at the national level of government, activists appeal to powerful international interests in the hope of compelling the obstructing authorities to change their position (Keck and Sikkink 1998; Khagram *et al.* 2002). Unable to stop thousands of forced evictions and property seizures around the proposed Boeung Kak Lake redevelopment project in Phnom Penh, a network of housing and land rights advocates appealed in 2009 to the World Bank Inspection Panel on the grounds that a Bank-funded land titling programme should have applied to the lakeside residents. The network's previous community organizing and legal rights strategy had encountered difficulties due to internal capacity limitations and the lack of unity among affected urban residents, as well as a widespread perception that the government and investors would work around the law when it suited their interests. The World Bank panel eventually found in favour of the complainants and put a temporary hold on lending to Cambodia in August 2011 (Tran 2011). Under pressure, the authorities offered a compromise outcome to reserve some space in the redevelopment area for evicted families, which although too late to help many evictees, shows the potential of the boomerang approach.

Cross-border connections

A Prey Lang network representative recounts that when villagers in the forest began to organize, they went to initiate a dialogue with a group of Vietnamese labourers who were clearing land for a rubber plantation in the forest. When the Vietnamese workers saw local residents approaching, they fled and later claimed they were under attack.

This anecdote illustrates a level of mistrust between Khmer and Vietnamese in which honest attempts at dialogue can easily be misinterpreted. Communication on the government-to-government level, in contrast, is strong. Indeed, the rubber workers are in Cambodia thanks to an agreement between a confederation of Vietnamese state-owned enterprises and the Cambodian government. Civil society contacts have been fewer. NGO delegations from Vietnam have visited Cambodia, and some exchanges have taken place on capacity building, ethnic issues and counter-trafficking, but these contacts have not yet yielded in-depth or long-lasting ties. To the extent that Cambodian and Vietnamese networks do cooperate, it is most often in the context of a regional campaign, such as Save the Mekong.

Cambodian NGOs have participated in regional networks for some time, dating from the UNTAC period and contacts formed in refugee camps on the Thai border. Vietnamese involvement is more recent. Indeed, in the case of the Save the Mekong Coalition, the participation of Vietnamese NGOs is unprecedented (Hirsch 2010: 320). The first major network forum to address effects of mainstream Mekong dams in Vietnam was organized in January 2010 at Can Tho University. As one of the Thai-based network partners describes, 'at the beginning, Save the Mekong used space at the regional level when it was not possible to do advocacy directly in Vietnam. Vietnamese groups used the regional platform to report back to Vietnam. That created more space'.

Even if the immediate benefits of conferences and study tours are unclear, the personal relationships arising from them have the potential of developing later into joint actions. These opportunities, however, are generally only open to individuals who speak English and are able to obtain external funding. Community network members, such as from CPN and Prey Lang, have had few chances for cross-border exchange. In autumn 2011, for the first time, a group of Cambodian community facilitators including Prey Lang network members travelled to the Earthrights International Mekong School in Chiang Mai, Thailand.

The potential benefits of increased connections between Vietnam and Cambodia are indisputable. The advocacy issues profiled in this chapter involve both countries: Vietnamese companies invest in rubber plantations and conduct logging operations in Cambodia, while dams planned for construction along the Mekong affect water flows in the Tonle Sap as well as the ecology of the Mekong Delta. Advocacy on the Mekong has facilitated new interactions among networks: since Vietnam is a downstream country, the effects of dam construction have raised public and official concern in a way not previously encountered in regard to downstream effects on Cambodia of Vietnamese dams on the Sesan River. 3SPN network members say they would like to increase collaboration with communities in Vietnam in addition to their existing contacts with VRN and PanNature. According to the current 3SPN coordinator, 'when the dams [on the upper Sesan in Vietnam] were being built, Vietnamese civil society didn't say anything. Now they are raising their voices, but the dams are done!' The coordinator has attended Save the Mekong meetings in Vietnam and hosted a 'media tour' for Vietnamese journalists to the Sesan. On the Vietnamese side, PanNature has begun to monitor Vietnamese investments in Cambodia, including logging, land concessions and mining. But overall, such advocacy connections are still limited.

Cultural and historical factors certainly play a role. Memories of Vietnam's occupation of Cambodia are not too distant, and the loss of the Mekong Delta region[7] remains a legacy that can be exploited for political purposes. In this context, efforts at cross-border advocacy, or even youth exchange, risk escalating sensitive issues of national security. Despite these political fears, and a substantial language gap, Cambodian and Vietnamese activists often relate well personally to each others' experiences. Cambodians can learn from Vietnamese tactics of engaging authorities through dialogue and alliance-building, and Vietnamese can benefit from the community organizing and rights-based approaches practised in Cambodia. Networks in each country may well choose to keep their core network strategies intact, but selecting from multiple strategies could lead to more creative advocacy.[8]

Conclusion: the varied meanings of networks

Civil society networks in both Vietnam and Cambodia demonstrate the existence of more underlying activism than is often publicly acknowledged. Observers who restrict their views of civil society to registered NGOs or intermediary associations miss much of the diversity and vibrancy that is actually occurring. Innovations in civil society organizing are taking place primarily in informal and issue-based advocacy networks, such as the cross-sectoral Vietnamese alliances and Cambodian community networks profiled in this chapter. These networks have the potential to influence not only the specific issues they advocate on, but the entire socio-political terrain in which they operate. As one Cambodian activist states, 'political parties and NGOs have been unable to change Cambodia.... We will continue as networks. We will rise up and speak for the people. We are Cambodia's civil society'.

While keeping this vision in mind, it is essential to realize that both Cambodian and Vietnamese networks have their respective strengths and weaknesses. At present, Cambodian networks have autonomy from state control and influence at the cost of limited access to policymakers. Although they operate independently from authorities, they are only able to draw on a weak reserve of bridging social capital. Vietnamese advocacy, in contrast, can usually rely on a fair hearing from at least one part of the state, as well as from a literate and educated public that can boast high levels of newspaper readership and access to the internet. Despite having less autonomous space, networks in Vietnam have achieved a degree of policy impact. Arguments based on expert scientific opinion have widespread traction. By involving sympathetic local and central government officials in networks, activists can sometimes use one part of the state to counterbalance another, a form of 'jujitsu advocacy' combining embedded approaches with appeals to public opinion (Wells-Dang 2012).

These strategies are less evident in Cambodia, where most networks have weak linkages to government and limited alliances and dialogue with other elites. In spite of an ostensibly multi-party system and decentralization programme, the Cambodian state appears less open to influence from civil society than the Vietnamese state. The greater autonomy of Cambodian networks from the state has not necessarily resulted in more successful outcomes. In the Cambodian case it is harder to engage in multi-level advocacy in a small country with less fragmentation of power across levels and bureaucracies. The presence of opposition parties has little, or even a negative, impact: networks avoid them for the practical reason that they are not seen as effective and association with them may result in a political backlash from the ruling party. Several international NGO representatives in Phnom Penh conclude that the Cambodian government is simply less open to dialogue and 'intelligent argument', since rational appeals do not get far in what they describe as a state characterized as 'a kleptocracy pure and simple'.

Media strategies are important in both countries, but in contrasting ways. In Vietnam, the state-owned print and online media plays a more positive role as a sounding board for public opinion than many observers assume. In Cambodia, activists have successfully used international media to reach a wider audience and overcome the limited circulation and freedom of domestic newspapers and television. Cambodian networks benefit from a larger domestic NGO sector, in which registration and operations have generally been smoother than in Vietnam. With greater international connections, civil society in Cambodia has also had more exposure to the language of human rights and civic participation. In part due to this influence, Cambodian networks have engaged in more community organizing than their counterparts in Vietnam, where authorities are still wary of the political potential of direct organizing. The 'boomerang strategy' for leveraging international actors has not been adopted in Vietnam, since the central government and large state-owned enterprises are less susceptible to public pressure (Ly, this volume). In fact, calls for external intervention or open protest can easily boomerang back onto the activists themselves if authorities frame them as tools of foreign interests.

From another viewpoint, Vietnamese networks have less need of such pressure tactics, since channels for participation within the system already exist to a certain extent, and the national government is not necessarily the main source of blockage. The engagement strategies of Vietnamese advocates have had a stronger impact on policy to date than the more confrontational 'civil society versus the state' approaches of some Cambodian activists. Given this observation, it may be worth re-examining assumptions about the intractability of the Cambodian state to well-targeted engagement; there may be more diversity and venues for pluralism than many actors think (Feuer, this volume).

Networks in both countries face a significant challenge of mediating between elite and community interests, which often parallels the urban–rural divide. Some Cambodian rural communities have self-organized into networks, but are still isolated from NGOs in Phnom Penh. In Vietnam, most NGOs and networks are based in major cities, with limited membership and capacity in rural provinces. The advocacy strategies selected by Vietnamese networks are focused on reaching power-holders and elites, not expanding their membership base. Networks that receive donor funding are at risk of becoming dependent on grants, rather than striving for accountability to their local constituencies. These risks are lower in community networks, where almost all network members are volunteers. It is precisely community networks, however, that can benefit most from international linkages, not primarily for funding but to build transnational alliances and share advocacy strategies.

Both Cambodian and Vietnamese networks face challenges in their national political contexts. As Cambodia's ruling party consolidates its power, one scenario might be that the Cambodian civil society context becomes more like Vietnam – and consequently less like the idealized model of an autonomous civil society. If networks cannot advocate openly using their current repertoire, they may shift to more informal tactics. As Vietnamese advocates have found, linkages to government can sometimes lead to positive outcomes. Whether political trajectories in Cambodia and Vietnam converge or separate, networks in both countries will continue to have much to learn from each other's structures, strategies and aims of inclusive social change.

Notes

1 Research for this chapter was conducted while living and working in Vietnam, with frequent visits to Cambodia (including nine in 2011 alone). A total of over 50 semi-structured interviews were conducted with network coordinators and members in both countries between November 2010 and December 2011. Since some respondents prefer to remain anonymous, no personal details are given in citations of interview data. An earlier version of this chapter was presented to the Washington Indochina Roundtable, Johns Hopkins University School of Advanced International Studies (USA) in November 2011.
2 VUSTA currently has over 600 members, of which 240 are registered local NGOs (VUSTA 2011). With a stated mission to 'build networks of NGOs', VUSTA considers itself a network and claims to be the most effective Vietnamese organization in policy advocacy. While VUSTA arguably has more of a state than civil society character, its

members and leaders participate in numerous networks and contribute to opening space for advocacy of others. VUSTA's structure does not include working groups or facilitation of horizontal links, but members have formed multiple, overlapping issue-based networks of their own without interference.

3 The focus in this chapter on advocacy strategies as a characteristic activity of civil society networks does not imply that other network functions are less important: successful networks balance external advocacy with services to their members (Wells-Dang 2012).

4 The author is one of a handful of international individual members of VRN. All of the network's organizational members are Vietnamese, and most VRN meetings and publications are in Vietnamese language only.

5 The six RCC members are CDCam, FACT (a fisheries coalition that spun off from the NGO Forum), 3SPN, CIVS, Culture and Environment Preservation Association, and the NGO Forum itself.

6 This redundancy is seen in another Cambodian network, the Housing Rights Task Force in Phnom Penh, which has the NGO Forum as one of its members, while other core members are separately part of the NGO Forum. The Task Force, in turn, is a member of a Land and Housing Working Group that also includes some of the task force's individual members. When one of the task force's member organizations, Sahmakam Teang Tnaut (STT) was suspended by the Cambodian government for six months in 2011 for alleged 'illegal' activities in opposition to an ADB-financed railroad project, the multiple ties of this network enabled STT members to continue engagement through alternate pathways.

7 In Cambodia the Mekong Delta is sometimes referred to as 'Kampuchea Krom' (Lower Cambodia), with historical ties that remain politically contentious.

8 Comparative research on China and Vietnam finds that networks with multiple advocacy strategies and a diversity of members who 'wear different hats' are more effective overall in both short-term policy impact and longer term influence on political space (Wells-Dang 2012).

References

Anheier, H., Glasius, M. and Kaldor, M. (2003) *Global Civil Society 2003*, Oxford: Oxford University Press.

Baird, I. (2009) *Best Practices in Compensation and Resettlement for Large Dams: The Case of the Planned Lower Sesan 2 Hydropower Project in Northeastern Cambodia*, Phnom Penh: Rivers Coalition in Cambodia.

Bass, S., Annandale, D., Phan Van Binh, Tran Phuong Dong, Hoang Anh Nam, Le Thi Kien Oanh, Parsons, M., Nguyen Van Phuc and Vu Van Trieu (2010) *Integrating Environment and Development in Viet Nam: Achievements, Challenges and Next Steps*, London: International Institute for Environment and Development.

Brown, D. (2011) 'Green on Red: Searching for "Suitable Solutions" to Vietnam's Environmental Crisis', paper presented at the Vietnam Update conference, Australian National University, Canberra, 17 November.

Castells, M. (1996) *The Rise of the Network Society: Volume 1*, Oxford: Blackwell.

CCD Cambodia (undated) 'Community Peacebuilding Network – CPN'. Online. Available at: www.ccdcambodia.org/main.php?p=cpn.php (accessed 14 October 2011).

Cohen, J. and Arato, A. (1992) *Civil Society and Political Theory*, Cambridge, MA: MIT Press.

Government of Vietnam (2002) Decision 22/QD-TTg of the Prime Minister on the Activities of Consultancy, Judgment and Social Expertise by the Vietnam Union of Science and Technology Associations, issued 30 January.

Government of Vietnam (2010) Decree No. 45/2010/ND-CP on the Organization, Operation and Management of Associations, issued 21 April.

Habermas, J. (1992) 'Further Reflections on the Public Sphere' in C. Calhoun, (ed.), *Habermas and the Public Sphere*, Cambridge, MA: MIT Press: 421–79.

Hannah, J. (2007) 'Approaching Civil Society in Vietnam', unpublished thesis, University of Washington.

Hirsch, P. (2010) 'The Changing Political Dynamics of Dam Building on the Mekong' in *Water Alternatives*, 3 (2): 312–23.

Ho, P. and Edmonds, R. (eds) (2008) *China's Embedded Activism: Opportunities and Constraints of a Social Movement*, London: Routledge.

Hughes, C. (2009) *Dependent Communities: Aid and Politics in Cambodia and East Timor*, Ithaca, NY: Cornell University Press.

IUCN (2011) 'Mekong Water Dialogues Vietnam National Working Group', unpublished meeting minutes, Ho Chi Minh City, 27 January.

Keck, M. and Sikkink, K. (1998) *Activists Beyond Borders*, Ithaca, NY: Cornell University Press.

Kerkvliet, B. J. T., Nguyen Quang A, and Bach Tan Sinh (2008) *Forms of Engagement Between State Agencies and Civil Society Organizations in Vietnam*, Hanoi: VUFO-NGO Resource Centre.

Khagram, S., Riker, J. and Sikkink, K. (eds) (2002) *Restructuring World Politics: Transnational Social Movements, Networks, and Norms*, Minneapolis, MN: University of Minnesota Press.

Krishna, A. (2002) *Active social capital: Tracing the roots of development and democracy*, New York: Columbia University Press.

Nguyen Huu Thien (2011) 'ĐBSCL nghiên cứu tác động của các đập thủy điện sông Mekong' [Mekong Delta research on the impact of Mekong River dams] in *Saigon Times*, 23 April. Online. Available at: http://mobile.thesaigontimes.vn/ArticleDetail. aspx?id=52233 (accessed 16 September 2011).

Öjendal, J. and Lilja, M. (eds) (2009) *Beyond Democracy in Cambodia*, Singapore: NIAS Press.

Prey Lang Community Network (2011) 'Prey Lang's "Avatars"' in *Prey Lang – It's YOUR Forest Too!*' Online. Available at: http://ourpreylang.wordpress.com/the-network/ (accessed 1 November 2011).

Putnam, R. (1993) *Making Democracy Work: Civil Traditions in Modern Italy*, Princeton: Princeton University Press.

Read, B. and Pekkanen, R. (eds) (2009) *Local Organizations and Urban Governance in East and Southeast Asia: Straddling State and Society*, London: Routledge Studies on Civil Society in Asia.

Thanh Nien News (2011) 'Scientists Question Environment Impact Assessments of Vietnam Power Projects', *Thanh Nien News* 15 July. Online. Available at: www.thanhniennews.com/2010/Pages/20110715165856.aspx (accessed 13 September 2011).

Thayer, C. (2009) 'Vietnam and the Challenge of Political Civil Society' in *Contemporary Southeast Asia*, 31 (1): 1–27.

Tran, M. (2011) 'World Bank Suspends New Lending to Cambodia over eviction of Landowners' in *Guardian*, 10 August. Online. Available at: www.guardian.co.uk/globaldevelopment/2011/aug/10/world-bank-suspends-cambodia-lending (accessed 3 November 2011).

Vasavakul, T. (2003) 'From Fence-Breaking to Networking: Interests, Popular Organizations, and Policy Influences in Post-Socialist Vietnam' in Kerkvliet, B. J. T., Koh,

D. W. H. and Heng, R. H.-k. (eds), *Getting Organized in Vietnam: Moving in and around the Socialist State*, Singapore: Institute of Southeast Asian Studies: 25–61.

Vietnam Rivers Network (2011a) 'Báo cáo tổng kết hoạt động Mạng lưới Sông ngòi Việt Nam 2011' [VRN Annual Report], distributed at VRN annual meeting, Hue, December.

Vietnam Rivers Network (2011b) 'Nhận diện tác động xã hội của hai dự án Thủy điện Đồng Nai 6 và 6A' [Identifying social impacts of the Dong Nai 6 and 6A Dam projects], *Bản tin VRN* [Newsletter], 4–5 August.

Wells-Dang, A. (2012) *Civil Society Networks in China and Vietnam: Informal Pathbreakers in Health and the Environment*, Basingstoke: Palgrave Macmillan.

5 Civil society and political culture in Vietnam

Nadine Reis

Introduction

The idea that a vibrant civil society is beneficial for the political and social development of a nation has been popular at least since de Tocqueville's (2008 [1835]) analysis of nineteenth century America. In the twentieth century, the idea of civil society has gained popularity in particular due to the democratic movements in Eastern Europe since the 1970s, making it a central point of reference in the debate about democratization processes (Klein 2001: 19). Further, Putnam's work on Italy and the US has been highly influential, showing the positive relationship between high levels of civic engagement, a strong associational life, and the functioning of political institutions (Putnam 1993, 2000). Civil society has consequently entered Western governments' and international organizations' political agenda in developing countries, considered 'the key ingredient in promoting democratic development' (Jenkins 2001: 251). In short, 'civic groups figure large in visions of a better society' (Lichterman 2005: 395). Problematic about such expectations is not only to which extent civil society can meet them, but also the assumption that civil society is a universal concept. International donors mostly understand the concept of civil society in general terms; as 'the wide array of non-governmental and not-for-profit organizations that have a presence in public life, expressing the interests and values of their members or others, based on ethical, cultural, political, scientific, religious or philanthropic considerations' (World Bank 2010).

Dalton and Ong (2005) question whether such a definition can capture civic engagement in a one-party system like Vietnam, and in particular, whether the mere existence of civic organizations can be seen as a step towards democracy. As Lichterman suggests, civic engagement is not the same everywhere, but 'means very different things in different settings, with different consequences for public discussion and intergroup ties' (Lichtermann 2005: 394). Different settings may also create different civic customs that 'carry different potentials for realizing different kinds of collective goods' (ibid.: 389). How can we conceptualize the different settings under which civil society exists and operates? What kinds of 'collective goods' or social processes can be expected to emerge from civic engagement in Vietnam?

One way of understanding the diversity of civil society is to approach it from the perspective of (political) culture. Following Archer's critical realist approach to social theory, 'culture' is defined as 'referring to all intelligibilia, that is to any item that has the dispositional ability to be understood by someone', while a Cultural System is 'that subset of items to which the law of contradiction can be applied' (Archer 2005: 24). This chapter analyses the cultural dimension of civic engagement: the system of meanings and values under which citizens engage in their society as well as the knowledge that underpins the practices of active citizenship, and thus builds the situational basis for societal elaboration. Next to material-structural conditions, such as available resources, infrastructure, or limits posed by physical violence, cultural conditions are vital for civic engagement, since they shape social practices just like material structures do.

> [T]he [Cultural System] is the product of historical [Socio-Cultural] interaction, but having emerged (cultural emergence being a continuous process) then *qua* product, it has properties but also powers of its own kind. Like structure, some of its most important causal powers are those of constraints and enablements. In the cultural domain these stem from contradictions and complementarities.
>
> (Archer 2005: 25)

The question is thus how a specific Cultural System enables or constrains civic action in Vietnam, and how the practices of civic engagement may in turn reproduce or change it.

The chapter begins by outlining the emergence of the idea of civil society. I argue that the 'social imaginary' (Taylor 2004) is a particularly relevant element of political culture on which civic action draws. The idea of civil society is based on the historical legacy of the development of an independent economic sphere in Europe and the ideas accompanying this process. In making central the idea of free and equal individuals together making up society for mutual benefit, the modern social imaginary fundamentally differs from the Vietnamese social imaginary – which is based on the idea of hierarchical differentiation. After analysing the implications for the forms and meanings of civil society in Vietnam, I will discuss the constraints and possibilities for the rapidly increasing number of civic groups to bring about change.

Civil society in the 'modern social imaginary'

Political culture theory suggests that differences in attitudes about authority and power are key to the analysis of political systems and their development (Pye 1985; Bukovansky 2002). Therefore, an assessment of the potential of civil society for political development in Vietnam requires an understanding of the substantive content of the Cultural System in which the idea of civil society emerged, particularly attitudes to power. The idea of civil society is part of a Cultural System that Taylor (2004) describes as the 'modern social imaginary', which is 'the ways people imagine their social existence, how they fit together with others, how things go on between them and their fellows, the expectations that are normally met, and the deeper normative notions and images that underlie these expectations' (ibid.: 23). The social imaginary can thus be understood as the way(s) in which humans are imagined as social beings.

The social imaginary of Western societies started its 'long march' in Renaissance times and, over the centuries, turned from an elite idea into the common way in which ordinary people imagine their social surroundings (ibid.: 32ff.). The core of the idea is that of human beings forming society as free and equal individuals for their mutual benefit (ibid.: 4). The presumption of equality fundamentally distinguishes the new social imaginary from earlier ones.

> Premodern social imaginaries … were structured by various modes of hierarchical complementarity. The hierarchical differentiation is seen as the proper order of things. It was part of the nature or form of society. Any attempt to deviate from it turned reality against itself, society would be denatured.… The modern idealisation of order departs radically from this. Whatever distribution of functions a society might develop is deemed contingent. It cannot itself define the good; the basic normative principle is, indeed, that the members of society serve each other's needs, help each other, in short, behave like the rational and sociable creatures they are. The modern order vies no ontological status to hierarchy or any particular structure of differentiation.
>
> (Taylor 2004: 11f.)

This social imaginary is the core of the 'system culture' (Almond 1989: 28) of modern Western societies,[1] in which the idea of civil society plays a significant role. In its classical meaning 'civil' was a quality of society – the opposite of 'uncivilized' society (Kumar 1993: 376ff.). The privatization of economic activity, and the advent of the idea of a society formed of free and equal individuals in the eighteenth century, shifted its meaning. Civil society came to mean a societal sphere distinct from the state. Civil society is 'interpreted to signify a reality'; state and civil society are not only categories to be distinguished analytically, but also seen as referentially discrete or even causally independent (Dunn 2001: 53). The semiotic separation of state and civil society in the West means that the idea of civil society is an element of a specific Cultural System in which 'the state' is seen to exist for the benefit of free and equal individuals.[2]

As a sphere independent of the state, the privatized economy laid the ground for the second dimension of civil society, namely the notion of the public sphere, within which the requirements of privatized societal reproduction were secured. With the detachment of the economic sphere from the polity, a common interest of individuals emerges for the first time, which manifests in the central significance of the rule of law. Political interventions in a market without laws are incalculable, and thus fundamentally run counter to the degree of rationality required by individuals who are privately acting market participants. For the law to become law, that is, to apply to all without exception, the public itself, comprised of private individuals, has to take charge of legislation (Habermas 1989: 80ff.). This moment signified the final break with the imaginary of a hierarchically differentiated society, where authority (*Herrschaft*) is conferred only to a specific group of people. After all,

> [i]n its intention, the rule of the law aimed at dissolving domination altogether; this was a typically bourgeois idea insofar as not even the political safeguarding of the private sphere emancipating itself from political domination was to assume the form of domination. The bourgeois idea of the law-based state, namely, the binding of all state-activity to a system of norms legitimated by public opinion (a system that had no gaps, if possible), already aimed at abolishing the state as an instrument of domination altogether.
>
> (Habermas 1989: 81ff.)

Civil society not only achieved an identity different from the polity, but became, through its function of creating the public sphere, a moral requirement for the legitimacy of the state. The core requirement of this idea is the sovereignty of the people: all state activities are only legitimate when based on the opinion of the public. The public sphere stands, 'mentally, outside of the polity, as it were, from which to judge its performance' (Taylor 2004: 87).

> Government is then not only wise to follow [public] opinion; it is morally bound to do so. Governments ought to legislate and rule in the midst of a reasoning public. In making its decisions, Parliament or the court ought to be concentrating together and enacting what has already been emerging out of enlightened debate among the people....The public sphere is, then, a locus in which rational views are elaborated that should guide government.
>
> (Ibid.: 88ff.)

Civil society thus became a sphere whose function lies in the political intermediation between state and society (Klein 2001: 31).

However, in the modern idea, civil society is not only bound to the legitimization of the state as viewed in deliberative political theory. In occupying the domain between the individual and the state, civil society also invokes an idea of salvation. It is 'the attempt to grapple with the central problem of modern society: how to find a "third way" between "the atomization of competitive market society", on the one side, and a "state dominated existence", on the other'. Most commonly, this has referred to the space of groups and organizations where 'the individual develops the sense of social solidarity and civic participation' (Kumar 1993: 380).

Investigations of 'civic culture' (Almond and Verba 1963) found that the 'rationality-activist' model of citizenship cannot be seen as the only element of a functioning democratic state. 'Only when combined in some sense with its opposites of passivity, trust, and deference to authority and competence was a viable, stable democracy possible' (Almond 1989: 16).

The idea of deliberative democracy has been further criticized for being naïve in that it believes too much in the power of public debate (Ottmann 2006: 319). It would thus be too simplistic to view Western political culture(s) as devoid of passive subjects who trust or even subordinate themselves to political authority. Nevertheless, this does not affect the conception of civil society as a sphere distinct from the state, in and through which the moral idea of a society existing of equal individuals is continuously expanding, both in extensity (more people are claiming it) and in intensity (its demands are heavier) (Taylor 2004: 5). Today, this materializes in the claim of rights to privacy, property, publicity (free speech and association) and equality before the law (Cohen and Arato 1992: 345).

As a discursive structure, 'civil society' has spread from Europe around the world with the advent of colonialism. By establishing 'states', there was already an 'implicit distinction from civil society' (Kaviraj and Khilnani 2001: 4):

[T]he language used to describe, evaluate and express the experiences of politics are the same everywhere. For historical reasons, nearly all societies speak a Western language. It is a language which identifies states and civil societies, speaks of bureaucracies, political parties, parliaments, expresses political desires for the establishment of liberal, Communist or socialist political forms, and evaluates political systems in terms of democracy and dictatorship.

To what extent has the dissemination of terminology gone along with the dissemination of culture? How is society imagined in Vietnam, and what is the prevailing idea of the state?

The idea of the state in Vietnam

Traditional Vietnamese society and its political system were based on Confucian political philosophy, which employed the patriarchal family as the basic model for the political system and did not concede any political or civil rights to citizens. During the 1829–41 Minh Mang regency, printing was restricted based on the idea that ordinary people were incapable of making decisions and did not need to know how to write or read (Porter 1993: 4). A hierarchically structured society is traditionally believed to be in 'the nature of things', to represent 'the intrinsic structure of the universe' (Jamieson 1993: 16). Attitudes to power in Vietnam also involve a great deal of non-Confucian, in particular Buddhist, cultural heritage (Pye 1985: 238ff.). Nevertheless, the overall political Cultural System still differs fundamentally from the Western one in that it is of a distinctively hierarchical kind. The view of power and authority is paternalistic in emphasizing 'dependency and ... expecting superiors to be nurturing and generously supportive in both strength and wealth' (Pye 1985: 239). At the heart of the Vietnamese cultural heritage is also the idea that only proper social relationships following this natural order 'will produce social harmony, creating happy and prosperous families, villages and nations' (Jamieson 1993: 12). The rejection of Confucianism by the Communist movement did not mean the end of this imaginary.

> Like Confucianism, Marxism-Leninism gave legitimacy to the claims of the collective and the society over those of the individual.... For the fund of ancient wisdom and practice on which the legitimacy of the traditional Confucianist elite was based, the Vietnamese Communist movement substituted a 'scientific' system of thought that gave party leaders the ability to discern the truth and to point to the correct path.
>
> (Porter 1993: 7ff.)

Hue-Tam Ho Tai (1992: 259ff.) demonstrates that the victory of Marxist-Leninist ideology over liberalist and individualistic ideas in the 1920s can largely be attributed to its ability to unite the 'ingrained elitism' among the revolutionary vanguard with the promise of national independence ('the victory of the oppressed masses').

> By emphasizing the importance of class at the expense of the individual, Marxism-Leninism brushed aside the humanist concerns – in particular the desire for personal freedom and moral autonomy as distinct from social justice, equality, or political independence – that had brought so many young Vietnamese into revolutionary politics.
>
> (Hue-Tam Ho Tai 1992: 262ff.)

In spite of the liberalist movement in which the revolution originated, it finally ended in the reproduction of a Cultural System that placed the individual in the service of the collective. Elitism and anti-liberalism were deeply ingrained in the new leading ideology. As Lenin saw it, the selected cadre of vanguard revolutionaries was to take over the role of teachers who dictate the uneducated masses which way to go (Scott 1998: 148).

> the 'masses' in general and the working class in particular become 'the body', while the vanguard party is 'the brain'.... [T]he vanguard party not only is essential to the tactical cohesion of the masses but also must literally do their thinking for them.... Its authority is based on its scientific intelligence.... There is no need for politics within the party inasmuch as the science and rationality of the socialist intelligentsia require instead a technically necessary subordination; the party's judgments are not subjective and value laden but objective and logically inevitable.
>
> (Scott 1998: 149ff., citing Lenin)

Ho Chi Minh's political thought and the foundation of the Democratic Republic of Vietnam in 1954 embraced the decisively authoritarian Soviet model, in which human freedom was subordinated to the (party-defined) interests of the collective (Brocheux 2007: 187). This model, incorporating the idea of the infallibility of the Party, was strongly supported by the neo-Confucian principle of *Chính nghĩa* (exclusive righteousness) of the political elite, which, in this form, lived on in spite of the significant ideological differences between Confucianism and Marxist-Leninism (Gillespie 2002: 183). As Metzger (2001: 230ff.) assessed in the case of China,

> in addressing the question of political improvement, modern Chinese political thought has not turned toward a non-utopian, bottom-up approach. Based on the traditional optimism about political practicability, it still reflects the traditional paradigm of a morally and intellectually enlightened elite working with a corrigible political centre morally to transform society, instead of emphasising the organisational efforts of free but fallible citizens forming a civil society with which to monitor an incorrigible political centre.

This assessment resonates strongly with the Vietnamese case and explains the ethical justification of hierarchical differentiation in society. As in the Western imaginary, political decision-making should be based on a rational, enlightened view of the world. However, it is not public opinion that is enlightened, it is the political authorities (Taylor 2004: 88). In contrast, it is the Party that is the embodiment of reason. This worldview prevails until today, explaining why

> the very notion of an oppositional sphere, or a domain outside of the state, remains anathema – an affront even.... [T]he idea of an oppositional sphere simply does not fit with the philosophical underpinnings in which the Communist Party of Vietnam is rooted and still draws. To suggest otherwise is insulting because it is to question the party's commitment to the people.
>
> (Gainsborough 2005: 37)

If Vietnamese political culture differs in such a substantial way from the Western one, can civil society still be thought to exist, and in what sense?

Civil society in Vietnam

Unlike other international development terminology that has entered Vietnamese policy discourse, 'civil society' is normally not used in official documents or in the media (Hannah 2007: 103; Phuong Le Trong, this volume). Nevertheless, group membership is significantly higher in Vietnam than in other Asian and even Western countries (Dalton and Ong 2005: 33; Norlund 2007: 78). Moreover, the popularity of 'civil society' in international policy discourse has significantly increased the number of community-based organizations (CBOs) in Vietnam through donor engagement (Thayer 2008: 5ff.). Vietnamese mass organizations, as well as other organizations, 'try to pass themselves off as "genuine" civil society groups out of self-interest' (ibid.: 13). In what way do civil society practices in Vietnam differ from those in the West, and what is their foreseen and actual role in society? From a cultural perspective, the answer to this question lies in the ways civic engagement 'fits' the Cultural System.[3] Two 'ideal types' of active citizenship in Vietnam can be identified.

The first type, foremost manifested in the mass organizations (Women's Union, Farmers' Union, Youth Union and Veterans' Union) and professional organizations (Bach Tan Sinh, this volume), has to be understood in relation to the role of the public sphere. The public sphere in Vietnam cannot be understood as an independent, public expression of private people in opposition to the state. In the democratic West, the public can be regarded as part of the societal sphere of private persons (Habermas 1989: 30). In Vietnam the public cannot be seen as such, since there is no binary idea of state and society as separated spheres. The public in Vietnam, rather, must be viewed as a sphere of education: there is no private, and thus no public, independent of the party state. Public discourse is not debate between private individuals, but rather public opinion controlled through the state apparatus. The public sphere is, so to speak, the sphere where the one-party state accesses the people, and where the party's policies and values are transmitted to the different groups in society (cf. Rittersporn *et al.* 2003: 14). Therefore, the government's strategy is to initiate and direct the participation of citizens in social groups (Dalton and Ong 2005: 33). The mass organizations are, next to the state and party organizations at every administrative level, the core instrument for ensuring the effective education of the masses. This is evident, for example, in water supply and sanitation, where it is the task of the Women's Union to communicate party views on environmental and hygiene issues to the people, following a clear top-down approach.

> The Women's Union has the function of mobilization and communication on good hygiene and sanitation, improving the awareness of the people, training.... We get the decision about the strategy from the provincial People's Committee.
>
> (Interview, Women's Union, Tra Vinh province, 10 July 2008)

> We train and mobilize the women [on district level] to become facilitators in communication and education for rural water supply and sanitation. The rural women should participate in the protection of the environment, improvement of hygienic latrines, collecting waste, digging holes for collecting chicken and duck droppings, and establishing families with good health.
>
> (Interview, Women's Union, Can Tho province, 3 June 2008)

> We try to communicate about environmental issues to all members of the Women's Union. To protect health, the people have to use well water, install hygienic latrines and drink boiled water.

[NR: *How do you cooperate with the Women's Union on provincial level?*] Cooperation is not the right expression. We get the decision from the provincial level and we follow.

(Interview, Women's Union, Co Do district, Can Tho province,
11 July 2008)

Women's Union officers are appointed by the party.

[NR: *How did you become the leader of the WU?*] Previously, I worked in the hamlet, then the commune suggested that I work in the commune. I became the deputy manager, and after a few years, I became the leader.

[NR: *Who from the commune suggested you for the commune Women's Union, was it the People's Committee?*] No, it was people from the party.

[NR: *Does the party always appoint the leader of the Women's Union?*] Yes.

[NR: *Do you have to be a party member to become the leader of the Women's Union?*] I have been a member since 1998.

(Interview, Women's Union leader, Truong Xuan commune,
Co Do district, Can Tho province, 23 October 2008)

The mass organizations can thus be seen as the 'civil arm' of the party apparatus, through which the political elite propagates its views on virtually all aspects of life. To illustrate, the Women's Union is also responsible for 'communicating' the party's two-child policy to the population through 'birth control officers' active in the communes. Hence, the Vietnamese social imaginary implies that the public, in the sense of society as a whole, is fully entitled to control the private (cf. Rittersporn 2003: 413).

The second 'ideal type' of active citizenship in Vietnam relates to the moral imperative for devoting oneself to the wellbeing and harmony of the societal whole. One of the components of the Vietnamese Cultural System, with origins in Buddhist rather than Confucian thought, is a morality steeped in self-sacrifice and 'destruction of the ego' (Pye 1985: 238ff.). Civic engagement can thus be seen as a way of becoming a 'good' citizen. The agents of this project of civic engagement can be individuals as well as collectives.

On the individual side, the water sector can exemplify the cultural representation of this kind of civic engagement. In order to supply the rural areas in Can Tho City with clean domestic water, provincial authorities began to install water supply stations with piped networks at the end of the 1990s (Reis 2012: 74ff.). However, as research has revealed, the budget of the provincial agency responsible for rural water supply is so low that the operation and management of the local water supply stations is essentially dependent on the commitment of individuals. The stations are commonly constructed on the property of a household willing to donate a piece of land (usually in their back yard) for constructing the station; they then take over its management. The task involves maintaining the station and tubes, washing the water container, collecting water fees from households, implementing minor repairs and installing household connections. However, the station managers are not government employees, and only receive a small allowance of VND140,000 (approx. US$7.43) per month. In addition, they receive VND2,500 for every household that uses more than $3\,m^3$; i.e. a manager whose piped water is used by 100 households can receive VND390,000VND (approximately US$20.72) per month.

How many days the station managers work for the water supply station depends on how often the water container is cleaned and how frequently repairs are needed. Station managers stated that they worked between three and 16 days per month,[4] and represented their work as a personal commitment for the community.

> I do not consider the money from [the government agency] as a salary. It is just for serving the people.
>
> (Station manager, Thanh Quoi commune, Vinh Thanh district,
> 23 September 2008)

> I do not consider the money I get as a salary, I just do it because I want to serve the people.
>
> (Station manager, Truong Xuan commune, Co Do district,
> 23 October 2008)

> The salary for the station management is not too much; but because the government invested to serve the people, I also work to serve the people.
>
> (Station manager, Truong Long commune, Phong Dien district,
> 28 October 2008)

The salary of the managers is very little considering the considerable responsibility. Proper operation of the stations effectively depends on the commitment of the station managers. For example, the water quality depends on how often the container is cleaned. Therefore, authorities select families with a strong sense of civic duty.

> The land is usually offered by the families. They have to choose a family which has high social spirit. The area is usually 48 m².

> [NR: *What are the important characteristics of the families?*] High social spirit, responsibility, good health. If the guy is drunk all the time it is not good! [*laughing*].... In this area, the social spirit is the most important.
>
> (President, PC Thoi An ward, O Mon district, 15 September 2008)

The station managers in Can Tho are very kind. They have good social spirit. They manage the public property very well. The manager is supported by the local authorities and the communities very much.

(Head of Office, provincial water supply agency, 15 October 2008)

Similar to the idea of 'social spirit', the morality of civic engagement is illustrated by the conception of a 'good hamlet' (*Áp văn hóa*). Becoming a 'good hamlet' is achieved by 'creating a culture among the people' (interview, People's Committee Troung Long commune, Phong Dien district, Can Tho City, 2 March 2009).

The culture of 'serving' the wellbeing of society also materializes in CBOs, many of which were established after 1986 (Wischermann and Nguyen Quang Vinh 2003: 186). CBOs fulfil a prominent role in the policy of 'socialization'. The government encourages the establishment of non-profit organizations providing public services to citizens that the government is not able or willing to provide (CIEM/FES 2006: 19ff.). In 2005 an estimated 100,000 to 200,000 such groups existed in Vietnam; working in the health, education, environmental and religious sectors (Norlund 2007: 13). As pointed out by Waibel and Benedikter (this volume), in the case of irrigation management CBOs play a key role in the implementation of government policy.

It is necessary to clearly emphasize that socialization is to mobilize material, intellectual, and spiritual strength of the whole society to better meet daily demands of people on education, healthcare, culture, gymnastics and sports, [and to] better implement social equality in these fields.

(Address of Prime Minister Phan Van Khai to the National Conference, 26 July 2005, cited in CIEM/FES 2006: 23)

These words of the Prime Minister make the case for viewing CBOs as vicarious agents of the government, and as a manifestation of the idea that civic engagement is to serve the wellbeing of the society at large.

Discussion and conclusion

In the Vietnamese social imaginary, civic engagement takes place within the boundaries of the party state. Therefore, if 'civil society' exists in Vietnam, it cannot be seen as a sphere outside of the state, or even a sphere in which the activities of the state are guided and judged. On the contrary, 'active citizenship' in Vietnam functions as an important mechanism for the reproduction of the social imaginary, which can be understood to be the 'cultural property' of the one-party state (Reis 2012: 215ff.).

How does this analysis assess the changes in Vietnam since the economic liberalization of the late 1980s? Waibel and Benedikter (this volume) show that the reform process has produced a growing number, and new types, of civic organizations, such as religious groups, environmental groups, educational/cultural groups and business organizations. Thayer (2008: 13) recognized an increasing number of 'explicitly political organizations dedicated to the promotion of democracy, human rights and religious freedom' in Vietnam. Religious leaders and networks have been a particularly active source of political unrest.[5] Will these new groups initiate political change and transform Vietnam into a democracy? A simple answer would be that only history will tell: society is an open system. The political Cultural System is a structural condition, not a determinant, which means that the exercise of its causal powers is dependent upon their activation by people (Archer 2005: 25).

Nevertheless, as a structural condition, the Cultural System exercises its own powers on socio-cultural interaction because it engenders specific mechanisms that enable or constrain the variation, selection and retention of social practices. Social imaginaries possess discursively selective powers (Jessop 2008: 239). The key driver for the reproduction of the political Cultural System through civic action is that people become carriers of various structures as their behaviour is formed by processes of socialization, in particular cultural and cumulative social learning (Eckstein 1988: 792). It is for this reason that Dalton and Ong (2005: 41) found that civic groups in Vietnam, instead of developing political skills and interests (as postulated by classical civil society theorists), 'convey the values of hierarchy and collective decision-making that underlie the current communist regime'.

What if ideas that contradict the prevailing social imaginary still emerge? Clearly the reproduction of the Cultural System also depends on material-structural forces and the interests associated with them. 'Although there may be a plurality of ideas and interests at play in any given socio-political structure, the dominant legitimacy conceptions and rules constituting that structure will favor some sorts of interests and modes of action over others' (Bukovansky 2002: 43).

In Vietnam the cultural properties of the state are carried by the interests of one societal group, one which has expanded numerically with economic liberalization but one which has not diversified to the extent that conflicting political ideas would gain weight (Reis 2012: 217). The concentration of resources within a single elite, and its strong interdependence with a long-established idea of the state, creates a strong incentive for closing off the system against alternative ideas. The modern idea of equality has to be suppressed because it is subversive to the core features of social order. Hence, the prevailing Cultural System is protected, most notably, by the hindering or closing off information sources, anti-pluralist propaganda, and finally, physical violence against political dissidents.[6] In summary, the properties of the cultural and material structures of the Vietnamese state system provide more reason to assume that civil society actors will continue to contribute to the reproduction of social and political order rather than to democratic transformation.

Nevertheless, there are signs that civic action in Vietnam could push forward the 'modern idea' in a more modest sense. The central features of the Vietnamese Cultural System, emphasizing the creation of harmony through hierarchical order and elitist paternalism, may also be seen as a 'primary civilizational layer'

(Arnason 2003: 17) that is not only exceptionally capable of absorbing external ideas without disruption,[7] but also of adapting (to a certain extent) to new social realities. Until now, the strategy of the majority of civic organizations for introducing change has consisted of pushing the Cultural System to its internal limits rather than challenging the system by exploiting potential contradictions.

> [T]hey view themselves as representative of marginalized groups and lobby the state for change in policy. In this role Vietnamese NGOs attempt to negotiate and educate state officials rather than confront them as a tactic to bring about change. In other words, their activities were in direct support of existing government programs or in support of larger state-approved policy goals (national development or poverty alleviation).
>
> (Thayer 2008: 9)

By focusing on cultural complementarities instead of contradictions, their practices have strengthened the dominant Cultural System, but at the same time they may be able to initiate processes of structural elaboration. Rather than initiating a radical transformation process, civil society actors could bring about gradual change towards less controversial views in certain societal spheres. The first signs of such elaboration may be glimpsed in the field of environmental management (Wells-Dang, this volume), gender relations, and people living with HIV/AIDS (Wischermann 2011). It remains to be seen, however, to what extent the idea of equality (and which facets of it) can be accommodated and manifested within the Vietnamese social imaginary.

To conclude, the cultural conditions under which civic engagement takes place in Vietnam differ fundamentally from those in which the concept of civil society originated, and civic action thus also takes on different forms and meanings than in Western societies. By analysing the meanings of civic engagement in Vietnam, it has become clear that there is no automatic logic that 'civil society' functions for increased citizen participation in political decision-making and democracy. Rather, it depends on the demands civic actors make of their political leaders, and to what extent the Vietnamese state will become more of a project of the people than the project of a self-proclaimed enlightened elite.

Notes

1 In the following, the term 'modern' is used (in line with Taylor 2004) with reference to the dominant, European form of modernity, leaving open whether modernity can also exist in other forms (cf. Eisenstadt 2000).
2 I leave aside the debate on concepts of 'freedom and equality' in Western capitalism, and the practices of the idea/ideology of civil society in Western societies. This chapter focuses on how structures of meaning (or ideologies) emanating from a particular cultural setting find application in other contexts, like Vietnam.
3 The empirical material presented derives from a year of field research in the Mekong Delta on policy practices in domestic water supply and sanitation.
4 It is unclear how many hours they work per day.
5 See, e.g. UCA News, 2012.

6 For information on government restrictions and suppression in Vietnam see Human Rights Watch (2012). In response to recent popular movements in the Arab world, the VCP has, in particular, increased surveillance and repression of bloggers (Thayer 2012).
7 On the absorption of Western donor terminology as 'mobilising metaphors' (Mosse 2004: 663) in development cooperation in Vietnam, see Reis (2012: 185ff.).

References

Almond, G. A. (1989) 'The intellectual history of the Civic Culture concept' in G. A. Almond (ed.), *The Civic Culture revisited*, London: Sage: 1–36.

Almond, G. A. and Verba, S. (1963) *The Civic Culture. Political Attitudes and Democracy in Five Nations*, Princeton: Princeton University Press.

Archer, M. (2005) 'Structure, Culture and Agency' in M. D. Jacobs and N. Weiss Hanrahan (eds), *The Blackwell Companion to the Sociology of Culture*, Oxford: Blackwell: 17–34.

Arnason, J. P. (2003) *Civilizations in dispute*, Leiden, Boston: Brill.

Brocheux P. (2007) *Ho Chi Minh. A biography*, New York: Cambridge University Press.

Bukovansky, M. (2002) *Legitimacy and Power Politics: The American and French Revolutions in International Political Culture*, Princeton: Princeton University Press.

Central Institute for Economic Management (CIEM) and Friedrich-Ebert-Foundation (2006) 'Reforms on Public Service Supply in Vietnam' in *Working Paper 4* (2006). Online. Available at: www.ciem.org.vn/home/en/upload/info/attach/1169526210203_Reforms_on_Public_service_supply_in_Vietnam0606.pdf (accessed March 2012).

Cohen, J. L. and Arato, A. (1992) *Civil Society and Political Theory*, Cambridge: MIT Press.

Dalton, R. J. and Nhu-Ngoc T. Ong (2005) 'Civil Society and Social Capital in Vietnam' in G. Mutz and R. Klump (eds), *Modernization and Social Transformation in Vietnam. Social Capital Formation and Institution Building*, Hamburg: Mitteilungsreihe des Instituts für Asienkunde: 30–48.

de Tocqueville, A. (2008) *Democracy in America*. Online. Available at: http://ebooks.adelaide.edu.au/t/tocqueville/alexis/democracy/complete.html (accessed March 2012).

Dunn, J. (2001) 'The Contemporary Political Significance of John Locke's Conception of Civil Society' in S. Kaviraj and S. Khilnani (eds), *Civil society: History and possibilities*, Cambridge: Cambridge University Press: 39–57.

Eckstein, H. (1988) 'A Culturalist Theory of Political Change' in *American Political Science Review*, 82 (3): 789–804.

Eisenstadt, S. N. (2000)' Multiple Modernities' in: *Daedalus*, 129 (1): 1–29.

Gainsborough M. (2005) 'Rethinking Vietnamese Politics: Will the Real State Please Stand Up?' Online. Available at: www.bristol.ac.uk/politics/grc/bvp/bvpworkingpapers/rethinking.doc (accessed February 2008).

Gillespie J. (2002) 'The Political-Legal Culture of Anti-Corruption Reforms in Vietnam' in T. Lindsey and H. Dick (eds). *Corruption in Asia*, Sydney: Federation Press: 167–200.

Habermas, J. (1989) *The Structural Transformation of the Public Sphere: An Inquiry Into a Category of Bourgeois Society*, Cambridge: MIT Press.

Hannah, J. (2007) *Local Non-Government Organizations in Vietnam: Development, Civil Society and State-society Relations*, Doctoral dissertation, University of Washington.

Hue-Tam Ho Tai (1992) *Radicalism and the Origins of the Vietnamese Revolution*, Cambridge, London: Harvard University Press.

Human Rights Watch (2012) *World Report 2012: Vietnam.* Online. Available at: www.
hrw.org/world-report-2012/world-report-2012-vietnam (accessed July 2012).

Jamieson, N. L. (1993) *Understanding Vietnam*, Berkeley, Los Angeles, London: University of California Press.

Jenkins, R. (2001) 'Mistaking "Governance" for "Politics": Foreign Aid, Democracy, and the Construction of Civil Society' in S. Kaviraj and S. Khilnani (eds), *Civil society. History and possibilities*, Cambridge: Cambridge University Press: 250–68.

Jessop, B. (2008) *State Power. A Strategic-Relational Approach*, Cambridge, Malden: Polity Press.

Kaviraj, S. and Khilnani, S. (2001) *Civil Society: History and Possibilities. Introduction*, Cambridge: Cambridge University Press.

Klein, A. (2001) *Der Diskurs der Zivilgesellschaft: Politische Hintergründe und demokratietheoretische Schlussfolgerungen* [The discourse of civil society: Political background, and implications for democracy theory], Opladen: Leske + Budrich.

Kumar, K. (1993) 'Civil Society: An Enquiry into the Usefulness of an Historical Term' in *British Journal of Sociology*, 44 (3): 375–95.

Lichterman, P. (2005) 'Civic Culture at the Grassroots' in M. D. Jacobs and N. Weiss Hanrahan (eds), *The Blackwell Companion to the Sociology of Culture*, Malden, Oxford, Carlton: Blackwell: 383–97.

Metzger, T. A. (2001) 'The Western Concept of Civil Society in the Context of Chinese History' in. S. Kaviraj and. S. Khilnani (eds), *Civil Society: History and Possibilities*, Cambridge: Cambridge University Press: 204–31.

Mosse D. (2004) 'Is Good Policy Unimplementable? Reflections on the Ethnography of Aid Policy and Practice' in *Development and Change*, 35 (4): 639–71.

Norlund, I. (2007) *Filling the Gap: The Emerging Civil Society in Viet Nam*, Hanoi.

Ottmann, H. (2006) 'Liberale, republikanische, deliberative Demokratie' [Liberal, republican, deliberative democracy] in *Synthesis Philosophica*, 42 (2): 315–25.

Porter, G. (1993) *Vietnam: The Politics of Bureaucratic Socialism*, Ithaca, London: Cornell University Press.

Putnam, R. (1993) *Making Democracy Work: Civic Traditions in Modern Italy*, Princeton: Princeton University Press.

Putnam, R. (2000) *Bowling Alone: The Collapse and Revival of American Community*, New York: Simon and Schuster.

Pye, L. W. (1985) *Asian Power and Politics. The Cultural Dimensions of Authority*, Cambridge, London: Belknap Harvard.

Reis N. (2012) *Tracing and Making the State: Policy Practices and Domestic Water Supply in the Mekong Delta*, Vietnam. Berlin: LIT.

Rittersporn, G. T., Behrends, J. C. and Rolf, M. (2003) 'Öffentliche Räume und Öffentlichkeit in Gesellschaften sowjetischen Typs: Ein erster Blick aus komparativer Perspektive. Einleitung' [Public spaces and the public in Sowjet type societies: A first glimpse from a comparative perspective], in Rittersporn, G. T., Behrends, J. C. and Rolf, M. (eds), *Sphären von Öffentlichkeit in Gesellschaften sowjetischen Typs* [Public spheres in Sowjet type societies], Frankfurt am Main: Peter Lang: 7–21.

Scott, J. (1998) *Seeing Like a State. How Certain Schemes to Improve the Human Condition Have Failed*, New Haven, London: Yale University Press.

Taylor, C. (2004) *Modern Social Imaginaries*, Durham and London: Duke.

Thayer, C. (2008) *One-party Rule and the Challenge of Civil Society in Vietnam.* Online. Available at: www.viet-studies.info/kinhte/CivilSociety_Thayer.pdf (accessed March 2012).

Thayer, C. (2012) *Background Briefing: Vietnam's Draft Decree on Internet Management.* Online. Available at: http://de.scribd.com/doc/89937585/Thayer-Vietnam-s-Draft-Decree-on-Internet-Management (accessed June 2012).

UCA News (2012) *Church Protests 'Illegal Arrests'.* Online. Available at: www.ucanews.com/2012/01/11/church-protests-illegal-arrests-of-christians (accessed July 2012).

Wischermann, J. (2011) 'Governance and Civil Society Action in Vietnam: Changing the Rules From Within. Potentials and Limits' in *Asian Politics & Policy*, 3 (3): 381–411.

Wischermann, J. and Nguyen Quang Vinh (2003) 'The Relationship between Civic Organizations and Governmental Organizations in Vietnam: Selected Findings of an Empirical Survey' in Kerkvliet, B. J. T., Koh, D. W. H., and Heng, R. H.-k. (eds), *Getting Organized in Vietnam: Moving in and around the Socialist State*, Singapore: Institute of Southeast Asian Studies: 185–233.

World Bank (2010) *Defining Civil Society.* Online. Available at: http://go.worldbank.org/4CE7W046K0 (accessed March 2012).

6 Enclosing women's rights in the kitchen cabinet?

Interactions between the Vietnam Women's Union, civil society and state on gender equality

Nora Pistor and Le Thi Quy[1]

Introduction

Vietnamese civil society working in the fields of women's rights and gender equality was considered fragile during the mid 2000s. Over the course of just half a decade, the landscape of organizations promoting these issues developed remarkably. Supported by the government's stronger commitment in these areas, this process has been driven by international directives, practical implementation of related policy, and numerous projects by the emerging civil society. The Vietnam Women's Union (VWU), with its hybrid character as a semi-state, semi-civil society organization and with long-standing ties to the Vietnamese Communist Party (VCP), is playing a major role in the development of the progressive issues of women's rights and gender equality while maintaining a generally conservative position. In this chapter we argue that, despite its frequent classification as being part of civil society, the VWU is merely fulfilling the function of a state propaganda instrument that reaches down to communities at the grassroots level. Its existence allows the government to abdicate its responsibility for dealing with the subject, leaving the real civil society to take on the risk of increasing participation in advocacy and policy development, and to bravely address delicate topics on which the VWU often prefers to maintain a silent position. As a result, the opportunities of influencing state policy remain limited for both the VWU and for other civil society organizations (CSOs).

This chapter explores interactions of the VWU with the government and the emerging civil society actors, such as the newly formed networks, highlighting some remarkable achievements and shedding light on the remaining challenges and risks.

Civil society organizations on gender and women's rights issues in Vietnam: an overview

The Asian Development Bank's 'Gender Report' from 2005 assessed civil society working on women's rights and gender equality (hereafter together referred to as women's rights) as weak and in need of support, noting that, without support, these issues 'would fall off the political agenda' (ADB 2005: 58). The report summarizes that, 'as such, civil society ... in terms of critical engagement with the government, is somewhat lacking in Viet Nam'. The civil society working on women's rights was largely considered to be echoing the programmes of the Vietnamese state-sponsored mass organizations, especially those of the VWU, particularly as there were not many other organizations of a governmental nor non-governmental kind to be taken into account.

Despite this negative assessment in 2005, the current picture is a different one. Indeed, numerous Vietnamese CSOs are now active in advancing women's rights. Some non-governmental organizations (NGOs) have specialized in women's issues with rather small-scale projects at the grassroots level, such as the 'Little Rose Shelter',[2] which has, since 1992, provided a safe place for young girls who have been victims of human trafficking or who are at high risk of becoming victims. Research institutions such as the Center for Gender, Family and Environment in Development, established also in 1992, represent some of the first women-oriented Vietnamese NGOs focusing research on reproductive health and related health topics (Tran Thi Van Anh et al. 1997: 57). Others organizations working on research and a broad spectrum of women's topics include the Center for Education Promotion and Empowerment of Women, the renowned Center for Studies and Applied Sciences on Gender and Adolescents,[3] the Research Center for Gender and Development belonging to the Hanoi University of Social Science and Humanities, and the Center for Promoting Development for Women and Children. In addition, in the 1990s, three significant networks all directly targeting women's and children's issues, have emerged within the civil society community:[4] The Gender Communication Network comprises 20 NGOs according to its own account, the Domestic Violence Prevention Network has 22 member NGOs, and the Network for the Empowerment of Women (NEW) has 60 NGOs. Collectively, these offer a wide landscape of potential for interactions between civil society and the state.

Although most of these organizations and networks undertook the discursive shift from the 'women in development' approach (WID) to the more inclusive approach of 'gender and development' (GAD) in the mid 1990s, the understanding of gender equality remains limited. The shift to GAD generally coincides with a broadening of analytic perspective to categories such as gender relations within the household and at work, within marriage and outside of it, to sexuality, and to the impact of kinship (Werner et al. 2002: 15). The combination of Confucianism within the socialist ideology, and the impacts of the economic reform (Đổi Mới), have been nominally examined from a gender perspective since 1986, yet it is striking that gender equality is still mainly understood as a synonym for the equality of women, recognizing women as the only vulnerable and discriminated gender in Vietnam. Homosexuality, for example, is being neglected in the discussion about gender, having been officially labelled a 'social evil' by the Vietnamese government. As Rydstrom comments:

Homosexuality, pornography, prostitution, drug and alcohol addiction, gamb-
ling, theft, abuse and violence as well as paintings (e.g. pin-up calendars),
music videos and music referring to sex … have been linked with 'social
evils' by the Vietnamese government. 'Social evils' is a category widely
associated with the types of sexual practices condemned as being 'dirty'
(*bẩn*) … which, in turn, are linked with assumptions about HIV and AIDS.

(Rydstrom 2006a: 284)

There are few Vietnamese CSOs supporting the interests of lesbian, gay, bisex-
ual, transgender and intersexual persons, and even fewer donor organizations
interested in supporting this target group in Vietnam. The diverse rights and
challenges of these persons, as well as their gender identities, are only starting to
be addressed by the civil society and the media in conferences and meetings on
gender equality, although, at least so far, the LGBTI community remains largely
under-explored (US State Department 2011: 38).

An umbrella for these organizations, centres and networks is being provided
by the Gender Action Partnership (GAP), which is chaired by the Ministry of
Labour, Invalids and Social Affairs (MOLISA), the ministry responsible for the
implementation of gender equality and gender mainstreaming (with considerable
support of UN Women). GAP was created under the secretariat of the National
Committee for the Advancement of Women (NCFAW) in 1999 as an inter-
ministerial committee to bring together members from the 63 provincial Committees for the Advancement of Women. Today, GAP comprises around 45
member organizations in a partnership of relevant governmental agencies,
national and international organizations, networks, as well as CSOs. Its explicit
aim is to provide a space for CSOs to present their projects, advocate for specific
causes and promote their organizations to governmental agencies, international
organizations and donors.[5] Often, however, GAP is seen as initiated and dominated by the government and donors such as UN Women, a fact that might result
in a hesitant participation and filtered expression of needs and interests by the
civil society actors.

The development of an organizational landscape since the early 1990s, which
was strongly reinforced after the beginning of the millennium, can be viewed as
the *second feminist wave* in Vietnam, focused less on the details of the discourse
on women's rights and more on concrete activism and the realization of a higher
quantity of qualitatively improved projects to support women. Though, as Soucy
(2000: 124) suggests, unlike its earlier Western equivalents, Vietnamese feminism does not seem to challenge the hegemonic masculine structure but rather
'tends to become only a vehicle for carrying broader policy issues; it has become
a Trojan horse of nationalism', manifesting itself as a quiet, rarely critical, social
development without aspirations of transformation into a genuine political
movement. While the first feminist wave was, in contrast to the second, closely
linked to a socialist liberation movement (against the French colonial regime)
(Tran Thi Van Anh *et al.* 1997: 52), it did not aim at improving women's
rights in the frame of a human rights approach but – following the communist

model – looked at integrating women into the nationalist struggle for freedom and encouraging the participation of women in the process, defeats and achievements of political and social development (Turley 1972). While a human rights approach would have argued for the rights of all women based on their being a human being, the first feminist wave, initiated and lead by the state, focused on military, economic, demographic and social needs. In this respect, the state enlisted women to fight in the war, materially support the country's economy, and bear children to counteract the human losses in society. Analysing the inherent contradiction of the constructed image of the Vietnamese women, Soucy points out that, 'it depicts women as being labourers and freedom fighters, purportedly showing how women are equal to men, while maintaining the primacy of the traditional roles and responsibilities' (Soucy 2000: 124).

Little research on the current new wave of feminism has been undertaken so far by the organizations working on the topic of women's rights; in fact, analytical and empirical research about the feminist and gender movements from within civil society in Vietnam seems to be non-existent. The lack of a 'critical' stance regarding women's rights and gender issues, and the 'chaotic situation' for NGOs having to operate without formal laws (Kerkvliet 2003: 3), are two contributing factors to the negative assessment of civil society working on these issues up to 2005 (ADB 2005: 58). Since then, with international support and heightened awareness within society about women's rights, the circumstances have become more attractive for new CSOs and NGOs to establish and implement projects. Considering the recent mushrooming of initiatives and projects throughout the country, which appear to be following an action- and interaction-centred approach as suggested by Wischermann (2010: 9), an immense increase of civil society activity in the field of women's rights is evident. Despite this, international NGOs and donors often choose the VWU as a partner, given the fact that it can provide the necessary organizational structure, capacities and long-term experiences at the central, provincial and community level.

Paper doesn't blush: Vietnam's policies on women's rights and gender equality

Written along Marxist principles, the first Vietnamese Constitution of 1946 already recognized the necessity of equality between men and women and codified it in a simplistic form. The Law on Marriage and Family of 1959 confirmed this principle (Turley 1972: 798). The Vietnamese Constitution, in its current form since 1992, provides for gender equality in a broad sense for all citizens of the country in all areas of 'political, economic, cultural, social (life) and in the family' (National Assembly 1992: 11), in line with the wording of the International Convention on the Elimination of all Forms of Violence against Women (CEDAW).[6] A year after the new constitution was written, in 1993, the NCFAW was established with a mandate to advise the Prime Minister, support the implementation of the five-year Plans of Action for Women's Advancement, and support the achievement of gender equality (ADB 2005: 32). According to a decision of the Prime Minister in 2008, this inter-sectoral body, filled by representatives from various ministries and mass organizations, and headed by the female minister of MOLISA, the vice-minister of MOLISA and the president of the VWU,[7] is tasked with researching and coordinating interdisciplinary initiatives concerning the advancement of women. Despite the positive signal sent by institutionalizing a political forum for advancing women's issues, NCFAW remains a recommending entity without legislative or executive powers.

The new Law on Marriage and Family of 2000 formalizes equal rights for marriage and divorce, guardianship for children, and child rights, similar to the law of 1959 (National Assembly 2000). However, the minimum age for women to marry was set at 18, while for men it is 20, a simple clause that is symbolic of unequal treatment of women, and one which fortifies gender stereotypes to the disadvantage of women, and may result in higher violability of younger women (Martignoni 2001: 11).

In November 2006 the Government of Vietnam took the step of approving the Law on Gender Equality, leading to the establishment of the Gender Equality Department in MOLISA (National Assembly 2006). The law explicitly but vaguely states that 'all acts of discrimination against women and all acts damaging women's dignity are strictly banned'. The Law on Gender Equality tends to narrow the focus on gender equality to the immediate social and family life by consistently referring to these gendered areas of female responsibility throughout the legal document, while other important issues for the realization of gender equality, such as equal economic opportunity, equal work and pay, and possibilities for equal political decision-making, seem to play a minor role. The implementation of the Law on Gender Equality is supported by three decrees as well as various policies and directives aiming to enhance the realization of gender equality, such as the Party Directive of 1994, which enforced the 20 per cent quota for women in the Party and governmental organizations (NORAD 2010: 9ff.). However, since there are neither legal nor practical consequences if this quota is not met, the scope for implementation of this, and many other related policies, remains limited.

MOLISA is the government focal point for the CEDAW follow-up reports mandated by the CEDAW Committee since 2007.[8] Under this framework, a National Strategy for the Advancement of Women in Vietnam was approved by the government for the period 2002–10, and a second one for the period 2011–20, highlighting the importance of gender equality for national socio-economic development. Along with this National Strategy, a National Targeted Program on Gender Equality for the period 2011–15 was developed in July 2011 with the aim of

> making a fundamental transformation in the public awareness to promote behavior changes in substantial gender equality; to make steps towards bridging the gender gap and promoting women's status in areas where there is actual occurrence or high risks of inequality.
>
> (Government of Vietnam 2011: Article 1)

The National Assembly, in turn, supervises the process of mainstreaming gender in legal documents as well as in the 1992 Constitution, as provided for in the Law on Gender Equality. The development of these strategies was strongly supported by UN agencies, especially the new entity of UN Women, which was counting on the active participation of civil society.

One of the topics within MOLISA's purview that has been a matter of intense discussion since 2006 is the unequal retirement age of 60 for male and 55 for female civil servants, as codified in the Labour Law of 1960.[9] The differential treatment is officially justified on the grounds that women need to take care of their household responsibilities, and the belief that elderly women are physically weaker than men. Ironically, this provision was meant – and is considered by more than 85 per cent of the population (male and female) according to a survey by the Vietnam Academy of Social Sciences – as preferential treatment to the advantage of women, allowing them more time to take care of their health and family (World Bank and ILSSA 2009: 21; Rama 2001: 18). However, a different study published in 2005 found that:

> There was uniform opposition to the idea of an earlier retirement age for women among all the stakeholders interviewed for this project.... The consultations produced a strong consensus that the retirement age should be the same for both women and men with the option for retiring earlier extended to both.
>
> (Kabeer *et al.* 2005: 19)

A consequence of this provision is that fewer women are allowed to participate in vocational training after reaching a certain age as they would have to retire shortly thereafter, and there is correspondingly less opportunity for women to reach high-level and better-paid positions. From an economic perspective, 'the gender bias represents a financial burden to the pension system' (World Bank and ILSSA 2009: 36) while, from a rights-based perspective, it results in a clear violation of the provisions of CEDAW demanding a substantial equality between women and men. Based on the UN recommendations on the implementation of the CEDAW in Vietnam (UNIFEM 2009: 233), both the official CEDAW report prepared by state agencies (Government of Vietnam 2005), and the NGO CEDAW reports (so-called 'shadow reports') facilitated by NEW (Gencomnet 2006; Gencomnet 2010), address the disadvantages and discrimination of the unequal retirement age. While all reports agree on the importance of an equal retirement age for men and women without any distinction based on sex, the new models currently under discussion still foresee an age gap of either three or five years. The official government report states that 'in a bid to address these problems, the VWU and other relevant agencies are working on proposals to the Government on measures to be taken in the near future' (Government of Vietnam 2005: 17).

Current trends at VWU suggest, however, that any such proposals will likely not advocate for drastic changes to the unequal retirement age.

With the enactment of the Law on the Prevention and Control of Domestic Violence in 2007, the high prevalence of domestic violence was acknowledged by the Government of Vietnam, which also assigned state agencies as well as non-governmental organizations and civil society to jointly implement the legal provisions. Perhaps reflecting their mixed feelings about acknowledging this phenomenon, it was the Ministry of Culture, Sports and Tourism, and not MOLISA, that was named the state managing agency for this law, thereby taking on responsibility for the provision of counselling and support services for victims of domestic violence.[10]

Aside from these selected legal inconsistencies to achieve gender equality, weak participation of the VWU and civil society in policy formulation, and the fragmentation of implementation, have led to convoluted bureaucratic procedures and the prolongation of administrative and legal processes.[11] This scattering of responsibilities in the topics of gender equality and domestic violence – topics that are genuinely intertwined with each other and which require high administrative collaboration – suggests a lack of unity regarding the promotion of women's rights in Vietnam.

On the social inappropriateness of gender equality

Despite positive achievements well documented in various development reports in the fields of health, education, economy and politics, the understanding of gender equality and the role of women and men in Vietnamese society, as lived by the people and watched over by civil society and the VWU, is still indicative of unequal relations between women and men. The current nationwide movement led by the VWU, which was started in 2010, encourages women to strive for a 'mutual assistance among women' in the economic development of households.[12] This has reinforced the taken-for-granted responsibility of women in the domestic sphere and revealed the stubbornness of the patriarchal hierarchies deriving from Confucian social traditions, which have discriminated against women on the basis of an inherent assumption of the superiority of men over women (Rydstrom 2006b: 333).[13]

In Vietnamese society, strong gender stereotypes and gender-specific identifications influence the appropriateness of behaviour, appearance, and the forms of expressions between men and women of different ages. Examples of these stereotypes can be found in nearly all areas of everyday life, such as the carrying out of ritual ancestral worship, which is reserved for men due to their 'innate honour' (Long *et al.* 2000: 26); in the responsibility for the maintenance of 'happiness in the family', which lies exclusively within the female sphere regardless of the husband's actions (Long *et al.* 2000: 29); as well as in numerous proverbs in the Vietnamese language that bear discriminating connotations against women (Khuat Thu Hong *et al.* 2009: 236ff.).

Initiatives addressing gender-related discrimination are often classified as inappropriate or unsuitable for Vietnamese society, even by representatives from the VWU and members of CSOs who are actively promoting women's rights.

This was the case, for example, with the topics of domestic violence and trafficking in women and children. During the set up of the first pilot project to support female victims of domestic violence through shelter and counselling services, the VWU opposed the idea of a shelter project as they found this to be inappropriate for Vietnamese society and they disagreed about the prevalence of domestic violence (Hardinghaus 2009: 93). Despite this initial denial, the prevalence of domestic violence has been evidenced in nationwide research conducted in 2010 and has, since then, found wide-ranging support from state authorities and international donors to local development partners (General Statistics Office Vietnam 2010).

A similar resistance was encountered in the first projects to prevent trafficking in women and children that was to be implemented from 1997 to 2000 by the Youth Research Institute in cooperation with the VWU (Le Thi Quy 2000). It was not until 2000 that the first publication on trafficking of women was printed, revealing that, indeed, human trafficking constituted a major problem in Vietnam, especially in the provinces bordering Cambodia in the south and China in the north, with an estimated tens of thousands of women and children being trafficked since 1998 (Le Thi Quy 2000; Gencomnet 2010). Before that no research project and no literature was made available in Vietnam, and the topic was regarded too sensitive to be discussed publicly.[14] As a result, the first initiatives to support victims of human trafficking were established after research was carried out in 2000 by the Research Center for Gender and Development, the Institute for Tradition and Development, the Centre for Promoting Development for Women and Children, the international NGO Nordic Assistance Vietnam, as well as the VWU through its Center for Women and Development. Initiatives sponsored by CSOs and the VWU are now increasingly being supported by the government, international organizations, and the media. In fact, cooperation between the police and civic service providers are being fortified, and the partnership between the government and VWU has been defined by the recent Anti-Human Trafficking Law (National Assembly 2011).

These remarkable achievements show that civil society is daring to challenge the status quo (under certain conditions) rather than reproducing gender discrimination in the existing socio-political setting. CSOs have been playing a catalytic role in advancing taboo topics such as domestic violence, human trafficking and LGBTI rights by overcoming the initial resistance of governmental agencies through independent research, persistent advocacy and international support.

The elephant in the house: the Vietnam Women's Union

The VWU is the biggest mass organization under the umbrella of the Fatherland Front. A review of available reports shows that the classification of the VWU as part of the civil society is highly contested (Norlund 2007: 9). In fact, some reports list the union as part of the national machinery for gender equality (ADB 2005); others call it a 'quasi-state, quasi-NGO mass organization' (Angeles 2000: 7). Despite its frequent classification as a civil society organization domestically

(Norlund 2007: 11), the VWU constitutes, *de lege*, a part of the political system of Vietnam.[15] It is affiliated with the government through its participation in politics, policy development and its presence in various official organs, and with its status as a formally recognized consulting and commenting body.

The structure of the VWU echoes that of the Communist Party, with a governing body made up of 15 women leaders who are announced for five-early terms at the National Women's Congress. This central authority branches out in a rigidly hierarchic pattern down to the provinces, districts and communes, with its decisions being made in a top-down process (JICA 2011: 15ff.). In practice, however, the local chapters of the VWU enjoy some degree of autonomy in the implementation of their programmes. This informal autonomy, however, can be restricted by the local Provincial People's Committees.[16] A brief overview of the VWU's historical background and the political context will help shed light on its role and current position.

A civic mass organization under Leninist ideology

In socialist revolutionary ideology, bodies such as the VWU stem from the need to mobilize women to help liberate the country; in the case of Vietnam, first from French colonialism and later from American imperialism. Along with optimism for the liberalization of the country and equality of all people, the VWU's social programmes designed in the aftermath of the American War designated the place for women in society by assigning them explicit tasks in the nationalist struggle, thereby contributing to the construction of a new female role in times of revolution.

The innovative nature of this role lay in its combining of the stereotypical role of women as mothers responsible for reproducing and nurturing society with the extraordinary war-related task of replenishing the dwindled male labour force.[17] The underlying ideology acting to improve women's status in society was alimented by the necessity to maintain the mostly agricultural economy of the country with the female labour force while men were fighting against the foreign aggressors; needless to say, women were not allowed to fight in the regular army (Turley 1972: 797). Women participated mostly as informal war workers or volunteers, thus not benefiting from any post-war indemnification.

The era of *Đổi Mới*, starting in 1986, brought about the beginning of fundamental change, not only in economic terms but also in terms of social development, which caused a decline in the public sector and produced a consequent shift of female labour into the informal sector and home-based work (Werner 2002: 35). Along with economic disadvantages faced by women at this time, gender-related changes also resulted in increasing responsibilities of women for family healthcare, and – with the concurrent deconstruction of traditional gender roles – an increase in domestic conflict (Long *et al.* 2000: 29). The VWU contributed to national development through capacity building and the improvement of the living standards of women through various programmes, campaigns and projects. At the same time, many of these initiatives reproduced conventional stereotypes such as kind-heartedness and altruism, typical female attributes deriving from Confucian traditions (Schuler *et al.* 2006: 385ff., see also Le Thi Nham Tuyet 2005).

Since the 1990s, the prominent VWU campaign for women to 'Study Actively, Work Creatively and Build Happy Families' was launched, implying additional responsibilities and burdens for women, including increasing the household's economic status through new enterprise, enhancing capacities and knowledge, as well as taking care of the well-being of the family. Even engendering happiness of the family and of its members – an emotion that can hardly be obtained through a governmental top-down process for economic development and stability (Kwiatkowski 2011: 3) – was defined as the task of a good wife (Schuler *et al.* 2006). With the new millennium, the VWU continued in the same direction, namely supporting the economic and social development of women by promoting women's dual roles in the family and income generation. At the same time, the VWU became increasingly engaged in regional and international cooperation. From 2002–7, the goals of the VWU were vaguely codified,

> to raise the all-sided capacity and knowledge, and improve the material and spiritual livelihood for women, to effectuate gender equality. To cultivate the Vietnamese women who are patriotic, knowledgeable, healthy, dynamic, innovative, well-cultured, kind-hearted, and attentive to social and community interests.
>
> (VWU leaflet: undated)

The operational objectives of the VWU in this period were focused on building up the capacities of the organization, enhancing international and regional networks, exercising its role as a policy recommending body, supporting the implementation of existing laws, improving the 'qualities and capacities' of Vietnamese women, and 'building plentiful, equal, progressive and happy families' (ibid.).

From society or for society?

The question remains open how to position the VWU and what the reasons are for the difficulties of its classification. According to the NGO Resource Center of the Vietnam Union of Friendship Organizations (VUFO NGO Resource Center), in the VWU's own view, it is being classified as part of civil society:

> [T]he [Women's] union and other [mass organizations] are part of civil society on two grounds. First, they represent sectors of society. Second, they are not state-managed entities (*không phải là cơ quan quản lý nhà nước*). True, they are organizations within the state system, but given that their role is to represent societal functions and that they are not state-managed, these informants claim they are part of civil society.
>
> (VUFO NGO Resource Center 2008: 20)

The Vietnamese concepts of the notions of NGO and civil society are even more vague than their Western-derived analogues (Wischermann 2004: 205). While there is no agreed definition for civil society in the Western academic community, Thayer (2008: 13) summarizes its characteristics for the case of Vietnam as follows:

> When the term civil society is used in discussions with foreigners it generally refers to Vietnamese organizations closely linked to the state. These organizations try to pass themselves off as 'genuine' civil society groups out of self-interest. The so-called NGOs sector in Vietnam is a site of struggle over normative ideals between foreign donors and the one-party State.

The Vietnamese term for non-governmental organization (*tổ chức phi chính phủ*) literally means organization not of the (main) government. According to Norlund (2007: 10), this includes mass organizations such as the VWU, which are, in fact, organizations created, supported and directed by the VCP. In contrast, the Vietnamese term for civil society (*xã hội dân sự*) (see Phuong Le Trong, this volume) has a strong connotation of work *for* the community or even 'social' work;[18] thus in Vietnamese, it is not exclusively the nature of the organization that matters for its classification as belonging to civil society, but also the function and purpose of its work. In short, a simple dichotomy of governmental versus civil or non-governmental, cannot be applied to Vietnam.

The VWU has been active in communities, advocating in a populist manner for the comprehensive development of women and the realization of women's rights (Fforde 2011: 171). It has, among other achievements, gained a strong reputation for supporting ethnic minority women and poor women in rural areas. Its prominent micro-credit programme has further contributed to high popularity at the grassroots level as it lends special support to poor women. In this respect, we suggest understanding the self-characterization of the VWU as belonging to civil society as more closely resembling a situation in which its purpose is to work *for* the society.

Narrow windows of influence

Within a legal framework allowing various forms of political participation, the Government of Vietnam acknowledges the importance of the VWU, and its close links to society, by conceding to it the role of advising the Fatherland Front and allowing to to provide a check on the executive. As such, the VWU was appointed as one of 30 members of the Drafting Committee for the Amendment of the Constitution in the current constitutional reform process. This would, in theory, confer a remarkable potential for political influence in the field of women's rights. Furthermore, according to Decree Number 163 of 1988, the government needs to consult the VWU on issues concerning women and children, which suggests a significant role for the VWU in sectoral policy development (ADB 2002: 34). That said, the actual degree of involvement conceded to the VWU varies from case to case.

In 1999, with the intention 'to strengthen the close tie between the people and the Party and the State', the Law of the Vietnam Fatherland Front was issued. In Article Two of this law, the Fatherland Front is assigned responsibility to supervise the activities of the state and its functionaries, to represent people's opinions, and issue recommendations to the Party and the state, to support the administrative body of the state, and to support the people's legitimate interests. Despite this, in the list of priority topics of the Resolution of the Eleventh National Congress of the Communist Party, women's rights and gender equality are not mentioned. Evidently, in its movements and programmes, the VWU is following the VCP's directive without openly pressing for the inclusion of critical issues on the Party agenda. Since the VWU is financed partly by the state budget, there is an influence on the VWU's spending and independence, but with increasing support from international donors, the budgetary influence of the state may decrease (JDR 2009: 113). Thus far, however, neither budgetary nor technical sovereignty have been given to the VWU.

The restricted space for intervention by the VWU amounts to limited potential for political influence on decision-making processes. However, the VWU is continuously consulted by various governmental organs, especially when it comes to commenting on 'traditional women's topics' such as education and health. As such, the VWU is complementing the line ministries in their responsibilities, specifically MOLISA, which is responsible for mainstreaming gender in all governmental institutions and programmes, the Ministry of Education and Training in its endeavours for equal education access, and the Ministry of Health on reproductive health issues.

In practice, whether acting under the influence of the Vietnamese state or international donors, the VWU generally applies a pragmatic approach to its operations, implementing them based on the possibilities and constraints with a focus on the practical needs of the female population. Through its structure and communication channels down to the grassroots level, the VWU is an efficient agent for gathering the views and voices of the people and conveying them in an amplified way towards the state. This capacity, for example, can be used when the Fatherland Front reports during the opening sessions of the National Assembly's plenary meetings (JDR 2009: 113). Although this rarely takes place, it is one clear forum in which the National Assembly, the Party and the government can be addressed with the challenges and constructive criticism of the society.

With regard to its populist outreach, the VWU, like the other mass organizations (but to a lesser degree), has developed structures present at every level of the administration, which allows it to reach and mobilize the masses. On the provincial level, most aspects related to women's rights, such as awareness-raising and efforts to reduce female poverty, are commonly shifted to the VWU – this being an opportunity for governments to escape difficult responsibilities. Especially at the local level, the state agencies acknowledge their lack of awareness and limited capacity to advance women's rights issues. In the end, the reality that is created on the ground includes a national government that has established a formal organ for women's rights and gender issues but yet concedes only limited influence to that organ (the VWU), preferring to retain decision-making power within the VCP and to itself; at the provincial and local levels, the VWU cadres are recognized as the only potentially capable agents, though without the allocation of sufficient resources to implement their tasks. Thus, with the existence of the VWU, its limited resources and minor influence on decision-making processes, local governments tend to cold-shoulder women's rights in their constituencies.

'When the buffalo and the ox fight, flies and mosquitoes get squashed'

In contrast to other civil society organizations, the VWU is prominent due to its massive membership and its close relationship with the state. While the VWU represents itself as an inflated, strong, CSO, Vietnamese NGOs appear to be 'vulnerable, caught as they are between the dominant powers of state and donor, depending on the former for their social and legal legitimacy and on the latter for the lifeblood of funding' (Hannah 2007: 172).

This situation can be one of the factors hindering cooperation with smaller-scale civic organizations, which have difficulties viewing the VWU as an equal partner, since, as the World Bank reports, 'its sheer size and presence makes it difficult for alternative forms of civil society organizations aimed [at] promoting gender equality to flourish' (World Bank 2011: 90).

Nevertheless, efforts by the VWU to enhance the collaboration with civil society on an equal basis, e.g. by technical cooperation at the central level and in the provinces, are becoming more common.[19] At the same time, according to many accounts, CSOs increasingly invite the staff of the VWU, especially in the communes, to participate in their development projects. However, as suggested by Werner (2002: 44), attempts at cooperation from both sides are still overshadowed by hesitation and mistrust given the fact that the VWU also plays the function of watchdog over other civil organizations, which it does more often than observing the activities of state agencies. Nevertheless, civil society outside of mass organizations maintains the potential to compensate for some of the weaknesses of the VWU, such as its overly bureaucratic structure, its hesitation to utter criticism, and its adherence to traditional values by applying more innovative models and high quality projects in the field of women's rights. With this perspective in mind, a closer cooperation between civil society and the VWU needs to be envisaged.

The government is showing increased interest in the work of civil society and conceding some, if limited, space for advocacy and action; such as during the consultation meeting of representatives of civil society with UN Women on the occasion of the finalization of the seventh and eighth CEDAW reports of 2012 (ibid.). According to its own accounts, NEW has been able to contribute to the drafting of the Gender Equality Law, the Law on Domestic Violence, and the Law on Human Trafficking through recommendations and participation in consultation meetings with the government that allow for community models and the views of the grassroots to be presented. Noteworthy is that the presidium of NEW consists of former government officials from various agencies, as well as from governmental research institutes which initiated the establishment of new civic organizations upon their (usually compulsory) retirement. Thus, it can be imagined that the identity and views of personnel formerly working in the governmental sector may even be perpetuated through civil society. This can be viewed as alliance-building with the government (as suggested by Wells-Dang, this volume), or, as we interpret, as a denigration of civil society precepts in the field of women's rights, marked by a dearth of independent civil society agents who are 'actors in their own right' (a condition called for in the Accra Agenda for Action (OECD 2008: 18)).

Conclusions

Vietnam looks back at a long development of promoting equality between women and men. The commitment of the government is evident in its policies and at the institutional and structural level. Along with the improvement of the judiciary, a process of including more comprehensive impact-oriented methods has been initiated by the relevant governmental agencies in order to improve the quality of women's lives. However, between the laws and everyday practice, big gaps remain.

The VWU, other mass organizations, CSOs, and networks have become important driving forces to advance women's rights on behalf of citizens. The significance of Vietnamese civil society has increased even beyond the borders of the country through participation in regional and international activities that allow the sharing of common concerns and knowledge. However, in the end, the capacity of CSOs and the VWU for consulting on and influencing the development, implementation and monitoring of policies in the field of women's rights remain limited.

The organizational boundaries between civil society and the VWU as an organization *of* the masses and *for* the masses are not easily delineated; the massive, traditional VWU is often perceived as a facet of civil society with limited political influence, while the recently established NEW, which networks a large amount of NGOs together, is headed by, and likely influenced by, the perspectives of former government officials. The emerging initiatives of the VWU and CSOs generally share a common goal of advancing women's rights, although the VWU maintains a more conservative approach that is capable of flexibility only within a narrow state-mandated agenda.

In sum, the VWU's position between the government and society engenders an ambiguous picture of hesitant civil society action. Despite, and perhaps due to, its vague positioning and set of roles, the VWU's structure is ubiquitous within the Vietnamese system, which suggests a sustainable presence. With its massive outreach capacities, it represents a chance of bringing about change. However, the VWU finds itself in urgent need of modernizing its structure in order to avoid getting lost in its own bureaucracy; of showing more openness towards a post-feminist viewpoint by widening its mandate from the classical women's topics to a gender equality perspective; and of fulfilling its role of critical advocacy and monitoring agent vis-à-vis the government. A stronger cooperation with civil society can support these functions since civil society actors have demonstrated their capability of following more modern approaches and initiatives in topics perceived as 'too sensitive' by the VWU. To start with, analytical research with a critical perspective on the VWU and from within the VWU needs to be initiated or,[20] as we have suggested, the VWU might end up reproducing gender stereotypes within the system and the society, or even hindering the modernist tendencies of the CSOs. By doing so, it would increase its own political isolation, enclose women's rights in its own designated *kitchen closet*, and play but a token role in the process of gender mainstreaming in Vietnam.

Notes

1 The authors, Nora Pistor and Le Thi Quy, combine practical experiences from within the sector of the Vietnamese civil society and the VWU. Pistor has gained insights as an advisor to the Center for Women and Development, one of the departments of the Vietnam Women's Union, through a partnership with the Deutsche Gesellschaft für Internationale Zusammenarbeit (GIZ). Le Thi Quy is director of the Research Center for Gender and Development at the University of Social Science and Humanities, Hanoi, and the president of the recently established Network for the Empowerment of Women (NEW).
2 See the website of the Little Rose Shelter at: www.hcs.harvard.edu/~rose/whoweare.html (accessed 15 November 2011).
3 See the website of the Center at: http://csaga.org.vn/Desktop.aspx/HomeEn/ (accessed 15 November 2011).
4 The currently available references do not offer a comprehensive list of Vietnamese NGOs and CSOs working on women's issues. The JICA Country Gender Profile for Vietnam (JICA 2011: 50 *et seq.*, provides a compilation of organizations and gender projects in Vietnam up to December 2010, covering eight governmental organizations (including the Vietnam Women's Union), 12 international organizations, and only two NGOs (including the National Committee for the Advancement of Women, which is also an inter-ministerial committee located inside MOLISA). Even the NGO Resource Center, an organization established by the Vietnam Union of Friendship Organizations (VUFO), which receives part of its budget from the state for the purpose of facilitating information transfer as well as sharing and enhancing the dialogue between NGOs, does not broach the issue of women's rights despite counting 130 member INGOs (as of January 2010) of many different sectors. A working group on 'Women in Development' existed at the NGO Resource Center in 1992 but is not in operation anymore (see Hannah (2007: 166)) and the website of the Center at: www.ngocentre.org.vn/ (accessed 11 December 2011). Currently, the annual gender mapping conducted by the Gender Action Partnership provides the most complete overview of organizations, governmental as well as non-governmental, along with implemented and planned projects in the field of women's rights. As only members of the partnership get to participate in the mapping exercise, the list is not exhaustive; in particular, small-scale civil society initiatives are not being taken into account.
5 Even the GAP focuses nearly exclusively on the 'classical' women's issues when discussing gender equality.

6 See the full text of CEDAW online, at: www.un.org/womenwatch/daw/cedaw/text/
   econvention.htm (accessed 25 October 2011). Although Vietnam was one of the first
   countries to become a signatory to CEDAW in 1982, it has expressed reservations
   about the implementation of the Convention's paragraph 1 Article 29, and has not yet
   signed the optional protocol, which would provide the right of individual redress for
   aggrieved citizens.
7 In 2005 the NCFAW was headed by the president of the VWU. This can be interpreted
   as having resulted in a strong influence of the VWU over this body, but consequently
   also in a low impact for the NCFAW over governmental decision-making procedures.
8 See the website of UN Vietnam at: www.un.org.vn/index.php?option=com_content&
   view=article&id=1083%3Anational-structures-for-gender-
   equality&catid=116%3Awhat-we-do&Itemid=1&lang=en and MOLISA at http://
   english.molisa.gov.vn/ (both accessed 21 November 2011).
9 The Labour Code contains an extra chapter on separate provisions concerning female
   employees (Chapter X), granting equal rights in all aspects of work to female workers
   and providing favourable conditions for female employees, such as preferential treatment in the recruitment processes, the right to prenatal and postnatal leave of four
   months, the provision of sanitary facilities, crèches and kindergartens 'where a high
   number of female employees are employed' (italics by authors). Curiously, women in
   their 'menstruation period(s) [are] entitled to 30 minutes off in every working day
   with full pay', according to Article 115.
10 The National Plan of Action to Prevent and Control Domestic Violence, developed by
   the Ministry of Culture, Sports and Tourism, has set a target that by 2015, 40 per cent
   of the detected victims of domestic violence will receive legal and social counselling
   as well as healthcare support at specialized establishments, while 70 per cent of the
   perpetrators of domestic violence may receive free counselling services.
11 To compare with a case indicative of more concentrated responsibilities, please see
   the description of Cambodia in Hiwasa (this volume).
12 These formulations are used for the current nationwide movement of the VWU
   (2010), available online at: http://hoilhpn.org.vn/newsdetail.asp?CatId=66&NewsId
   =819&lang=EN (accessed 20 November 2011).
13 According to Confucian philosophy, a woman has to be obedient in three familial
   relationships: towards her father before she gets married, towards her husband once
   she is married, and towards her own son after her husband dies.
14 From an interview with the presidium of NEW, March 2012.
15 Law of the Vietnam Fatherland Front (1999).
16 From interviews with representatives of the VWU cadres in the provinces of An
   Giang and Soc Trang, March 2012.
17 Under the leadership of President Ho Chi Minh, war-related propagandist imagery of
   women was referenced in a speech on the occasion of the VWU's anniversary in
   1966:

> From the beginning of the first century A.D. when the two Trung sisters rose up
> to fight the enemy and save the nation, until now, whenever our country has
> faced danger, our women have contributed whatever they could towards the
> cause of national liberation. Our people are grateful that our mothers from North
> and South alike have born and raised our nation's generations of heroes. Under
> the socialist system, tens of thousands of women have become specialists in dif-
> ferent fields and, as cadres, serve as directors and vice-directors of factories,
> leaders of farming cooperatives, presidents of People's Committees, and general
> secretaries of Party cells…. And so, the women of Vietnam from ancient times
> until now, from South to North, from young to old, are truly heroes.
>
> (Excerpt from the speech on the anniversary of the VWU on 20 October 1966,
> quoted from the homepage of the VWU)

18 The notion of *xã hội*, meaning both society or social, and *dân sự*, meaning civil or civic, which can be understood as civil/civic society or social civics. The latter stresses the social orientation of the organization's work while the former includes all organizations that are not, at least not entirely, governmental and which can be working in all sorts of fields, not necessarily in the social field.
19 From an interview with the presidium of NEW, January 2012.
20 A comparison to the developments of the All-China Women's Federation could provide useful lessons on the process of organizational change of a women's mass organization. For a start, see Howell (2003).

References

ADB (2002) 'Women in Viet Nam', country briefing paper, Manila, Philippines: Regional and Sustainable Development Department and Mekong Department, Asian Development Bank.

ADB (2005) 'Viet Nam: Gender Situation Analysis', Asian Development Bank.

Angeles, L. C. (2000) 'Women, Bureaucracy and the Governance of Poverty in Southeast Asia: Integrating Gender and Participatory Governance in Poverty Reduction Programs in the Philippines and Vietnam', paper presented at the DEVNET International Conference on 'Poverty, Prosperity, Progress', University of Victoria, Wellington, New Zealand, 17–19 November.

Fforde, A. (2011) 'Contemporary Vietnam: Political Opportunities, Conservative Formal Politics, and Patterns of Radical Change' in *Asian Politics & Policy*, 3 (2): 165–84.

Gencomnet (2006) 'Vietnam NGOs', report on CEDAW Implementation in Vietnam, Hanoi: Gender Communication Network.

Gencomnet (2010) 'NGO Report on CEDAW Implementation in Vietnam' (with assistance from Actionaid Vietnam, Embassy of Switzerland in Vietnam), Hanoi: Gender Communication Network.

General Statistics Office Vietnam (2010) *Keeping Silent is Dying. Results from the National Study on Domestic Violence against Women in Viet Nam*, Hanoi: General Statistics Office. Online. Available at: www.gso.gov.vn/Modules/Doc_Download.aspx? DocID=12579 (accessed 5 July 2012).

Government of Vietnam (2005) 'Consideration of Reports Submitted by States Parties under Article 18 of the Convention on the Elimination of All Forms of Discrimination against Women. Combined fifth and sixth periodic reports of States parties', CEDAW/C/VNM/5–6, Viet Nam.

Government of Vietnam (2011) 'Decision Approving the National Program on Gender Equality for the Period of 2011–2015', No: 1241/QĐ-TTg.

Hannah, J. (2007) 'Local Non-Government Organizations in Vietnam: Development, Civil Society and State-society Relations', unpublished thesis, University of Social Science and Humanities in Ho Chi Minh City, Vietnam.

Hardinghaus, B. (2009) 'Das Haus der Madame Thuy' [The house of Madam Thuy] in *Der Spiegel*, 8: 92–6. Online. Available at: www.spiegel.de/spiegel/print/d-64197243. html (accessed 5 July 2012).

Howell, J. (2003) 'Women's Organizations and Civil Society in China: Making a Difference' in *International Feminist Journal of Politics*, 5 (2): 191–215.

JDR (2009) 'Joint Donor Report to the Vietnam Consultative Group Meeting' in *Vietnam Development Report 2010. Modern Institutions*, Hanoi, December 3–4.

JICA (2011) 'Country Gender Profile: Viet Nam', Final Report, Japan International Cooperation Agency.

Kabeer, N., Tran Thi Van Anh and Vu Manh Loi (2005) *Preparing for the Future: Forward-looking Strategies to Promote Gender Equity in Vietnam*, Hanoi: United Nations and World Bank.

Kerkvliet, B. (2003) 'Introduction: Grappling with Organizations and the State in Contemporary Vietnam' in Kerkvliet, B. J. T., Koh, D. W. H. and Heng, R. H.-k. (eds), *Getting Organized in Vietnam: Moving in and around the Socialist State*, Singapore: Institute of Southeast Asian Studies: 1–24.

Khuat Thu Hong, Le Bach Duong and Nguyen Ngoc Huong (2009) *Sexuality in Contemporary Vietnam. Easy to joke about but hard to talk about*, Hanoi: Knowledge Publishing House.

Kwiatkowski, L. (2011) 'Prolonging Suffering: Domestic Violence, Political Economy, and the State in Northern Vietnam', Working Paper No. 299, Gender, Development, and Globalization Program, Center for Gender in Global Context, Michigan State University.

Le Thi Nham Tuyet (2005) *Images of Vietnamese Women in the 21st Century*, Hanoi: Thế Giới Publishers.

Le Thi Quy (2000) *Prevention of Trafficking in Women in Vietnam*, Hanoi: Youth Research Institute and Labour and Social Affairs Publishing House.

Long, Lynellyn D., Le Ngoc Hung, Allison Truitt, Le Thi Phuong Mai and Dang Nguyen Anh, (2000) 'Changing Gender Relations in Vietnam's Post Đổi Mới Era', Policy Research Report on Gender and Development, Working Paper Series No. 14, Washington, DC: World Bank.

Martignoni, J. B. (2001) 'Implementation of the Convention on the Elimination of All Forms of Discrimination against Women by Vietnam', Committee on the Elimination of Discrimination against Women, 25th session, 20 June 2001, Geneva: World Organization Against Torture (OMCT).

National Assembly (1992) '1992 Constitution of the Socialist Republic of Vietnam (as amended 25 December 2001)'. Online. Available at: www.vietnamlaws.com/freelaws/Constitution92(aa01).pdf/ (accessed 1 July 2012).

National Assembly (2000) 'The Marriage and Family Law'. Online. Available at: http://moj.gov.vn/vbpq/en/Lists/Vn%20bn%20php%20lut/View_Detail.aspx?ItemID=373 (accessed 1 July 2012).

National Assembly (2006) 'Law on Gender Equality'. Online. Available at: www.csaga.org.vn/Desktop.aspx/News/Library/LAW_ON_GENDER_EQUALITY/ (accessed 1 July 2012).

National Assembly (2011) 'Law on Prevention, Suppression against Human Trafficking', Translation of Draft Law submitted to the National Assembly for passage (provided by United Nations Inter-Agency Project on Human Trafficking, UNIAP).

NORAD (2010) 'Gender Review Report. Royal Norwegian Embassy Viet Nam', NORAD Report June 2011 discussion. Hanoi: Norwegian Agency for Development Cooperation.

Norlund, I. (2007) *Filling the Gap: The Emerging Civil Society in Viet Nam*, Hanoi. Online. Available at: www.snvworld.org/files/publications/filling_the_gap_cs.pdf (accessed 29 June 2012).

OECD (2008) 'The Paris Declaration on Aid Effectiveness and the Accra Agenda for Action', Organization for Economic Cooperation and Development. Online. Available at: www.oecd.org/dataoecd/11/41/34428351.pdf (accessed 29 June 2012).

Rama, M. (2001) 'The Gender Implications of Public Sector Downsizing: The Reform Program of Viet Nam', Policy Research Report on Gender and Development, Working Paper Series No. 19, Washington, DC: World Bank.

Rydstrom, H. (2006a) 'Sexual Desires and "Social Evils": Young women in Rural Vietnam' in *Gender, Place and Culture*, 13 (3): 283–301.

Rydstrom, H. (2006b) 'Masculinity and Punishment: Men's Upbringing of Boys in Rural Vietnam' in *Childhood*, 13 (3): 329–48.

Schuler, S. R., Hoang Tu Anh, Vu Song Ha, Tran Hung Minh, Bui Thi Thanh Mai and Pham Vu Thien (2006) 'Constructions of Gender in Vietnam: In pursuit of the "Three Criteria"' in *Culture, Health & Sexuality*, 8 (5): 383–94.

Soucy, A. (2000) 'Vietnamese Warriors, Vietnamese Mothers: State Imperatives on the Portrayal of Women' in *Canadian Women Studies/Les Cahiers de la Femme*, 19 (4): 121–6.

Thayer, C. (2008) 'One-Party Rule and the Challenge of Civil Society in Vietnam', presentation to 'Remaking the Vietnamese State: Implications for Vietnam and the Region', Vietnam, Workshop, City University of Hong Kong, 21–22 August .

Tran Thi Van Anh and Le Ngoc Hung (1997) *Women and đổi mới in Vietnam*, Hanoi: Woman Publishing House.

Turley, W. S. (1972) 'Women in the Communist Revolution in Vietnam' in *Asian Survey*, 12 (9) 793–805.

UN General Assembly (1979) 'The Convention on the Elimination of All Forms of Discrimination against Women, CEDAW', Online. Available at: www.un.org/womenwatch/daw/cedaw/text/econvention.htm (accessed 25 October 2011).

UNIFEM (2009) 'Tuyển chọn các khuyến nghị chung CEDAW' (Compilation of Selected CEDAW General Recommendations), Hanoi: United Nations Development Fund for Women.

US State Department (2011) 'Sexual Orientation/Gender Identity References', US Department of State, Human Rights Reports, Washington, DC: US State Department.

Vietnamese Women's Museum (2009) *Images of Vietnamese Women in Propaganda Posters (1954–1975)*, Hanoi: Nhà Xuất Bản Phụ Nữ.

VUFO NGO Resource Center (2008) 'Forms of Engagement between State Agencies and Civil Society Organizations in Vietnam: Study Report', Hanoi: Vietnam Union of Friendship Organizations (VUFO) NGO Resource Center.

VWU (undated) *International Integration of Vietnam Women's Union*, Hanoi: Swedish International Development Cooperation Agency. Online. Available at: http://hoilhpn.org.vn/newsdetail.asp?CatId=66&NewsId=819&lang=EN (accessed 20 November 2011).

Werner, J. (2002) 'Gender, Household, and State: Renovation (Đổi Mới) as social process in Viet Nam' in Werner, J. and Bélanger, D. (eds), *Gender, Household, State: Đổi Mới in Viet Nam*, New York: Southeast Asia Program: 29–47.

Werner, J. and Bélanger, D. (2002) 'Introduction: Gender and Viet Nam Studies' in Werner, J. and Bélanger, D. (eds), *Gender, Household, State: Đổi Mới in Viet Nam*, New York: Southeast Asia Program: 13–28.

Wischermann, J. (2004) 'Towards Good Society? Civil-society Actors, the State, and the Business Class in Southeast Asia – Facilitators of or Impediments to a Strong, Democratic, and Fair Society?' in Heinrich Böll Foundation (ed.), *Towards good society: Civil society actors, the state, and the business class in Southeast Asia – Facilitators of or impediments to a strong, democratic, and fair society?*, Berlin: Heinrich Böll Foundation: 201–52.

Wischermann, J. (2010) 'Civil Society Action and Governance in Vietnam: Selected Findings from an Empirical Survey' in *Journal of Current Southeast Asian Affairs*, 29 (2): 3–40.

World Bank and ILSSA (2009) *Women's Retirement Age in Vietnam. Gender Equality and Sustainability of the Social Security Fund*, Hanoi: World Bank and Institute of Labour Studies and Social Affairs.

World Bank (2011) 'Viet Nam Country Gender Assessment', Hanoi: World Bank and Vietnam Development Information Center.

7   Civil society engagement in the fight against the HIV/AIDS epidemic in Cambodia

Frédéric Bourdier

Introduction

Health sector development in Cambodia has largely been conditioned by external players, beginning with the colonial French and continuing with the Vietnamese and international development agents (Bernader *et al.* 1995). Healthcare infrastructure and public institutions created during and after the colonial period were left in ruins after the revolution (Ovesen and Trankell 2010) and serious reconstruction only began when the Vietnamese liberated and occupied the country from January 1979 to the end of 1989 (Mysliwiec 1988). Abandoned hospitals had to be reconstructed in order to function at a basic level. Before the 1990s, funding to improve services started to come from outside sources (Lanjouw *et al.* 1999). Indeed, the late 1980s saw an increasing number of NGOs and international agencies inaugurating new health infrastructure and initiating projects in a growing number of provinces (Khus 2000). From the 1990s onwards, and in the face of persistent insecurity and political instability, most of Cambodia's development efforts were undertaken under the auspices of, and in cooperation with international NGOs, bilateral agencies and, although not without critique (Jennar 2010; Oxfam International 2003), the United Nations. This historical legacy largely engendered a dependent relationship between Cambodia and the aid community.

At the same time as changes in healthcare were progressing, the notion of 'civil society', which had, for decades, been a 'forgotten concept',[1] started timidly to reappear. It received increasing attention by the turn of the century. The objective of this chapter is to focus on this period by following the sharp resurgence of what might be known as 'civil society', from 2005–7. I chose these three years because they correspond to a crucial moment in the visibility of civil society in relation to health questions. For Cambodia, the health sector in this period is emblematic in the analysis of the emergence of civil society for two reasons: first, because some members of the civil society engaged directly with health initiatives at the international level with the expectation of subsequently receiving better recognition and visibility at the national level; and second, because Cambodia signed up to a worldwide strategy encouraging people's involvement in the struggle against malaria, tuberculosis, HIV/AIDS and other communicable diseases. Following Clayton's framework (1996), this chapter aims to elaborate how, and under which conditions, civil society is in a position to contribute to healthcare development and, in particular, to the struggle against the HIV/AIDS epidemic. Keeping in mind that access to care became a key issue during this time, specifically the quest for universal provision of antiretroviral treatment (ART),[2] the beginning of this chapter will examine the issue of access before enlarging its scope to broader aspects of civil society participation.

During 2005–7, the combination of NGO interventions, national health policies and international guidance coming from the United Nations resulted in an innovative orientation towards grassroots participation in health development. In particular, a new kind of local actor, collectively the people living with HIV (PLWHIV), were expected to collaborate with health decision-makers and planners by strengthening the implementation of the programmes, acting as interlocutors with the general population, collecting relevant health information, and providing care and support to their peers. Substantial financial support, mainly provided by the Global Fund (GF),[3] offered new opportunities to mobilize individuals to engage in civil society. As a result, during this period increasing numbers of people living with HIV/AIDS became either career professionals or volunteers involved with the epidemic (Bureau 2010).

Beyond the rhetoric of participation, little is known about the mechanisms that have enabled PLWHIV and other actors from civil society to contribute to improving the health management system through their professional, technical and ideological positioning. This chapter attempts to elucidate this area of investigation. The team of researchers (composed of French and Cambodian researchers) carried out long-term open interviews and participatory observation methodologies, primarily in Phnom Penh, as well as a systematic review of the literature dealing with health activities. Suggestions made in the text derive from this fieldwork as well as personal observations.

National meanings and interpretations of social mobilization

A common statement elaborated and repeated in most parts of the world by international experts, health developers and policy planers is that social mobilization has become valuable in and of itself as a tool for contributing to development, particularly in lesser-developed countries like Cambodia.

An ideological shift

Since the turn of the century, civil society's involvement in development efforts has been increasingly recognized by development agencies and governments as an essential tool for promoting better governance and improving responsiveness of national policies and programmes. Nowadays, most international aid providers agree that civilian cooperation is crucial for expressing the needs and the views of populations targeted by development programmes. A declaration elaborated by the former United Nations Secretary-General, Kofi Annan, argues that the civil society sector should serve as a critical element for holding accountable external agencies involved in HIV/AIDS policies. Domestically, the first generation of social activists envisioned civil society as a supplementary means for ensuring that the national government invests in qualitative, affordable, equitable and accessible healthcare and treatment. On a more practical level, selected representatives of the population should keep an eye on the protection of human rights and should verify that the government is held accountable for the fulfilment of these goals.

Although discussions concerning mobilization did not achieve a strictly uniform agreement, a more theoretical and fundamental consensus has materialized, at least on paper (WHO 2004). In general, however, the need for mobilization was taken for granted by the majority of international agencies, but less so by the national government which has oscillated between resistance and openness. For the government, social mobilization has not necessarily been viewed as an unavoidable approach or a crucial strategy. It enables people to organize for collective action by pooling resources and building the solidarity required for resolving common problems and working towards community advancement. It was also said to be a process that empowers people to organize their own democratic self-governing groups or community organizations, which enables them to initiate and control their own personal and communal development. It contrasts with participatory programmes initiated and designed either by government or by external organizations. In fact, it was this division that created programmatic dilemmas and often made such an ideology difficult to accept by civil servants and Cambodian decision-makers.

Legacy of the past and flexible appropriations

The socio-cultural and political context implies different interpretations of mobilization, which, in addition to local dynamics, need to be understood and adjusted in order to facilitate successful implementation. To that end, the first step of the present analysis involves clarifying not only the vernacular relevance but also the meaning of some concepts embedded in the international discourse, such as social mobilization, collective action and community participation, which are supposed to be exported, rearranged and implemented in Cambodia.

First, culminating in the extremist Maoist regime of Pol Pot (1975–8), the Cambodian historical authoritarian political context has not allowed people to spontaneously gather or organize as groups looking toward a common perceived interest; particularly when it comes to addressing grievances, protesting against the abuse of human rights, or opposing authoritarian local governance. This continued, but with much less brutality, during the Vietnamese occupation. However, since 1993, when the first national election was organized with the assistance of the United Nations, local people have started to be encouraged to work as groups and form associations, unions and NGOs. Based on the idea that civil society must participate in order to reinforce the bold process of democratization, one goal was to involve organized citizens (e.g. from self-help groups, care associations, local NGOs) in national governance and possibly a few decision-making processes.

However, this has led to comments by both external and internal observers, as well as a few written studies, questioning whether the chosen persons actually represent civil society (Gollogly 2002; Bourdier 2006). It can be observed that not all movements and activities of established groups necessarily stemmed from people's voluntarism or actually served the common interest they claimed. Indeed, it became generally accepted that involvement was driven by material motivations, whereby people submitted to training and performed service for their own economic interest. In addition to supporting development, they were seeking new opportunities that would enable them to be financially comfortable (Ou and Kim, this volume). The self-interest guiding personal participation could seriously divert initiatives from their original objectives (i.e. the well-being of target groups). On the one hand, it is neither surprising nor wrong that people pursue personal gain, but frequently it comes at the detriment of the beneficiaries.[4] Indeed, common goals shared between development practitioners and beneficiaries were rarely a central focus. On the other hand, the task was not easy; most representatives of civil society who were part of the small, emerging, NGOs were facing increasingly discriminatory organizational obstacles, including opposition to both their participation in public debates and their contribution to the implementation phase that followed.

Second, mobilization cannot be separated from the idea of 'community participation'. This concept has often been oversimplified and translated in a technical fashion by Khmer and Western developers, while local people have more complex understandings or use other Khmer terminologies. *Sahakum* is associated with the existence of a group of people or restricted social unit living in a delimited area, having a moral socio-religious contract for helping each other.[5] This can be the village, the commune or the *sangkat* (downtown residential area).[6] In the context of the HIV/AIDS epidemic, the phrase *kochorum robo sahakum* refers to community participation in its colloquial definition; it involves people living nearby, including administrators, families and monks. But there can be factions due to social frictions, resulting in a loss of cohesion in the *sahakum*. The original *sahakum* is transformed into divergent and competing sub-groups, in which case the imported notion of community participation falls into a vacuum. Worse, this may accentuate internal divisions and exacerbate inequalities. In comparison, *samakum* is an association of people who voluntarily gather as a group and share common interests. In its formal manifestation, members of the same *samakum* register and pay fees. For example, the Phnom Penh based Antiretroviral Users' Association (AUA), which acts as a lobby group for increasing the quality of health services, is an archetypal *samakum* working for specific interests that are not systematically shared by the population. The last term for community participation is more inclusive but less frequently employed in the context of HIV/AIDS: *sangkum* comprises the whole society, even if it can be disaggregated into social units like *sangkum krusar*, which references family matters in society. Unlike other countries, such as Brazil (Parker 1997; Bourdier 2011), the HIV/AIDS epidemic in Cambodia has not galvanized the national community by socio-economic categories, sex, or otherwise. However, during our fieldwork we met national decision-makers, implementers and observers who considered that such a collective movement could be initiated, as has already been demonstrated for other situations that have demanded national mobilization.[7] They personally believed (indeed, they frequently used this evasive term), but did not try, or dare to try, to put collective movement into practice. Despite their beliefs no concrete action was taken and no social and political mobilization was ever initiated.

Besides the nuances in terms surrounding community mobilization, which are not only linguistic but full of socio-cultural implications, a fundamental element is the emphasis on autonomy and self-reliance in community participation. It has been demonstrated elsewhere (Crewe and Harrison 1998), and it remains valid from my personal observations in Cambodia, that people's participation rarely covers everyone in an identifiable community. Often, power is diverted by local elites who have a strong voice in decision-making; participation means little to the voiceless majority who have little access to resources and power. Other distinctions can be made between an authentic participation that involves the typical criteria (empowerment, self-decision, ideological autonomy) and a pseudo-participation that limits community involvement to the mere implementation, or ratification, of decisions already made by external bodies (Cooke and Kothari 2001). The latter type of manipulation has been analysed in a study dealing with the so-called participation of the ethnic minorities in Ratanakiri province (Bourdier 2008).

Because of the loose definition and internal divisions, the concept of community remains ambiguous. A few authors remain satisfied to describe it as the smallest unit (after the family) of socio-spatial organization, often evoking the idea of the ideological homogeneity of a village. Failing to reflect on the local context, imported Western theories about the concept of community participation tend to regard 'people' as a systematic and unified group potentially able to be mobilized for collective action. International NGOs, in particular, have misunderstood this dynamic. A few anthropologists like Soizick Crochet (2000: 45–77) and Jan Ovesen and his colleagues (1996) have demonstrated that persons living in a so-called community often have nothing more in common with each other than that they live in the same area, perhaps belonging to the same religious or political group. This means that they do not systematically share similar challenges or have collective goals, which is contrary to what the idealistic concept of community participation implicitly suggests. Moreover, its implication is unclear for decision-making processes regarding the formulating of policies, planning, and the implementation of economic and social development programmes. Under these conditions, the ideals of autonomy and self-reliance pertaining to a group of concerned persons can hardly be taken into account.

In the Cambodian social context of health, mobilization is rather associated with its technical, and not political, dimension. Implicitly formulated with this restriction, 'technical assistance' was supposed to be the main axis of a process in which leading agencies should grant low budgets to grassroots-level groups, associations and small local NGOs for their involvement in particular activities. Among the responses understood as priorities, community participation was definitely put forward, although it was misinterpreted as I already mentioned. However, a few important NGOs managed to develop partnerships with a number of grassroots NGOs and associations. But these leading organizations were mostly working under the US Agency for International Development (USAID) and were obligated to match the conditions and ideologies of the international donors, whose policy was devoted to home-based care, care-support and home visits rather than access to ART (at least up to 2004). Funds for local groups rarely existed for more than one year and these recipients were constantly monitored and evaluated, sometimes by persons having limited country experiences, poor qualifications and low motivation. Leaders of various NGOs and community-based organizations (CBOs) remembered that they had to spend their time writing endless reports, plans and updated strategies. Ironically, little time could be devoted to the implementation of the project itself. Reciprocity and interaction between the donors and recipients were not encouraged.[8] Ultimately, money remained available if local NGOs kept up their activities along a very specific scope of intervention that was imposed by external agencies.

Although not explicitly stated, personal interviews indicate that donors, along with the international NGOs they fund, maintain that such guidance is theoretically adequate to promote and encourage a gradual process of local NGO self-reliance. The logic is that once the funding period is completed, both local NGOs and grassroots-level NGOs will have developed their capacity to run autonomously. This is referred to as the 'trickle down effect'. But the expected percolation from top to bottom is more hypothesis than fact, especially when necessary qualifications, such as creativity and access to an enlarged knowledge base has not been provided during the process. In the end, bureaucratization and administration became the primary activities encouraged, when more attention should have been directed at the projects' beneficiaries.

National governance as step toward social visibility of civil society

The epidemiological outbreak[9] of HIV/AIDS and the energetic public measures that followed have been depicted elsewhere (Bourdier and Gnep 2011: 67–116), but we should keep in mind that Cambodia became the most affected Southeast Asian country in the late nineties, with the HIV adult prevalence rate reaching 3 per cent in 1997. After considering new transmission routes, the years 1994–5 showed the highest rates of infection. Transmission routes were, in decreasing order, male clients of sex workers (nearly 75 per cent), husband to wife (15 per cent), sex workers themselves (7 per cent) and mother to child (3 per cent). The prevalence went down to 2.2 per cent in 2001 and was against reduced to 0.9 per cent in 2003 (UNAIDS 2006). Since then, it has been reported as low as 0.7 per cent in the United National General Assembly Special Session of HIV/AIDS in 2009. The most recent data provided by the government shows an 'expected' rate of 0.6 per cent in 2011.[10] Even if sex workers (both male and female) continue to remain the most vulnerable group, the other two transmission routes (husband to wife and mother to child) are significant contributors. To summarize, Cambodia's response to the epidemic has been depicted as one of the few 'success stories' (along with Brazil, Thailand and Uganda) in reversing the trend of the epidemic, as shown by declining prevalence. In addition, the number of adults with HIV/AIDS receiving ART has increased dramatically, with more than 50 per cent of patients receiving ART by 2005. As of September 2005, 12,355 active patients were receiving ART, of which 1,071 were children.[11] According to national authorities, the scaling-up of treatment was reinforced in the aftermath of the 'universal access' strategy promoted by the UN. It reached nearly 90 per cent of people who needed the treatment in 2007, and it reached 99 per cent at the end of 2011, according to official sources from the Ministry of Health. But what can we say about the contribution of civil society to this encouraging result?

As elaborated above, some public measures were launched promptly after the first HIV case was made made public in 1991 (e.g. national policy, prevention measures, condom promotion, health system strengthening, authorization for massive NGO intervention, etc.). Other measures (e.g. early diagnosis and access to care and treatment) were introduced without overly significant delay. In the coming years, but mostly during and after 1995, some members of civil society infected by the virus, specifically in Phnom Penh, decided to join together and form a group. They were encouraged by the local NGO *Khana* to raise their voice and to combat social discrimination. After some time this group was followed by others. Some of them eventually came to be recognized and registered as civil society entities, but not before 1998. When the discovery of new effective ART was announced during the International AIDS Conference, some civil society groups expanded and spread their activities to wider social networks. In this context, they continued to develop primary activities at the grassroots level (e.g. referral, practical health information, human rights' awareness, hospital guidance, social welfare, access to treatment, general care, etc.) but started to recognize that access to ART would become the most important issue in Cambodia. Their activities led them to reach out to persons at home (home-based care activities) and to eventually accompany patients to the main hospitals where the first international NGOs were conducting medical operations at the end of the 1990s.[12] Nevertheless, the availability of funds devoted to this first 'spontaneous' generation of civil society was not only restricted but extremely conditioned by top-down decisions. Budgets were frequently provided for a short period under the cover of umbrella organizations (like the HIV/AIDS Alliance), which consolidated funds from abroad in order to distribute small incentives to minor local groups via well-established local NGOs like *Khana*. The performance of the groups representing civil society was, in spite of notable exceptions, restricted to home-based care activities. While this was necessary, it was hardly sufficient. Advocacy (for human rights, healthcare, equal and non-discriminatory access to treatment) was also one of their objectives, but was not always encouraged; it was not yet considered a priority by most donors, either nationally (Ministry of Health, National AIDS Authorities, provincial health departments, etc.) or internationally (USAID, World Bank, many religious NGOs, etc.).

It was in this socio-political environment that a Cambodian civil society emerged with an intention to contribute to the fight against the epidemic. This was not a general and widespread movement as had happened in other countries in the world (such as those in Africa and South America), but it was unquestionably present and was not at risk of disappearing. Some members of civil society organizations were committed to promoting better care and treatment for the infected population. At the same time, external funding from various agencies (bilateral, multilateral, private, etc.) let to the creation of local and international NGOs able to implement their own programmes, most of them with the intention of involving communities. However, a preliminary study showed that, of the numerous HIV/AIDS projects which existed before 2000, many have long since disbanded (Crochet 1998).[13] Most of the health actors from international NGOs used to work in isolation due to frequent ideological and methodological disagreements. For many years health initiatives in Cambodia were atomized and characterized by contradiction, controversy and competition. The situation changed in early 2000 with the government's attempt to enforce a national HIV/AIDS policy. Local authorities, together with international NGOs, bilateral institutions and UN agencies started to share the responsibility for supervising and monitoring efforts to fight the disease, and started providing access to treatment.[14]

A new worldwide solidarity

The year 2002 is key because it saw the creation of the GF and its rapid financial support to Cambodia. It facilitated the elaboration of a national health policy by enabling new management and organizational developments which were previously unthinkable, including making the participation of civil society official and financially feasible as opposed to something 'to be shown' anecdotally. In the beginning, that participation was not clearly articulated and most of the health actors declared that it was a challenge to maintain a coherent overview of the current situation (Pillai et al. 2004). It was unclear who was doing what, even for those working in a similar geographical area. Lack of coordination prevailed among external agencies like the UN, whose organizations had separate agendas, sometimes with externally imposed and overlapping interventions (Curtis 1998). Further, many of the NGOs considered each other as potential rivals for funding. Institutional bridges between development agents remained fragmented and exceptional. As a result, comprehensive understanding of the social, political, economic and cultural dynamics influencing the trend of the epidemic remained limited because agencies working on AIDS issues rarely shared information, data and analyses. As a result, health officials were unwilling or uncomfortable dealing with a civil society that was, from their point of view, barely integrated.

The situation has changed with Cambodia having benefited from more than ten years (2002–12) of GF money. This funding partner has facilitated innovative programmes, including an ART distribution project that has required the recruitment of hundreds of 'patient experts' who can all be considered part of civil society (Bureau 2010). To illustrate, in 2002, US$101 million worth of grants, through four rounds of funding, were for the HIV/AIDS component alone, making the GF one of the largest sources of funding for combating HIV/AIDS. Studies conducted locally have been completed; some, concerning the GF, were written during its early phase of implementation (Wilkinson 2004). Since 2002 further rounds of funding have been proposed every year, changing the dynamics of the process of ART delivery as well as ensuring a better visibility of the participation of civil society. However, no system is perfect. In particular, administrative barriers made small associations reluctant to apply for GF grants. Many of the smaller organizations had insufficient human resources to meet the required system of documentation and to write regular reports demonstrating transparency in the execution of their programmes. Government bodies and bigger NGOs felt more comfortable because they were in a position to employ staff to concentrate on administration and management of the GF funding.

Projects implemented under the GF regulations and mechanisms differ based on organizations and social actors (Brugha *et al.* 2002). A significant determinant is the role of health actors and their interactions during proposal-writing and implementation, which includes procurement, training, public relations, monitoring, capacity building, as well as material and human resources management. All these activities theoretically have direct implications for the quality of care related to HIV treatment. These fundamental activities are supposed to be handled by the contribution of the civil society, but can only be engaged in with support of funded NGOs. Without these partnerships, smaller-scale actors in civil society can hardly implement programmes and activities on their own.

In every domain of intervention, a social institution acting as a sub-recipient (to the government, who is the principal recipient) is supposed to comply with GF requirements. After years, and due to external criticism, the international organization from Geneva has adapted its position. It tries nowadays to have a lighter structure by providing flexibility for the implementation strategy and by strengthening health structures as a whole. But most of the social actors who are associated with sub-recipients continue to argue that the rules laid out by the GF, to which institutional beneficiaries are bound for the implementation of the activities, have virtually no voice.[15] This occurs because ART procurement and operational guidelines are controlled by the principal recipient based in the Ministry of Health, in which the civil society is only theoretically represented.

Promoting communication and homogeneity at the health organizational level

Over time, some improvements have become observable. The government officers in charge of health project planning – including GF coordination and supervision – deserve recognition for their attempt to integrate and work with some members of civil society. They developed skills for health management and for creating information and structural links with the sub-recipients who received the money. The GF has become an incentive for strengthening networks and encouraging dialogue between social actors working at different levels in the various domains of HIV/AIDS intervention. In spite of ongoing resistance by a small number of international NGOs to coordinate their activities with the national programme, a local agenda aimed at better governance was developed from 2005–6. Its goal is far from being achieved, but a process has been initiated among individual parties who recognize that effectiveness relies on their mutual interdependence. Furthermore, the funding mechanisms reward the beneficiaries not only for going into the field but also force them to sit together around a table and monitor every single account. Such financial and logistic issues provide a new economic credibility to the government, in spite of some problems with corruption (local and international) that the GF cannot prevent alone.

There are other constructive ongoing processes. One is linked to the ideological independence (not related to financing) and freedom of expression offered by an independent organization such as the GF that maintains its role as a funding agency, intervening only lightly in the contents of the projects submitted. The GF, which is morally neutral,[16] acts indirectly as a counterweight against agencies that not only fund, but also attempt to shape the ideological orientations of the programmes they support. The GF provides incentives but does not interfere, or at least does so very little, in the choice of the programmes. The sub-recipients, should they want to strengthen civil society participation, thereby have a free space to implement activities under the sole condition of respecting management, transparency and reporting mechanisms.

The relative freedom and security offered by the GF prevents the hegemonic influences of powerful agencies arriving with huge amounts of funding and trying to influence development procedures with a strict moralistic approach or with a revisionist version of an 'appropriate response' to HIV/AIDS. The Emergency Plan for managing the HIV/AIDS epidemic coming from the US Bush administration (Pepfar), in 2003, is emblematic of such an initiative. Its policy has been justified by controversial scientific methods, sometimes severely criticized by activists, academic researchers, national and international NGOs (NGO Forum 2004). The GF, in contrast, allows national and alternative programmes, mostly those that encourage the mobilization of society and which would otherwise not be supported.

The safety valves act at another level. An institution does not systematically exercise control over its own members. For instance, while USAID has no choice but to outwardly comply with the conditions put forward by the Emergency Plan, people working within the agency accept modifications to the otherwise well-articulated Emergency Plan (promotion on fidelity, abstinence and restriction to condom use, limitations of generic drugs, ban on projects focusing on sex work). Some of these individuals have previously worked as medical or political activists, sometimes belonging to militant groups like Act-Up. It is not uncommon to find some of them actually recruited by USAID and then internally fighting within the institution. Such an alternative space of negotiation exists in practice, even if it is not written on paper. In other words, it would be a mistake to categorize social actors involved in a particular institution as obedient agents or unconditional 'soldiers' of their organization. On the contrary, some individuals are strong supporters of a bottom-up approach and try their best to act on behalf of civil society, or at least as part of civil society.

External interferences in national policy and civil society mobilization

The GF openly supports 'institutional capacity building'. Broadly speaking, members of GF-supported institutions include the whole chain of social health actors, from implementers to representatives of civil society. The GF has increasingly been pushing for a more formal and a more standardized way of implementing grants by encouraging the creation of different assemblages: self-help groups, community-based organizations, medical staff assistant groups, care groups, etc. In spite of these efforts, GF support has led to greater dominance by the government and less involvement of civil society. In spite of its initial expectation, the GF has not yet provided sufficient tools to counter government control by creating more channels for a civil society contribution liable to lead to active mobilization. This point requires greater investigation and will be elaborated upon below.

A 20-year inheritance transformed by growing mistrust

At the intervention level, it could be expected that decisions and strategies proposed by various social health actors (from national decision-makers to members of civil society) would be complementary. This has been hardly the case, but is not surprising given that a health system is also a social and political system (Hours 2001). Its evolution depends on the quality and the nature of relations between social agents. But, in the case of Cambodia, limited mechanisms have been created to enable the cross-fertilization of ideas among actors from different professions belonging to either national or international agencies.

A conducive social environment for cooperation has yet to be established. Active partnership at the national level remains a challenge, even if some local NGOs and Cambodian doctors have managed to organize sustainable active collaborations in some public health clinics.[17] Indeed, the long-term control over local health officials by international bodies has had a negative impact. This approach, taken for granted over the years by external developers, can often be interpreted as deliberate manipulation and has led to strong reactions by national leaders in the field of HIV/AIDS. Over time, some national figures managed to obtain positions that they do not want to share anymore, mostly with 'non-educated' people.[18] Furthermore, it is commonplace to find contempt for non-Khmers who, despite poor awareness of the socio-cultural and political reality, want impose ready-made ideas in Cambodia. National HIV/AIDS professionals hardly accept criticism from foreign counterparts and do not hesitate to drive them away if they insist on a direction which is not perceived as a priority. Moreover, some of these international agents are accused of 'spoiling civil society' by giving them ideas from outside and not respecting 'local traditions'.[19]

A new expression of civil society

New forms, or expressions, of civil society cannot be fully understood without analysing the broader health context in which they have emerged. For the last 20 years, it has been repeated that the emergence of civil society was a crucial factor for health improvement in general. With the HIV pan-epidemic, civil society was offered a key role for the improvement of the national programme against HIV/AIDS. In the first section I outlined some of the ambiguities contained in such a discourse, mostly when it meets practice. Although civil society mobilization was strongly encouraged at the international level by the UN in 2002, and even became a more formalized subject of interest at the national level in the foregoing years, its implementation and its acceptability deserve to be scrutinized in the diverse socio-cultural context of Cambodia. After long-term observations and interviews with NGO representatives, we found that Khmer civil society was not able, from 2002–5, to work autonomously (Bourdier and Ou 2005; Bureau 2010). We already mentioned that the government, with GF mechanisms, was in a position to act as leader for the debate and controlled the privilege of decision-making due to its position as principal financial recipient. It had the capacity to control financial transactions and subsequently had more facility to control and pressure NGOs and CBOs. This can be interpreted as a constructive effort in terms of national governance, as, indeed, it had been understood among development agents in Cambodia.

Then came the time for 'normalization' under the auspices of the UN, with consequent financial encouragement from international agencies in Geneva. Important funding to implement the participation of civil society throughout the developing countries came to be available mostly through the Global Fund. Before the early phase of the civil society mobilization encouraged by the UN in the early 2000s, a few members of society had already become official 'representatives' of the civil society and been granted opportunity to meet civil groups from other countries and participate in exchange tours, seminars and meetings. When returning, they passed their knowledge and lessons learned from abroad to colleagues and friends (see Wells-Dang, this volume). As a result, people eventually came up with an idea of how to work as an autonomous group and tried to cultivate their civil society representation. People who have recently started to be involved in the national struggle against HIV/AIDS in Cambodia often have similar backgrounds based in grassroots activities. But only a few prominent activists have actually emerged. This means that the hoped-for objectives of civilian leadership were not fulfilled. Instead, individuals appeared to be reluctant to engage themselves in the long term. This might be because of budgetary constraints, fear of repression (a political syndicate activist's assassination and details of recent imprisonments published in newspapers focus people's minds on this possibility) and lack of any decentralized system that could have strengthened their unity or at least augmented their courage to assume positions of responsibility. In addition, despite a growing activism occurring in other spheres of development activities (Landau 2008), there was little space for open public debate and, in hindsight, few candidates in the health sector were really in a position to lobby on behalf of the HIV/AIDS campaign.

From this period onwards, however, the number of PLWHIV who started working in the health sector grew dramatically (exact figures are not available). This trend started in 2005 and carried on until 2011. A new social visibility was emerging. But who are they and what are they doing? Often they are employed by the national programme, international agencies, and by small local NGOs with their extended networks in the villages. Most of them are voluntary while a few are working under contract and have a mandate to fulfil specific tasks. Despite this, a two-year study showed PLWHIV are not welcome to take personal and collective initiatives. Ongoing research beyond this period goes in the same direction (e.g. Pen and Bourdier 2011). Most of the people studied by Eve Bureau (2010) recognize that they lose their freedom once they have been integrated into normative healthcare interventions. They cannot raise unexpected issues that have not been previously approved at the top level. Apart from very exceptional cases, they have little choice but to comply with external constraints and priorities. Negotiation is not a prevailing dynamic; they are rarely invited to join public debates (or do so as mere observers) and very few of them are in a position to attend official meetings or even conferences and events where they could raise their voices, which *is* the case in other countries such as Brazil, Thailand and Uganda. Most of the infected persons who became 'expert patients'[20] are expected to fit into the pyramidal hierarchy. Political mobilization is absent, even though there are many who would be motivated to join and put pressure on the government to open up public debates on sensitive issues like the long-term sustainable availability of generic drugs, access to second line treatments, the lack of medical care for opportunistic infections, top-up fees that patients have to pay, and absence of equitable social and nutrition support.

The link between government, international agencies, funded organizations, local NGOs, and PLWHIV involved in the fight against the epidemic can be categorized more in terms of allegiance than cooperation (Bureau 2010). The hierarchy is somewhat more complex than it appears, but it seems that any autonomous mobilization at the grassroots level is interpreted by the majority of decision-makers as an attempt at destabilization or as a threat to national sovereignty. Emerging militants and social groups who started criticizing some achievements claimed by the government, or by international agencies, have been denied access to public and official meetings where they could have justified their declarations and contributed positively to reorient national health policies.

Recent considerations

Social mobilization initiatives as they have been understood, reappropriated, and put into operation in Cambodia during the last decade, can be divided into two tendencies. In the first category, some NGOs funded by external donors are mandated to promote community involvement and grassroots-level NGOs that are supposed to strengthen HIV/AIDS awareness, mass media communication, volunteer training, social support and access to care. These small groups are selected and strongly guided by the bigger NGOs that fund them. In the second category, which has become 'thinkable' only recently but still remains uncommon, are individuals and people organizing themselves more independently and eventually managing to be registered as an association, CBO or NGO. In contrast to the first category, they encourage advocacy, sometimes through overseas networking alliances with southern hemisphere movements in India and Thailand, or with activist groups in Europe (see Wells-Dang, this chapter). They are more prone to oppose and criticize government policy. This tendency is relatively spontaneous, but sometimes organized via worldwide networks, and the civil society members aspire to be autonomous as much as they can. In contrast, the groups in the first category have more links with planned and 'polished' initiatives already prepared, supervised and controlled by the government and leading international NGOs.

As a result, civil society in Cambodia has become divided. Look, for example, at the scaling-up of ART delivery: for some patients anxious to follow government policies, it has been perceived largely in its quantitative dimension, i.e. the more patients under treatment the more successful the health policy is deemed to be. Qualitative aspects, which are, in fact, essential for the infected populations have so far been neglected. It came to a point that an emerging section of the civil society, which we can say is more 'wilful', started to mobilize around this unique issue. Even in the first category, although still minority voices, some NGO workers and social activists raised their voices and started commenting that it would have been better to avoid the quantitative focus, and insist instead upon the more fundamental socio-medical aspects, including adequate access to opportunistic treatment, better counselling for HIV testing, free exams, rehabilitation efforts and economic support for vulnerable populations.

Although more examples could have been presented, apart from a few exceptions that may allow us to forecast future changes, the majority of them would have led to similar observations. Our findings show that the nature of the link between government, international agencies, international NGOs, and small local NGOs, is more about subordination than genuine cooperation and can be characterized more in terms of participative obedience than autonomous mobilization. Manipulation of local NGO activities appears to be the standard norm not only when it is related to HIV/AIDS activities, but also when it concerns other health development issues.

Conclusion

At this point we may wonder about the emergence of relative autonomy in civil society in the coming future. Isolated actions, hesitant attempts, early signs and scattered aspirations obviously exist. But if social mobilization, as it is guardedly realized in Cambodia, does not manage to empower people or allow them to become intellectually independent, it will neither inspire or harness the creativity of the population nor will it promote autonomous decision-making. Additionally, the potential for advocacy is still limited as long as community participation is de facto inhibited by the government. Cambodia's recent history clearly shows that when community participation becomes fashionable, and when international intervention increases such participation's systematic activity, one of the government's main responses has been to control and absorb it into the framework of its own policy rather than let it become a potential alternative voice for the people.

To more specifically address the meaning of community participation at the grassroots level, medical staff and volunteers perceive community more generally as a group of people including family, neighbour, authority, villager and monks. As a slogan, 'mobilizing communities to respond to HIV/AIDS' has been promoted by a funded NGO under the control of a bilateral agency. But the meaning of the slogan has been neither sufficiently defined nor explained in detail. One blurry justification claims that 'HIV/AIDS community participation' comprises the contribution of infected persons as well as the solidarity of the social environment towards reducing stigma and discrimination and increasing psychological and social support. Unfortunately, such an aspirational statement does not provide methodological tools for executing any strategy that will take into account the socio-cultural logic and predisposition of the society. Yuvany Gnep's work focusing on monks' involvement in the cultural context of Cambodia (Gnep 2006; Bourdier and Gnep 2011) demonstrates that there is evidently a need to pursue broader research on this issue.

Through the observation of dominant practices related to national health interventions intended to encourage people's participation, I have noted that decisions from the top have shaped, if not formatted, the population's initiatives. Even over an apparently unpoliticized issue like HIV/AIDS, the creativity and enterprise of ordinary people has been subsumed by the superficial and questionable fashions of imported advice. If the situation does not evolve, it may allow the grip of imposed officialdom to suppress popular choice and individual freedom.

Popular mobilization has to be re-invented. At the same time, there is an incredible potential to reactivate a related concept of collective participation. The strength of the country resides not only in people's aspirations towards justice and access to healthcare and treatment, but also in the behaviour of certain government representatives, whose function it is to communicate with the movement. These individuals, such as Dr Tia Phalla from the National AIDS Authority, are sincerely willing to promote cooperation more constructively with civil society by encouraging a more open space of negotiation. Resolutions over the following years will reveal more about the future outcome.

Notes

1 This was due to successive political regimes from the 1970s to the late 1980s.
2 In the late 1990s Cambodia was the most HIV-affected country in Southeast Asia.
3 The Global Fund is a Geneva-based international agency which is receiving money from developed countries in order to fight HIV/AIDS, malaria and tuberculosis in developing countries.
4 Based on personal enquiries with a leading medical and political activist, Ms Mony Pen (2008).
5 Typically, *sangkum* is accompanied with *samaki* (solidarity) and *ataun oknia* (indulgence), two cultural values in Cambodian Theravada Buddhism.
6 *Neak sahakum* refers to villagers.
7 For example, in 2009 when the Preah Vihear temple and its borderlands were invaded by Thai nationalists.
8 A few funding NGOs like Action Aid and Christian Aid acted as collaborators in Cambodia. They also showed sincere willingness to interact constructively at the grassroots level with the small groups receiving financial support from them. Unfortunately, they did not represent the mainstream position and their funding capacity was limited.
9 The first HIV case was diagnosed in Phnom Penh in 1991 (blood donor).
10 This epidemic projection was still awaiting verification when this chapter was finalized.
11 Data available online, at: http://data.unaids.org/pub/Report/2006/20060801_cambodia_turning_tide_en.pdf.
12 From 2000–4, only five NGOs (operating in five different hospitals in the capital, plus one in Siem Reap Province) were receiving infected persons for treatment. ART was provided at first by MDM (*Médecins du Monde*) then by MSF France (*Médecins sans Frontières*) and by MSF Belgium/Holland.
13 There were more than 120 NGOs working in the HIV/AIDS shere in Cambodia before 1998.
14 This does not necessarily mean that civil society is unified. Indeed, even by 2012, the few groups maintaining a certain visibility were marked by internal conflicts, mutual distrusts and ideological disputes.
15 Personal interviews with a civil society's representative of the Global Fund in 2011.
16 So far, no counter example has been identified in Cambodia.
17 Personal observations in Kampot, Oddar Meanchey and Battambang provinces.
18 All outspoken HIV/AIDS activists that I know have repeatedly received this kind of subjective dismissal by national decision-makers, specifically during periods in which they enjoyed a recognized position, whether abroad or in Cambodia. For instance, Ms Pen Mony, whose voice had a tremendous international impact at the beginning of the Mexico Conference, and Ms Dy Many, who participated in different meetings of the UN General Assembly Special Session.
19 This is a recurring statement orally communicated by national decision-makers to local activists. Information: Ms Mony Pen (2010).
20 This is the accepted official title position devised by international agencies.

References

Bernander, B., Charny, J., Eastmond, M., Lindahl, C. and Öjendal, J. (1995) *Facing a Complex Emergency: An Evaluation of Swedish Support to Emergency Aid to Cambodia*, Stockholm: Swedish International Development Cooperation Agency.
Bourdier, F. (2006) 'Policies and Politics Behind the Path for Access to Treatment Against HIV/AIDS in Cambodia' in W*orking papers in contemporary Asian Studies*, 18, Lund: Centre for East and South-East Asian Studies, University of Lund (Sweden).

Bourdier, F. (2008) 'Indigenous Populations in a Cultural Perspective: The Paradox of Development in Southeast Asia' in *Anthropos*, 103: 1–12.

Bourdier, F. (2011) 'Entre gouvernement et agences internationales: la part d'autonomie des ONG brésiliennes dans la lutte contre le sida' in F. Eboko and F. Bourdier (eds), *Les Suds face au sida. Quand la société civile se mobilise*, Paris: Institut de recherche pour le développement: 21–37.

Bourdier, F. and Gnep, Y. (2011) 'Le réveil de la société civile: mobilisations profanes et religieuses dans la lutte contre le sida au Cambodge' in F. Eboko and F. Bourdier (eds), *Les suds face au Sida. Quand la société civile se mobilise*, Paris: Institut de recherche pour le développement: 67–116.

Bourdier, F. and Ou, H. (2005) 'Mobilisation sociale et accès aux antirétroviraux au Cambodge', Face à face 7.

Brugha, R., Starling, M. and Walt, G. (2002) 'The First Steps: Lessons for the Global Fund' in *The Lancet* 359 (9304): 435–8.

Bureau, E. (2010) 'Anthropologie d'une norme globalise: La participation profane dans les programmes de lutte contre le sida au Cambodge', unpublished thesis, University of Bordeaux 2.

Clayton, A. (1996) *NGOs, Civil Society and the State: Building Democracy in Transitional Societies*, Oxford: Intrac.

Cooke, B. and Kothari, U. (eds) (2001) *Participation: The New Tyranny?* London/New York: Zed Books.

Crewe, E. and Harrison, E. (1998) *Whose Development? An Ethnography of Aid*, London/New York: Zed Books.

Crochet, S. (2000) 'Cet obscure objet du désir' in R. Brauman (ed.), *Utopies sanitaires*, Paris: Le Pommier: 45–77.

Crochet, S. (1998) *Activités et idéologies des agences internationales en charge des programmes sida au Cambodge*, Paris: Centre National de Recherche Scientifique, Université de Nanterre/CNRS.

Curtis, G. (1998) *Cambodia Reborn? The Transition to Democracy and Development*, Washington, DC: Brookings Institution Press.

Gnep, Y. (2006) 'Initiatives bouddhistes contre le sida au Cambodge Enjeux thérapeutiques, religieux et identitaires autour de stratégies de développement communautaire', Master en Anthropologie sociale, Université de Marseille.

Gollogly, L. (2002) 'The Dilemmas of Aid: Cambodia 1992–2002' in *The Lancet*, 360 (9335): 793–8.

Hours, B. (2001) *Systèmes et politiques de santé: De la santé publique à l'anthropologie*, Paris: Karthala.

Jennar, R. M. (2010) *Trente ans depuis Pol Pot: Le Cambodge de 1979 à 2009*, Paris: L'harmattan.

Khus, T. (2000) *Country Study: Non Governmental Organizations in Cambodia*, Phnom Penh: Silaka.

Landau, I. (2008) 'Law and Civil Society in Cambodia and Vietnam: A Gramscian Perspective' in *Journal of Contemporary Asia*, 38 (2): 244–58.

Lanjouw, S., Marcrae, J. and Zwi, A. B. (1999) 'Rehabilitating Health Services in Cambodia: the Challenge of Coordination in Chronic Political Emergencies' in *Health Policy and Planning*, 14 (3): 229–42.

Mysliwiec, E. (1988) *Punishing the Poor: The Internal Isolation of Kampuchea*, London: Oxfam UK.

NGO Forum (2004) 'NGO letter from the 26th March 2004 to the Office of the Global

AIDS Initiative, (petitioned by 385 U.S. and international organizations)', Washington, March 2004.

Ovesen, J. and Trankell, I.-B. (2010) *Cambodians and their Doctors: a Medical Anthropology of Colonial and Post-colonial Cambodia*, Copenhagen: NIAS Press.

Ovesen, J., Trankell, I.-B. and Öjendal, J. (1996) 'When Every Household is an Island: Social Organization and Power Structures in Rural Cambodia' in *Uppsala Research Reports in Cultural Anthropology*, 15, Uppsala, Sweden: Department of Cultural Anthropology, Uppsala University.

Oxfam International (2003) *Cambodia's Accession to the WTO: How the Law of the Jungle is Applied to One of the Poorest Countries*, Geneva.

Parker, R. (1997) *Políticas, Instituições e AIDS: Enfrentando a Epidemia no Brasil*, Rio de Janeiro: Jorge Zahar Editor/ABIA.

Pen, M. and Bourdier, F. 'Responses and Claims of the Civil Society in Relation with the HIV/AIDS National Policy in Cambodia', paper presented at the HIV/AIDS Symposium, Phnom Penh, 16 November 2011.

Pillai, G., Donaldson, B. and Keang, S. 'A Directory of Organizations Implementing or Supporting HIV/AIDS Activities in Cambodia and a Compilation of Abstracts submitted to the XV AIDS Conference', Phnom Penh, 11–16 July 2004.

UNAIDS (2006) *Turning the Tide: Cambodia's Response to HIV/AIDS 1991–2005*, Phnom Penh: UNAIDS/National Aids Authority research document.

Wilkinson, D. (2004) *The Global Fund to Fight AIDS, Tuberculosis and Malaria*, Phnom Penh: Cambodia Country Coordination Mechanism.

World Health Organization (2004) WHO Asian Civil Society Conference on Macroeconomics and Health, Colombo, Sri Lanka, 27–8 April, Geneva: WHO.

8 Changing gendered boundaries in rural Cambodia

Community-based organizations as a platform for empowerment

Ayako Hiwasa

In Cambodia, women's participation in politics and the public sphere is often viewed as limited due to rigidly defined gender roles, a gendered public-private divide (Lilja 2008: 55) and the hierarchical nature of society. After three decades of war, however, political stability and socio-economic growth as well as development interventions have challenged traditional gender norms and opened space and opportunity for change (Aing 2004; Hill and Heng 2004). This movement was galvanized in the early 1990s by Cambodian non-governmental organizations (NGOs) backed by international donors. The first Cambodian NGO and women's organization, Khemara (see Ou and Kim, this volume; Frieson 1998) was established in 1991, followed by women's movements and initiatives by civil society organizations (CSO) such as Amara, which focused on gender-based violence (see Öjendal, this volume). Many of the larger Cambodian NGOs are headed by Cambodians returning from overseas to join in efforts to rebuild society. In addition to the influence of returnees, these organizations are financially dependent on, and influenced by, the agendas of donors (Malena and Chhim 2009; Ou and Kim, this volume). Concepts of gender and gender equality are imported into the Cambodian development agenda through international aid programmes and policies influenced to a great deal by Western feminist discourse (Hiwasa 2010; Mohanty 1984). This is partially responsible for the gap cited by a number of scholars between Phnom Penh-based professional NGOs and the communities they serve (Malena and Chhim 2009; Ou and Kim, this volume).

Despite the rapid growth of Cambodian NGOs, the shortcomings of top-down development approaches to development in the 1980s (Cooke and Kothari 2001) encouraged a growing trend in participatory approaches to development that led to the establishment of many grassroots associations and community-based organizations (CBO) as a way to promote community engagement in local development (Malena and Chhim 2009). Compared to the traditional form of CBOs based on religion, such as pagoda associations (see Ehlert, this volume) and Buddhism for Social Development Action (Öjendal, this volume), modern associations and grassroots CBOs outside of the religious sphere are relatively new and their impact is considered limited in facilitating citizen–state relationships due to their small scale (Malena and Chhim 2009).

This study looks into the detail of how women's groups, a modern form of CBO facilitated by a livelihood improvement project in Takeo province, have provided a platform for women's empowerment[1] and filled some of the 'gap' in intermediaries referenced by Öjendal (this volume). Unlike most professional NGOs headed by elites (see examples in Ou and Kim, this volume), these women's groups consist of voluntary members who share some degree of mutual interest as well as personal outlook and are headed by elected leaders. Case studies in four villages provide evidence that despite the fact that women's groups initially focused on livelihoods rather than gender-specific issues, they have ultimately initiated processes of women's empowerment, and gone on to challenge traditional gender norms. I will argue that these groups open up opportunities for ordinary women to participate in public space. In addition, they present the potential for a more autonomous and self-sustaining form of CBO that can link the masses – women in this case – and the public sphere.

In my discussion, I take a postmodern feminist approach for understanding how women's groups have challenged power relations and become active in the public sphere, which has previously been considered a male-dominated domain. The postmodern feminist approach (McNay 1992; Parpart 1993; Parpart and Marchand 1995; Jackson and Pearson 1998) accepts and understands the power of discourse to situate women's voices and experiences in the specific historical, spatial and social context. My attempt here is to contextualize these voices and bring them into discussions about the formation of civil society in Cambodia.

This chapter is based on ethnographic fieldwork undertaken in 2007 and in 2011 (Hiwasa 2010).[2] The methods of data collection include participant observation, in-depth individual interviews using semi-structured guidelines, and focus group discussions. Over the course of five months, I made frequent visits to four villages, attended relevant meetings, and lived in the homes of female leaders over two months in two out of four of the villages in the study.

Changing gender norms in Cambodia

Gender relations have undergone substantial changes as economic, social and political development opened up new opportunities for women outside of the household (Derks 2008; UNIFEM *et al.* 2004). A number of factors have contributed to these changes, including skewed demographic patterns resulting from the toll of civil wars, free market reforms, economic pressures, educational attainment, political decentralization, gender mainstreaming policy, and the adaption of an anti-domestic violence law (Derks 2008; Frieson and Chan 1998; Kim and Öjendal 2011; Nakagawa 2006). Although there is change in this field, reigning gender norms still firmly place women lower than men, despite the fact that women have played a comparative role as income providers for their families and are now viewed as a driving force for economic development (UNIFEM *et al.* 2004; Nakagawa 2006; Hun 2004).

Relations in Khmer society are determined by a combination of factors such as reputation, political position, wealth, sex and age (Ebihara 1968; Ledgerwood

1992; Öjendal, this volume). Women are compelled to conform to traditional gender norms in order to develop and maintain their status in the social hierarchy (Ledgerwood 1992).

Traditional gender norms

Gender ideologies and cultural ideals often place conflicting demands upon women. A woman should be shy, soft and sweet in her communication, avoid speaking loudly, move without being heard, and she must be protected, ideally never leaving the company of her relatives before her marriage. Such ideals for proper behaviour and attitudes in the household, and interactions with her husband (Zimmerman 1994: 24), are elaborated and widely taught through the *chbap srey* (Women's Code of Conduct). For example, a woman's anger with her husband or with family members is described as a fire that she can extinguish with her calmness (Ledgerwood 1996: 124). The *chbap srey* is written in rhyme and children used to sing some parts of it at school until it was recently taken off the curriculum. Some elements of the *chbap srey* are still passed on from generation to generation (Aing 2004).

Another aspect of the proper woman is that she must know how to run a household and manage its finances. One of the symbolic women, or *srey kroup leakkh* (perfectly virtuous woman), in Khmer mythology named *Mea Yoeng* exemplifies the qualities of an ideal woman, which rarely exists in reality (Aing 2004). A *srey kroup leakkh* is obedient to her husband (Nakagawa 2006) but also presents the image of an intelligent woman. In the folk tale, Mea Yoeng helps in educating her husband to become a valued servant of the king instead of a poor fisherman. It portrays images of a wife who acts as an advisor to her husband as well as acting as his servant (Ledgerwood 1992, 1994).

New patterns of behaviour and employment

All of the traditional ideals described above form part of the foundation of women's lives. These ideals inform new patterns of behaviour in a variety of situations in the changing society (Ledgerwood 1992: 5). During the reconstruction period, the population was imbalanced due to war-related casualties (Hill and Heng 2004; Ledgerwood 1992: 7). In rural areas, women bore the burden of performing typically male tasks, including heavy agricultural work such as ploughing and construction, in addition to traditionally female duties in agriculture such as planting, transplanting, harvesting, milling and marketing (Frieson and Chan 1998; Kraynanski 2007; Ledgerwood 1992: 7). In urban areas, employment with the government and state-run factories opened up new opportunities for women (Ledgerwood 1992).

After market reforms took place in early 1990s, the growth in the industrial sector encouraged women's labour migration. Labour intensive and export-oriented manufacturing sectors, mainly garment and shoe production, grew rapidly and opened up employment opportunities for low-skilled labour (Derks

2008). Garment factories alone employed more than 300,000 workers in 2010, of which 85 per cent were women; most of the factories prefer a female work-force (Better Factories Cambodia 2010 and 2006; NGO-CEDAW and CAMBOW 2011; interviews with several mothers of factory workers in November 2011).

As rural households struggle to make ends meet, there is a strong push factor for young women to work at factories far from home. While sending unmarried daughters away from home is generally considered inappropriate (Derks 2008), economic necessity has increasingly overridden this (Aing 2004). This has resulted, on the one hand, in an increase in the number of women in waged employment (MoWA 2009; NIS *et al.* 2006; NIS *et al.* 2011), but, on the other hand, with women disproportionately occupying low-skilled and low-paid jobs, which remains a concern regarding the impact of women's employment (NGO-CEDAW and CAMBOW 2011).

Decentralization and women's participation in the public sphere

Since decentralization and deconcentration reform was put into effect by the election in 2002, the number of women in the public domain has increased, especially at the commune council level (Kim and Öjendal 2011). However, the increase in the number of women appointed does not necessarily translate into an increase in active participation. Women who are elected as council members, or appointed as assistants in charge of women's and children's affairs (Women and Children Focal Points, hereinafter 'the focal points') face many challenges and struggle to meet the expectations placed upon them (Kim and Öjendal 2011; Wild 2006).

Due to prevailing gender norms, women persistently see themselves – and are seen by men – as inferior to, and in the service of, men, which prompts many to stay home to take care of the household. Work outside of the household is generally considered to be in the male domain. In rural areas especially, women lack self-confidence and often do not vote for female candidates because they do not feel confident having women as leaders (workshop with women community leaders, 18 November 2011). Within the conservative and politicized party system, women struggle as party candidates during election campaigns (Kim and Öjendal 2011). Nevertheless, the fact that there are more women in leadership roles, and strong advocacy efforts through campaigning and the media, sends a signal to the population. It is generally accepted and viewed as a concrete sign of change; even relatively conservative villagers often say, 'women have equal rights as men now because women can take up leadership positions' (interviews in 2007 and 2011). To move beyond this first step, a shift in social norms upheld by both men and women is necessary for achieving gender equality (Wild 2006; Kim and Öjendal 2011).

Development discourse and the role of the government in gender issues in Cambodia

The ideas of gender and gender equality were brought primarily by international development agencies to Cambodia. The term 'gender' is not found in the Khmer language and new concepts carry ambiguous meanings. As in other developing countries, gender and development (GAD)[3] became an important policy agenda in the 1990s, and a gender mainstreaming framework is now an integral part of the national development strategic plan in Cambodia. In 2004, the prime minister pronounced that, 'women [are] the backbone of the economy and society' (Hun 2004) when he introduced the so-called Rectangular Strategy. The Rectangular Strategy is the political platform which recognizes the importance of fostering the environment for gender equality. The National Strategic Development Plan operationalizes the Rectangular Strategy and includes gender equality as one of the priority areas.

The Ministry of Women's Affairs (MoWA) and the Cambodian National Council for Women make up the national machinery to promote gender equality. Both institutions play central roles in implementing gender mainstreaming in all the development efforts in partnership with line ministries and donors. The ministry launched the first five-year strategic plan, Neary Rattanak (Women are Precious Gems) in 1999, and is currently implementing the third five-year strategic plan (2009–13). Civil society is mentioned as one of the stakeholders in these policy documents; however, they do not articulate or elaborate on the role of CSOs or CBOs in realizing their agendas, despite the focus placed on community participation. The ministry leads the technical working group on gender with memberships of other ministries, donors and NGOs, which helps to coordinate work on gender and facilitates knowledge-sharing within the policy framework. In one of the latest joint initiatives, MoWA published music videos that present alternative ways of understanding masculinity in Cambodia and celebrate the wide range of diverse and respectful female roles in Cambodia. The videos promote positive attitudes towards gender equality amongst young people, offering progressive images of masculinity, modern self-confident women, and equal partnerships. By intention or lack of space, however, the videos do not show images of women in decision-making roles or as community leaders.

In the vernacular, the word *yender* (gender) already implies equal rights for women. The term 'women's empowerment', or *phdal amnach oy satrey* in Khmer, means the provision of power to women (MoWA 2006). *Yender*, therefore, is inherently political as it implies activism and assumption of power by women. Comparing 2011 to 2007, I noticed that more people are aware of the term *yender* when I was interviewing both female and male leaders, and people use the term with greater familiarity.

A platform for empowerment: the case of women's community-based organizations

The livelihood improvement project entitled, 'Improvement of Livelihood of Small Farmers in Tram kok' (ILFARM-TKK, hereinafter 'the project') was implemented by the Cambodian Centre for Study and Development in Agriculture (CEDAC[4]) between 2003 and 2009.[5] The primary objective of the project was to promote ecological agriculture technologies through farm-to-farmer extension, and establishing associations that help improve the livelihood of small landholders. By the end of the project in 2009, CEDAC had facilitated 169 farmer associations with 5,087 members in a district containing 223 villages. Typically, local people establish a central farmer association and subsequently set up sub-groups according to the specific interests of the villagers. Usually, this included groups focused on saving, organic rice production, and ecological livestock raising. Groups targeting specific population segments, such as women and the very poorest, are also created depending on the leadership and interest of each village.

In 2004, CEDAC realized that the participation of women tended to be low despite the fact that women played an essential role in applying the agricultural technologies CEDAC was promoting (i.e. the System of Rice Intensification (SRI) and the improved making of compost). A study conducted in 2004 about the association building process and gender mainstreaming found that women feel more comfortable speaking out and expressing their opinions and ideas in women-only groups. In villages where female CEDAC community workers were placed, women's groups were often set up first. One of the case villages described below is a good example of this. The evaluation report also recommended that exclusive women's groups can function as an incubator to foster leadership in women, particularly if the group is set up early on, which helps prepare women to speak out and participate in the general farmer association meetings. The report also suggested diversifying the activities beyond what are typically 'suitable for women' (Kusakabe 2004).

Background to the case studies

Four women's groups in four villages within four communes were selected as case studies in Tram kak district for the original study. Instead of examining the four cases in isolation to one another, this section extracts some themes that are relevant to the message of this book.

All four villages are located between 7–20 kilometres from the district centre where the major market, public offices and NGO offices (including CEDAC and microfinance institutions) are located. The numbers of households range between 100 and 150 in villages A and C, between 250 and 300 in village B, and between 150 and 200 in village D. The majority of villagers rely on rain-fed agriculture, primarily focusing on rice cultivation, livestock and fish, and vegetables on a small scale for home consumption and cash sales. Many men are hired on occasional construction projects, such as building and repairing roads, houses and community facilities. Others work as motorcycle taxi drivers, teachers, policemen and local authorities. A significant number of young women migrate to cities to work at garment factories and provide a cash income to their rural families.

Small grocery shops, battery charging stations, and rice milling stations are common family-owned businesses in the communities. Grid-quality electricity services and piped water have not reached the villages yet. The villagers collect wood as cooking fuel and use candles, kerosene, and lead acid rechargeable batteries for lighting.

Khmers are very pragmatic in their residency patterns. They live wherever the conditions are most suitable, which changes over time (Ebihara 1977, cited in Ledgerwood 1992), but with a preference for matrilocal residence.[6] In all four villages, the woman's side of the family lives close to each other within the same village and such family ties seem to provide a background support mechanism for women. Of nine women in leadership positions in the four villages, seven are originally from the village they live in.

In agriculture, the division of labour is based on the composition of the household (Ledgerwood 1992) and is generally not based on sex, except that a few physically demanding tasks such as ploughing and making field levees typically fall to men. Labour exchange between relatives and neighbours is common during busy times of the year. Outside of cultivation, the division of labour in common activities such as fishing, gardening, taking care of livestock, collecting firewood, fetching water and other similar tasks vary slightly depending on the family composition and the availability of labour. Such divisions have not changed very much from the pre-revolutionary period as noted in Ebihara's (1968: 682) ethnographic work.

Two categories of task, however, follow strict divisions of labour by sex: household maintenance and finance. Both of these fall in the domain of women. There is an unchallenged view that household chores and caring for the elderly, sick and young siblings remains the exclusive responsibility of women and girls (Aing 2004; Velasco 2001; Ledgerwood 1992). Even though a majority of interviewees believe that both boys and girls have equal rights to education and support the idea of educating girls, families often hold their daughters back to provide for their family (Hiwasa 2010). Women are also responsible for family finances (Ledgerwood 1996: 143) and literally responsible for all financial transactions including decision-making over everyday expenditure, family savings, and the taking of loans.

Decision-making in the household, in contrast, is relatively mutual. All the households I interviewed said they make decisions together, especially about important matters concerning their families; however, it is hard to know how this plays out in practice.

Women's group activities

Women's groups usually meet once a month for one or two hours. The number of members is between 15 and 40. Each women's group has a leader, deputy and a secretary elected by the members, which demonstrates that they share a consistent formal structure. The leaders are generally the outspoken ones who have relatively good literacy and numeracy skills. The members learn various agricultural techniques such as SRI, home gardening, compost making, and livestock raising. Meetings usually start with information being shared and discussion of some hot topics such as how to cope with insects if they are destroying rice fields, how to prevent dengue fever and diarrhoea during the rainy season, incidences of violence in the village, and so forth. The common activity in all the women's groups, and the primary interest of most members, is collective savings. At every meeting, the total capital, amount collected, and current total lending are announced. The interest rate for lending is around 3–4 per cent per month and members share the capital earned through lending at the end of the term.

Practical utility and social relevance of women's groups

What makes women's group activities attractive for the members? One of the great achievements of women's groups is to improve the skills of women in

Figure 8.1 Women's group meeting in one of the case study villages.

managing their livelihoods. Given the general impoverishment in rural areas, women are typically most concerned with their hard economic reality rather than social status or gender inequality. Improving the situation in their households often requires that women fulfil practical needs such as increased productivity and crop diversification, easy access to financial resources through savings activities, and income generating activities (mainly livestock). Because women are in charge of the financial management of households, easy access to credit through group savings seems to be one of the most important and practical reasons for women to join women's groups. All of the women interviewed in the four villages mentioned it as a benefit of participating in women's groups. Most of the husbands also agreed. And even though some women's groups disbanded when outside facilitation by CEDAC was discontinued, group savings remain active.

In general, women are more likely to say they are happier after experiences in women's groups and, due to improving livelihood skills gained through group exchange and savings activities, many women are satisfied by their capability to feed their families. And as long as it helps the family to save money and provide a culturally embedded educational outlet, husbands are generally supportive about their wives' engagement in women's groups (interviews with husbands in 2007).

Indirect impacts of women's groups

This is not to say that women's groups only promote the stereotypical role of women within traditional boundaries. While the main purpose of women's groups is to improve livelihood-related skills and techniques, the opportunity presented by meeting, sharing ideas, exchanging experiences, and solving problems creates a culture of mutual help and strengthens social capital among women. Many women exhibit an overall improvement in their self-esteem by being able to improve their living standard. The non-livelihood effects are captured by various narratives highlighted by members of women's groups in case study villages (interviews and focus groups, 2007):

- women can cooperate and help each other
- women can be leaders like men
- women dare to speak out like men and can express themselves
- women can participate in the public sphere and have an understanding and knowledge of politics
- women have roles beyond the household.

Many of these elements are outlined by an enthusiastic women's group member in village A:

When I join the group, I can learn from other women; how they do things in their families ... when I join a meeting of the group, we get to know each other and improve cooperation. It's better than before. Before, I only stayed

Figure 8.2 A member of the women's group speaking out at a public meeting.

at home and knew people around the house.... But after we formed the women's group, I got to know other women and dared to make jokes with them ... when I became a member of the women's group, we could save money, exchange experiences with others, and help each other. For example, when I don't have enough crops, the members share with me. If I have crops and they don't have enough, I share with them ... we learn about food processing such as preserving cucumber. I didn't know how to do it. If the members know how to pickle the cucumber well and preserve them for a long time, they share the knowledge with me ... when I go to learn new technologies, I share what I learned with the members, and when they go, they share with me.

(Interview, July 2007)

Association building contributes to the creation of social capital, which is expressed by increased happiness, connection with other women, and sharing access to information and ideas. Before they joined, many members of women's groups perceived themselves to be like 'frogs in a well', who are blind and ignorant. Many of them articulate their constrained situation in the household with the saying *satray bongbal chongkran mun chom* (women cannot even come out from behind the cook stove), which prescribes housework as women's primary role, and undervalues their capacity for growth (Hiwasa 2010). The narratives regarding the impacts of women's groups suggest that this perception is changing as a result of having opportunities to learn new skills and techniques, sharing ideas and experiences, participating in workshops, going on exposure trips outside of their villages, and speaking out in public.

Emergence of grassroots leadership

The presence of strong female leadership seems to be an essential element for the success of and continuous development of women's groups. The characteristics of active leaders vary from community to community, but one common way in which women develop leadership motivation and skills is by reflecting on males around them and negotiating their position in relation to the male members of their families (Frieson 2001). The case studies below present two types of female leaders: those whose husbands hold political positions and those who are divorced.

Wives of local political authorities

Two female leaders of the women's group in village A are the wives of the village chief and the deputy village chief. Their marriages to men in positions of authority do not necessary translate to a leadership role for themselves, but this opens certain avenues for learning and acting. The folk tale *Mea Yoeng*, mentioned earlier, describes a wise wife who is expected to be industrious and shrewd in supporting her husband's attempts to be successful. His success is therefore facilitated and dependent on the woman behind him. One Khmer proverb relates, 'If you do not listen to the advice of a woman, you will not have any rice seed next year'. Such proverbs and tales like *Mea Yoeng* symbolize the important supporting role women play for men.

A leader of the farmer association and deputy leader of the women's group named Bopha,[7] in her late 40s, said 'I didn't join [associations in the beginning] because my husband is already a leader' (interview, July 2007). The family has five daughters, and Bopha used to sell vegetables at the nearby market and raise animals to support her family as her husband's earnings as a deputy chief is minimal. Initially, she did not take part in any group activities. Her eldest daughter had joined earlier when the group was at an early stage. Bopha eventually replaced her daughter when she married, which is how Bopha became involved. When the time came to formalize the group, Bopha was elected as a leader. Her husband was not fully supportive initially because the family income declined. As Bopha became increasingly active and busy attending meetings and training, she stopped selling vegetables and raised less livestock. He became critical about his wife not maintaining the living standard of the family but he conceded that, 'she is also the wife of the deputy chief of the village, so I cannot say anything' as he would lose face as the deputy chief if he did not support her (interview in village A, July 2007).

The leader of the women's group and wife of the village chief, a woman named Pay in her early 60s, had long desired to form an association for women but admitted that she did not know how to do so. CEDAC's project interested her and helped her to put her ideas into action. Pay leveraged the opportunity presented by CEDAC's project in the village to challenge the power structure and her husband. Even as the wife of the village chief, traditional social norms limited her capability to take any direct initiative without the intervention of an external actor like CEDAC.

Pay's husband, who is in his early 70s, has held leadership roles since 1979, and primarily acted within traditionally circumscribed gender roles and value structures, which largely deny women's participation in the public sphere. He described the changes to this situation:

> Before, women didn't have rights. But now, women have equal rights [as men]. [Women] can know and join meetings and understand. Even if they are illiterate, they can join, listen and get some ideas.... In the past, there was no plan for women [to participate in public affairs]. No plan from society for women. Regardless of whether it is far from home or close, women didn't have a chance to join.
>
> (Interview, July 2007)

It seems that it was only possible for these women leaders to organize a women's group with external facilitation and technical support. Establishment of women's groups has created a public sphere where women's participation is justified and encouraged, at least regarding improvements in their households and communities. After achieving significant improvement in their livelihood and fostering mutually supportive relationships, both the chief and deputy chief acknowledge the importance of women's participation in the development of their communities. Indeed, the village chief is proud of the women's group in village A having achieved more than women's groups in other villages (interviews, September 2007 and November 2011).

Divorcee – strong independent women

Divorced women are typically seen as lower in status and, consequently, they have to be very strong to raise their family without much male support. However, they are also more independent and free to do as they like (interview with a divorcee, 2007). The women leaders in villages B and D are divorcees who separated from their husbands due to domestic violence and raised their young children alone, which contrasts with the leadership figures presented above from villages A and C.

In village B, one of the women leaders, Veasna, raised seven children by herself. She worked as a nurse during the Khmer Rouge period and continued to work as a health-related volunteer in the village for many years. She was elected as a deputy chief of the village after four years of active engagement with the farmer association and women's group. Another leader, Saran, who is somewhat quieter than Veasna, also raised seven children by herself. She divorced around the time of the birth to her seventh child. Saran was eventually appointed leader of the women's group. She emphasized her appreciation of the women's group as a venue where women can discuss their struggles. In fact, she thinks that the women's group is one of the most important groups in the village because:

> Women face many difficulties. For example, for women who have a husband … many husbands do domestic violence, so women need to stand up for themselves. For those women who don't have a husband, it is diffi-cult to raise children alone. So we discuss, exchange ideas and find a way to solve the problems in the family.
>
> (Interview with Saran, September 2007)

As divorcees, they have struggled to raise their children and are aware of the dif-ficulties other women face with domestic violence. This generates respect for their leadership from many women in their villages.

In discussions with women leaders about the issues related to persistent domestic violence (carried out in a workshop, November 2011), it emerged that women often fear that they will be looked down upon, lose income and male labour, lose security, and will be a poor model of marriage for their children. As a result, many women do not dare to divorce but rather tend to tolerate domestic violence. Veasna, the deputy chief and the leader of the farmer associ-ation in village B regularly argued that women should not tolerate violence because of social norms, advocating instead for building self-esteem and their capacity to earn a living independently. In addition to showing solidarity towards divorcees, the female leaders in villages B and D strongly emphasize the importance of women's capacity to earn income as key to their autonomy and independence.

Women's groups as a link between the masses and other actors

Women's groups create various links between different actors: women's groups, other CBOs/CSOs, local authorities and the national government. They play a role in potentially filling the lack of 'intermediaries' in society because of their broad grassroots coverage (see Öjendal, and also Ou and Kim, this volume). As of January 2012, over 700 women's groups facilitated by CEDAC exist through-out the country. A network called the National Women Farmers' Network (NWFN) is active in organizing national-level activities involving women's groups. NWFN operates under the umbrella of the Farmer and Nature Network, the farmer association federation formally registered with the Ministry of Interior. In the first general meeting of the NWFN, organized in October 2007, the five tentative committee members were elected by the participants (see Figure 3). As of March 2012, NWFN has 390 member groups representing 8,291 women in ten provinces.

Figure 8.3 Five tentative committee members of NWFN.

The NWFN organizes quarterly meetings for capacity building and sharing best practices and other relevant information at the national level. However, the provincial and district levels are still somewhat disconnected and the results of the national-level meetings do not benefit every group member because the network lacks financial capacity to organize sufficient training and meetings (email correspondence with director of the national farmer association). Should the NWFN improve its financial capacity and organizational structure to involve other stakeholders effectively, the network has the potential to be an intermediary body (see Öjendal, this volume).

Women's groups as hubs for development cooperation

The success of women's groups has attracted attention from local authorities and the national government as well as other NGOs working in different sectors such as child issues, education and health. Many of these actors have asked women's groups to be hubs for their activities. For example, a facilitator from one local NGO focusing on teaching women about reproductive health asked the leader of a women's group to gather the members for training (this was observed in all four case study villages). Women's groups also play a role in disseminating information to all the women in the villages. Women's groups are so often used to coordinate activities with other NGOs (i.e. to collect members for meetings) that, if

Figure 8.4 A facilitator from a local NGO teaching the members of a women's group about birth spacing.

they are ever dissolved, it becomes difficult for other organizations to reach people (interview with the promoter in one of the case villages, November 2011).

Women's groups and local government

Some of the women active in women's groups and farmer associations are involved in commune monitoring committees, which evaluate development activities implemented by the commune council.[8] Committee members participate in monthly meetings of the commune council to monitor delivery of services and expenditure, as well as to help to improve the relevance, efficiency and transparency of the activities (Ngin 2008). For example, an unmarried woman in her late twenties from village A, who is the secretary of the women's group and farmer association, and another women's group leader are active members of commune monitoring committees. They are knowledgeable about current activities at the commune councils and share information from the committee meetings with neighbours and members of the women's group. Another example is the female leader of the farmer association and a deputy chief in village B, who helped the commune council to organize a village meeting to identify the priorities of the village for the annual development plan. The presence of CBO members at commune council meetings is a great opportunity for CBOs to bring up the needs identified within CBOs, as well as to collaborate with the commune council (Ngin 2008).

Women's groups and the state

The staff from the district office of MoWA and the focal points from commune councils are often invited to attend the women's forum, which is a quarterly gathering of women leaders in the district organized by CEDAC since 2007. It is not only an opportunity for female grassroots leaders to learn from each other and share their experiences, but also to advocate their needs and to be heard by government officials. These opportunities, however, do not necessarily yield tangible outcomes because there are no clear terms between the project and MoWA, and no budget allocation for collaboration on advancing women's interests to the provincial level. While more linkage with the government (see Wells-Dang, this volume), in this case between MoWA and commune councils, can strengthen the advocacy power of women's groups, without a specific framework for involvement in the project, it is challenging to forge a link between female grassroots leaders and the government officials as there is no order and budget allocated from MoWA (interview with district staff, September 2007).

Sustainability and dependency of CBOs

Sustaining externally initiated groups based on voluntary participation can be a challenge given uncertainty of funding. At the end of the project in 2009, CEDAC left one of the case villages entirely but remained engaged with new projects in the other three villages. Nevertheless, all of the women's groups continue to be active in different ways.

In the village without CEDAC's presence (Village D) after 2009, the women continued saving activities and working together without a formal structure (as of November 2011). The leader of the women's group, who is a divorcee and committee member of the commune monitoring committee, remains pivotal for various development activities in her village. In village C, however, the group was dissolved in 2009 when the leader quit due to illness and none of the other members wanted to take over her responsibilities. However, they reorganized themselves as a savings group on their own initiative in 2011. In village A, where the women's leaders are the wives of local authorities, the women continued with savings activities but shifted their focus to the farmer association, which they hoped to formally register with the Ministry of Interior, in addition to continuing their engagement with CEDAC. In village B, where divorcees are the leaders of the women's group, the activities generally focus on group savings and reducing violence in their village, and maintain their group activities.

Regardless of CEDAC's presence, each women's group has chosen how they want to continue their activities based on their leadership and interests. Even though they were externally initiated, the women's groups have demonstrated the capacity to grow on their own and engage with other stakeholders.

Blurring the gendered division of roles and social spaces

It is almost a slogan in Cambodia that 'women now have the same rights as men' when both women and men regard the changes to women's status in recent years. Practically, however, equal rights have advanced only superficially (Kim and Öjendal 2011; Hiwasa 2010) as the traditionally hierarchical nature of Cambodian society persistently prevents women from equal access to public decision-making (Malena and Chhim 2009). This begs the question: are women and men ready to go beyond the traditionally defined roles they play in public and private, within and outside the household? Although this is changing, it seems that attitudes in the personal and private domain are more resistant to change than in the public domain (interview with women leaders and government officials, 2007 and 2011). The deputy chief of one of the case villages, who is also the husband of the farmer association leader, described this change in the following narrative:

> In the past, I didn't understand [why it was important for women to join] and I was not comfortable with it. Before, if a wife went to the field, the husband wouldn't do any housework and would wait until the wife comes home.... When I was young, if a wife went out and came back, the wife and husband would have an argument [because a meal is not ready]. It's not like that now. In my village, awareness of villagers about domestic violence has increased.... If a woman goes to plough the field, the husband cooks the meals. Not so many husbands wait around for their wives to come home and do the housework.
>
> (Interview, November 2011)

Figure 8.5 A woman ploughing her land.

The deputy chief refers to ploughing, one of the farming activities that has traditionally been a man's role, and cooking and housework, which are traditionally women's roles, to illustrate the change in the attitude towards gendered roles in the private domain. In some cases, however, this change does not come easily. For example, one official of the department of Women's Affairs in Tram kak district complains that even though she has a full-time and respectable position in a public office, her husband does not help her with any housework (interview in September 2007). Changes in the private domain, particularly attitudes towards household chores, have yet to become mainstream. The burden of household duties and child rearing continue to pose a challenge for women trying to be active in the public sphere. Nevertheless, many husbands that I interviewed expressed encouragement for their wives to participate in the women's group. If their wives occasionally join an all-day workshop far from home, they would cook and take care of the children at home (interviews with husbands between July and October 2007). This attitude indicates men's growing acceptance of going beyond the traditionally defined division of public and private space.

From women's issues to gender issues

Development approaches have shifted from focusing on women, a half of the story to gender, to the social construction of gender relations which critically look at the power relationship between men and women in specific context. In practice, however, workshops about women's empowerment and gender equality typically exclude men. Organizers think that women feel more comfortable talking about sensitive issues without having any male presence. This was probably true in the beginning of the project as women were getting used to the idea of speaking out at public gatherings (CEDAC 2004; Kusakabe 2004). However, female leaders now agree that it is necessary to have male leadership present in meetings discussing domestic violence and women's leadership roles in society in order to gain understanding and support from their male counterparts. Among other things, this helps to create an enabling atmosphere for more women to become active outside of their households (workshop in November 2011).

A similar change is perhaps necessary in the content of female-oriented programming. For example, the training provided by CEDAC to the leaders of women's groups focuses on skills related to household work, such as how to balance nutrition, improve kitchen hygiene, and how to care for health issues particular to women and children. Kusakabe (2004) criticized that the content of this training is overly focused on skills that are 'suitable' for women, which perpetuates women's traditional roles in the household rather than challenging them.

Conclusion

Empowerment, in contrast to the way the term is often employed in development, is not merely capacity development in the sense of livelihood improvement.

Indeed, livelihood-focused activities of women's groups can be criticized for reproducing and emphasizing women's traditional roles in the household. However, by applying a postmodern feminist perspective to the context of rural Cambodia, this type of empowerment can be understood as a logical step for women to improve their status as well as to fulfil cultural ideals that enhance their self-esteem. By enhancing their capacity to improve the livelihoods of their households and communities, they earn respect from male counterparts and local leadership and fortify their sense of self-worth. As a result, both women and men more often proclaim that 'women can now come out from behind the cook stove' and that women are no longer 'a frog in a well'. By bringing women together (in women's groups) and cultivating social capital that provides support, female leaders are coming out to challenge the boundaries of traditional gender norms. When women themselves not only redefine what is possible for them but also become figures in case studies, one can say that empowerment is at least under way.

This success in engaging women in group activities fosters a culture of women's participation in the public realm, a place where the majority of women never had access to before. None of the female grassroots leaders in these case studies had the opportunity to be an active agent in the public sphere prior to their participation in a women's group. These women can be considered as pioneers and role models, and it will be interesting to observe whether participation will spread to women more generally (i.e. not only to divorcees and wives of village leaders).

This chapter presents women's groups as 'artificial' seeds of CBOs that not only advance women's participation in the public realm, and generate local civil society, but also provide stepping stones to national engagement (Öjendal, this volume). Women's groups at the village level can reach out and raise their agendas more broadly by leveraging, among others, the women's forum at the district level as well as national networks. Nonetheless, these groups do require some facilitation and capacity building for female grassroots leaders in order to get organized, sustain and differentiate their activities, raise funds, strengthen their networking capacity, and actively partner with other stakeholders. The growth of CBOs shows great potential in advancing gender equality from the grassroots level.

Notes

1 For a more detailed discussion of the concept of power, see Hayward (1998), and Mosedale (2005: 250). For a more detailed discussion, and definition of, empowerment, see Rowland (1997: 13), Parpart *et al.* (2002: 4), Kabeer (2003; 2005), as well as Alsop *et al.* (2006).
2 These results were published as a monograph through VDM Verlag Dr Müller in 2010 with minor edits from the original 2008 thesis accepted by the Royal Tropical Institute, Amsterdam.
3 The GAD approach focuses on the social construction of gender relations. The approach in GAD is more critical in its perspective of women's subordinate status relative to men. This is a reflection of the failure of the previously promoted approach,

women in development (WID). WID regards women's subordination in terms of their exclusion from the market and limited access to, and control over, resources (Revees and Baden 2000) but lacks consideration of power relations, which underlie the causes of such subordination.

4 The acronym CEDAC derives from the French name of the organization, the Centre d'Etude et de Développement Agricole Cambodgien.

5 It was financed by Japan International Cooperation Agency.

6 Newly married young women who live far from their own mother and relatives feel anxious and lack social support compared to those who live near their own mothers and relatives throughout their pregnancy, delivery and post-partum periods (Hiwasa 2010).

7 All the personal names used in this chapter are pseudonyms in order to protect the confidentiality of the study participants.

8 This is a good governance project supported by PACT, financed by the US Agency for International Development.

References

Aing, S. (2004) 'A Comparative Analysis of Traditional and Contemporary Roles of Khmer Women in the Household: A Case Study in Leap Tong Village', unpublished thesis, Royal University of Phnom Penh.

Alsop, R., Bertelsen, M. and Holland, J. (2006) *Empowerment in Practice: From Analysis to Implementation*, Washington, DC: World Bank.

Better Factories Cambodia (2006) *Cambodia Garment Industry Workforce Assessment: Identifying Skill Needs and Sources of Supply*, Phnom Penh: US Agency for International Development.

Better Factories Cambodia (2010) *Cambodia's Garment Industry Rebounds from the Global Economic Downturn*, Phnom Penh: US Agency for International Development.

CEDAC (2004) *Annual Report: Improving Livelihood of Small Farmers in Tram kak April 2003 – March 2004*, Phnom Penh: Centre d'Etude et de Développement Agricole Cambodgien.

Cooke, B. and Kothari, U. (2001) *Participation: New Tyranny?* London: Zed Books.

Derks, A. (2008) *Khmer Women on the Move: Exploring Work and Life in Urban Cambodia*, Honolulu: University of Hawaii Press.

Ebihara, M. M. (1968) 'Svay: A Khmer Village in Cambodia', unpublished thesis, Columbia University.

Frieson, K. (2001) *In the Shadows: Women, Power and Politics in Cambodia*, CAPI Occasional Paper 26, Victoria: Center for Asian-Pacific Initiatives.

Frieson, K. and Chan, S. (1998) *The Role of Women's Organizations in Post-Conflict Cambodia*, US Agency for International Development.

Hayward, C. R (1998) 'De-Facing Power' in *Polity*, 31 (1): 1–22.

Hill, P. S. and Heng, T. L. (2004) 'Women are Silver, Women are Diamonds: Conflicting Images of Women in the Cambodian Print Media' in *Reproductive Health Matters*, 12 (24): 104–15.

Hiwasa, A. (2010) *Now Women are Different: An Effective Strategy for Women's Empowerment in Rural Cambodia*, Saarbrücken: VDM Verlag.

Hun, Sen (2004) *The Rectangular Strategy for Growth, Employment, Equity and Efficiency in Cambodia*, Phnom Penh: Royal Government of Cambodia.

Jackson, C. and Pearson, R. (eds) (1998) *Feminist Visions of Development: Gender analysis and policy*, London: Routledge.

Kabeer, N. (2003) *Gender Mainstreaming in Poverty: Eradication and the Millennium Development Goals: A handbook for policy-makers and other stakeholders*, Commonwealth Secretariat, Canadian International Development Agency, the International Development Research Centre.

Kabeer, N. (2005) 'Gender equality and women's empowerment: A critical analysis of the third Millennium Development Goal' in *Gender and Development*, 13 (1): 13–24.

Kim, S. and Öjendal, J. (2011) 'A Gendered Analysis of the Decentralisation Reform in Cambodia', ICLD Research Report No. 2, Visby: Swedish International Centre for Local Democracy.

Kraynanski, J. N. (2007) 'Women Walking Silently: The Emergence of Cambodian Women into the Public Sphere', unpublished thesis, Ohio University.

Kusakabe, K. (2004) *Association Strengthening and Gender Mainstreaming in Improving Livelihood of Small Farmers in Tram kak (ILFARM-TK) Project*, Phnom Penh: Centre d'Etude et de Développement Agricole Cambodgien.

Ledgerwood, J. (1992) *Analysis of the Situation of Women in Cambodia*, Phnom Penh: United Nations Children's Fund.

Ledgerwood, J. (1994) 'Gender Symbolism and Culture Change: Viewing the Virtuous Women in the Khmer Society "Mea Yoeng"' in Ebihara, M. M., Mortland, C. and Ledgerwood, J. (eds), *Cambodian Culture since 1975: Homeland and Exile*. Ithaca, NY: Cornell University Press, 119–28.

Ledgerwood, J. (1996) 'Politics and Gender: Negotiating Changing Cambodian Ideas of the Proper Woman' in *Asia Pacific Viewpoint*, 37 (2): 139–52.

Lilja, M. (2008) *Power, Resistance and Women Politicians in Cambodia: Discourses of Emancipation*, Copenhagen: NIAS Press.

Malena, C. and Chhim, K. (2009) *Linking Citizens and the State: An Assessment of Civil Society Contributions to Good Governance in Cambodia*, Washington, DC: World Bank.

McNay, L. (1992) *Foucault and Feminism: Power, Gender, and the Self*, Cambridge: Polity Press.

Mohanty, C. T. (1984) 'Under Western Eyes: Feminist Scholarship and Colonial Discourse' in *Boundary 2*, 12 (3): 333–58.

Mosedale, S. (2005) 'Policy Arena, Assessing Women's Empowerment: Towards a Conceptual Framework' in *Journal of International Development*, 17 (2): 243–57.

MoWA (2006) *Gender Terminology*, Phnom Penh: Ministry of Women's Affairs.

MoWA (2009) *Neary Rattanak 3: Five Year Strategic Plan of Ministry of Women's Affairs 2009–2013*, Phnom Penh: Ministry of Women's Affairs.

Nakagawa, K. (2006) *More Than White Cloth? Women's Rights in Cambodia*, Phnom Penh: Kim Long Printing House.

Ngin, C. (2008) 'Farmers' Associations in Cambodia: Internal Functions and External Relations', unpublished working paper, Chiang Mai University.

NGO-CEDAW and CAMBOW (2011) *Implementation of the Convention on the Elimination of All Forms of Discrimination Against Women In Cambodia, 2010*, Phnom Penh: Cambodian NGO Committee on CEDAW and the Cambodian Committee for Women.

NIS, DGH and ICF Macro (2011) *Cambodia Demographic and Health Survey 2010*, Phnom Penh, Cambodia and Calverton, Maryland, USA: National Institute of Statistics (Cambodia), Directorate General for Health (Cambodia), and ICF Macro (USA).

NIS, NIPH and ORC Macro (2006) *Cambodia Demographic and Health Survey 2005*, Phnom Penh and Calverton, Maryland, USA: National Institute of Statistics (Cambodia), National Institute of Public Health (Cambodia), and ORC Macro (USA).

Parpart, J L. (1993) 'Who is the "Other"?: A Postmodern Feminist Critique of Women and Development Theory and Practice' in *Development and Change*, 24 (3): 439–64.

Parpart, J. L., and Marchand, M. H. (1995) 'Part 1 – Exploding the cannon: An Introduction/Conclusion' in J. L. Parpart and M. H. Marchand (eds), *Feminism/postmodernism/development*, London: Routledge: 1–22.

Parpart, J. L., Rai, S. M. and Studt, K. (2002) *Rethinking Empowerment: Gender and development in a global/local world*, New York: Routledge.

Razavi, S and Miller, C. (1995) 'From WID to GAD: Conceptual Shifts in the Women and Development Discourse', Occasional Paper 1, Geneva: United Nations Research Institute for Social Development, United Nations Development Programme.

Rowland, J. (1997) *Questioning Empowerment: Working with women in Honduras*, Oxford: Oxfam Great Britain.

UNIFEM, WB, ADB, UNDP and DFID (2004) *A Fair Share for Women: Cambodia Gender Assessment*, Phnom Penh: The United Nations Entity for Gender Equality and the Empowerment of Women, World Bank, the Asian Development Bank, the United Nations Development Program, and UK Department for International Development.

Velasco, E. (2001) *Why are Girls not in School? Perceptions, Realities and Contradictions in Changing Cambodia*, Phnom Penh: United Nations Children's Fund, Swedish International Development Cooperation Agency.

Wild, M. (ed.) (2006) *Gender Mainstreaming and Decentralization: An Assessment of the Process with Recommendations*, Phnom Penh: Ministry of Women's Affairs.

Zimmerman, C. (1994) *Plates in a Basket will Rattle: Domestic Violence in Cambodia*, Phnom Penh: The Asia Foundation, US Agency for International Development.

9 Mobilizing against hydropower projects

Multi-scale dimensions of civil society action in a transboundary setting

Ly Thim

Introduction

At the end of February 2000, a sudden flood swept away properties and claimed lives among the communities living along the Se San River in Ratanakiri province, Cambodia. Due to the unusual timing and intensity of the flood for the dry season, a preliminary media investigation revealed that the tragedy was caused by sudden water release from the Yali-Falls Dam, located upstream on the Se San River in Vietnam. This chapter uses a civil society lens to look at how the response to this and other harmful dam impacts have been organized at different levels. As a framework, this chapter employs an actor-oriented approach to social interfaces for analysing conflicts, in which contestation over resources, practices, knowledge and value take place between social actors. This chapter views the evolution of civil society as an organic process, in which affected people and sympathetic parties create and reinvent new types of interfaces to achieve wider representation and national voice. At these interfaces, institutions are founded and grow in scale and differentiation with the aspiration of meaningfully influencing national politics. This is a form of gradual empowerment and strategic inclusion. Because boundaries of various types continually crop up, multi-scale cooperation often becomes necessary to achieve larger goals.

Methods of data collection

This chapter is based on the results of the author's PhD research conducted for the Center for Development Research (ZEF) at the University of Bonn, including fieldwork in Cambodia, Vietnam and Laos from May 2007 to February 2008. This study mainly employed qualitative methods of data collection using semi-structured interviews, focus group discussions, informal interviewing, and participant observation, focusing on both the local level and with relevant non-governmental organizations (NGOs), international organizations and government officials in Cambodia, Vietnam and Laos. Some 45 of 60 villages located adjacent to the river were studied with a view towards uncovering community perception towards hydropower dams and their activities, focused on coping with the changing river flows and managing transboundary concerns of the entire Se San River basin. Secondary data collection on certain subjects was carried out throughout this period and continued until the end of 2009.

For this chapter only the affected communities in Ratanakiri province were selected for investigation (see geographical location in Figure 9.1). The choice of this province is instructive because (1) it borders on Vietnam and is therefore proximate to the dam site, (2) it constitutes a significant cohort of people living along the Se San River, (3) the affected population were informed about potential dam impacts by local and international NGOs as early as 2000, which has sharpened their opinions and perspectives, (4) the presence of local NGOs and the community-based Se San protection network is active in this region, and (5) the affected communities in Vietnam are not considered in the scope of this study because this study is about responses of transboundary issues where Cambodian local communities petition their own government to find solutions with the Vietnam government.

An actor-oriented approach to social interface: the landscape of civil society

In this chapter the concept of social interface in the context of civil society concerns the dynamics of negotiation between different actors operating with different agendas, and at different scales. It allows us to analyse the processes by which affected communities and civil society actors respond to development processes, develop strategies for dealing with intervening parties, and use local resources to shape the actual outcome of potential policy interventions. The actor-oriented approach, developed primarily by Norman Long, is useful in analyses of situations in which various actors repeatedly interact and fight over resource use and meaning in the development process.

Long (1989) develops the social interface perspective within the actor-oriented approach as an analytical tool for understanding cultural diversity, social cleavages and conflict inherent in the processes of development and policy intervention. Interfaces are seen as the dynamic social spaces where conflictive or cooperative interaction take place (Long 1989) and convey the idea of some kind of face-to-face encounter between individuals with differing interests, resources and power bases (Arce and Long 1992; Long 2001: 177). The study of interfaces is also concerned with the analysis of discontinuities, characterized by discrepancies in social interest, cultural interpretation, knowledge and power. These discontinuities are mediated and transformed at critical points of confrontation and linkage (Long 2001: 89). Interface analysis reveals the dynamic and contingent character of the struggles and interactions that take place, showing how actors' goals, perceptions, interests and relationships are reshaped by the process.

The flooding from the Yali-Falls Dam prompted the emergence of groups and social networks on both sides of the border, creating open interfaces around the issues of flood control, river flows, compensation and vulnerability. However, interfaces contain within them many levels and forms of social linkage and discontinuity. Because of such discontinuities in spatial and institutional coherence, the Cambodian groups grew and differentiated themselves so as to harmonize their mutual interfaces and create a more unified and powerful voice. However, as Arce and Long argue (1992: 214)

> studies of interface should not be restricted to observing what goes on during face-to-face encounters, since these interactions are in part affected by actors, institutional and cultural frameworks, and resources that may not actually be physically or directly present.

Indeed, the group formation and stabilization of interest-group interfaces was driven partly by foreign aid and accompanying frameworks of rights, empowerment, and social mobilization. So although the methodology of interface analysis focuses upon specific social interactional processes, the analysis is situated within these broader institutional and power fields (Long 1989).

Although interface interactions presuppose some degree of common interest, Long (2001) points out that interface analysis is also concerned with multiple realities made up of potentially conflicting social and normative interests and diverse and contested bodies of knowledge. Negotiations at the interface are sometimes carried out by individuals who represent particular groups or organizations. Their position is inevitably ambivalent since they must respond to the demands of their own groups as well as to the expectations of those with whom they must negotiate. One should, however, not assume that because a particular person 'represents' a specific group or institution that he or she necessarily acts in the interests, or on behalf, of his or her fellows (Long 2002). Long and Long (1992) posit that it is in the field of intervention that struggles over social meanings and practices take place. In short, one should not assume that harmonious cooperation along interfaces necessarily means an absence of conflict. Therefore, when looking at responses to development intervention one should look at who is part of the conflicts and how these conflicts are fought. Long refers to these contexts as arenas, or 'social and spatial locations where actors confront each other, mobilize social relations and other cultural means for the attainment of specific ends' (Long 2001: 59).

The concept of arena is especially important for identifying the actors and mapping out the issues, resources and discourse entailed in particular situations of disagreement or dispute (ibid.). The analysis of arenas, however, is not limited to local actors or settings only, but also takes into account distant actors and social networks which shape the social processes, strategies and actions that take place in these localized settings. Hence, studies of social interfaces analyse how matters of scale and complexity shape organizing practices of civil society. By and large, for most observers, civil society in the Cambodian context mostly refers to NGOs, local associations, and local community networks (see a survey in Öjendal's introduction to this volume). In this chapter, however, civil society may also be defined as 'organized activities by groups or individuals either performing certain services or trying to influence and improve society as a whole, but they are not part of government or business' (Jørgensen 1996). In addition, civil society is not only limited to organizations but also includes networks (see Wells-Dang, this volume).

Transboundary hydropower impacts on Se San River: the source of conflict

The Se San River originates in the central highlands of Vietnam and flows through the two Vietnamese provinces of Kon Tum and Gia Lai, before descending through two provinces in the northeast of Cambodia, Ratanakiri and Stung Treng, before finally feeding into the Mekong. A map of the Se San River is found in Figure 9.1.

The Se San River is well-known for its hydropower development potential. The total capacity of energy that can currently be generated from this river is estimated at 2,600 megawatts (MW). Six hydropower projects with a combined capacity of about 1,800 MW are located in Vietnam, while five others with a combined capacity of approximately 800 MW, are found in Cambodia.

The Yali-Falls Dam was the first large hydropower dam constructed on this river located in the territory of Vietnam. Construction of the dam, with a potential capacity of 720 MW, began in 1993. By 1996, villagers living along the riverbanks in two downstream districts (Oyadao and Andong Meas) of Ratanakiri province in Cambodia began to experience the impacts of the dam's development in the form of intense flooding as early as September 1996. During the

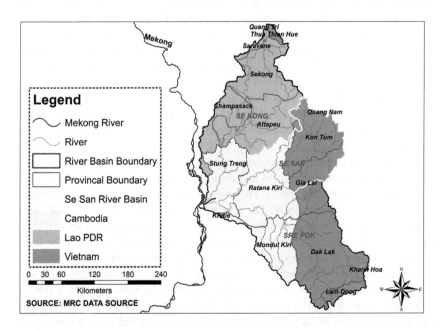

Figure 9.1 Overview of the Se San River Basin.

1996 floods the villagers were not aware of the Yali-Falls Dam construction and, at that time, according to their ethnic cultural belief, they assumed that the floods were caused by the angry spirit of the water. One villager described that, 'after the excessive floods, our villagers gathered and held a ritual ceremony to worship the river water spirit, but, not long after the ceremony we observed more changes in river water such as more extreme fluctuation, surges and dirty water' (focus group discussion, 2007).

After the 1996 events, the riverbank villagers started to search for information regarding the changes in river water particularly from communities living upstream in Gia Lai province, which is located just downstream of the Yali-Falls Dam in Vietnam. The ethnic Jaray community living in Oyadao and Andong Meas districts, who are often in contact with their ethnic minority counterparts in Vietnam for reasons relating to commodity exchange, reported that, referring to the Yali-Falls Dam, the floods were caused by large-scale dam construction in Vietnam. The information circulated within the community was that the dam builders used poor Vietnamese cement instead of Japanese cement, which caused the dam to break and flood downstream. After recognizing that changes in water flow were being caused by dam construction, the riverbank villagers in Oyadao and Andong Meas districts stopped holding ritual ceremonies. Similar cultural beliefs and practices were also abandoned by riverbank villagers in the downstream districts of Taveng and Veunsai, who became aware of the dam impacts after flood events in February 2000.

The landscape of civil society: responses to dam impacts

The February 2000 flood event caused by water release from the Yali-Falls Dam was identified as a watershed moment, in which conflict over water resource use in the Se San basin began to emerge and take shape. The main parties were the affected communities in Cambodia and the dam owners in Vietnam. The essence of the actor-oriented approach is the concept of 'agency', which attributes to the individual actor the capacity to control social relations and devise modes of coping with life (Long 2001). Because of the heterogeneity of actors involved, groups with different interests engaged in the conflict in ways that reflected their collective capacity and reach within different socio-political levels. At the local level, responses began to emerge concretely as a result of interaction between the affected communities and staff from local and international NGOs working in Ratanakiri province. The section below outlines how civil society evolves and differentiates itself from its informal roots to into formalized structures, typically graduating from groups, to organizations, to networks, and from local to national and international levels.

Creating social space to fight dam development and impacts

After the February 2000 flood events, staff from various NGOs in Cambodia began to form the Provincial Se San Working Group (PSWG) at the provincial level. Oxfam America and the NGO Forum of Cambodia (NGOF) had been paying a visit to Ratanakiri province and collaborated with the local organization, Non-Timber Forest Products (NTFP), to investigate and study dam-related impacts on river flows. The PSWG identified that human resources should be mobilized locally with technical assistance from international experts while funds could be obtained from Oxfam America through the NTFP project. Although an unlikely alliance, this cooperation set the stage for many further ones. With the availability of financial resources, a survey team was established and led by an international consultant through NTFP, which also drew in individuals from provincial government departments, such as the Agriculture, Forestry and Fisheries Department, Environment Department, and Rural Development Department. In addition to these institutional partners, indigenous peoples originating from the Se San River basin in Ratanakiri province were also involved in the survey.

The team surveyed all the villages located along the Se San River in Ratanakiri province between April and May 2000, resulting in a 43-page report entitled 'A Study of the Downstream Impacts of the Yali-Falls Dam in the Se San River Basin in Ratanakiri Province, Northeast Cambodia'. The report documented the impacts of the Yali-Falls Dam construction, including the serious consequences upon livelihoods among downstream communities in Cambodia since late 1996, and called upon the Cambodian government to begin addressing the issue and negotiate with Vietnam. Through this report, the affected communities living along the Se San River made several significant statements and issued a number of appeals to the government:

- The Vietnam Government, and those international organizations, foreign countries and companies who supported them in building the Yali-Falls Dam should take responsibility for the losses that local people have already experienced, including the loss of life and the loss of livelihoods. Compensation will need to be provided on a continual basis if the impacts from the dam are not alleviated.
- The villagers living along the Se San River would like to see the Yali-Falls Dam decommissioned, and the Se San River returned to its natural state. However, if this is not immediately possible, strong measures need to be adopted to mitigate the downstream impacts in Cambodia, including releasing water from the dam in a way that replicates natural flows.

(Fisheries Office 2000: 38)

After the study had been released, activity at local level did not stop, but actually intensified with the establishment of a local grassroots NGO called Se San Protection Network (SPN), which was to advocate for social and environmental protection for riverbank communities. SPN was formally launched in 2001 and was quickly followed by the establishment of the Se San Community Network (SCN), aimed at strengthening networking at village level in order to more effectively disseminate and collect information on dam issues and to mobilize community support for advocacy initiatives. The local-level SCN consists of focal persons and elder groups from district and village levels and, by early 2004, was active in all 60 affected villages in Ratanakiri. By the third quarter of 2005, SPN extended its working location to two other rivers (Sre Pok and Se Kong) which join the Se San River about 10 km before entering the Mekong River. As a result, SPN was then renamed the 3S Rivers Protection Network (3SPN). At the national level, 3SPN networks with various NGO partners to advocate on behalf of constituents in order to put pressure on government agencies to protect the environment and the social well-being of riverbank communities. Such advocacy includes restoration of the rivers, livelihood promotion

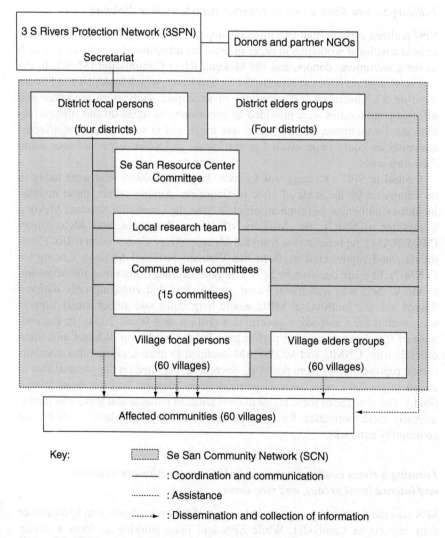

Figure 9.2 3SPN and its Se San Community Network (SCN).

and compensation for dam-related impacts. At the international level, 3SPN and its allies established ties with international organizations, which it can potentially leverage to help stop dam building and/or fight for compensation.

Strategies and choices of Se San Protection Network

SPN, and later 3SPN, have employed various strategies to influence river basin development policy at national and international levels, which I will present below.

Utilizing Se San River issues to generate transboundary dialogue

SPN realized early on that an important step for promoting their cause would be to hold a national workshop in order to draw the attention of major players, such as the government, donors, and the Mekong River Commission (MRC). In the first workshop on issues relating to the Se San River, which took place in Phnom Penh on 27 November 2002, findings of an impact study were presented and affected communities were provided an opportunity to speak up and suggest resolutions. Furthermore, the workshop was organized in such a way that affected communities could be motivated to participate and address the audience using their own words.

Central to SPN's strategy was to invite key stakeholders who were likely to be influenced by the scale of civic participation. Among others, these invitees included Cambodian government officials from the Cambodia National Mekong Committee (CNMC), the Ministry of Water Resources and Meteorology (MOWRAM), representatives from the Mekong River Commission (MRC) Secretariat, and representatives from the Vietnam National Mekong Committee (VNMC). In a late decision by SPN's Se San Steering Committee, the invitation to the VNMC was withdrawn based on the view that engaging only national figures and the multilateral MRC would help build and attract initial support from within the Cambodian government (Hirsch and Wyatt 2004). In the end, none of the above-mentioned parties attended the workshop. While Cambodian officials from CNMC and MOWRAM declined to attend, citing other commitments, representatives from the MRC Secretariat declined on the grounds that to attend might have been seen as partisan since Vietnam had not been invited (ibid.). The absence of these major players tends to indicate that there was fundamentally little motivation for listening and answering complains made by the community networks.

Forming a rivers coalition network: linking local actions to national and international arenas, and vice-versa

SPN was the first local group created as part of the civic response to hydropower dam impacts in Cambodia. While SPN had been working to form a strong network at the local level, the idea of forming a broader coalition group (eventually called the Se San Working Group (SWG)) was initiated in 2003 by a coalition of three Cambodian NGOs including SPN, the NGO Forum on Cambodia (NGOF), and the Culture and Environment Preservation Association (CEPA). The main aim of this coalition group was to strengthen inter-group solidarity and to advocate for policy reform in cross-border hydropower development in order to mitigate the negative impacts on communities living downstream of the Se San River in Cambodia. While the role of SPN was to establish and strengthen SCN at the local level in Ratanakiri province (CEPA performed similar tasks in Stung Treng province), NGOF took on the responsibility of supporting and coordinating advocacy efforts at the national level. As a result, national-level advocacy initiatives were often coordinated via NGOF. For instance, NGOF assisted local communities in sending their statement demanding resolutions and compensation to the Cambodian prime minister. Supporting this coalition group were also international NGOs and an advisory group that included many development INGOs and other water and natural resource-specific NGOs working globally.

Due to the fact that dam building grew significantly on the Sre Pok and Se Kong Rivers, which merge into the Se San before flowing into the Mekong in Stung Treng province, the 3SPN coalition, formalized in 2005, included these rivers as well. By 2007 3SPN was joined with a new coalition network called Rivers Coalition in Cambodia (RCC), in response to the expanding efforts to manage dam-related issues in the entire territory of Cambodia (see also Wells-Dang, this volume).

Building the capacity of the network

While structures for civic engagement at local level had become well-established, 3SPN believed that the next step was to strengthen and build the capacity of the local network in order to enable members of SCN to not only be able to understand and gain knowledge about dam-related issues, but also to be in a position to act upon this knowledge to claim their rights regarding shared water resources. Central to this strategy, 3SPN started developing opportunities for local network members to access training, workshops, study tours and meetings, all of which has significantly improved their ability to learn, express their opinions, organize their communities, carry out advocacy work, analyze the causes of problems that they encounter, and strengthen their planning, documentation and reporting skills. With access to this capacity-building programme, the local network members have become more confident in their capacity to leverage public forums and better able to articulate their concerns, needs and complaints to elected representatives at all levels, especially to top government officials (SPN 2005). For instance, since 2003, a statement has been drafted annually by the representatives of SCN and sent to the prime minister informing him about impacts from hydropower development and seeking solutions.

Formally researching and documenting the situation

After realizing the relevance of the plight of the Se San and other local rivers internationally, 3SPN recognized that cooperation with national and international stakeholders was critical for acquiring technical, political and legal assistance. Through the RCC, which serves as a communications platform for member groups, 3SPN and other groups have produced a number of studies and reports documenting the wide range of impacts of hydropower construction, including social and cultural aspects, economic issues and legal aspects. These studies have served as a basis for increasing public and stakeholder awareness, engaging international donors, and creating space for dialogue between Vietnamese and Cambodian actors and authorities. As mentioned above, the first example of such a documentation effort was the impact study jointly conducted with NTFP between April and May 2000. Although the physical impacts were claimed to have occurred since mid-1996, this participatory study process provided a chance for most of the population living along the Se San River to become aware of, and formally document, the widespread impacts of the dam only in 2000. These studies serve as both public awareness measures and as platforms for communities to press the Cambodian government to negotiate with Vietnam.

In this spirit, 3SPN has been strengthening the capacity of local network members by promoting community-based research for SCN teams. In order to do so, 3SPN provides training on research methodology, data collection techniques, analysis and reporting, as well as in structuring and editing reports to finalize them for publication. While the research conducted by local communities constitutes internal efforts to improve civic engagement, local members are also increasingly aware that such reports serve as evidence in ongoing disputes over the actual impacts of hydropower development and provide a basis for initiating dialogue and increasing public and stakeholder awareness (Trandem 2008).

One of their achievements is the research on 'Abandoned villages along the Se San River in Ratanakiri Province, Northeastern Cambodia', which was conducted by 17 local researchers from SCN teams between May and July 2006. With technical and financial assistance from the 3SPN Secretariat, the report was published in August 2007. It documents homesteads that have been abandoned and households that have moved away from the river to resettle on higher ground due to the degradation of fisheries and water quality, as well as fears of dam structural failures. The 68-page report, which was printed in colour in both Khmer and English, is an indication of how local community network members have built up their capacity by moving from verbal expression to formal written documents that can be used as tools for advocacy and propaganda for reaching a much wider audience. The published report also provides an empowering effect (see a similar situation in Hiwasa, this volume) that increases incentives for engaging in further civic action in other domains. Moreover, the reports can be used by SCN teams to disseminate their research findings to the affected communities along the Se San River for building awareness and raising the level of advocacy support at the grassroots level.

Outcomes and challenges

This section discusses the outcomes and challenges resulting from the advocacy work of groups responding to hydropower development in Cambodia. The two most prominent outcomes identified include the growth in community awareness and support for advocacy, and the acknowledgement of dam impacts by the Vietnamese and Cambodian governments.

Community awareness and support for advocacy

Most of the population living along the Se San River became aware of the effects of Yali-Falls Dam only after the first comprehensive impact study was carried out by NTFP in 2000. Although some upstream communities were nominally aware of the dam earlier than this study (some as early as 1996), information prior to 2000 was sketchy and not much understood. During the process of the Rapid Rural Appraisal for the study, the team methodically informed communities about the reasons for observed changes in the river flow. The study not only resulted in wider awareness about the effects of Yali-Falls Dam, it also provided a launching point for communities to appeal to government, as well as national and international agencies, to restore their livelihoods and to potentially help stop dam construction on the Se San River. Indeed, after this study, SPN was set up, and local communities, as described in detail above, began formally participating in network advocacy activities in order to receive, among other things, compensation and acknowledgment of their situation. Since 2001 at least 500 individual members from grassroots level have been involved in the network, representing hundreds more in their communities. In short, since the formation of this network, affected communities have received regular information on current events regarding the river and dam construction, and can participate in meetings, workshops and other forums that increase their legitimacy and create opportunities to advocate for intervention.

Acknowledgement of dam impacts

Through the community network's advocacy efforts, the Vietnamese and Cambodian governments eventually acknowledged that the Yali-Falls Dam has caused negative impacts downstream. According to Trandem (2008: 111–12),

> the first recognition came in the form of a verbal apology at a November 2002 conference, when a representative of Vietnam's Ministry of Industry stated 'we are very sorry for the losses of the people living downstream on the Se San River, caused, of course, by releasing water from Yali Falls dam's reservoir in February 2000' (SPN 2003). The second acknowledgement came in August 2003, when, at the recommendation of SPN, the CNMC sent a facsimile to VNMC, stating the concerns of the Se San villagers and requesting that Vietnam respond accordingly.

The acknowledgements of dam impacts described above led to two significant responses by Vietnam. First, Vietnam began construction in November 2004 of the Se San 4A re-regulatory reservoir, located about one kilometre from the Cambodian border. As stated by the government of Vietnam, the rationale behind this reservoir is to provide re-regulation of the intermittent outflow from the upstream hydropower projects, thereby providing a steady flow without daily variations into Cambodia (SWECO 2007). This meant that the erratic daily water level fluctuations, which downstream communities often complained of, would be solved; although the problem of water quality would remain. Second, an Environmental Impact Assessment (EIA) was conducted in November 2005, evaluating the past impacts and future risks of the dam on social, economic, cultural and environmental dimensions. The findings of this report, including proposed mitigation measures, were presented to the Cambodian government on 5 July 2007.

Challenges facing local communities and the Se San Protection Network

Even though the Cambodian and Vietnamese governments have acknowledged the impacts of Yali-Falls Dam on the Se San River, there has yet to be any mitigation or compensation for affected communities in downstream Cambodia, and Vietnam continues to build more dams on the river. Furthermore, access to information about ongoing hydropower development, and the river's hydrology, remains restricted (Trandem 2008). Additionally, the two successes of the community network's initiative, outlined above, demonstrate, perhaps unsurprisingly, the necessity of perpetuating and expanding upon monitoring and advocacy efforts.

First, while the construction of Se San 4A re-regulatory reservoir mitigates the most dramatic effects of hydropower development (i.e. flooding events), there is no guarantee that water quality will be improved or that Vietnam will maintain its control over water flows. Indeed, it is possible that Vietnam could turn this reservoir into an additional hydropower dam at a later date. Even though Vietnam assured Cambodia that this reservoir will only be used to stabilize water flows downstream, at least one Vietnamese news outlet has indicated that Se San 4A will become another hydropower dam with a capacity of 60 MW, scheduled for completion in 2010 (Than Nien News 2008).

Second, even though a Vietnamese EIA for hydropower development on the part of Se San River in Cambodia *has* been conducted, and demonstrates that the Yali-Falls operation *has* disrupted the river flow, there have been concerns about the process of this assessment and its eventual implementation. For example, while about 100 participants from Cambodian government agencies, and local leaders from affected areas, attended the presentation of the EIA, SPN and its allies, surprisingly, boycotted the meeting. They argued that because the EIA report was delivered to them only a week before the workshop began, they had insufficient time to review it and respond to questionable issues; additionally, they were offended that representatives of the affected communities were not invited. After the EIA was presented, disputes centred on how Vietnam would translate compensation and mitigation measures outlined in the report into real action, including setting up aquaculture programmes, developing alternative livestock and crop systems, introducing electricity supply, erecting drinking water and sanitation systems, improving healthcare infrastructure, and acting on measures to prevent erosion.

Conclusion

> The ability to influence others or to pass on a command (e.g. to get them to accept a particular message) rests on the actions of a chain of agents [...] and power is composed here and now by enrolling many actors in a given political and social scheme.
>
> (Long and Long 1992: 23)

The foregoing discussion shows that civil society, consisting of a group of local and international NGOs has, since 2000, been leveraging the community network model to advocate for policy reform and better river basin management to address the consequences of transboundary hydropower development. Since 2001 this community network has been established and strengthened through capacity building and institutionalization spearheaded by the SPN Secretariat. Over subsequent years of this network's operation, affected communities not only became well-aware of hydropower development and its consequences through information dissemination, but have increasingly joined in local, national and international advocacy efforts. Around 500 members representing affected communities have directly participated in (3)SPN's activities, calling on the Cambodian government to negotiate with Vietnam, and documenting the reasons why they deserve compensation. This is just one indicator showing how the affected communities became engaged in advocacy.

Achieving success in the long term, however, has also been furthered by the SPN Secretariat's initiatives to establish linkages from local to national and international levels, and to formalize these movements. While perhaps the minimal role of a local community network is to disseminate information on dam impacts to affected communities, and to document these impacts, SPN also helps local community network members to carry out their own research and documentation, and thereafter facilitates the distribution of these reports to concerned agencies at national and international levels in order to press Vietnam for compensation. Through SPN activities such as supporting community-based research, forums and workshops, local communities are able to speak to policy-makers at national and international level about dam impacts on local livelihoods, and to call for action at all political levels. Over time, and as other similar movements joined forces, NGO coalition networks formed to mobilize foreign NGOs and donors in Cambodia and abroad to press for policy reform in river basin management and for justice for affected communities.

Through the community network's efforts the Vietnamese government has publicly acknowledged that the Yali-Falls Dam has been negatively impacting upon local livelihoods in downstream Cambodia. These efforts have also yielded some redressive action to mitigate effects felt by local communities. Although the promised interventions have caused new concerns, the construction of the Se San 4A re-regulatory reservoir near the Cambodian border, and the formal drafting of an EIA covering the Cambodian part of the Se San River, are considered tangible achievements. These successes, however, seem to be associated with other challenges such as the failure to agree on measures for compensation for, and restoration of, local communities. While affected communities have been receiving strong support from NGOs in the field of advocacy, most affected communities continue to face problems with water quality and food shortage; there is a limit to what national NGOs and the government can achieve. On the one hand, this implies that local network activities must persist to suit other purposes. On the other hand, as long as problems persist, the drive for advocacy weakens participation of affected communities. Some affected community members perceive that the local community network has not produced any tangible results; there has been no compensation from Vietnam and livelihoods continue to be impacted by the deteriorating river system. Therefore, the challenge is to promote the living conditions and livelihoods of local communities while maintaining advocacy and pressure for policy reform.

References

Arce, A. and Long, N. (1992) 'The dynamics of knowledge: Interfaces between bureaucrats and peasants' in N. Long and A. Long (eds), *Battlefields of Knowledge: The Interlocking of Theory and Practice in Social Research and Development*, London and New York: Routledge.

Fisheries Office (2000) *A Study of the Downstream Impacts of the Yali-Falls Dam in the Se San River Basin in Ratanakiri Province, Northeast Cambodia*, The Fisheries Office, Ratanakiri Province in Cooperation with the Non-Timber Forest Products (NTFP) Project, Ratanakiri Province, Cambodia.

Hirsch, P. and Wyatt, A. (2004) 'Negotiating Local Livelihoods: Scales of Conflict in the Se San River Basin' in *Asia Pacific Viewpoint*, 45 (1): 51–68.

Jørgensen, L. (1996) 'What are NGOs Doing in Civil Society?' in C. Andrew (ed.), *NGOs, Civil Society and the State: Building Democracy in Transitional Societies*, Oxford: International NGO Resource and Training Center (INTRAC): 36–55.

Long, N. (ed.) (1989) *Encounters at the Interface: A Perspective on Social Discontinuities in Rural Development*, Wageningen, Netherlands: Wageningen Agricultural University.

Long, N. (2001) *Development Sociology: Actor Perspectives*, London: Routledge.

Long, N. (2002) 'An Actor-oriented Approach to Development Intervention', background paper prepared for APO Meeting, Tokyo, 22–26 April.

Long, N. and Long, A. (eds) (1992) *Battlefields of Knowledge: The Interlocking of Theory and Practice in Social Research and Development*, London: Routledge.

Se San Protection Network (2003) 'Learning from Transboundary Environmental Conflict' in *Mekong Update and Dialogue* 6 (4): 5–6, Sydney: Australian Mekong Resource Center.

SPN (2005) *Evaluation Report of the Se San Protection Network Project from December 2001 – July 2005*, Banlung, Cambodia: Se San Protection Network.

SWECO (2007) *Final Report: Rapid Environmental Impact Assessment on the Cambodian part of the Se San River due to Hydropower Development in Vietnam*, SWECO Grøner in association with Norwegian Institute for Water Research, ENVIRO-DEV, and ENS Consult. Hanoi: Electricity of Vietnam.

Than Nien News (2008) *Banks finance $51 millions for hydropower plant*, 16 January 2008. Online. Available at: www.thanhniennews.com/business/?catid=2&newsid=35069 (accessed 9 March 2008).

Trandem, A. (2008) 'A Vietnamese/Cambodian Transboundary Dialogue: Impacts of dams on the Se San River' in *Development*, 51: 108–13.

Part III
Traces and tendencies

10 Tracing the discourses on civil society in Vietnam

A narrative from within

Phuong Le Trong

Introduction

This chapter attempts to make light of the heterogeneous conceptualizations of civil society in Vietnam by academics, representatives of organizations, and policymakers. To this end, my goal is to sift through the various concepts of civil society and analyse their place in the state's self-image and their influence on the establishment and functioning of established and nascent non-governmental organizations (NGOs). Written in the absence of a clear legal framework in Vietnam, this discussion will focus on how civil society is rather unevenly taking shape as a consequence of discussions in the media and certain scientific circles, and of accumulating facts on the ground. A chapter on Vietnam, however, cannot ignore the role of the state, but the key issue for the understanding of the nature of the contemporary system in Vietnam is assessing the relative strength of state and society when they square off and interact (Koh 2006).

Beyond issues of consensus and dissent, this chapter assesses how social constructionism, authority and the political status quo impact on conceptions of civil society. In this chapter, the evolution of civil society is analysed through two interlinked approaches: (1) 'structural dominance', which suggests that there is little space for society to self-regulate or influence the party-state other than through approved channels in the multi-layered hierarchy (Koh 2006: 2–3); and (2) the 'accommodating state', which sees state–society relations as characterized by tolerance, responsiveness and mutual influence, and the provision of space for society to manoeuvre beyond the party-state norms and perhaps even influence them. In practice, these two approaches are not mutually exclusive. Rather, as will become clear later in the chapter, they reflect the idea that state–society relations are dialogical and that the Vietnamese state is usually 'domineering' and 'accommodating' at the same time (Koh 2006: 10). This is further clarified by the approach to the conceptualization of civil society of many Vietnamese observers, who strategically respond to and also shape definitions derived from international (Western-dominated) discourse. The current trends are mixed in their expression; the population increasingly associates civil society with associations and social organizations, but it is sometimes regarded by Vietnamese scholars as a model of democratization and/or a third sector acting in partnership with the state. Illuminating how these different models are shaped and legitimated in Vietnam is the goal of this chapter.

The paper begins with an initial linguistic analysis of civil society terminology and its embeddedness in various narratives of Vietnamese social history. The paper continues with discourse analysis of conceptions and contributions to civil society from international and Vietnamese sources.

Civil society vernacular in Vietnam

Between international scholars of civil society and local Vietnamese academics, there is a general consensus that civil society is, at the same time, both old and new. In addition to the newer wave of NGOs and other manifestations from development discourse, civil society is also viewed as a built-in element of the Vietnamese party-state system, and as a fundamental piece of traditional village and regional governance. In its abstract form, civil society is understood as an inclusive and ubiquitous part of social relations. The cleavages in the debate appear when one party or another tries to specify what is *not* civil society. In this section, I explore some of the narratives that inform this civil society debate by drawing out the various themes from Vietnamese texts and syntax.

Some Vietnamese authors argue that civil society has been demonstrably present throughout the nation's history. The director of the Vietnam Institute of Development Studies, Đặng Ngọc Dinh, a sociologist, proposes the following definition (2006: 14):

> Through research, we found that civil society in Vietnam has existed for a long time. In simple words, they are the social organizations located outside the state, and outside the activities of the market, outside the family, with the aim to connect people together to work for a common goal. In this sense, the important components of civil society are associations, groups of people, in communities, with community cohesion.

This view is based on the idea that Vietnamese civilization has integrated, and successful, social institutions based on a vernacular form of civil society. In this respect, the difference between 'traditional social space' and 'civic space' is always something tacit in the assessment of Vietnamese civil society. Some Vietnamese scholars even suggest that civil society can be considered *habitus*, in that it lies in people's unconscious cultural framework and is reproduced in an organic way (see Đặng Việt Phương and Bùi Quang Dũng: 2011). Nguyễn Mạnh Cường (2009) stresses these shared mental models and organic practices are inherent to Vietnamese society:

> according to the common notion, civil society is actually not a strange realm to Vietnam. In ancient times, the community, village, village relationships, mutual caring were clearly characterized by traditional cultural values, beliefs, community, sharing responsibility for joint tasks.

This formulation, with its nationalistic undertones, is perhaps a response to the implicit suggestion in Western discourse that civil society is part of being a modern 'civilization'.

The yearning to achieve 'civility' (*văn minh*) is idiomatically connected with the advancement of culture (*văn hoá*). The meaning of *văn minh* refers to those qualities associated with developed societies: education and health standards, economic discipline, real prospects for prosperity and political order. At the same time, the *văn minh* discourse in Vietnam links these criteria to elements of spiritual strengthening, to revitalized traditions that embody the state's newest vision of modernity. From a sociological perspective, focusing on rules that constitute a society, 'civility is critical not just for private, personal relationships, but also for relationships of power and authority' (Pye 1999: 765). Pye (ibid.: 767) suggests that a feature of Southeast Asian cultures, which applies to Vietnam, is that civility is also wrapped up in the idea of strict rules for conducting social relations. So even though civil society may be viewed as a desirable modern aspiration, its growth must contribute not as a rowdy oppositional force, but as a promoter of harmony in society.

It is, then, unsurprising that, at least within academic circles in Vietnam, there is almost common acceptance and recognition of the importance and necessity of civil society (see Bach Tan Sinh, this volume). The majority of texts appearing in recent years in Vietnam favour a definition of civil society that views it more generally as a model for the formation of something like a prosperous, idealistic, communal society. The *Communist Review* – a journal adhering largely to the official Party line – has printed that civil society is 'a society marked by autonomy, benevolence and solidarity, that promotes and serves the interests of the community; people that are not selfish individuals who are enslaved to the market, but mindful of the needs of others' (Tạp chí Cộng sản 2007).

The trend of viewing civil society exclusively as some kind of 'moral community', however, is coming under question due to globalization and the input of various international and multilateral organizations. It has been increasingly identified with formal associations and social organizations, although not necessarily with advocacy. For example, Nguyễn Thanh Tuấn (2007), a Party theorist, considers civil society as a domain of social life, including all organizations and associations with self-regulated, self-managed activities conforming to the basis of the constitution and the law, that will debate, monitor and coordinate with government. This increasing technocratic dimension of civil society is reflected in the vernacular usage and meanings of civil society.

Within Vietnamese language, and in popular usage, the concept of civil society itself has progressively experienced a linguistic shift towards a more benign understanding of state–society relationships. Currently, the term '*xã hội dân sự*' (civil society) is widespread among Vietnamese scholars. Rather than dualism and antagonism between state and citizen, it stresses the two-way interaction between state and society. This interaction, mediated by civil society, is based on the principles of community spirit and communitarianism rather than competition. More concretely, civil society is meant to serve first and foremost as an interlocutor between legal persons, their mutual relations, and the state. In contrast to this, the formerly popular term '*xã hội công dân*' (citizen society, relating to Habermas' concept of '*Bürgergesellschaft*') connotes a more confrontational relationship between state and the politically mature 'công dân' (citizens). The effect of this linguistic shift has been to reduce the spirit of individualism and liberalism of 'civil society' found in '*xã hội công dân*' by assigning to 'civil society' the aspects of community spirit and harmony implied by the term '*xã hội dân sự*'. By employing '*xã hội dân sự*' in their work, Vietnamese scholars and journalists implicitly emphasize this positive meaning of civil society.

In practical usage, the more benign term '*xã hội dân sự*' is often conceptually boiled down to a more technically-oriented reference to civil society organizations (CSOs). This was demonstrated in the report, 'Image of civil society organizations in the Vietnamese press', published by the Institute of Social Studies, Economics and Environment on 19 December 2011. The research was carried out with several newspapers and internet portals covering issues on Vietnamese NGOs and CBOs, and international NGOs. According to the results,

> in a year, the media carried 472 news articles referring to these organizations. The contents of the news confirmed the usefulness of CSOs for the people, and viewed CSOs as having a complementary role to the state in social activities, policy debates, as well as monitoring and inspection activities of state agencies.

Although this report covers CSO activities and some of their confrontational activities, the word 'civil society' is rarely used in comparison to the more concrete 'civil society organizations'.

Intellectuals in Vietnam, in contrast, do not shy away from the terminology of civil society but instead often bury the definition in moral platitudes and ideals of virtuousness, in which civil society is repositioned as an abstract force that does not imply negative feedback between the state and society. Đặng Ngọc Dinh (2006), for example, suggests that civil society is more of a 'forum', in which state and market activities are facilitated by social enforcement and by taking care of the moral aspects of society. He writes,

> Civil society supports people to follow the law and reflects the aspirations of the people. If government institutions act on the basis of law, the market operates according to the pursuits of profit, civil society is still subject to the law and to the market, but it enforces the moral, promotes the humanity and the community.
>
> (Đặng Ngọc Dinh 2006)

He cautions, however, that 'one should not regard civil society as in opposition to the government or assume that the government does all the work so that people do not need civil society. One can say, civil society and government are complementary to each other' (ibid.). In an interview with the magazine *Tuổi Trẻ cuối tuần*, he answered the question, 'Why has civil society long been considered a sensitive issue, and not discussed in VN?'

> The reason is that in some countries there are some attempts to use the civil society opponents of the government to create instability. So some argue that if we continue research and dissemination of civil society in Vietnam, it would proceed to tap the opposition to the government. One should understand that civil society is a diverse field and we need to examine its negative and positive sides. Even people also know very little about civil society. Therefore it is necessary to study and understand the role and impact of civil society, first of all the scientific research community, managers.
>
> (Đặng Ngọc Dinh 2006)

In this answer, Đặng Ngọc Dinh hints at some of the contradictions in the civil society debate in Vietnam that I have traced in this section. Civil society is, on the one hand, viewed as a moral imperative in the context of civilization, that has historical roots and should be understood in its vernacular context. On the other hand, the potentially critical standpoint of civil society can be considered a political liability and must be carefully managed. In this regard, for the state, which is strategically interested in reinforcing its grip on society, civil society presents both opportunities and risks. As I present below, the state has two broad approaches for getting the most out of civil society: structural dominance and accommodation. Although these two approaches oftentimes overlap and complement each other when looking at the dynamic on the ground, it is instructive to look at which approaches inform the arguments of different parties under certain conditions, which is a task I turn to now.

Structural dominance in Vietnamese state action

Vietnam has been represented as a country in which the monopoly on decision making is firmly held by the state and bureaucracy. While *đổi mới* beginning in 1986 represented a turning point in state–society relations, these changes were generally limited to the economic field (e.g. rights of free enterprise, repealing economic prohibitions, privatization of state-owned enterprises, etc.). Despite policies like that of 'socialization' (see Waibel and Benedikter, this volume), many cultural and social institutions are still managed, or remain under direct control of, the state. What can be said of *đổi mới* is that it stimulated expectations for, and academic literature on, political change in the field of Vietnam studies. Although there is no reading consensus, one concept widely drawn from concerning post-*đổi mới* state–society relations in Vietnam is the idea of the 'dominating state' (Kerkvliet 2001: 242) or 'mono-organizational system' (Thayer 2009: 12). Together, these terms acknowledge the Party's hegemonic control over state institutions and other organizations through penetration by Party cells and committee structures. If one abides exclusively by this view, there is little space for manoeuvre beyond the scope of the Party-led command structure. The composite terms 'mono-organizational socialism' and 'bureaucratic socialism' are typical characterizations of such systems, indicating that individuals and social organizations are essentially compelled to become members of the state structure. Political participation can thus be restricted to feedback on state policies through official channels, such as mass organizations and a few other acceptable associations.

These state-dominated organizations, which can be viewed as forms of 'semi-civil society' or 'quasi-civil society', serve as channel for state control as well as a tool for, or source of, legitimation. The rise of CSOs in recent years, and the skills and strategies utilized by CSOs in relation to the state, are in part dependent on the stage of social mobilization and political transition. The mass organizations are essential to the Party because they provide an immediate force for mobilization, and they enable the Party to control key social groups. The Party, in fact, places members from the Central Committee in leadership positions to steer the organizations. But these organizations are not just used for the purpose of mobilization and control. They also serve a semi-democratic function by providing social groups with a channel for expressing their interests, albeit in a tightly controlled manner. These organizations act as the Party's ears in society. Particularly from a Western civil society perspective, this control structure inevitably raises questions about civil society's autonomy from the state. Nascent organizations are typically 'absorbed' into the state early on through the various processes associated with official registration. This lack of granted autonomy may have prevented the development of certain groups, particularly the opposition, but it has also proved decisive for groups as they grow and differentiate. This was the case for what was Vietnam's first independent policy-oriented research think tank. In September 2007 the Institute of Development Studies, a non-profit organization, was founded by an interdisciplinary group of influential academics and intellectuals. Only two years later, the board decided to close down the institute as a protest against Decision 97/2009/QD-TTg. This decision 'allows' (*cho phép*) people to associate in restricted ways, and civic organizations to be established under specific conditions (see Wischermann 2011: 391). As a result of this decision the institute encountered state regulations that the founding members considered counterproductive and in conflict with the functioning of an autonomous body. This question of autonomy becomes even more critical in parts of society where the state has an abiding interest in maintaining control.

Most commonly, organizations and associations operating in the areas of culture, education and community tend to be at the centre of the government's 'nationalization' (*nhà nước hoá*) and 'administration' (*hành chính hoá*) polices. These two terms blur the distinction between intervention (the official language says 'state management' of ministries and departments) and the delegation of functions to professionals attached to various social institutions. Professionals can find themselves nominally given posts, only to be continually directed how to carry out their work. This current situation for many such organizations can be characterized similarly to that of the state-owned enterprises and collectives in the subsidization period before *đổi mới* (see Pistor and Le Thi Quy, this volume). For some other sectors, however, *đổi mới* entailed a detachment of state management functions from production and business functions.

The disparity in expressions of *đổi mới*-period liberalization for certain actors compared to others has implications for the state–civil society divide because it illuminates the strategic considerations in the state's willingness to give up social control. According to Koh (2006: 21), state–society relations are 'between actors and institutions of governance on the one side, and the subjects of governance on the other side, but the distinction between them is not always clear-cut'. In Vietnam, one finds a lack of clear delineation between state and society (Kerkvliet 2001; Heng 2004), which is consistent with other communist regimes. The Vietnamese state equipped itself with a network of mass organizations placed under the umbrella of the Vietnam Fatherland Front, while officially prohibiting autonomous organizations. For a while, these networks ensured the Party's penetration into every sector and level of society, including the private lives of the individual (Heng 2004: 145; Koh 2006: 2). The intention of the Party to play an interventionist role is reflected clearly in existing laws (Landau 2008: 251). Outside observers have frequently commented on this aspect of Vietnamese society. Koh (2006: 7) argues that, because the state's machinery brings 'the party-state into every home', a private sphere independent from the state does not exist. Due to the lack of distinction between the private and public realms, Drummond (2000: 2377) finds it difficult to detect a public sphere in Vietnam, at least when applying a Western concept of civil society. She also sees little in the way of an historical basis for civil society, suggesting that the 'social vacuum ... has been filled by the authority of the emperor/state with little place for Western-style public discussion or expression' (Drummond 2000: 2512382). The Vietnamese state can be imagined as reaching down into communities, intervening in a 'top down' manner to manipulate or plan society. Civil society, in this vertical topography, appears as the middle latitude, the zone of contact between the 'up there' state and the 'on the ground' people, snug in their communities. Following Leninist doctrine, the state is seen as the organismic human body, possessing such 'higher functions' as reason, control, and regulation, guarding against the irrationality, passions, and uncontrollable appetites of the lower regions of society (see also Reis, this volume).

To provide legitimacy to this top-down, patriarchal relationship between state and society, a narrative of the rule-of-law state is often referenced by Vietnamese academics. The terminology 'rule-of-law' was officially used for the first time in the documents of the Eighth Party Congress in June 1996, as documented by social researcher Trương Trọng Nghĩa (2004). His impressions from this event, and subsequently, is that,

> The rule-of-law state is a democratic state, and vice versa. It is understood to be a state embodying the law, but also abiding by the law. It makes laws to govern relations between the state and its citizens, state-to-state relations,

the relationships of citizens to one another, and the state itself (in contrast to the feudal state, which makes laws to govern others).

As the importance of a rule-of-law state increases apace with economic liberalization, an expectation arises that civil society has the basic building blocks to take shape. Following this line of thinking, Trần Ngọc Hiên (2008), a social scientist who often publishes in the *Communist Review*, argues that, in the 'gradual reorganisation of the apparatus according to the nature of the "rule-of-law"-state of the people. . . ., civil society's role as controller of the state is a crucial factor'. Indeed, he goes as far as suggesting that:

> Where the market economy is, there must be also the 'rule-of-law'-state and civil society. These three parts build up a system of political and economic institutions. However, the completion of the institutional system is based entirely on the interaction between the three parts. This is the process of democratization.'
>
> (Trần Ngọc Hiên 2008)

Trần Ngọc Hiên (2008) notes that the switch to a market economy in 1986 had 'set the first brick' of democratization, followed by the 'second brick' with the defining of the rule-of-law in 2001; the Party, however, has so far has 'not dared to set the third brick (civil society)' to 'provide the full basis for a relationship between the political and economic institutions of our country'. Trương Trọng Nghĩa (2004), foreshadowing this state of affairs, warned that economic liberalization does not automatically reconcile the inherent 'differences between the socialist rule-of-law state and a bourgeois rule-of-law state'.

In practice, the Vietnamese party-state asserts the right embodied in a socialist rule-of-law state to regulate, in a top-down manner, state–society relations (which includes civil society). In particular, the autonomy of civil society is not viewed as an important concern, which leads to a more proactive form of state involvement and intervention in civil society. By extensively drawing on narratives of harmony and organic partnership between the party-state, the economy and society, the rule-of-law state aims for all-encompassing national unity enforced by hegemony. For this endeavour, civil society serves as an important legitimating sphere. The activities of civil society, if high consensus can be achieved, would strongly promote the mobilization of energy, initiative and the ability to initiate a very wide variety of achievements for the development process, and thus will implicitly reinforce the power and the presence of the state, as well as strengthening national unity. But it should be emphasized that this consensus can only be achieved through the establishment of hegemony over civil society by strategically configuring the legal and practical conditions by which CSOs operate, and voluntary activities orient themselves (Trần Hữu Quang 2010: 22). In other words, consensus and legitimacy are sought by forming a state-centred ideology around civil society. The hegemony, whether cultural or social, is thus built on consent as well as coercion.

This approach to long-term control, as suggested by Koh (2006: 10), is referred to as 'accommodation'. More closely reflecting 'functional substitution' than command and control, the 'accommodating state' makes use of CSOs to meet social needs while, at the same time, exploiting them to maintain (or even reinforce) state rule. As I demonstrate below, Vietnam is also embracing the idea of civil society in a manner that retains and reproduces the socialist system.

The accommodating state

Western scholars tend to assume that, since *đổi mới*, there is room for dialogue and negotiation between the state and civil society (Heng 2004: 148). Because the Party's grip on society has weakened in some respects (see Thayer 2008: 5), this conclusion is not altogether surprising. However, the ultimate outcome of the contest between state and society for space is more dynamic than many observers perhaps initially believed. According to the accommodating state approach (Koh 2006), there is a constant interaction that takes shape through resistance or coercion between residents, local officials and the party-state. In searching for suitable descriptions for this dynamic in Vietnam, Womack (1987) has characterized the party-state as being 'mass regarding' or 'quasi-democratic', a view that gained backing when observers began noting that the state tolerated some participation by organizations outside the mono-organizational framework in the 1990s (Koh 2006: 3). One of the primary explanations for this phenomenon is that the state increasingly found itself with inadequate resources to implement its policies, which led to compromises regarding the engagement of CSOs. Proponents of this interpretation suggest that not only must the state tolerate more activities, but that social groups resist state control to shape society and influence state policy. White (1985, in Heng 2004: 147) calls attention to situations where pressure from various spheres of society has led to significant policy changes. In this section, I demonstrate how this contention has been conceptualized by academics and policymakers, and how the state attempts to transform its weakening command-and-control structure into an opportunity.

The dominant representation of civil society since the mid-2000s has aimed at pre-empting the idea that civil society might be oppositional or countervailing, instead preferring to render it as a modern and positive force that works with the state for development. Distancing civil society from oppositional content, Lê Bạch Dương (2008), a sociologist, suggests that the creation of associations in the field of economy, science and technology, and the service sector after *đổi mới*, have led to the establishment of a so-called 'third sector'. According to the essence of these representations, civil society is not a 'threat' to the government, nor is acting 'against' the government, but instead is able to play a complementary role in addressing the challenges the country is facing. The first priority remains promoting economic development, which may potentially, in time, lead to political development. Võ Khánh Vinh (2008: 24), a sociologist, for instance, argues that, 'the development of a market economy creates the foundation, especially the economic basis for the implementation and operation of civil society'. He stresses that, in particular, 'the rapid changes of our country to a modern civilized market economy are the most important prerequisites for the formation, mobilization and development of civil society' (ibid.: 32). Echoing this sentiment at the policy-maker level, the former National Assembly Chairman Nguyễn Văn An (2007) declared that, 'Moving towards a society of the rule-of-law means moving towards a civil society with a very high extent of self management, self-organization of the people. Then the state will get ever smaller, as Marx said.' In other words, only in a stimulating economic environment can civil society move from its position of partnership and subservience as a 'third sector' to 'full-fledged' civil society in a normative democratic sense (Võ Khánh Vinh 2008: 24–5).

Establishing civil society as a partner in development, however, is not a concrete activity that the state can undertake. References to the term civil society (*'xã hội dân sự'* or *'xã hội công dân'*, see above) are only reluctantly used in Party and state documents but, as suggested by Nguyễn Thanh Tuấn (2007), a Party theorist, the state and the Party are interested in 'establishing an institutional and legal basis for civil society'. In other words, the economic liberalization of *đổi mới* has obliged the state to work quietly to provide a platform for civil society, without overtly promoting it.

> The socialist-oriented market economy, based on the socialist rule-of-law-state and advancing toward integration into the international economy, has and continues to engender many ideas, even controversial ones for society about the role of civil society organizations in relation to the Communist Party and the rule-of-law.
>
> (Nguyễn Thanh Tuấn 2007)

The state's accommodation to civil society, and toleration of potentially destabilizing ideas mentioned by Nguyễn Thanh Tuấn, are linked to the need for political legitimacy in a liberal market economy. In a limited way, the state's commitment to economic growth and modernization has also compelled it to provide reluctant support to some emerging ideas and practices associated with civil society. Concerning this trend, Koh (2007: 235) has suggested that indeed, 'the state has conceded more ground to society by relaxing a wide range of controls'. The development of professional associations and other types of charity CSOs, for example, is seen as part of a modernizing market-based society (see Bach Tan Sinh, this volume).

Reinforcing the socialist rule-of-law-state, however, entails distinguishing between the political system and civil society, and laying out some form of democratic relations between them. An article that can be considered official, which is published on the website of the Ministry of Justice, states:

> Democratization in the socialist rule-of-law-state requires the diversification of forms of public organizations, the diversification of forms of democratic practices of the people. The people are not merely exercising their role as

subjects through the state's institutions and political system but also can perform their democratic rights through social organizations, professional industry, associations, and religious communities. Therefore, the political system has to reform relations and modes of their impact on civil society and create conditions for civil society formation and development.

(Nguyễn Xuân Tùng 2011)

Although forms of democratic participation appear to be officially sanctioned in such statements, in practice social forces may influence policy only through organizations and mechanisms that the state itself dominates. Dixon (2004: 25–6) regards this as a form of 'soft authoritarian-corporatism', in which the state's approach to society is based more on incentives and coercion than direct intervention.

This approach also characterizes the recent efforts at strengthening the rule-of-law by restructuring institutions so that they support integration into the international market. For example, instead of using state power to spur production and clamp down on corruption, the state has generated measurable indices to be used for creating transparency and competition. In 2006 the Vietnam Chamber of Commerce and Industry started surveying competitiveness in the provinces through the Provincial Competitiveness Index (*Chỉ số năng lực cạnh tranh cấp tỉnh*). From a position of scepticism and opposition at the beginning, provinces now view improvements in index rankings as a goal to strive for. In 2011 they launched a new survey on ministerial-level implementation of business laws, called the Ministerial Effectiveness Index (*Chỉ số hiệu quả hoạt động xây dựng và thi hành pháp luật kinh doanh*). The first report about these indices was released in December 2011. Such indices are presented as a tool for measuring local economic mobility and state efficiency and transparency. However, this type of 'mobilizational corporatism' (Kerkvliet 2001: 243) or 'mobilisational authoritarianism' (Turley 1993: 269–70) could also be viewed as a way for the state to push a top-down agenda while simultaneously prestructuring and controlling avenues for public criticism.

According to this logic of 'soft authoritarianism', civil society and the state comprise a general social system of a country in which the state is to conduct coercive force and civil society is to participate in the implementation of this hegemony by creating consensus among members of society. By definition, civil society activities are thus not directed against the state since the state and (civil) society are not to be conceived as an antagonistic pair. Based on the writings of many Vietnamese academics, although civil society is theorized as offering a source of 'critical feedback' (*phản biện*), it is nonetheless understood in this sense as a 'partner' of the state. Tương Lai (2005), a senior sociologist, emphasizes this involvement of the people vis-à-vis the state, suggesting that:

civil society is the equal partner of the state, and not the tail of the state. The essential idea is that the state provides the conditions for people to be truly involved in planning, policy implementation and monitoring the state; to exercise social criticism towards the state, including evaluating the quality and behaviour of government officials.

The essence of the accommodating state is hard to place in such statements, but it is implied that civil society is empowered on one level to provide critical feedback, but in the role of partner rather than in the role of opposition. How the state practically envisions this taking place has been discussed above in detail, but in general it includes creating bureaucratic transparency and proximity, and channelling feedback in a moderated manner through various sanctioned organs. To some degree, this has occurred because of the state's diminishing capacity for direct control and the need for different strategies to shore up and legitimize continued structural dominance through state–society relations.

New paths in Vietnamese civil society

Vietnam finds itself in a struggle to conceptualize the state–society relationship since *đổi mới*, with one of the main arenas being that of civil society. Indeed, Vietnam is as much in the midst of an economic transformation as in the middle of a dynamic dialogical process, wherein the relative strengths of state and society remain contested. Although it is still an abstract and fluid concept to the majority in Vietnam, civil society is becoming a new reference point for understanding, and for studying, changes in the country's political culture. The advent of *đổi mới* has meant a circumscribed role for the state in certain domains but, as I have argued here, the state still has many tricks up its sleeve for reinforcing its position and leveraging soft power. This is particularly visible in the academic and policymaking debates about civil society which I have reviewed above. In Vietnam, state agents tend to prefer a conceptualization of civil society in the abstract (i.e. connotations of modernity, civility, development) and support the controlled rise of CSOs, particularly those providing specific technical services that can be transparently registered and provide bureaucratic access to local areas. However, there is more hesitation and equivocation about identifying civil society as a national-level movement, which seems to imply opposition to the state. It is somewhere between the state's dissolution of power and the agency of new forms of civic engagement that the unsteady view of civil society in Vietnam begins to emerge. This process of negotiation, to be sure, is also informed by historical views of civil society and the contemporary discourses.

Indeed, the civil society discourse in Vietnam traverses the pre-modern, a society based on vernacular understandings, through socialism, to a modern orientation on civil society including touches of democratization. The expectations of civil society are growing, and with this comes a struggle to appear mature, sophisticated and interactive, able to establish mutually respectful, if contentious, state–society relations. Put in perspective, the state finds itself trapped in between the need for popular legitimation and its historically-rooted and ideological position of control. By being domineering and strategically accommodating at the same time, the state manages to remain a dominant force driving the country. As a result, the distinction between the meaning of 'civil society' in its technical dimension of service delivery by local development NGOs, and in its political dimension of a 'public space [where] Vietnam's one-party state can be challenged by the non-violent political mobilization of ordinary citizens' (Oscar Salemink referenced in Thayer 2009: 12), seems to get absorbed in the debate around the harmony between the state and the civic sphere in accordance with the principle of modern socialist development.

Most Vietnamese scholars see civil society as a kind of buffer between the low and the high, an imagined middle zone of contact or mediation between the citizen, the family, or the community, on the one hand, and the state, on the other. This is exemplified by the sociologist Hồ Bá Thâm (2009):

> in the strict and modern sense, we just have a proto civil society; only if there is real rule-of-law-state, civil society can develop. There is no legitimate state power without strong civil society and vice versa. In postmodern times, civil society is no longer based on individual rights anymore, but mainly based on social organization. With the socialization process increasing, society requires civil society and it will actively build civil society.... Civil society functions as a bridge between the individual and the state.

However, practically speaking, civil society is now increasingly less of a buffer between state and society in terms of social welfare provision and economic development. Approaches which predominantly focus on the formal institutions of politics turn out to be incomplete for the provision of a deeper understanding of state–society relations. As Heng (2004: 147) notes, 'they pay little attention to discrepancies between what the state has proclaimed as policy and what people in society actually do'. Indeed, civil society (in aggregate) seems to have a subtle stake in the transformation of political culture. Contributing to this is also an increasingly strong connection between international and Vietnamese civil society. For example, international media and attention (including the Vietnamese diaspora) have begun to play a more focused role in various contentious activities.

Changes in Vietnamese conceptions of state–society relations are also being strongly informed by emerging local dynamics. As Thayer (2009: 5) argues, 'the all-encompassing matrix of party hegemonic control over society has been continually challenged from below'. In particular, this shift in the cultural environment and power structures is being prompted by actors such as the mass media, intellectuals and cultural groups, as well as the organized and/or spontaneous appeals of individual persons. Reflecting the uneasy position of the state vis-à-vis these groups, Vũ Duy Phú, a sociologist, proposes the concept of a 'knowledge-based civil society' (*xã hội dân sự thông thái*), based on building the 'rule-of-law-state of the people, by the people and for the people', under the leadership of the Party. This includes striving to become a 'knowledge society' whose members are well-educated, take part in voluntary activities for the common good, and build good social governance by incorporating themselves into state functions through organizational channels, in compliance with laws. As such, it would fulfil well the role of an equal counterpart, equal partner of the rule-of-law-state. Civil society thus becomes a factor in carrying out 'socialization policy', counteracting the ill effects of an unscrupulous market, and being an agent of the state's 'soft power' to build a modern society (Vũ Duy Phú 2008: 345–55).

All of these discourses and practices from 'below' exert influence on the country's political culture and pose challenges for the state in some way. Political culture plays a significant role in the political transition as ideology, beliefs, values, and other cultural factors underlie political relations, behaviours and institutional reforms. The change of political culture is both a necessity for, and in turn a result of, the development of civil society. The state is interested in a sort of 'compromise' that would help to bring balance into the political and cultural discourse around civil society (see also Wischermann 2011: 25, and Hannah 2007: 174), but has shied away from granting autonomy or creating relations based on negative (oppositional) feedback. Nevertheless, the growth and differentiation of civil society is increasingly placing emphasis on the promotion of civic awareness, the internalization of foreign civil society values and ideals, participation and participatory culture, and on the capability to check the power of the party-state through various means. The party-state increasingly has no choice but to further accommodate civil society in ways that may begin to erode state dominance, or to hold on stubbornly to the declining model of a 'strong rule-of-law-state'. Whether the state is up to this task, and whether the economy and social sphere fall in line with the state, is still very much up in the air.

References

Cao Huy Thuần (2004) 'Xã hội dân sự?' [Civil Society] in *Tạp chí Thời đại mới* [New Age – Vietnamese Review of Studies and Discussions], 3 (November). Online. Available at: www.tapchithoidai.org/ThoiDai3/200403_CHThuan.htm (accessed July 2012).

Đặng Ngọc Dinh (2006) 'Đừng sợ xã hội dân sự!' [Don't be afraid of civil society!] in *Tuổi trẻ cuối tuần* ['Youth' weekly], 21 May. Online. Available at: http://tuoitre.vn/Chinh-tri-Xa-hoi/138839/Dung-so-xa-hoi-dan-su.html (Accessed July 2012).

Đặng Việt Phương and Bùi Quang Dũng (2011) 'Các tổ chức xã hội tự nguyện ở nông thôn đồng bằng sông Hồng: Liên kết và trao đổi xã hội' [Voluntary civic organizations in the Rural Red River Delta: Networking and Social Exchanges] in *Tạp chí Xã hội học* [Sociology Review], 4 (2011), Hanoi: 31–45.

Dixon, C. (2004) 'State, Party and Political Change in Vietnam' in D. McCargo (ed.), *Rethinking Vietnam*. New York: Routledge: 15–26.

Drummond, L. (2000) 'Street Scenes: Pratices of Public and Private Space in Urban Vietnam' in *Urban Studies*, 37 (November): 2377–91.

Drummond, L. and Thomas, M. (eds) (2003) *Consuming Urban Culture in Contemporary Vietnam*, London and New York: Routledge.

Hannah, J. (2007) *Local Non-Government Organizations in Vietnam: Development, Civil Society and State-society Relations*, Seattle: University of Washington.

Heng, R. H.-k. (2004) 'Civil Society Effectiveness and the Vietnamese State – Despite or

Because the Lack of Autonomy', in L.H. Guan (ed.), *Civil Society in Southeast Asia*, Singapore: ISEAS Publications: 144–66.

Hồ Bá Thâm (2009) 'Xã hội dân sự, tính đặc thù và vấn đề ở Việt Nam' [Civil Society, Characteristics and Issues in Vietnam] in *Tạp Chí Sinh Hoạt Lý Luận* [Magazine of Debates], 1. Online. Available at: http://chungta.com/Desktop.aspx/ChungTa-Suy Ngam/Van-Hoa/Xa_hoi_dan_su_tinh_dac_thu/ (accessed July 2012).

Kerkvliet, B. J. T. (2001) 'An Approach for Analysing State-Society Relations in Vietnam' in *Journal of Social Issues in Southeast Asia (SOJOURN)*, 16 (2): 238–78.

Koh, D. W. H. (2006) *Wards of Hanoi*. Singapore: Institute of Southeast Asian Studies.

Koh, D. W. H. (2007) 'Modern Law, Traditional Ethics, and Contemporary Political Legitimacy in Vietnam' in S. Balme and M. Sidel (eds), *Vietnam's New Order: International Perspectives on The State and Reform in Vietnam*. New York: Palgrave Macmillan: 217–36.

Landau, I. (2008) 'Law and Civil Society in Cambodia and Vietnam: A Gramscian Perspective' in *Journal of Contemporary Asia*, 38 (2): 244–58.

Lê Bạch Dương (2008) 'Xã hội dân sự khỏe, nhà nước khỏe' [Healthy civil society, healthy state] in *Pháp luật* [Law], HCMC, 23 April. Online. Available at: http://sinhviennganhang.com/diendan/showthread.php?t=7690 (accessed July 2012).

Nguyễn Mạnh Cường (2009) 'Xã hội dân sự Việt Nam' [Vietnamese Civil Society] in *Tia Sáng* [Tia Sáng Magazine]. Online. Available at: www.tiasang.com.vn/Default.aspx?ta bid=62&CategoryID=3&News=3053 (accessed July 2012).

Nguyễn Thanh Tuấn (2007) 'Xã hội dân sự: từ kinh điển Mác – Lê-nin đến thực tiễn Việt nam hiện nay' [Civil society: From classical Marxism-Leninism to Vietnam's present conditions] in *Tạp chí Cộng sản* [Communist Review], 132 (12). Online. Available at: www.tapchicongsan.org.vn/Home/Nghiencuu-Traodoi/2007/451/Xa-hoi-dan-su-Tu-kinh-dien-Mac-Lenin-den-thuc.aspx (accessed July 2012).

Nguyễn Trung (2006) 'Bàn về Vốn xã hội' [On social capital] in *Tạp chí Tia sáng* [Tia Sáng Magazine], 22 April. Online. Available at: www.tiasang.com.vn/Default.aspx?tab id=87&CategoryID=16&News=1777 (accessed July 2012).

Nguyễn Văn An (2007) 'Xã hội dân sự trong mắt chuyên gia' [Civil society seen by professionals] in *Pháp luật* [Law] HCMC, 31 December. Online. Available at: phapluattp. vn/206987p0c1013/2008-xa-hoi-dan-su-trong-mat-chuyen-gia.htm (accessed July 2012).

Nguyễn Xuân Tùng (2011) 'Xã hội dân sự trong quá trình đẩy mạnh xây dựng nhà nước pháp quyền XHCN tại Việt Nam' [Civil Society in The Process of Building the Socialist Rule-of-Law-State in Vietnam], Ministry of Justice, 5 December. Online. Available at: http://moj.gov.vn/ct/tintuc/lists/nghin%20cu%20trao%20i/view_detail.aspx?ItemID =4445 (accessed July 2012).

Pye, L. (1999) 'Civility, Social Capital, and Civil Society: Three Powerful Concepts for Explaining Asia' in *Journal of Interdisciplinary History*, 29 (4): 763–82.

Thayer, C. A. (1992) 'Political Reform in Vietnam: Doi Moi and the Emergence of Civil Society' in R. F. Miller (ed.), *The Development of Civil Society in Communist Systems*, Sydney: Allen and Unwin, 110–29.

Thayer, C. (2008) 'One-Party Rule and the Challenge of Civil Society in Vietnam', presentation to Remaking the Vietnamese State: Implications for Vietnam and the Region, Vietnam, Workshop, City University of Hong Kong, 21–22 August.

Thayer, C. (2009) 'Vietnam and the Challenge of Political Civil Society' in *Contemporary Southeast Asia*, 31 (1): 1–27.

Trần Hữu Quang (2010) 'Hướng đến một khái niệm khoa học về xã hội dân sự' [Towards a scientific concept of civil society] in *Tạp chí Khoa học xã hội* [Social Scientific Review], 4 (140): 10–23.

Trần Ngọc Hiên (2008) 'Kinh tế thị trường định hướng xã hội chủ nghĩa với nhà nước pháp quyền và xã hội dân sự nước ta' [Socialist market economy and rule-of-law and civil society in our country] in *Tạp chí Cộng sản* [Communist Review], 787. Online. Available at: www.tapchicongsan.org.vn/Home/Nghiencuu-Traodoi/2008/629/Kinh-te-thi-truong-dinh-huong-xa-hoi-chu-nghia-voi-nha.aspx (accessed July 2012).

Tương Lai (2005) 'Nhà nước pháp quyền và xã hội dân sự' [Rule-of-law and civil society] in *Tạp chí Nghiên cứu lập pháp* [Review of Law Studies], 11. Online. Available at: diendankienthuc.net/diendan/kien-thuc-triet-hoc/9382-nha-nuoc-phap-quyen-va-xa-hoi-dan-su.html (accessed July 2012).

Trương Trọng Nghĩa (2004) 'The Rule of Law in Vietnam: Theory and Practice' in *The Rule of Law: Perspectives from the Pacific Rim*, The Mansfield Center for Pacific Affairs, New York. Online. Available at: www.mansfieldfdn.org/backup/programs/program_pdfs/10nghia.pdf (accessed July 2013).

Turley, W. S. (1993) 'Party, State, and People: Political Structure and Economic Propects' in M. Selden and W. S. Turley (eds), *Reinventing Vietnamese Socialism: Doi Moi in Comparative Perspective*, Boulder: Westview Press: 257–76.

Võ Khánh Vinh (2008) 'Một số vấn đề lý luận về xã hội dân sự' [Some theoretical issues on civil society] in *Tạp chí Khoa học xã hội* [Social Scientific Review], 4 (116): 21–35.

Vũ Duy Phú (2008) 'Phát triển xã hội dân sự thông thái tương ứng với nhà nước pháp quyền hiện đại là nhiệm vụ quan trọng của Việt Nam trong thế kỷ XXI' [The development of a knowledge-based civil society in accordance with the modern rule-of-law state is crucial for Vietnam in the XXI. Century] in Vũ Duy Phú (ed.), *Xã hội dân sự – Một số vấn đề chọn lọc* [Civil Society – Selected Issues], Hanoi: 345–55.

NN (2007) 'Xã hội dân sự' [Civil society] in *Tạp chí Cộng sản* [Communist Review]. Online. Available at: www.tapchicongsan.org.vn/Home/Nghiencuu-Traodoi/2007/452/Xa-hoi-dan-su.aspx (accessed July 2012).

Wischermann, J. (2011) 'Governance and Civil Society Action in Vietnam: Changing the Rules From Within. Potentials and Limits' in *Asian Politics & Policy*, 3 (3): 381–411.

Womack, B. (1987) 'The Party and the People: Revolutionary and Post-revolutionary Politics in China and Vietnam' in *World Politics*, 39 (4): 479–507.

11 NGOs and the illusion of a Cambodian civil society[1]

Sivhuoch Ou and Sedara Kim

Introduction

In early development economics (back to the 1960s), the interventionist state was considered the central and driving force of development; from the 1980s, the neo-liberal counter movement in development theory has taken stage, seeing the state as the major drawback to development and giving a greater role to the market (Mohan and Stokke 2000). This dramatic shift, particularly in the wake of the Cold War, has triggered development policy and aid transfers to be framed under what Robinson (1994) terms a 'New Policy Agenda' (Edwards and Hulme 1995, 1996). Under the Agenda, non-governmental organizations (NGOs) are considered central agents, playing an important role by exerting organized pressure on autocratic and unresponsive states, and thereby supporting democratic stability and good governance, providing welfare services to those who could not be reached by markets, and strengthening the thriving civil society (Edwards and Hulme 1995: 4; Mohan and Stokke 2000; Moore 1993; Pearce 1993; Robinson 1996). The agenda is not monolithic in that its content varies from one official donor to another; however, all cases are driven by two poles: neoliberal economics and liberal democratic theory (Moore 1993). The trend to utilize NGOs to fulfill those roles has led to the mushrooming of NGOs both in the north and the south,[2] especially in the 1980s and 1990s (Carroll 1992; Edwards and Hulme 1995, 1996; Hulme and Michael 1997). In practice, the emergence of NGOs and roles in development 'represent both an opportunity and a danger' (Edwards and Hulme 1995: 5). One main avenue of criticism questions whether the creation of NGOs has actually translated into the building of civil society (see, for instance, Carothers and Ottaway 2000). Other critical questions have centred, inter alia, around the following issues:

- NGOs' positioning between the public and the private sectors; for instance, (Uphoff 1995: 18) contends that 'NGOs are best considered as a sub-sector of the private sector'
- NGOs' ineffectiveness in terms of sustainability and popular participation (Edwards and Hulme 1995)
- NGOs' accountability orientation upwards, away from the grassroots (Desai and Howes 1995; Shah and Shah 1995)

- NGOs' failure to democratize their own structures which impedes their downwards accountability to the beneficiaries (Carroll 1992)
- Local people's manipulation of foreign aid in the name of NGOs for their own advantage (Sampson 1996).

Despite these lingering questions, from the early 1990s Cambodia has experienced exponential growth of NGOs. By the end of 2010 official figures showed that 2,982[3] local organizations[4] were registered with the Ministry of Interior (CCC 2012). While NGOs have contributed quite substantially to the nation's development (Curtis 1998; Merla 2010; SPM 2003, 2006), this should not immediately indicate the presence of a strong civil society but rather reflects the strong presence of the donor community in Cambodia (SPM 2006: 13). In addition, the shortcomings listed above, which are well documented for Cambodian NGOs and often related to donor intervention, raise questions about the 'content' of these NGOs. Indeed, the core discussion of this chapter, which examines the sheer number of these NGOs, asks to what degree they constitute a civil society and possess civil society characteristics as envisioned in theory and practice by the donors under the New Policy Agenda? Have NGOs been able to meet those expectations or have they formed an illusion of a civil society? To respond to the research question, we make use of secondary data and of qualitative interview results from about 20 NGOs, international NGOs and research institutes obtained at two different periods (in 2009 and between October 2011 and February 2012). This chapter pays particular attention to NGOs at the national level for three reasons. First, NGOs are popularly considered a key player in contemporary Cambodia. Second, though there is sizeable body of recent research on NGOs at the national level, the critical question asked in this chapter remains unanswered. Third, although Cambodia has its own distinct and organically formed civil society comprising pagodas, as well other types of groups and movements (Carmen and Chhim 2009; Collins 1998; Ebihara 1968; Ehlert, this volume), NGOs outnumber these actors.

The chapter is structured in the following way. First, we lay out the analytical and theoretical framework. Second, we explore the characteristics of Khmer society and the history of civil society, which provides contextual background informing the question of the growth of NGOs. Third, we will delve into discussions of NGO characteristics emerging from the interplay between the external support and the local societal structure. Finally, we suggest why and how NGOs have been shaped by this interplay.

Framing the chapter

Khilnani (2001) propounds that civil society is often marked by ambiguities and difficulties, and that contradictions arise because there are multiple meanings of the term in the Western tradition itself. While the concept is often interpreted from different perspectives,[5] a widely quoted definition is that by White (1994: 337–8), who defines civil society as an intermediate associational realm between state and family populated by organizations which are separate from the state, enjoy autonomy in relation to the state and are formed voluntarily by members of society to protect or extend their interests or values.

The term NGO is also subject to definitional ambiguity as well. This study adopts a generally accepted definition by Clarke (1998: 2 3), defining NGOs as 'private, non-profit, professional organizations with a distinctive legal character, concerned with public welfare goals'.[6] Since the building of civil society via the support to and creation of NGOs has been one of the major initiatives of donors under the New Policy Agenda, the chapter uses this intersection as a backdrop to examine the characteristics of Cambodian NGOs. According to the definition by Clarke above, and in line with donors' expectations and various theoretical discussions (e.g. Carroll 1992; Edwards and Hulme 1995), NGOs are primarily supposed to (1) *act accountably* to the targeted beneficiaries; (2) develop an *identity* conforming to the going definition of NGOs; (3) *represent* the masses by connecting with beneficiaries in a way that makes them responsive to their needs and demands, and; (4) possess a *democratic governance structure*,[7] which is crucial since they are tasked to improve the state governance and act as role models. If NGOs possess these qualities, it is hoped that they would be both means (as catalysts to strengthen civil society) and ends (they would become civil society organizations themselves). However, if they fail to support and constitute civil society, NGOs would then only represent an illusion of civil society.

Cambodian societal traits

The Western conception of civil society does not fit comfortably with Cambodian society given its culture, history (Mabbett and Chandler 1996), and repression by the state during the last three decades (Ovesen *et al.* 1996, Ojendal, this volume). Historically, civil society has mostly included a realm of religiously based relations (Collins 1998; Ebihara 1968; Ledgerwood 2002). In rural areas, where around 80 per cent of Cambodians live, the village is not home to durable and functionally important groups or voluntary associations aside from family and kinship ties, and those of the Buddhist monastic structure. Ebihara (1968: 181) concurs that 'a striking feature of Khmer village life is the lack of indigenous, traditional, organized associations, clubs, factions, or other groups that are formed on non-kin principle', and, in later work, that Khmer community households in the 1960s were bound together not organizationally but by socially embedded reciprocity supporting 'institutions' of kinship, proximity and familiarity (Ebihara 1974: 306).

This loose structure is not only a consequence of the wars, as is often implied; indeed, it has been documented even in the colonial period (Chandler 2008; Delvert 1961; Hughes and Conway 2003). And if compared, the Khmer traditional society has had less of a sense of community than many other agriculture-based Asian societies (Hughes 2003). Until now, the lack of participation, solidarity and collective action in rural areas remains a widespread phenomenon (Chea *et al.* 2011; Ros *et al.* 2011). A recent survey indicates that social capital in rural society remains mostly unchanged since the end of the wars (CDRI 2012). More specifically, the survey (as well as other qualitative accounts, such as Kim 2011), find relatively strong social capital in terms of bonding among relatives and familiars, but little that bridges communities and almost none supporting vertical linkages (ibid.).

Civil society, NGOs at a glance

The term civil society (*sangkum civil*) does not exist in the Khmer dictionary or in common conversation; it is a completely imported concept. In Khmer, only the word society (*sangkum*) is used. As illustrated above, historically speaking, Cambodian society is not conducive to the formation of associations or organizations beyond kinship, and while some civil society-like groups (which are formed beyond kin level) are emerging, they are only found in particular contexts, such as trade unions, which are mostly established in the garment industry (Henke 2011).[8]

From the early 1990s, the term civil society has been widely circulated and used in Cambodia, often without clear understanding about what it exactly means. Most commonly, this term is used in reference to the nearly 3,000 NGOs operating across the country, most of which were established with the influence and financial support of international donors rather than under local initiative (Carmen and Chhim 2009; Un 2006). In 1991 there was only one NGO called *Khemara*[9]; throughout the early 1990s, however, the number of NGOs mushroomed, an incident variously described as 'a short burst followed by an explosion' (Burnip 1997: 24–5).[10] The United Nations Transitional Authority in Cambodia (UNTAC), operating under the assumption that an organic Cambodian civil society was close to being absent, supported the creation of local NGOs (especially human rights groups) to, among other things, safeguard democracy and guarantee against state repression. NGO representatives and their leaders were often unhesitatingly labelled 'civil society' in the media (Hughes 2003). Under the New Policy Agenda, the international community also promoted NGOs that provided basic services to the people in a similar fashion to other countries where state institutions are extremely weak and unresponsive.

NGOs are commonly known in Khmer and among local citizens as *angka*, a word meaning 'organization' but bearing additional connotations. Common citizens have mixed feelings regarding the concept of *angka*. On the one hand, *angka* recalls a recent tragedy in society, referring to the administration of the totalitarian Pol Pot regime notoriously known to have killed almost two million people. On the other hand, people also use the word *angka* to refer to the emerging development practitioners, as well as democracy and human rights groups, which they believe to have good intentions to assist society. The word, however, does bear some shadow of its former connotation. For many, *angka* is also associated with resources, good employment and a class distinct from the private sector and the state; local people typically refer to the staff of *angka* as being separate from them because they are salaried and educated people, and often stay somewhat detached from normal citizens.[11]

In short, *sangkum civil* is a new concept in circulation and NGOs are a popular manifestation that is born of external intervention, yet inevitably embedded using the cultural and linguistic distinctions of local society.

Analysing the substance of NGOs

Using the four-point framework laid out above for assessing the content of NGOs, this section scrutinizes some of the tangible characteristics of contemporary NGOs, looking at donor efforts in the social, cultural and historical context of Cambodia.

Accountability to whom?

Apparently, NGOs in Cambodia are largely dependent on donors for financial support and thus risk orienting their accountability upwards to donors rather than downwards to beneficiaries; this is well explained by both existing empirical studies and our own latest data. For the purposes of this study, accountability is defined as 'the means by which individuals and organizations report to a recognized authority (or authorities) and are held responsible for their actions' (Edwards and Hulme 1996: 967). It is such an important aspect that a large study conducted by the Cooperation Committee for Cambodia, Cambodia's largest umbrella NGO that covers Cambodia's civil society sector,[12] views the upwards accountability of NGOs as the primary governance challenge.

> Most accountability practices are predominantly upward.... As most NGOs are donor dependent, their decision making, not unexpectedly, is influenced greatly by their donors/development partners. In defining strategic focus or directions ... the priority concerns or issues of communities become secondary to donor priorities and agenda.
>
> (CCC 2010: 31–2)

Un (2006) echoes that financial dependence compels NGOs to compromise their own agendas and sometimes pursue those of their donors, for financial survival; this causes NGOs to become submissive, which damages the downward accountability so important to local NGOs. Carmen and Chhim (2009), likewise, contend that financial dependence induces local organizations to superimpose foreign concepts and agendas upon local cultural, political and social realities. From the early 1990s until recently, there have been few indications that Cambodian NGOs would be able to survive without external resources. Out of 16 NGOs studied by Ou (co-author of this volume) in 2006, only one was able to secure 50 per cent of their headquarters' expenses from local resources; two provincial branches of the same NGO, however, were still largely dependent upon donors' support. The other 15 NGOs admitted that they would collapse immediately without external assistance (Ou 2006). Although it was found that well-established NGOs have more bargaining power and thus manage to claim more downwards accountability, the majority of NGOs remain fairly submissive, making them vulnerable to compromising their accountability (ibid.).

Norman (2010) and Khlok *et al.* (2003) observe that Cambodian NGOs often subscribe to contemporary ideas such as empowerment, gender, participation and sustainability to please donors rather than to respond to the demands of beneficiaries. Furthermore, over time, and as NGOs face more fierce competition to secure funds, donors are increasingly in a position to impose their expectations and agendas on applicant organizations (Norman 2010: 186). Pressure from the donors can often be felt right down to local NGO counterparts in the country, who have increasingly complained about difficulty in getting funding and the level of competition for it. This is the case, for instance, in the decentralization and deconcentration sectors. One informant told the authors in interview: 'We suffer from a lack of funding support; though we have fundraising strategies in place and I work through weekends until I get sick, funding remains unsecured' (interview, Phnom Penh, 27 December 2011). A representative of an international organization who has closely watched the funding trend for NGOs commented that, 'As of the end of 2011, whenever and wherever there is a grant, NGOs crowd in like ants gathering to eat sugar'.[13] A provincial NGO director acknowledges that striking a good balance between working directly for beneficiaries and serving donors is a critical matter as funding is getting more scarce.[14] As NGOs become worried about their survival and are increasingly occupied with resource mobilization, the time and energy left to serve their target groups comes into question.

NGOs and the crisis of identity?

If NGOs are tasked with building civil society in ways envisioned by the donor community, their long-term identities as independent units come under question. In describing the response to the emerging development or aid market (especially relevant in the 1990s), Norman (2010: 180–1) states that external support

> resulted at first in the rise of a multitude of Come-and-go NGOs (ComeN'GOs) that were specifically targeting donor funding for entrepreneurial motivations, often disbanding once projects had expired. These NGOs start new projects, not because of bottom-up demand from societal needs, but because of the top-down supply of resources from donors.

Adding to this, Nowaczyk (2009: 25) reported on the incidence of corruption within NGOs, and in particular that some NGOs were 'set up for employment purposes rather than assisting the poor'. While opportunism manifests more subtly for many NGOs, some NGOs would appear to have been established less for the sake of their supposed beneficiaries and more for the benefit of their staff.

Inside NGOs, other questions emerge, particularly regarding their capacity and effectiveness and the implications that this has on the long-term identity of NGOs sector-wide. In the early days (from early 1990s), NGOs were treated as child-like and supported in almost all areas, from computer networking to financial accounting, writing proposals, advocacy work and how to conduct relations with the press and government; furthermore, they struggled in terms of retaining qualified staff (Hughes 2003). Hughes noted that as far back as 1996, NGO leaders complained about high staff turnover and about training that was conducted endlessly because of high staff turnover rates.

The situation has not changed much since 1996. A recent complaint comes from the executive director of one NGO:

> Our NGO used to be a big one supported by eight large donors; however, since its funding has shrunk, a number of potential and qualified staff have left for better paid jobs at international NGOs (INGOs), ADB, WB.
> (NGO No. 7, interview by the authors, Phnom Penh, 27 December, 2011)

A number of issues arise here. First, though the positions left vacant by departing NGO staff are usually filled, and the organizations still function to serve those intended, the high turnover already indicates that people commit themselves less to the beneficiaries and the cause, and more to their own career advancement. Second, after around two decades, NGOs are still complaining about the lack of capacity as pointed out above. However, if one looks underneath these complaints, one often finds that the discontinuity caused by pursuing shifting donor whims has brought about skill fragmentation. NGO staff often run from one organization to another, or from NGOs to the private sector, or to multilateral agencies, embassies, etc., mostly in the hope of higher pay, and often abandoning accumulated skillsets. This effectively leaves their former workplaces with a deficit in trained personnel and continuity. The plight of beneficiaries is adversely affected by this high level of turnover. Having critically addressed this state of affairs, we step back and recognize that Cambodia was in a dramatic post-conflict reconstruction period in the early 1990s, leading to poor career advancement potential in the public and private sectors, which may contribute to the opportunistic nature of NGO staff. Despite the immaturity of the job market during this period, these NGOs were established, as outlined by donors, to benefit vulnerable people. But this aim has been compromised by the rent-seeking behaviour of the sector as a whole.

Instead of changing, this dynamic appears to be becoming entrenched. Some NGO staff have enjoyed remaining in their comfort zone and are not committed to making situational change that supports beneficiaries at the expense of their own working conditions. They are accustomed to working in the 'conventional style' of the 1990s, a unique donor-driven period in which NGO staff did not necessarily have to reflect critically on what a civil society 'worker' should be like. A donor representative, commenting on the proceedings of a workshop in which NGO staff discussed criteria for recruiting partners, narrated that, people are now used to focusing on the technical aspects and organizational structure (professionalism) but I feel something is missing, as civil society strengthening is more than just the technical and organizational strength. The question is the identity of an organization and the question of what makes a difference. NGO or CBO staff have to put the beneficiaries in front of themselves but they complain that doing so is very demanding and difficult and they wish to stick to their old style of working.

(INGO No. 1, interview by the authors, Phnom Penh, 22 December 2011)

The authors, having worked on, and been involved in, this sector for around a decade, have witnessed similar incidents and anecdotally agree with the perception of the informant above. Distance from beneficiaries, however, is in some cases exaggerated further. Another INGO representative raised concerns about provincial NGO staff viewing themselves as superior to the beneficiaries. In the following quote this informant strategizes about how to teach the provincial staff to adopt a villager-friendly attitude:

NGO staff often behave like outsiders coming from the provincial town, not from the locality. I will put forward some simple strategies to make NGOs work on a more equal basis with the local people, say, by asking them to park their cars far away from the people's houses and take a walk into the communities, wearing very casual clothes, speaking the language of the local people so that they will feel comfortable working with NGOs. But there is still a long way to go.

(INGO No. 2, interview by the authors, Phnom Penh, 28 December 2011)

The type of mindset, that privileges working conditions and valuing one's own professional image over the welfare of beneficiaries, manifests itself in a reticence to leave one's comfort zone, and remains an ever-present hurdle in the way of civil society advancement in Cambodia.

Connecting with or remaining aloof from the masses?

While participation on the part of beneficiaries is often deemed crucial to ensure that NGO activities respond to people's needs, the poor connection of NGOs with the masses has remained an unsolved challenge. As funds grow scarce,[15] this problem is only exacerbated further. Several studies using empirical evidence share this view. Studies by a Swedish consulting firm working on development aid management noted that Cambodian NGOs had low levels of voluntary and public participation (SPM 2003, 2006). Others authors note that, because NGOs are often externally created and not organically formed, they tend to lack grassroots links (Carmen and Chhim 2009; Khlok *et al.* 2003). Characterizing this, Un (2004: 272) considers the Cambodian NGO sector as a 'civil movement without citizens'. Hughes (2003: 162) suggests that the emergence of professional NGOs, typically with an inward orientation focusing on internal functioning along Western norms of management practice, and bias in the recruitment of urban elites, has produced a gap between the NGO movement and the rural villages they consider as their 'members'. Yonekura (1999), adding to this, remarks that NGOs generally performed poorly in representing the target beneficiaries. Wells-Dang (this volume) even highlights that well-organized Cambodian rural community networks can come to be detached from Phnom Penh-based NGOs.

Paradoxically, past successes in working closely with vulnerable people sometimes serves to create distance between NGO staff and beneficiaries. This is the case for a large NGO working on community development in 348 villages. The NGO sends their staff to the villages, where they remain working and living with the people for years in extremely remote areas untouched by the state and other services. Although they are considered relatively successful compared to other NGOs in the same field, a negative trend has emerged over time. On the one hand, the NGO workers engage closely with the people to empower them; on the other, the social cleavages of these inherently different groups become increasingly stark. The increasing salaries paid to NGO workers contrasts with the more static position of target beneficiaries, which only serves to distance them from local people, thereby hindering the continued empathy necessary for remaining passionate about the cause. A former staff of the NGO related,

> There is a problem occurring along with the NGO's success stories. Some staff have worked in the communities for 20 years and their salaries have risen to a very comfortable level that they find places them in a comfort zone they do not want to leave. The issue is that they are no longer innovative and some of our activities get stagnant.
>
> (CSO No. 5, interview by the authors, Phnom Penh, 1 December 2011)

Governance structure

Many accounts of the NGO sector in Cambodia note the weak internal governance. Cambodians have been steeped in development discourses that are influenced by democratic principles such as accountability, transparency, equality and mass participation. Although good governance, an additional principle, is usually a stated part of the vision of many NGOs, it is not uncommon to find NGOs 'owned by' the founders and 'characterized by autocratic, hierarchical, and centralized management, with patron–client relationships [as the] dominant feature' (Richardson 2001: 7). A recent case study of a Cambodian NGO revealed that, despite being well funded, the NGO had not internally replicated civil society values. For instance, although the staff were well educated, decision-making and authority rested almost entirely with the executive director (Gellman 2010: 90–1). A similar trend was also anecdotally observed in NGOs beyond the case examined (ibid.). Such a key governance deficit is noted in a CCC study (2010: 31) as well, which posits that, 'transparency is mainly understood in financial terms and rarely in terms of decision making processes. The practice of democracy is limited'. This undemocratic and hierarchical structure of NGOs has largely not improved over the years according to an empirical analysis conducted between 2003 and 2006 (SPM 2006). A recent informal interview, with a colleague who has a work relationship with a Phnom Penh-based NGO and its network, illustrates this observation:

> I can see how authoritarian her leadership is. She does not only exercise dominance over the staff but also owns the organization; she has fired staff she dislikes and sometimes recruits her own family members and relatives. For the network itself, it is getting more difficult to manage to ensure effectiveness because now they have secured some funding and every member fights to run the secretariat.
>
> (Social researcher, interview by the authors, Phnom Penh, February 2012)

Perhaps the most worrying manifestation of poor governance in NGOs is what Nowaczyk (2009: 24–5) suggests from her recent study, namely that, 'the overwhelming evidence ... is that NGOs are both forced into corruption and experience it'. Nowaczyk's study notes that 82 per cent of her survey respondents 'had been aware of some form of corruption in their own or other organizations in the past year'. Furthermore, she reports such irregularities as staff claiming per diems for fieldwork they did not conduct, managers producing fake receipts, nepotism, etc. Related to that, Nowaczyk further noticed that some NGO managerial staff face pressure to permit corruption, or they face extreme difficulties in enforcing anti-corruption policies. For instance, there were no avenues for resolving issues such as receiving death threats from staff they had dismissed or accused of engaging in corrupt practices (ibid.: 26).

Putting the illusion into perspective

Two primary objectives of donors under the New Policy Agenda are to support NGOs to provide services directly to people, and to strengthen civil society more generally. Over the past two decades, NGOs have made strides in fulfilling the former but have been less effective in carrying out the later objective. Specifically, many NGOs (1) remain more upwardly accountable (to donors) than downwardly accountable (to beneficiaries); (2) identify disproportionately with their professional status rather than their duty to beneficiaries; (3) are detached from the grassroots they are supposed to work with and serve; and (4) lack the democratic structures they often exhort as development agents. As a result, the extent to which NGOs share civil society characteristics and strengthen civil society is compromised. This is not to generalize that all (types of) NGOs lack these defining attributes, or that these attributes consistently apply to all NGOs and all sectors, but that a general trend with national character is observable. Öjendal (this volume) highlighted the plurality of 'civil societies' in Cambodia, while this chapter argues that one of them – the externally supported NGOs – are a questionable constituent of civil society.

Who is responsible for this illusion?

Why have NGOs in Cambodia developed in this manner? Internationally, the case of Cambodia is not unique; indeed, the idea that *he who pays the piper calls the tune* is quite pervasive in literature upon NGOs in general. Edwards and Hulme (1995: 5–6) explain that the dependence of NGOs on foreign aid puts them in the risky position of being co-opted by others' (donors) agendas and erodes their independent social base. Similarly, in her provocative paper entitled 'NGOs' Seat at the Donor Table: Enjoying the Food or Serving the Dinner?', Hudock (2000: 17) argues that the relationships between donors and NGOs are regrettably unequal, with 'Donor–NGO relationships [having] been dominated and even dictated by donors' largely because donors provide the development resources. This is illustrated by a surprisingly frank acknowledgement from the former Cambodian country director of Médecins Sans Frontières Belgium

> I have to confess that sometimes we come in and say 'we want to do this', and we don't even bother asking if this is what [Cambodians] want. It is true that we are very arrogant – sometimes too much.... The problem with the NGOs today is that they are funded by donors, so what they do, and I cannot blame them, is follow where the money is going. It's very tricky.
>
> (Berneau, cited in Strangio 2009)

Looking deeper into the root of the problem, a donor representative commented that,

> part of the current civil society problem was caused by INGOs and donors themselves in the design process; they were responsible for, in the early 1990s, establishing NGOs without discriminating and examining what types they should assist and what consequences would arise out of their support. More importantly, it must be noted that some INGOs are like consultancy firms which carry out their activities improperly and often produce ill consequences for local partners.
>
> (INGO No. 1, interview by the authors, Phnom Penh, 22 December 2011)

Several commentators in the early 1990s speculated about whether Cambodia would survive the flood of foreign aid, even though it had survived the Khmer Rouge tragedy and the economic embargo of the 1980s. It was already conspicuous from the 1990s that there was too much money chasing NGOs (see Öjendal, this volume) and a very favourable environment in which they could grow. The international community was enthusiastic about the opening of the country and there seemed to be no overarching planning concerned with building the NGO sector. Although, as mentioned earlier, Khmer society and culture are not particularly conducive for the kind of NGO formation and civil society development hoped and envisioned by donors, the UN and attendant donors barely seemed to notice this. Although we acknowledge that several promising forms of social energy have emerged in recent years (see, for instance, Ngin 2004; Wells-Dang, this volume; Hiwasa, this volume), considerable potential has also been left unfulfilled. Insufficient legislation or standards for managing the NGO sector is one explanation for the poor performance of many NGOs in terms of account-ability to beneficiaries (Mayhew 2005). That said, the counterproductive charac-teristics and operational problems have remained unchallenged by many NGOs and their staff, which has exacerbated any problems created initially by the donor community. Because many people have personally benefited from this state of affairs in the name of development, they also bear responsibility.

Khmer society and its culture: inhibiting or enhancing NGO formation and success?

In terms of numbers, Cambodian society and culture have little impact on the landscape of civil society over the years – the context is not conducive to auto-nomous group formation. NGOs have emerged almost exclusively in reaction to resource availability, as demonstrated in the World Bank study by Carmen and Chhim (2009). The content of these organizations, however, does respond to cul-tural and societal traits. With little experience in forming groups, NGOs were set up much like companies (Öjendal, this volume), or by learning from trial and error, or by modelling their foreign counterparts (Hughes 2003). With a basis in salaried staff and a 'market' that depended on donor demand, the fate of NGOs has waxed and waned in time with the vagaries of overseas aid to Cambodia. Öjendal (this volume) considers that contemporary civil society has reached a point of 'normalization' – the externally funded NGO sector is fading away or sustaining itself unconventionally, whereas others are transforming into social enterprises, businesses or being absorbed into government (Feuer, this volume). Those that cannot reinvent themselves and manage the transition will fall out. In Cambodia, NGO formation (at least when observed at the national level) has had little to do with whether a culture of civil society is evolving or is static. Instead, rather superficially, it has followed the money flow. In other words, the shrink-ing or expanding of the NGO sector is not an indicator for cultural and social inculcation of civil society behaviour. However, one critical cultural factor, namely the difficulty in generating internal democratic culture, appears to have prevented NGOs from empowering themselves and evolving with the times. Democratic principles have failed to anchor in the way NGOs work, allowing hierarchy, class cleavages, patronage, nepotism and autocracy to pre-empt civil society tendencies and render NGOs an illusion, rather than a constituent part, of civil society.

Notes

1 This work and the title are inspired by the arguments in 'Promoting Democracy: NGOs and "civil society"' (Chapter 7) in Caroline Hughes (2003) *The Political Economy of Cambodia's Transition, 1991–2001*.

2 The north refers to aid-giving countries, while the south is understood to constitute developing countries receiving aid.

3 Additionally, around 8,000 modern Community Based Organizations (CBOs) are operational in Cambodia's 13,000 villages, mostly funded by overseas development aid (Carmen and Chhim 2009; Henke 2011).

4 According to an official in charge of NGO and association registration at the Ministry of Interior, two types of organizations are registered: local NGOs and associations. However, in practice, there is no clear distinction between the two as they operate on similar basis (see Ou 2006).

5 For a critical discussion on civil society there are many detailed references (e.g. Chandhoke 2001; Chandhoke 2007; Hyden 1997; Kaviraj and Khilnani 2001).

6 'Within this definition, NGOs include philanthropic foundations, church development agencies, academic think tanks and other organizations focusing on issues such as human rights, gender, health, agricultural development, social welfare, the environment, and indigenous people.' (Clarke 1998: 3).

7 Other assumed performances of NGOs as stated by the authors above include focusing on poverty alleviation, cost effectiveness, sustainability, flexibility and innovation. The four points are fundamental in that they are widely expected by donors as documented in literature and policy documents.

8 In addition, although union membership appears quite significant, ranging between 160,000 and 377,000 according to different sources (or 40 per cent of Cambodia's labour force (Makin 2006), 'overall unionization remains low' as unions are weak and not financially independent and political space beyond strikes at the factory level has shrunk following the murder of Chea Vichea, a high profile union leader (Henke 2011: 293).

9 The name *Khemara* literally means Khmer. It is the first NGO led by a Cambodian, established with the primary objective of tackling women's and children's issues.

10 The sudden rise of NGOs is due to several potential reasons such as the favourable atmosphere enabled by UNTAC, the availability of plentiful financial support, and the availability of educated human resources repatriated from the border camps (Hughes 2003; Ou 2006).

11 Both anecdotal evidence and our 2009 fieldwork in six villages, in three different communes, in three different provinces, confirms this (see Thon *et al.* 2009).

12 The study claims to cover the whole NGO sector because it both examines some individual NGOs as well as all of the networks representing NGOs that are registered with the CCC.

13 INGO No. 2, interview by the authors, Phnom Penh, 28 December 2011.

14 NGO No. 11, interview by the authors, Battambang, 6 October 2011.

15 It is necessary to note that while the feeling shared among most of the informants is that funding is generally in decline, one NGO director warned (in a phone interview by the authors, August 20 2012) that not all of the NGO sector suffers from reduced funding levels; for instance, he pointed to the case of NGOs working in the human rights arena, whose funding support remains stable largely because human rights abuse cases have not declined over the years and have thus attracted continuous attention and resources from donors.

References

Burnip, D. A. (1997) *Developing Cambodian NGOs through Partnerships*, Brattleboro, Vermont: School for International Training.

Carmen, M. and Chhim, K. (2009) *Linking Citizens and the State: As Assessment of Civil Society Contributions to Good Governance in Cambodia*, Washington, DC: The World Bank.

Carothers, T. and Ottaway, M. (eds) (2000) *Funding Virtue: Civil Society Aid and Democracy Promotion*, Washington, DC: Carnegie Endowment for International Peace.

Carroll, T. F. (1992) *Intermediary NGOs: The Supporting Links in Grassroots Development*, West Hartford, CT: Kumarian Press.

CCC (2010) *Reflections, Challenges and Choices: 2010 Review of NGO Sector in Cambodia*, Phnom Penh: Cooperation Committee for Cambodia.

CCC (2012) *CSO Contribution to the Development of Cambodia 2011*, Phnom Penh: Cooperation Committee for Cambodia.

CDRI (2012) *Survey Report on Social Capital and Sustainable Development in Cambodia*, Phnom Penh, Cambodia: Cambodia Development Resource Institute.

Chandhoke, N. (2001) 'The "Civil" and the "Political" in Civil Society' in *Democratization*, 8 (2): 1–24.

Chandhoke, N. (2007) 'Civil Society' in *Development in Practice*, 17 (4): 607–14.

Chandler, D. (2008) *A History of Cambodia*, 4th edition: Silkworm Books.

Chea, C., Nang, P., Whitehead, I., Hirsch, P. and Thompson, A. (2011) 'Decentralized Governance of Irrigation Water in Cambodia: Matching Principles to Local Realities', Working Paper No. 62, Phnom Penh, Cambodia: Cambodian Development Resource Institute.

Clarke, G. (1998) *The Politics of NGOs in South-East Asia: Participation and Protest in the Philippines*, London: Routledge.

Collins, W. (1998) *Grassroots Civil Society in Cambodia*, Phnom Penh: Centre for Advanced Study.

Curtis, G. (1998) *Cambodia: Reborn? The Transition to Democracy and Development*, Washington DC and Geneva: Brookings Institution Press and the United Nations Research Institute for Social Development.

Desai, V. and Howes, M. (1995) 'Accountability and Participation: A Case Study from Bombay' in M. Edwards and D. Hulme (eds), *Non-governmental Organisations: Performance and Accountability Beyond the Magic Bullet*, London: Earthscan.

Ebihara, M. (1968) 'Svay, a Khmer village in Cambodia', unpublished thesis, Columbia University.

Ebihara, M. (1974) 'Khmer Village Women in Cambodia' in C. Matthiasson (ed.), *Many Sisters: Women in Cross-Cultural Perspective*, New York: Free Press.

Edwards, M. and Hulme, D. (eds) (1995) *Non-governmental Organisations: Performance and Accountability Beyond the Magic Bullet*, London: Earthscan.

Edwards, M. and Hulme, D. (1996) 'Too Close for Comfort? The Impact of Official Aid on Nongovernmental Organizations' in *World Development*, 24 (6): 961–73.

Gellman, M. (2010) 'World Views in Peace Building: A Post-conflict Reconstruction Challenge in Cambodia' in *Development in Practice*, 20 (1): 85–98.

Henke, R. (2011) 'NGOs, People's Movements and Natural Resource Management' in C. Hughes and U. Kheang (eds), *Cambodia's Economic Transformation*, Copenhagen: NIAS Press.

Hudock, A. C. (2000) 'NGOs' Seat at the Donor Table: Enjoy the Food or Serving the Dinner?' in *IDS Bulletin*, 31 (3): 14–18.

Hughes, C. (2003) *The Political Economy of Cambodia's Transition, 1992–2001*, London: Routledge.

Hughes, C. and Conway, T. (2003) *Understanding Pro-Poor political change: The policy process*, London: Overseas Development Institute.

Hulme, D. and Michael, E. (eds) (1997) *NGOs, States and Donors? Too Close for Comfort?* London: Macmillan Press.

Hyden, G. (1997) 'Civil Society, Social Capital, and Development: Dissection of a Complex Discourse' in *Studies in Comparative International Development*, 32 (1): 3–30.

Kaviraj, S. and Khilnani, S. (eds) (2001) *Civil Society: History and Possibilities*, Cambridge: Cambridge University Press.

Khilnani, S. (2001) *The Development of Civil Society*, Cambridge: Cambridge University Press.

Khlok, S., Ouch, P. and Nil, V. (2003) *Margin to Mainstream. An Assessment of Community based Organizations in Cambodia*, Washington, DC: World Bank.

Kim, S. (2011) 'Reciprocity: Informal Patterns of Social Interaction in a Cambodian village' in J. Marston (ed.), *Anthropology and Community in Cambodia: Reflections on the Work of May Ebihara*, Victoria, Australia: Monash University Press.

Ledgerwood, J. (2002) *Cambodia Emerges from the Past: Eight essays*, Dekalb, IL: Southeast Asia Publications, Center for Southeast Asian Studies, Northern Illinois University.

Mabbett, I. and Chandler, D. (1996) *The Khmers*, Oxford: Blackwell.

Makin, J. (2006) *Cambodia: Women and Work in the Garment Industry*, Phnom Penh: ILO's Better Factory Cambodia and The World Bank's Justice for the Poor.

Mayhew, S. H. (2005) *Journal of Development Studies*, 41 (5): 727–58.

Merla, C. (2010) *Civil Society Empowerment and Democratic Governance in Cambodia*, Phnom Penh: United Nations Development Programme.

Mohan, G. and Stokke, K. (2000) 'Participatory development and empowerment: The dangers of localism' in *Third World Quarterly*, 21 (2): 247–68.

Moore, M. (1993) 'Good government? Introduction' in *IDS Bulletin*, 24 (1): 1–6.

Ngin, C. (2004) 'Strengthening NGO Accountability through Beneficiary Participation: Lessons from Cambodia NGOs', unpublished thesis, Nagoya University.

Norman, D. J. (2010) 'Interrogating the Dynamics of "Cosmopolitan Democracy" in Theory and Practice: The Case of Cambodia', unpublished thesis, University of Birmingham.

Nowaczyk, M. (2009) 'Between a Rock and a Hard Place: Organizations and Institutionalized Corruption in Cambodia', unpublished thesis, Open University.

Ou, S. (2006) 'Understanding Cambodian NGOs' Relationships with International NGOs: Focus on CNGOs' Autonomy and Sustainability', unpublished thesis, Waseda University.

Ovesen, J., Trankell, I.-B. and Öjendal, J. (1996) 'When Every Household is an Island: Social Organization and Power Structures in Rural Cambodia' in *Uppsala Research Reports in Cultural Anthropology 15*, Uppsala, Sweden: Department of Cultural Anthropology, Uppsala University.

Pearce, J. (1993) 'NGOs and Social Change: Agents or Facilitators?' in *Development in Practice*, 3 (3): 222–7.

Richardson, M. (2001) *NGO Sector Report*, Phnom Penh: Cambodia NGO Support Network.

Robinson, M. (1994) 'Governance, Democracy and Conditionality: NGOs and the New Policy Agenda' in A. Clayton (ed.), *Governance, Democracy and Conditionality: What roles for NGOs?* Oxford: INTRAC.

Robinson, M. (1996) 'The Role of Aid Donors in Strengthening Civil Society' in A. Clayton (ed.), *NGOs, Civil Society and the State: Building Democracy in Transitional Societies*, Oxford: INTRAC.

Ros, B., Ly, T. and Thompson, A. (2011) 'Catchment Governance and Cooperation

Dilemmas: A Case Study from Cambodia', Working Paper 61, Phnom Penh, Cambodia: Cambodia Development Resource Institute.

Sampson, S. (1996) 'The Social Life of Projects: Importing civil society to Albania' in C. Hann and E. Dunn (eds), *Civil Society: Challenging Western Models*, London and New York: Routledge.

Shah, P. and Shah, M. K. (1995) 'Participatory Methods for Increasing NGO Accountabillity: A Case Study from India' in M. Edwards and D. Hulme (eds), *Non-governmental Organisations: Performance and Accountability Beyond the Magic Bullet*, London: Earthscan.

SPM (2003) *Civil Society and Democracy in Cambodia: Changing Roles and Trends. The Fifth Report of the Sida Advisory Team on Democratic Governance*, Stockholm and Phnom Penh: SPM Consultants.

SPM (2006) *Civil Society and Uncivilized Politics: Trends and Roles of Cambodian Civil Society and Possibility for Sida Support. The Eighth Report of the Sida Advisory Team (SAT)*, Stockholm and Phnom Penh: SPM Consultants.

Strangio, S. (2009) 'Plotting an NGO Exit Plan' in *Phnom Penh Post*, Phnom Penh, Cambodia, 24 July.

Thon, V., Ou, S., Eng, N. and Ly, T. (2009) 'Leadership in Local Politics of Cambodia: A Study of Leaders in Three Communes of Three Provinces', Working Paper Series No. 42, Phnom Penh, Cambodia: Cambodian Development Resource Institute.

Un, K. (2004) 'Democratization Without Consolidation: The Case of Cambodia, 1993–2004', unpublished thesis, Northern Illinois University.

Un, K. (2006) 'State, Society and Democratic Consolidation: The case of Cambodia' in *Pacific Affairs*, 79 (2): 225–45.

Uphoff, N. (1995) 'Why NGOs are not a Third Sector: A Sectoral Analysis with some Thoughts on Accountability, Sustainability and Evaluation' in M. Edwards and D. Hulme (eds), *Non-governmental Organisations: Performance and Accountability Beyond the Magic Bullet*, London: Earthscan.

White, G. (1994) 'Civil Society, Democratization and Development (I): Clearing the Analytical Ground' in *Democratization*, 1 (2): 375–90.

Yonekura, Y. (1999) 'The Emergence of Civil Society in Cambodia: Its Role in the Democratization Process', unpublished thesis, University of Sussex.

12 Proto civil society

Pagodas and the socio-religious space in rural Cambodia

Judith Ehlert

Introduction

> Because of the Khmer Rouge, these people became less than animals. They
> lost the power to conduct their own lives. And it will take a long time to
> overcome this – several generations.
>
> (*New York Times* 1995, quoted in Ledgerwood and Vijghen 2002: 109)

After Cambodia opened to the international community in 1992 with the advent
of UN peacekeeping operations and elections, Western researchers rediscovered
a country which was, for many years, isolated due to civil war, auto-genocide
and the politics of the Cold War. Access to this grimly fascinating and untouched
country caused international donor agencies and Western scholars to launch
themselves enthusiastically into studies on rural society and its socio-cultural
fabric (Curtis 1998: 110; Hughes and Öjendal 2006: 415). As a product of those
heady days, literature dating back to the 1990s offers somewhat ambivalent perspectives on the traditional forms of social cohesion and community dynamics in
Cambodia. These early inquiries neglected the culturally situated spaces of social
and spiritual belonging presented to Cambodians by Buddhism. Instead, and as
detailed in Ou and Kim (this volume, see also Öjendal, this volume), foreign
donors imposed their visions by investing heavily into the creation of NGOs,
turning what was once an isolated country into a buzzing 'NGO haven' (Chap
2005: 5). The 1991 Paris Peace Accords not only signified an end to the many
years of civil war through the United Nations Transitional Authority in Cambodia (UNTAC, 1992–3) and subsequent disarmament and organized elections
(see St John 2005: 407), but also initiated training and information programmes
on human rights and democratic values (Mong Hay 1998; Khus 2004). Thousands of civilian and military advisors were pushing for democracy and development in a country that was assumed to be something of a social 'tabula rasa' (see
Öjendal, this volume). Although associational activity was certainly present and
had been likely recovering since the end of the Khmer Rouge in 1979, the
UNTAC era might appear to be a 'take-off' period for civil society. Cambodia
became an international aid market 'importing' development knowledge,
particularly concepts such as democratization and related virtues like good

governance and civil society (see Freske 1999). The consequent mushrooming of international and national NGOs was largely perceived as an important means of promoting democratic values and improving livelihoods.

This chapter is based on a literature review and on empirical data collected in 2006 during a four-month study in four different communes in Kampong Thom and Kampot province. While this study primarily examined the role of rural community-based organizations (CBOs) in the context of good governance (see Ehlert 2007), fieldwork also revealed that the pagodas constitute one of the most important focal point in people's lives. This chapter explicitly goes beyond this dominant narrative of externally facilitated organizations present in much of the academic writings and reports about Cambodian civil society, focusing instead on the local socio-religious spaces that have historically centred around Buddhist temples or pagodas. This type of 'proto civil society', which is embedded in people's everyday realities and social coexistence, forms the empirical backbone of this chapter. As we shall see, social life and ceremony in rural Cambodia – activities concerning birth and death, festivals, rituals and the reproduction of societal norms (see Monychenda 1998: 9) – continue to be shaped by the presence of the local Buddhist temple and community. The development and politics orientation that predominates in popular development discourse tends to focus on formalized spaces and sectors to the detriment of phenomena that do not immediately fit into predefined categories. The exploratory perspective in this chapter aims to crack open this rather formalistic view by accounting for the dynamically emerging social spaces and the diversity of actors that are often part of everyday life (see Lachenmann 1997). The perspective taken up in this chapter focuses on the interplay between religion, externally created groups, and the role of the state and the market economy (see Marston 2009) in order to look more comprehensively at the socio-cultural transformations going on in Cambodia. In this period of change, religion in Cambodia has also stayed continuously in motion (see Ovesen *et al.* 1996: 76), providing at once a glimpse of embedded tendencies stemming from the religious sphere, and of alternative understandings of the changes in civil society in contemporary Cambodia. In accordance with Hann and Dunn (1996: 3), I argue that an anthropological perspective is needed to counterbalance the dominant civil society debates that 'have been too narrowly circumscribed by modern western models of liberal-individualism', and to broaden the view of civil society to include a 'range of informal interpersonal practices' that have, and still do, constitute associational life in rural Cambodia.

This chapter begins with introductory briefs on the two main opposing schools of academic writing on Khmer socio-cultural legacies and the 'export' of the Western concept of civil society through UN intervention. Thereafter, I will challenge the post-conflict assumptions of social fatigue and fragmentation, nominally viewing local socio-religious mobilization around the temples as a form of civil society engagement with implications for rural development. The body of this text will account for, on the one hand, emic understandings of civic engagement and the loci of solidarity, which implies going beyond the overly politicized picture of state and society locking horns, instead looking at alternative space that 'naturally' fuels cultural belonging and stimulates social engagement. On the other hand, the religious sphere and its associational life must also be critically reviewed in terms of its growing politicization and monetarization. The chapter concludes by offering suggestions for an alternative understanding of civil society in Cambodia rooted in the religious realm of social life and how this can usefully complement studies on civil society that have exclusively focused on Cambodia as an 'NGO haven'.

In between Khmer socio-cultural legacies and global models of civil society

Due to the disruption in social continuity brought about by the Khmer Rouge, observers of Cambodia are left with the task of recreating a conception of associational behaviour prior to the revolution and squaring it with the distinct context after the revolution. Researchers are left to sift through historical pieces and disturbing memories, which do not always lend themselves to easy portrayal. Cambodians recoiled when the UN mission in the early 1990s applied the term 'democratization' to its purpose, recalling the brutal Pol Pot regime, which called itself *Democratic Kampuchea* (1975–9). A commune chief, remembering the time after the arrival of the UN in 1993, related that,

> When UNTAC came, the democratic regime started. This reminded some people of the democracy doctrine under Pol Pot. Because under Pol Pot they called it a 'democratic doctrine', too. They called it like this but in fact they killed the people with the hammer and axe and the gun – killing only.
>
> (Kampot province, 13 September 2006)

Maoist–communist ideology of a socially engineered peasant state contributed to the economic and socio-political revolution from 1975–9 in which over one million Cambodians were killed and half a million more left in exile (Chandler 1991: 236; see also Ou and Kim, this volume). By trying to erase all institutional legacies of former times, the Khmer Rouge wanted to commence year zero in Cambodian history; organized religion was destroyed, previous government institutions, private property and money were abolished, education suspended, urban–rural migration forced, and eating and working collectivized (see Blunt and Turner 2005: 76; Chandler 1991: 246/1).

The pioneering academic literature on Khmer society concerning the impact of such cruel experiences on social cohesion and community commonly falls into two schools. First, the 'atomized' school of thought (see Frings 1994; Ovesen *et al.* 1996) contends that in the aftermath of the revolution, social ties and networks beyond family and close kinship groups were systematically disrupted. Following this school of thought, the destruction of trust and social relations by the war and the Khmer Rouge doctrine have had long-term impacts on civil society. Downie and Kingsbury (2001:50) suggest that, 'During the Khmer Rouge period, through experience, people realized that they could not trust friends, neighbors, siblings or even their own children. This lack of trust has remained, and has hampered the development of civil society'. The title 'When Every Household is an Island' – a well-known book by academics from Uppsala University (see Ovesen *et al.* 1996) – is suggestive of a thoroughly individual-ized society. Evidencing this, Frings (1994: 61) argues that, although collective organizations emerged during the socialist puppet state under Vietnamese rule (1979–89), these were artificially imposed and participation was insincere.

The second school of thought, in contrast, argues that social cohesion and associational life in fact re-emerged after the war, though altered and weakened (Ebihara 1993; Ledgerwood 1998). Ledgerwood (1996: 140f.), for instance, gives ample evidence of intra-village cooperation including sharing food, donat-ing or lending cash, exchanging labour, and providing emergency assistance. Although the assistance provided may have shrunk, she would rather relate this to the villagers' limited resources than a priori to a lack of solidarity among neighbours (ibid.). Likewise, Luco (2002) portrays functioning local village and intra-village conflict resolution measures as another example of re-emerging social structures. In other writings, capitalism and monetarization of social rela-tions since colonialism, more than the Pol Pot regime, have had detrimental effects on the associational realm (see e.g. Springer 2010; Vickery 1992). In the same vein, Bit (1991: 24f.), argues that Western influence has introduced a regressive materialistic value system with wealth as a new standard for judging personal achievement. The encounter with modernization and ongoing develop-ment would thus facilitate the individualization of society and predilection for materialistic accumulation.

Despite the ambivalent views of scholars of Cambodian social organization and culture, some of whom are mentioned above, the 'atomized school' has almost become hegemonic, having been taken up by UNTAC in the rush to implement a Western liberal democratic model of civil society. Whilst enthusi-astically investing in the establishment of new formal social organizations man-dated to carry out rural development, the donor community overlooked or discounted 'less formal networks and mechanisms that have supported the village (particularly the poor) for generations' (Curtis 1998: 126). An observer since UNTAC, Curtis (1998: 128) takes a critical perspective on this approach by referring to the relevance of the Buddhist *sangha* (clergy):

> [I]t is surprising that the Buddhist *sangkha* was not utilized more specifi-cally with respect to community development and social service activities. For example, as much as the lack of social 'safety nets' was bemoaned, little effort was directed to one of the most important social service institutions in the country – the community *wat* [pagoda].

Instead, international efforts to reconstruct and democratize the terror-torn country channelled the bulk of resources and technical support starting in the early 1990s to civil society actors in the form of NGOs. Besides the proliferation of NGOs based in Phnom Penh, Village Development Committees (VDCs) were promoted nationwide starting in 1999, with one of the purposes being the management of incoming flows of international development aid. On behalf of donors and international NGOs, Cambodian CBOs initiated rice banks, cash associations and fishing communities at the village level (Kim and Ann 2005: 5f.). Ou and Kim (this volume) mention that about 3,000 NGOs have been registered in Cambodia, and consider these largely to be the result of foreign advisors attempting to stimulate a modern democratic regime by applying to civil society the same guiding principles as in Western models of liberal democracy. This model is nicely outlined in the chapters by Waibel and Reis (both in this volume). In brief, this model is strongly rooted in European intellectual discourse from where it developed into a contemporary universalist paradigm reinforcing the image of an ideal type dualistic state–society nexus. Practical implementation was inspired by events occurring at the end of the Cold War, whereby freedom movements led by NGOs became features of the political landscape in the developing and former socialist bloc countries. As a counterbalance to state dominance, these groups became an international benchmark for good governance (Weiss 2000: 799f.).

As Marston (2009: 228) indicates, '[the] term "civil society", of course, has larger implications than the existence of NGOs, although in Cambodia the terms are largely used interchangeably'. The strong technocratic orientation of development NGOs drew attention away from other civil society structures in rural Cambodia based on local cosmology and religion. According to Kent (2003: 19), the temple and the activities centred around it would provide social and moral guidance to the villagers:

> I find it useful … to examine the homogenising, centripetal power of the religious-magical-animistic realm of the pagoda and its attendant features. This may lead us towards the sources that Cambodians look to in their pursuit of moral order, legitimacy, trust and sharing – all of which are crucial in creating the fellowship that is essential to productive collective life. By giving serious attention to this field, it is possible that hitherto largely overlooked forms of solidarity may come to light and the 'collective spirit of Khmer culture may be unearthed.

In light of Kent's position, the following empirical account will look at the socio-cultural sphere of religion and the temple (*wat*) as a socio-religious space as expressions of agency in rural Cambodia, an important consideration with regard to civil society development. Whereas Ou and Kim suggest that NGOs are empty shells formally known as civil society, the pagoda activities will be viewed formally unrecognized, yet no less important, spaces of local solidarity and meaning.

The role of Buddhism and the socio-religious mobilization of the pagoda community

In Cambodia, 95 per cent of the population is Theravada Buddhist (German Federal Foreign Office 2012). Together with the Cambodian kingship, Harris (2001: 74) considers the Buddhist *sangha* as the second major institutional pillar of the society. During the upheavals of war in Cambodia, however, this institution, as well as many others, experienced considerable trauma. Under the Khmer Rouge, the Buddhist clergy was systematically destroyed, pagodas torn down and monks killed. From a level of about 60,000 ordained monks before the war, this number decreased to practically zero (Ledgerwood 2008: 149) as monks were either executed, defrocked or pressured by the Khmer Rouge to abdicate their religious beliefs (Kent 2003: 7). Cambodia experienced a 'virtual elimination of institutional Buddhism' (Harris 2001: 74). The strategic elimination of monks contributed to severe hardships in the Cambodian education and religious system since the pagoda provided classes in Khmer language and culture (Kent 2003: 4/7). On this subject, one commune chief recalled: 'During the Pol Pot regime, no one was left educated – both men and women. The pagoda and the school were burned down. So, there was nowhere we could learn or get educated' (interview, Kdei Doung commune, 7 August 2006).

In spite of this, Buddhist culture and the monkhood slowly re-emerged after the Khmer Rouge regime (Harris 2001: 73; Kobayashi 2008: 170), although it was initially strictly regulated and supervised in the subsequent Vietnamese-ruled regime (the People's Republic of Kampuchea). Allowed only along the Theravada monastic lineage, Buddhism was considered one of the mass organizations, comparable to, for instance, the Women's Union in Vietnam (see Pistor and Le Thi Quy, this volume). Because of their military suitability, men under the age of 50 were prohibited from (re)ordination (Kobayashi 2008: 170). Only in 1989 were young monks free to join different monastic orders again. Religious books were reprinted and newly published (Marston 2009: 227). After Vietnamese rule, the number of ordained monks continued to increase and, by 2005, had nearly reached pre-war numbers (Ledgerwood 2008: 149). Temples were also gradually rehabilitated and newly constructed – especially through the support of Khmer living overseas and the growing wealthy urban population in Phnom Penh (Kobayashi 2008).

Since the 1980s, Harris (2001) counts five forms of Buddhist groups spanning the full continuum from modernist to traditionalist religious orientations. These sects distinguish themselves by, for example, the language used in prayers and chanting (Pali and/or Khmer) and the belief in elements such as spirits (Kobayashi 2008: 179ff.). Furthermore, the sects differ on the bases of their involvement in political affairs, development orientation and social engagement, as well as in urban and rural outreach (Harris 2001). Whereas, for example, some orders have a stake in social questions such as HIV/AIDS education and care for the sick (see Bourdier, this volume), others refrain from such secular concerns and understand HIV/AIDS as a form of karmic punishment (Harris 2001).

Outside of the formal monastic structure, and originating especially from the refugee camps in Thailand, Buddhism-oriented NGOs with social agendas were established. 'Buddhism for Development' for example, formed in the camps in 1990 with the support of the Konrad-Adenauer-Foundation, and the 'Association of Nuns and Laywomen of Cambodia' funded by the Heinrich Böll Foundation, combine religion with social services (Marston 2009: 227ff.). Öjendal (this volume) presents the case of 'Buddhism for Social Development Action', as an issue-oriented NGO with a religious basis. Whereas some of those faith-based development-oriented NGOs are very successful, Marston (2009) questions the authenticity and sustainability of such Buddhism-oriented NGOs. According to him, most of them lack an actual connection to the grassroots level and the pagodas. This is partly explained by the imperatives of NGO-type professionalism for donor relations; hiring laypeople on the technical merits of resumés and job interviews, rather than religious integrity and direct involvement with monks and pagodas, facilitates technical service provision but distances the organization from its cosmological basis.

According to Nissen (2008), trust and moral integrity are automatically associated with local pagodas which are seen as bastions of social and moral order. The local relevance of the pagoda to this day came across clearly in an interview with a staff member of a Phnom Penh-based research organization, who made the following recommendation to me:

> I think, talking about Cambodia, if you leave out the role of the pagoda, you leave out a big part of the story.... A lot of things in local Cambodia get done through the pagoda. So it is a point that you should consider as well. You must have read an article a long time ago about pagodas and local traditional associations. We have the funeral association, the school support committee, which is a half traditional, half contemporary type organization. We all have these women's groups, which is quite modern, the fishery and forestry associations. But once again, if it is a traditional association it always has got to do with the pagoda.... The way that such associations are set up is quite abstract. They do not have regular meetings but they have key people. If a family member of mine dies, I call people who know exactly who to go to and they make an announcement in the pagoda or somewhere so that people come to contribute to prepare for the funeral. So it is quite active, although it is not very obvious, it is quite abstract.
>
> (Phnom Penh, 6 September 2006)

The pagoda associations had been the first after the Khmer Rouge to re-emerge on the scene as strong actors in developing self-help schemes and facilitating development and moral rehabilitation at a time when formal state institutions were fairly weak (Gyallay-Pap 2004: 36). According to Kim and Ann (2005: 5f.), local self-help groups in Cambodia can be categorized as organic and mandated groups. The authors define organic groups as 'indigenous associations and committees that have existed in communities for a long period of time and are collectively initiated by local citizens' in the framework of the local pagoda. In contrast to this, mandated groups are 'associations or organizations that are established by international NGOs or initiated by the government's regulations'. These definitions, as dichotomous as they are, reflect well on the current distinctions between groups in Cambodia since the opening-up of the country.

The pagoda represents a kind of umbrella organization under which not only self-help activities, but also general associational activity, can be incubated and legitimated. It offers a cosmological orientation and, at the same time, generates potential for community development and poverty reduction since pagoda associations, which help fulfil spiritual aspirations (*karma*, see below) are often voluntarily formed to respond to the pressing needs of the villagers (e.g. rice and credit) (Aschmoneit 2004). Besides the cash and rice associations (*samakum prak, samakum sraov*, respectively), other grassroots groupings under the pagoda include, for example, boat racing groups and funeral associations (Narak 1998). Boat racing activities are very popular in Cambodia. The men of the group go to the forest and cut a big tree from which they construct the boat. The boat is kept in the pagoda compound where the construction process is accompanied by worship and various ceremonies to collect money to support the rowers for training and travelling to Phnom Penh for the annual national race. The winning team of the annual Water Festival brings great honour to the pagoda (ibid.: 6). The support of the boat racing teams can be understood as an expression of local solidarity and identity of the temple community. According to a female councillor, the funeral associations constitute a similar expression of self-help and solidarity that also finds it origins in local self-help traditions and the religious sphere:

When a member of the funeral association faces a problem with the funeral ceremony all the other members can go and help by giving rice or money as merit. On the seventh day of the funeral, every member gives five kilogrammes of Cambodian noodle and coconut. They give it to the family who faces the problem. If one family is the poorest, or vulnerable, and a child of theirs is really sick but they cannot pay for the medicine, then the money collection association (*dharma* association) can invite the *achar* and the monks with the microphone to appeal to the people in the village to know about this and to support as much as they can.

(Kampot province, 13 September 2006)

Serving as an important reference point of solidarity, the supporting community of a temple (*chomnoh*) is, nevertheless, not geographically determined; people can choose to participate in the activities of a number of pagodas (Kobayashi 2008: 177). Kobayashi defines the *chomnoh* as an 'unbounded social group, defined by shared participation in the activities of a certain temple'. The temple community comprises the monks and nuns,[1] the *achar wat* (Buddhist laymen who organize ceremonies), the temple committee (working with secular issues), and ordinary people. The latter constituency not only includes the villagers but also people living in the cities as well as the Khmer diaspora abroad who come back to their homelands for certain festivals in the rural area. The relevance of the local temple for the Buddhist population was explained by one member of the pagoda committee as follows:

> The pagoda is like an evidence of Cambodia's tradition from the past. I try to collect the people, who are Buddhists, and they come to celebrate the ceremonies here – like the Khmer New Year or the Water Festival.... So they all try to protect the ancient culture that they had before and lost in the past during the Pol Pot regime. Today they try to protect it again.
>
> (*wat* committee member, Kampong Thom province, 7 August 2005)

Besides offering a cosmological orientation to Cambodian identity, pagodas fulfil a certain development function as well; they can appeal to the local population to contribute donations for small-scale projects in the commune, such as the construction of bridges. One of the local Buddhist laymen explained:

> The pagoda always helps, always participates in community development, too. In the ceremony, the Buddhists come from everywhere to celebrate in the pagoda and this is the time for the *achar* and the pagoda committee with the loudspeaker to tell about the planned construction (such as a bridge) and [to ask] who would like to participate to give the gift, the donation. But we do not say how much to give but they understand and help – not only the Buddhists but also the monks give a gift too, to support the construction. They think that when they give the gift for the community development, they can get a lot of merit for their next life.
>
> (Kampong Thom province, 16 August 2006)

As mentioned in the quote, gaining merit is the most basic rationality constituting the reciprocal relationships of everyday Buddhist life. Besides following the five Buddhist precepts,[2] other activities such as the financing of temple construction or repair, becoming a monk for a certain period of time, and giving gifts or daily food to the monks, all have positive effects on a person's reincarnation (see Ovesen *et al.* 1996: 38). This applies even to the distant Khmer diaspora, who have turned out to be a highly influential group of philanthropists. These material transactions correspond to symbolic transactions: donating money, rice or in-kind to the pagoda contributes to personal merit-making (*punna*) and influencing the person's *karma* (see Aschmoneit 2004: 26f.). This strong religious rationality was explained in an interview with an *achar*:

> Cambodians believe in the Buddhist religion, saying if you do good, you will receive good. If you do evil, you will receive evil. If you do merit, you will receive merit. The people believe in this and they always go to the pagoda very crowdedly and do merit for the good merit of their next life.
>
> (Kampot province, 19 September 2006)

Consequently, *karma* is the result of the merit people gained in former lives; in an article, Ledgerwood (2008) confirms the contemporary importance of merit-making – especially in the form of making offerings to monks, as donations to the temple, and contributions to building projects. Despite the importance of the rationality of merit-making, one has to nevertheless be careful not to exclusively understand donations as a manifestation of religious faith. These can also be understood as very secular expressions of social pressure and community obligation. In his article on Khmer Buddhist self-help organizations, Aschmoneit (2004: 28) explains that these groups function predominantly according to the principle of solidarity, and declares this to be the core of the success of the pagoda activities in rural Cambodia. This finding is supported by Sasse, who argues that the groups under the pagodas are considered more reliable and trustworthy than newly created groups since they derive legitimacy from a location marked by high solidarity, where work is typically carried out for merit and not for profit (Sasse quoted in Pellini 2004: 6f.).

Those latter statements, however, have stimulated some critical exchange. In the next section, the romantic and uncritical picture aroused by some scholars' presentation of the temple as a 'harmonious center of rural life' (Kobayashi 2008: 189) will be scrutinized in light of the growing politicization and monetarization of religion. This will be followed by some conclusions about the sociocultural realm of the pagodas and the relationship between these religiously bounded spaces and debates on civil society in Cambodia.

Co-optation and conflicts in modern Buddhist Cambodia

The high social status of monks and the trust vested in them is apparent in society, but the way in which it manifests on an individual basis speaks about the nature of this status on a national level. This was illustrated in an interview with a former monk who is now the village chief. To the question of why he thinks he might have been selected as village chief, he explained:

> One of the reasons was that I used to be a monk and I used to learn [about Buddhism] and so the people know about my character and behaviour. And so they think that I know what is good and what is bad by being a monk, what sin is and what is not.
>
> (Kampong Thom province, 9 August 2006)

This 'naturally-fuelled' trust in the moral integrity of the monkhood has, however, come increasingly under pressure. In contemporary Cambodia, public debates about the relationship between politics and religion are growing (see Sreang 2008). Kent (2003: 18), for instance, draws attention to the threat of co-optation: 'Financial support from secular organizations and from political leaders may also play a significant role in shaping the choices of the clergy, silencing the critical voice that has for centuries provided a moral check on the excesses of abusive leaders'. Whereas the state and politics are commonly distrusted by

Cambodians, the politicization of the monkhood represents a severe 'symbolic pollution of the whole society' (Nissen 2008: 283).

Furthermore, the opening up of the country created avenues beyond religion for people's cosmological guidance, as the following quote by a member of a local CBO illustrates:

> If we talk about solidarity, in the past when you asked each other for some fish, they would give you without asking for payment. But today if you only want some spices, you have to buy. Only one fish, you need to buy. Everything you need to buy. So they only think of money!
>
> (Kampong Thom province, 13 August 2006)

According to this CBO member, capitalism becomes an important rationality for guiding people's social interaction and competing with religiously based ideas of reciprocity and merit-making. This type of behaviour is more exhaustively discussed by Marston (2009), who describes the ways in which religion, the state, and the market creatively respond to, and reshape, each other. Within the scope of this paper, however, I will conclude with a discussion of whether an indigenous civil society exists in Cambodia (and if so, in what forms?) in light of the types of proto civil society enshrined in pagodas and the religious sphere.

Cambodian associational life: beyond an 'NGO haven'

In the brief depiction above, there are challenges evolving in the religious sphere around pagodas that still require further research. As Kobayashi (2008) points out, for example, the actual relationship between temple and community has been rarely researched. Perhaps due to pre-war nostalgia, temple communities are oftentimes taken for granted, portrayed uncritically as harmonious entities. In the light of overall societal modernization and growing external influences, internal negotiation processes within pagodas – looking at, for instance, the role of women or the relationship between the traditionalist elder and the moderate younger monks of the same pagoda – have to a large extent not yet been addressed. This chapter, while cognizant of these issues, has skirted the larger contestations in pagodas in order to focus more specifically on the potential presence and role of the religious realm in Cambodian civil society. I discuss whether and how Cambodian associational life constitutes more than an 'NGO haven'.

The primary conclusion of this chapter is that the cultural embodiment of Buddhism in the rural area is indeed a relevant component of people's associational lives. The enthusiasm of foreign development agencies intervening in Cambodia and creating civil society from the 'outside' largely failed to acknowledge the potential of indigenous self-help traditions. Shared religious practices constitute social spaces and a moral community whose existence proves that the dismissive perception that Cambodia is experiencing 'social fatigue' after the war is untenable. Instead, this associational space was simply disregarded by the development aid industry in its rush to apply familiar discourses to civil society development in the 1990s. This was evident at the annual meeting of the NGO Forum in 1996, at which the Venerable Moneychenda, a prominent Buddhist monk and himself head of a local NGO, sternly advised the international community of the need to strengthen indigenous groups instead of initiating long-term dependency by duplicating Western-style NGOs (see Curtis 1998: 136). Indeed, as I demonstrate, civil society in Cambodia was not inevitably an externally imposed sector as there were, and continue to be, actors and associations representing societal forces that predate UNTAC. The social spaces that emerge in the religious realm, which are based, among other things, on the rationality of merit-making, continue to function as strong social 'glue' for community cohesion in rural Cambodia. More likely than not, these spaces do not fit with, or even contradict, the Western understanding of civil society in the context of development. In fact, Kent (2003: 23) reports that she often heard Western NGO staff complain about villagers using the credit provided by the NGO for making donations to the pagoda instead of investing the money into their family business. Responding to this exasperation, Kent (2003) suggests the need to take an emic perspective when initially trying to elaborate the meaning of community and civil society in any given local cultural context, by

> [taking] the villagers' knowledge and will seriously, and [trying] to understand what it is that they value so highly and by which they set such store, but which does not necessarily correspond with the values promoted by the international community.
>
> (Kent 2003: 23)

In this respect, the interface between so-called expert knowledge, derived from the global model of civil society, and local knowledge, often results in the creation of 'systems of ignorance', meaning that development knowledge is automatically assigned a high status while the competences and the practices of everyday life and the cultural forms of the local population are disregarded (see both Lachenmann 2003 and Hobart 1993). I argue that the Western liberal democratic model of civil society is unable or unwilling to account for these diverse (and according to the rationality of the development aid industry, even 'irritating') forms of socio-cultural engagement, which are less formalized and thus less apparent, but which nevertheless strongly correspond to locally embedded modes of collective solidarity and belonging and represent alternative ways of dealing with problems of everyday life in the rural area. Forms of civil society and associational life can be subtle and do not inevitably need to have an explicit political agenda for the achievement of socio-political change. Nevertheless, given the role in shaping everyday life, providing safety nets, and their broad acceptance in society, I argue that not only Buddhist-oriented NGOs, but also less formalized self-help groups (which are both parts of socially engaged Buddhism), qualify as civil society in Cambodia.

While there has been a shift among scholars working on civil society that increasingly favours the acknowledgment of actual activities of civil society (instead of only looking at formalistic organizations) (see Kerkvliet *et al.* 2008), conspicuously absent are discussions on civil society with a more (micro) cosmological orientation. This view would seek out the often-overlooked spaces of belonging, cultural identity, and meaning that might be a fundamental basis for civic engagement. In order to understand such emic grounds of associational life, one cannot leave aside the changing socio-cultural experiences and knowledge that make up the subtle framework that guides people's actions.

Notes

1 Although there are a large number of (older) nuns, pagodas are dominated by monks. The head nun is subordinate to the pagoda committee, which itself is headed by a monk (Ramage *et al.* 2005).
2 Refrain from killing any living being, from stealing, from committing adultery, from lying and from drinking liquor – these constitute the five precepts by which one gains merit (Ovesen *et al.* 1996: 38).

References

Aschmoneit, W. (2004) 'Khmer Buddhist Self-Help Organizations and Development Cooperation', Civil Society in Southeast Asia Conference 7–8 June, Phnom Penh, Cambodia, Munich: Munich Institute for Social Sciences: 25–9.

Bit, S. (1991) *The Warrior Heritage: A Psychological Perspective of Cambodian Trauma*, Le Cerrito, California: Seanglim Bit.

Blunt, P and Turner, M. (2005) 'Decentralisation, Democracy and Development in a Post-Conflict Society: Commune Councils in Cambodia' in *Public Administration and Development*, 25 (1):75–87.

Chandler, D. P. (1991) *The Tragedy of Cambodian History. Politics, War and revolution since 1945*. Thailand/New Haven/London: Silkworm Books/Yale University Press.

Chap, S. (2005) 'Role of Media and Civil Society in a Democracy: A Cambodian Case Study', Working Paper No. 8, Phnom Penh: Cambodian Institute for Cooperation and Peace.

Curtis, G. (1998) *Cambodia Reborn? The Transition to Democracy and Development*, Washington DC and Geneva: Brookings Institute and UN Research Institute for Social Development.

Downie, S. and Kingsbury, D. (2001) 'Political Development and the Re-emergence of Civil Society in Cambodia' in *Contemporary Southeast Asia*, 23 (1): 43–63.

Ebihara, May M. (1993) '"Beyond Suffering": The Recent History of a Cambodian Village' in B. Ljunggren (ed.), *The Challenge of Reform in Indochina*, Cambridge, MA: Harvard University Press: 149–66.

Ehlert, J. (2007) 'Possibilities and Constraints of "Good Governance" in Rural Cambodia. Empirical Case Studies', unpublished thesis, University of Bielefeld, Germany.

Freske, S. (1999) 'Kambodscha: Die größte Demokratieexportunternehmung der Vereinten Nationen' [Cambodia: The biggest democratization machinery of the United Nations] in R. Hanisch (ed.), *Demokratieexport in die Länder des Südens? Schriften des Deutschen Übersee-Instituts Hamburg no. 35*, [Democracy export to the countries of the South? Writings of the German Overseas Institute of Hamburg], Hamburg: Deutsches Übersee-Institut Hamburg: 431–45.

Frings, V. (1994) 'Cambodia After Decollectivization (1989–1992)' in *Journal of Contemporary Asia*, 24 (1): 49–66.

German Federal Foreign Office (2012) 'Kambodscha', Online. Available at: www.auswaertiges-amt.de/DE/Aussenpolitik/Laender/Laenderinfos/01-Laender/Kambodscha.html (accessed 6 December 2012).

Gyallay-Pap, P. (2004) 'Civil Society and Religion in Southeast Asia: An Overview', Civil Society in Southeast Asia Conference 7–8 June, Phnom Penh, Cambodia, Munich: Munich Institute for Social Sciences: 35–6.

Hann, C. and Dunn, E. (1996) 'Introduction: Political Society and Civil Anthropology' in C. Hann and E. Dunn (eds), *Civil Society: Challenging Western Models*, London and New York: Routledge: 1–26.

Harris, I. (2001) 'Buddhist Sangha Groupings in Cambodia' in *Buddhist Studies Review*, 18 (1): 73–106.

Hobart, M. (1993) 'Introduction: The Growth of Ignorance?' in M. Hobart (ed.), *An Anthropological Critique of Development. The Growth of Ignorance*, London: Routledge: 1–30.

Hughes, C. and Öjendal, J. (2006) 'Reassessing Tradition in Times of Political Change: Post-War Cambodia Reconsidered' in *Journal of Southeast Asian Studies*, 37 (3): 415–20.

Kent, A. (2003) 'Recovery of the Collective Spirit: The Role of the Revival of Buddhism in Cambodia', Working Paper No. 8, Goteborg University, Department of Social Anthropology.

Kerkvliet, B. J. T., Nguyen Quang A. and Bach Tan Sinh (2008) *Forms of Engagement between State Agencies and Civil Society Organizations in Vietnam*, Hanoi: VUFO NGO Resource Center.

Khus, T. (2004) 'Cambodian Civil Society Movement', Civil Society in Southeast Asia Conference 7–8 June, Phnom Penh, Cambodia. Munich: Munich Institute for Social Sciences: 63–8.

Kim, S. and Ann, S. (2005) 'Decentralisation: Can Civil Society Enhance Local Government's Accountability in Cambodia? in *Cambodia Development Review*, 9 (3): 5–7.

Kobayashi, S. (2008) 'Reconstructing Buddhist Temple Buildings. An Analysis of Village Buddhism After the Era of Turmoil' in A. Kent and D. Chandler (eds), *People of Virtue: Reconfiguring Religion, Power and Morality in Cambodia Today*, Copenhagen: NIAS Press: 169–94.

Lachenmann, G. (1997) 'Zivilgesellschaft und Entwicklung' [Civil society and development] in M. Schulz (ed.), *Entwicklung* [Development], Opladen: Westdeutscher Verlag: 187–211.

Lachenmann, G. (2003) 'Savoir Local, etatique et Développementaliste: Quelle Interaction entre décentralisation et Société Civile?', Working Paper No. 343, University of Bielefeld, Sociology of Development Research Centre.

Ledgerwood, J. (1996) 'Politics and Gender: Negotiating Conceptions of the Ideal Woman in Present Day Cambodia' in *Asia Pacific Viewpoint*, 37 (2): 139–52.

Ledgerwood, J. (1998) 'Rural Development in Cambodia: The View from the Village' in F. Z. Brown and D. G. Timberman (eds), *Cambodia and the International Community: The Quest for Peace, Development and Democracy*, New York and Singapore: Asia Society and the Institute of Southeast Asian Studies: 127–47.

Ledgerwood, J. (2008) 'Buddhist Practice in Rural Kandal Province, 1960 and 2003. An

Essay in Honor of May M. Ebihara' in A. Kent and D. Chandler (eds), *People of Virtue: Reconfiguring Religion, Power and Morality in Cambodia Today*, Copenhagen: NIAS Press: 147–68.

Ledgerwood, J. and Vijghen, J. (2002) 'Decision-Making in Rural Khmer Villages' in J. Ledgerwood (ed.), *Cambodia Emerges from the Past: Eight Essays*, Northern Illinois University: Southeast Asia Publications: 109–50.

Luco, F. (2002) *Between a Tiger and a Crocodile: Management of Local Conflicts in Cambodia*, Phnom Penh: United Nations Educational, Scientific and Cultural Organization (UNESCO).

Marston, J. (2009) 'Cambodian Religion since 1989' in J. Öjendal and M. Lilja (eds), *Beyond Democracy in Cambodia: Political Reconstruction in a Post-Conflict Society*, Copenhagen: NIAS Press: 224–49.

Mong Hay, L. (1998) 'Building Democracy in Cambodia: Problems and Prospects' in F. Z. Brown and D. G. Timberman (eds), *Cambodia and the International Community: The Quest for Peace, Development and Democracy*, New York and Singapore: Asia Society and the Institute of Southeast Asian Studies: 169–86.

Monychenda, H. (1998) *Buddhism and the Making of Democracy in Cambodia: A Report to Cambodian Buddhist Council*, Phnom Penh: Cambodian Academic Network.

Narak, S. (1998) 'Historically Rooted Organisations in the Traditional Rural Community Stung District, Kampong Thom Province, Cambodia', PDP-Self Help Promotion/GTZ-Self Help Team, Kampong Thom, Cambodia: unpublished paper.

Nissen, C. J. (2008) 'Buddhism and Corruption' in A. Kent and D. Chandler (eds), *People of Virtue: Reconfiguring Religion, Power and Morality in Cambodia Today*, Copenhagen: NIAS Press: 272–92.

Ovesen, J., Trankell, I.-B. and Öjendal, J. (1996) 'When Every Household is an Island: Social Organization and Power Structures in Rural Cambodia' in *Uppsala Research Reports in Cultural Anthropology 15*, Uppsala, Sweden: Department of Cultural Anthropology, Uppsala University.

Öjendal, J. and Kim S. (2006) 'Korob, Kaud, Klach: In Search of Agency in Rural Cambodia' in *Journal of Southeast Asian Studies*, 37 (3): 507–26.

Pellini, A. (2004) 'Traditional Pagoda Associations and the Emergence of Civil Society in Cambodia' in *Cambodia Development Review*, 8 (3): 5–8.

Ramage, I., Pictet, G. and Lyhun K. (2005) *Girls and Buddhist Nuns. Research Report*, Cambodia: Domrei Research and Consulting.

Springer, S. (2010) *Cambodia's neoliberal order: violence, authoritarianism, and the contestation of public space*, Oxford: Routledge.

Sreang, H. (2008) 'The Scope and Limitations of Political Participation by Buddhist Monks' in A. Kent and D. Chandler (eds), *People of Virtue: Reconfiguring Religion, Power and Morality in Cambodia Today*, Copenhagen: NIAS Press: 241–56.

St John, R. B. (2005) 'Democracy in Cambodia – One Decade, US$5 Billion Later: What Went Wrong?' in *Contemporary Southeast Asia*, 27 (3): 406–28.

Vickery, M. (1992) 'Cambodia's Economy: Where has it come from, where is it going?' in T. Murano and I. Takeuchi (eds), *Indochina Economic Reconstruction and International Cooperation*, Tokyo: Institute of Developing Economies: 47–62.

Weiss, T. G. (2000) 'Governance, Good Governance and Global Governance: Conceptual and Actual Challenges' in *Third World Quarterly*, 21 (5): 795–814.

13 Voluntary or state-driven?

Community-based organizations in the Mekong Delta, Vietnam

Gabi Waibel and Simon Benedikter

The current debate on the development of civil society in Vietnam indicates that a large and growing number of community-based organizations (CBOs) exist in the country. By analysing the recent trajectories of CBO development in a rural area of Can Tho City in the Mekong Delta, this chapter critically challenges the idea of an emerging civil society independent of the state. The following background of the study starts with a brief introduction to the current understandings of Vietnamese civil society, in general, and CBOs, in particular.

Civil society in Vietnam – controversial approaches, fuzzy concepts

A couple of years after the introduction of *Đổi mới* Vietnam scholars started to investigate the emergence of civil society (organizations) and the uninterrupted growth in this body of literature suggests a continuous interest in the topic. Although the available publications generally exhibit considerable differences in theoretical and empirical approach, as well as in their eventual conclusions, a few aspects can be considered characteristic of the debate. First of all, the absence of an official definition of 'civil society' by the Vietnamese government led to a diverse and often confusing use of the term. As the concept of civil society is 'not widely recognized by the authorities yet' (Norlund 2007: 68), translations and interpretations between Vietnamese and English are also difficult. The 'invention' of terms, such as civic and issue-oriented organizations (Wischermann and Nguyen Quang Vinh 2003: 870),[1] takes the official discourse into account but these terms have not been widely adopted. In addition, there is a strong tendency in the literature to develop normative categories (Hannah 2007: 94), which indicates that civil society is often conceptualized as organizations with observable boundaries. Similarly, different classifications of civil society organizations have been developed, with a range of between four and nine group categories and organization types (for an example see endnote[1]) (e.g. Norlund *et al.* 2006; Sidel 1995; Wischermann and Nguyen Quang Vinh 2003). The differences between these classifications are partly due to the (frequently changing) legal framework. To date, no standardized typology of Vietnam's civil society exists (Menge 2009: 104).

Second, a considerable number of studies have been commissioned by international organizations, mostly donor agencies. A prominent example is the oft-quoted CIVICUS study, which claims to be 'the first step in identifying civil society in Vietnam' (Norlund *et al.* 2006: 17). CIVICUS defines civil society according to the mainstream of development cooperation as 'the arena, outside of the family, the state, and the market where people associate to advance common interests' (CIVICUS 2003). However, for the Vietnamese results, the study broadened the definition of civil society but ultimately acknowledges that 'civil society is not separated from the state' (Norlund 2007: 72). This example nicely illustrates Salemink's argument that international agencies, in order to carry out their mandate of development in places like Vietnam where the Western concept of civil society is not immediately applicable, is forced to redefine civil society to some degree (Salemink 2006). In fact, these agencies have a strong interest in employing civil society organizations as partners in development (projects); so far, however, the impact of donor-driven approaches on civil society development has hardly been subject to research in Vietnam (Bui The Cuong 2005: 97).

Third, research activities show a clear urban bias and expert interviews seem to be the predominant methodology employed. Anthropological and organizational studies 'from within' are basically missing, and little is known about how these organizations operate and how they manage their interfaces with the state. The range of findings also shows divergent experiences and practices between northern and southern Vietnam. With regard to rural-based associations, most studies stem from the north. In principle, CBOs are considered to be one type of 'civic organization' in Vietnam. Fourth, most of the literature views the relationship between the state and civil society organizations as the key issue, with a strong tendency to dichotomize between the two (Heng 2004: 144ff.).

Despite the diversity of approaches, gaps, and shortcomings, the majority of Vietnam scholars agree that 'civil society exists in degrees' in Vietnam (Kerkvliet 2003: 15) and that state–society relations have gradually changed since the 1980s. Legal reforms and economic liberalization provided the foundation for a growing organizational pluralism, whereby the predominant mono-organizational socialism, as described by Thayer (1995) in the beginning of the 1990s, has been partly transformed. In fact, before *Đổi mới*, private businesses were prohibited, and the few officially recognized non-state organizations were 'subsidized and managed by the state' (Bui The Cuong 2005: 94). In addition to new legal types of civil organizations, previously recognized organizations also continue to exist. The most prominent examples are the mass organizations, which were set up in the 1930s and are closely linked to the Vietnam Communist Party (VCP); their classification as civil society organizations however remains controversial (see Pistor and Le Thi Quy, as well as Bach Tan Sinh, both in this volume). This also holds true for a range of other organizations, which are connected to either state agencies or the Party (Norlund *et al.* 2006: 33f.). In fact, the boundaries between the state and civil society are far from clear and questions of a 'state-led civil society' (UNDP 2006: 8) are frequently raised.

The VCP continues to maintain its monopoly on political power, and restrictions for social organizations are still commonplace. Deficiencies in the legal framework also seem to be deliberate (the Law on Associations, initiated in the 1990s, is still pending). In principle, organizations are allowed to work outside the political sphere, and the state keeps track of, and control over, the registration processes and their activities (Gray 2003: 111). In general, non-state actors are still perceived as a potential challenge by the government (Vasavakul 2003: 25–6), although the so-called socialization of sectors such as health, education and environment aims at transferring state responsibilities to society, with private sector involvement being particularly encouraged.[2] This policy is often supported by donor and INGO projects and, consequently, there has been a wave of new organizations providing facilities and services (Salemink 2006: 118; Vasavakul 2003: 33–4). In line with this, numerous structural ties are supposed to guarantee the harmonious relationship with the state, and most civil society organizations portray themselves as collaborative partners of state agencies, working for the benefit of the country and its people (Thayer 2009).

The proliferation of community-based organizations – a strand of civil society development?

In July 2005 it was estimated that about 140,000 CBOs were operating in Vietnam (Sabharwal and Than Thi Thien Houng 2005: 4), and Norlund *et al.* (2006: 48) registered a 'boost' in the number of CBOs, with a 'remarkably high concentration in the South'. Nevertheless, there seems to be a lack of understanding of what the term CBO actually stands for, and the following definition illustrates its broad meaning:

> Collaborative Groups (CGs) – a term that is recently used to address those groups/organizations that operate at the grassroots level (commune or village) ... are also called community based organizations (CBOs) by development organizations (donors, NGOs). CGs exist in many forms, including for profit or non profit, or for economic, social, or cultural purposes, or as combined-purpose organizations.
>
> (People's Participation Working Group (PPWG) Vietnam 2007)

A variety of legal provisions issued in the context of *Đổi mới* reforms allow for different forms of association, but there is also evidence that CBOs emerge 'both within and at the margin of the state's regulatory framework' (Hy V. Luong 2005: 123; Kerkvliet 2003: 3). The currently available literature, which is definitely not exhaustive, provides information on different mutual aid groups, micro-credit and so-called rural collaborative groups, as well as faith-based organizations. The literature also indicates that CBO development varies spatially, depending to some degree on the combination of political and socio-cultural factors in different parts of the country. Historically speaking, the distinctions in local forms of traditional village and community life provided for a different foundation of grassroots development. In pre-colonial northern Vietnam, people lived in close proximity, and village affairs were managed and organized by local committees, clubs and professional groups (Grossheim 2004; Marr 2004; Pike 2000). In the Mekong Delta, in contrast, people settled along waterways and villages and remained loosely structured (Biggs *et al.* 2009; Jamieson 1995: 5). Community ties in the south generally remained weak, although peasants used to collaborate on land preparation, seeding and harvesting (Nguyen Ngoc De 2006: 69–70).

The regional differences in CBO development diverged further when, after independence (1954), northern and southern Vietnam ended up with different political regimes. Woodside (1976: 284) points out that, under colonialism and the first independent Saigon administration in the south, the development of 'uncontrollable rural organizations' was restricted and, as a result, peasants were hardly motivated to develop their organizational capacity. In northern Vietnam, to compare, the communist government integrated all forms of organization into the one-party-state structure; the increasing predominance of mass organizations worked to undermine formerly active institutions (Hy V. Luong 2005: 125). Another important policy measure of the new regime in the north was the collectivization of rural households, which was implemented in combination with land reforms. This policy was rigorously enforced and, after reunification (1976), continued nationwide, though with little success in the south, particularly in the Mekong Delta.[3] With *Đổi mới* and the return to household-based production in 1988, membership in agricultural cooperatives (*hợp tác xã*) and collective groups (*tập đoàn sản xuất*) finally became voluntary. As a result, the number of cooperatives significantly decreased and most of the collective groups dissolved. When the government issued new legislation in 1996 promoting so-called 'new-style cooperatives', farmers demonstrated a clear lack of interest (Le Meur *et al.* 2005: 37ff.; Nguyen Ngoc De 2006: 73–4).

What happened instead was the return to and (re)establishment of mutual self-help groups throughout the country. In northern Vietnam, such voluntary associations tend to be kinship-based and rooted in traditional institutions (Phan Dai Doan 2007: 56f.). Dang Thi Viet Phuong and Bui Quang Dung (2011) recently found a significant number of voluntary groups (*tổ chức xã hội tự nguyện*) in the Red River Delta, whose activities ranged from sports to traditional music, gardening, and the organization of community festivities. Migrants in big cities often engage in same-native-place associations of mutual assistance (Hy V. Luong 2003: 104). In the south, farmers started to initiate self-help groups to, for example, escape poverty traps (Hicks 2004), while ethnic minorities began building local safety nets (Taylor 2004: 265). Moreover, banking reforms and the breakdown of rural credit cooperatives led to the establishment of numerous savings groups (Seibel 1992: 64, 77f.). Similarly, other service gaps created by the collapse of rural collectives had to be filled by peasants (Kirsch 1997: 3) and, by the turn of the century, Fforde (2008: 17–18) documented the co-existence of formal (state-organized) and informal farmer groups. In the context of fundamental changes in the rural production system, farmers were compelled to engage in groups in order to manage pumping and drainage activities. Furthermore, governmental agencies continued to promote cooperative groups by offering incentives and technical equipment (Kono 2001: 77–8). To what extent group formation was 'voluntary' remains unclear.

Furthermore, it is a popular perception that 'NGOs' are initiated by foreign agencies and, indeed, numerous donor reports point out that a large number of CBOs have been set up in the context of project work (CIDIN 2006: 8). In fact, thousands of water and sanitation groups (Wyatt and Huynh Thi Ngoc Tuyet 2008), small-scale business clubs, micro-credit groups, and the like, have been established. These activities have closely followed national policies; microfinance schemes, for example, became a prominent instrument for poverty alleviation (Bloh 2007).

The trend of group formation is indicative of another shift in the policy framework. Following the enactment of the Grassroots Democracy Decree (1998), which provides the legitimate foundation for CBO development and 'participatory' approaches (Benedikter 2008: 66–77),[4] a range of other legal instruments, such as the regulation of water user groups, have been issued. In the Red River Delta, entities called clubs (câu lạc bộ) are registered under decree 88/2003/ ND-CP (Dang Thi Viet Phuong and Bui Quang Dung 2011), which regulates the organization and operation of certain types of association (Government of Vietnam 2003). Moreover, another decree (Decree 151) addressing the organization and operation of cooperative groups at commune level was enacted in 2007 (Government of Vietnam 2007).

Finally, despite widespread acknowledgements of the proliferation of voluntary associations, empirical research on CBO development is basically absent. In addition, strong regional disparities and a variety of responses to CBOs by local authorities are being reported (Kerkvliet et al. 2008). Kerkvliet et al. (2008: 46) therefore conclude that studies on CBOs should concentrate on concrete activities and what is physically happening in a given case study area. To that end, the following section presents the trajectory of group formation processes in Can Tho City and analyses current institutional change processes in a given environmental and socio-political context.

CBOs on the rise: insights from Can Tho City

In the framework of a large scientific research project on water resources management in the Mekong Delta,[5] a number of questions related to the interface between state management and water users have emerged. With a view to capturing institutional change processes, a survey covering 120 CBOs in eight different communes in Can Tho City was conducted in 2009–10. The survey was complemented by a series of interviews with state officials at district and provincial levels, and separate group discussions with local leaders and water users. Given the focus of water resources management, the following CBOs were included in the survey: 47 production groups (tổ hợp tác sản xuất), 12 irrigation groups (tổ bơm tưới), 56 micro-credit groups (nhóm tín dụng) engaged in water and sanitation, and one club *(câu lạc bộ)* and four groups which were involved in both production and micro-credit activities.[6]

Can Tho City is located in the heart of the Mekong Delta. Despite significant urbanization and modernization, rural production remains predominant. This includes, first and foremost, (irrigated) rice cultivation; but aquaculture and, to a lesser extent, horticulture, are also expanding. Water constitutes a major resource and state agencies undertake huge investments in flood management, salinity control, and the development of irrigation facilities (Evers and Benedikter 2009). Although water resource management is under state responsibility, water users get increasingly involved in managing the water for production and domestic use (Nguyen Xuan Tiep 2008: 297–9). A local narrative of CBO development, presented below, illustrates the origin of this shift (group interviews, October 2009):

In 1996, farmers experienced severe difficulties controlling water levels during the flood season. Following dramatic production losses, state agencies started to campaign for the formation of cooperative groups in fruit orchards and rice cultivation communities and, as a result, a number of self-help groups came into being. Other groups emerged when, as a result of dyke building, the nature of irrigation management changed. Pumping activities had to be coordinated and aligned with cropping calendars, and commune authorities strongly promoted and guided the process of establishing pumping groups (in 2004 in Thoi Dong commune, Co Do District, and in 2005 in Thanh An Commune, Vinh Thanh District).

From the mid-1990s, group formation was on the rise: In 2001 a total of 1,466 production groups were officially recorded, and by 2008 the number had more than doubled to 3,356 groups (DARD 2008: 18). Production groups tend to specialize in rice, gardening, fishery or aquaculture, but also include irrigation and pumping groups. In addition, a boost in micro-credit groups could be observed.[7] The data on the 120 groups covered by the survey demonstrate an acceleration of group formation from the mid-1990s. Interestingly though, 36 out of the 120 groups had formed out of previously existing agricultural collective groups or cooperatives.

According to the findings of the survey, the majority of respondents formed the new groups in order to share experience and knowledge, save costs and time, and improve their access to external support, including credit. The core activities of these production and irrigation groups include hydraulic works (dykes, canals and culverts), drainage and pumping, and mutual assistance for field preparation and pest management. As a minor activity, they engage in social welfare, while a few (less than 10 per cent) operate saving schemes.

Micro-credit groups (in this survey) aim at obtaining funds for improving their water supply and sanitation and also operate savings schemes. They also commonly engage in small enterprise development, notably animal breeding, farming and crafts. Education on family planning, hygiene and HIV/AIDS, as well as social welfare projects, round off their activity profiles.

The groups' scope of activities can change over time, and while some groups increase and diversify their activities, others may end up dissolving (although they might continue to exist on paper).

The majority of groups are active throughout the year (67 per cent). However, almost all irrigation groups and some production groups only operate seasonally, depending on the agricultural production cycle. The spatial scope of operation of CBOs tends to be limited: 34 per cent of the groups function at the hamlet level, while the rest stay within commune boundaries. In terms of membership, an average of 29–34 members was calculated, though differences among the groups are significant.[8] Group membership seems to be stable. Gender plays a very important role, with few micro-credit groups having male members and only one production group having predominantly female membership.

Internal and external regulations of CBOs

If one looks at common group formation processes, it is evident that mass organizations and state agencies often play a significant role. Furthermore, a set of formal requirements as well as (internal) rules and regulations indicate a strong tendency of formalization. Seventy out of the 120 groups surveyed reported that their establishment was initiated either by local authorities, usually the commune People's Committees or hamlet heads, or by the hamlet units of the Women's Union and Farmers' Association. In two cases, an international development agency played a role in encouraging group formation. Forty-four groups said that they were established on their own initiative. In all the communes surveyed, different types of community meeting were used to encourage people to become involved in self-help groups while local cadres frequently pointed out the benefits of mutual collaboration.

Most groups adopted a set of guiding principles, typically including some of the following stipulations: group members must be at least 18 years old (80 per cent) and need to be of moral and social integrity (68 per cent). The capacity to comply with financial contributions was a key requirement for taking part in both micro-credit groups (66 per cent) and irrigation groups (66 per cent), as farmers are requested to pay for joint pumping campaigns (contributions are based on the individual demand). Furthermore, 77 per cent of the production and 91 per cent of the irrigation groups require individual landholding as a prerequisite for membership. With regard to tasks and duties, basically all groups have developed internal regulations, such as compulsory attendance at group meetings. Compliance with such regulations is, however, considered weak in roughly a fifth of the groups. In addition, groups generally set up a leadership structure managed by a head, a deputy head and, in 94 per cent of the surveyed groups, a secretary. The head officially represents the group in external affairs and signs documents on behalf of the group. Less than a third (27 per cent) of the groups also appoint a treasurer. Financial management is thus not uniform: either the treasurer or the secretary is in charge of accounting, while the collection of fees falls under the secretary's (54 per cent), and the head's mandate (71 per cent).

Almost all of the surveyed groups were officially registered with either the People's Committee or a mass organization, and sometimes both. About a third of the groups were of the opinion that registration was a formal requirement (although not prescribed by law). In interviews, representatives of many groups noted that registration would improve their chances for accessing support schemes. The registration process seems to be uniform, requiring a few discrete steps (see Table 13.1). First of all, a list of group members is compiled, group leaders are elected, and group regulations are drafted. Based on our findings, the regulations are basically modelled on blueprints provided by local authorities and mass organizations, whose guidelines supposedly follow the provisions of Decree 151. As a next step, the minutes of the inaugural meeting, with a membership list attached, is submitted to a mass organization for approval. At this point a registration fee must be paid. In addition, most groups also seek the consent of the communal People's Committee, with the mass organizations often facilitating this by forwarding relevant documents.

As a result of this fairly standardized procedure for registration, mass organizations and local authorities are in a favourable position to keep track of, and intervene in, CBO development. The following quote illustrates how local officials closely monitor group establishment:

> All group members meet together with state representatives of the hamlet and the commune administration. In this meeting group candidates for leadership positions are elected by the members.
>
> (irrigation group, Thanh An Commune, Vinh Thanh District,
> Can Tho City, 2009)

One reason why it is important for local cadres to keep track of groups is because these data are then used to produce reports for more senior agencies, which – since the enactment of Decree 151 – officially encourage the development of farmer groups and hold local agencies accountable for the respective policy implementations. This is demonstrated openly in the following report:

> The district of Vinh Thanh at present has a total of 357 cooperative groups and 23 clubs, accounting for a total membership of 9,779 households, all of which are engaged in agriculture. Cooperative organizations and clubs ... need to be promoted as a type of collaborative organization of peasants that matches their practical needs in present-day agricultural production ... in order to develop effective production models.
>
> (Vinh Thanh District Office of Agriculture and Rural Development 2009,
> translation by the authors)

Table 13.1 Registration procedure for establishing a CBO

Type of procedure	Prevalence in groups (%)
Written application to mass organization	94
Consent of the People's Committee	96
Official membership list	45
Reporting scheme for meetings	34

The national policy of promoting and strengthening CBO formation under state guidance finds its expression in provincial government reports, such as those of Can Tho City, which encourage local cadres to act accordingly (DARD 2008). These efforts are embedded in the state-promoted concept of the so-called collective economy *(kinh tế tập thể)*, which ideologically stems from the pre-reform era but is still maintained as a key economic principle of the socialist-oriented market economy, as emphasized by the political leadership in the latest Eleventh Party Congress (Tạp Chí Cộng Sản, 21 August 2011). As Article 12 of Decree 151 states, cooperative groups have 'the right ... to participate in the elaboration and implementation of plans, programmes and projects in support of collective economy' and socio-economic development in general. In other words – farmer CBOs represent a vehicle to boost rural development, agricultural production and poverty alleviation.

Another revealing aspect of state–group relations is the involvement of officials in group membership and leadership (Norlund 2007: 84). With regard to the first aspect, local cadres were listed as members in 37 per cent of all the groups. As local cadres also do farming, this finding is not surprising. However, only nine groups (out of 120) reported that officials in state management functions also hold leadership positions. Instead, group leaders are more often than not affiliated with the local mass organization, as illustrated in Table 13.2.

In addition, 97 per cent of all groups consider themselves affiliated with a mass organization. This clearly demonstrates that mass organizations have an important role in CBO management. Moreover, they are in charge of implementing government policies and selected programmes, and can thereby offer incentives and further strengthen the state–group relationships. For agricultural development, training and advisory services, in close collaboration with the extension service, are provided to facilitate new production technologies and integrated pest management (Nguyen Ngoc De 2006: 76ff.), and subsidies can be offered. From the survey data on production groups, for instance, 93 per cent of them received training, 65 per cent advice, 12 per cent material support and equipment, and 30 per cent gained access to credit through the facilitation of the Farmers' Association. With regard to training and advisory services, it must however be critically examined whether this corresponds to farmers' demands. According to Nguyen Quy Hanh[9] (2011, personal communication), this is often not the case. In fact, state-run programmes must correspond with national policies – and these do not necessarily align with peasant's views and ideas (Dang Kieu Nhan *et al.* 2007: 169).

Table 13.2 Involvement of group leadership in mass organizations

	Membership in mass organization			Official function in mass organizations	
Group head (total 120)	95	79%	of whom	39	33%
Vice group head (total 120)	81	67%		8	7%

In the wake of the government's socialization policy, the collection of fees, the organization of labour campaigns, and the alignment of cropping and pumping schemes in accordance with the district and communal production targets are often carried out by CBOs (Benedikter and Waibel 2013). It can be assumed that, in return, CBOs are granted privileged access to existing support systems.

Finally, and as the sex-disaggregated data on group membership reveals, mass organizations pursue a gendered approach to community mobilization: male farmers affiliate with the Farmers' Association, while females predominantly engage with the Women's Union. Specifically, it appears that domestic waste management, health, and hygiene are considered 'women's issues', such that mainly women's groups are targeted for related training programmes.

The management of micro-credit groups in water and sanitation

For micro-credit groups, registration with the state is an administrative necessity. Individuals or households who lack the requested collateral for loan applications have a chance to apply for loans as members of a micro-credit group, but only groups which are registered with either the mass organizations or the state agencies can access such credit schemes.[10] The funds are mainly provided by rural banks as part of the implementation of national and local policies or development cooperation objectives. Agreements between the bank and mass organizations regulate their respective responsibilities. In general, mass organizations provide the guarantee to the funding institution on behalf of the group, support the administrative process of loan application, and supervise the correct usage and repayment of the funds (Dufheus 2007 cited in: Bloh 2007: 98; ILO 2005: 16). Notably, the Women's Union plays a prominent role in the formalized micro-finance sector (Bloh 2007: 19).

In Can Tho City, the Women's Union is generally involved in environmental protection, the development of water and sanitation facilities of rural households (a project of the Ministry of Agriculture and Rural Development (MARD) since 1999), and water treatment education (Vietnam Women's Union 2008). Since 2004 the Women's Union has operated as a credit facilitator for a large government programme which offers subsidized group loans for the construction of water supply and sanitation infrastructure (mostly household latrines) with a comparatively low interest rate over a period of three to five years (Reis and Mollinga 2009: 11ff.). The loans are granted by the Vietnam Bank for Social Policy[11] and the Women's Union actively promotes credit groups that qualify for these loans (Vietnam Women's Union and Social Bank for Policy 2003). Out of our sample, almost a third (30.9 per cent) of all the surveyed groups directly acknowledged that they were mobilized by the Women's Union.

With regard to their motivation to establish a micro-credit group, the raising of credit naturally ranks high (89 per cent); indeed, all groups intended to operate group internal savings schemes (probably with the purpose of eventually

qualifying for external credit schemes). So far, not all groups have been successful: less than half actually received a loan. Nevertheless, almost all the credit
groups indicated that they have benefited from their affiliation with the mass
organizations, as they have received training and advice. Indeed, capacity building appears to be a strong component in the relationship between mass organizations and CBOs. Capacity building includes a variety of activities, such as state
propaganda that benefits mass organizations, as well as technical or legal training
that benefits groups. It would be interesting to observe the ongoing development
of these groups. What will happen once they have paid back the loans? Will
group relations strengthen and alternative visions for group activities develop?

Relationships with other organizations and state agencies

Table 13.3 summarizes the different support structures reported by all CBOs
covered in the survey.

Although the affiliation with mass organizations is very strong, the local government apparently offers more support overall. Only nine groups stated that
they do not work with local government agencies at all. In comparison, 47
percent of all groups registered an increase in government support since the
group was established and since policies promoting so-called 'model groups'
began (Huynh Thi Phuong Linh 2012, personal communication). In general,
however, material support, in terms of funding or equipment, was reported to be
marginal. In any case, alternative support systems hardly exist and no development projects are currently run in Can Tho City.

The group's relationships with mass organizations and state agencies are,
however, far more developed than relationships between the groups themselves,
as evident in Table 13.4.

Table 13.3 External support received by CBOs (%)

	Equipment/production material	Training	Advice	Funding	Access to credit
Local government	8	76	63	5	38
Women's Union	1	49	40	1	21
Farmers' Association	6	62	46	0	18

Table 13.4 Level of cooperation: inter-group relations and group relations with other organizations (%)

	Same category of group	Other groups	Local government	Mass organizations	Social Bank
No cooperation	33	58	8	4	23
Low level of cooperation	42	39	42	10	17
Intensive cooperation	25	3	50	86	60

The highest level of inter-group interaction has been reported by irrigation groups (59 per cent intensive and 33 per cent low level of cooperation), while approximately a third of production and micro-credit groups do not cooperate with other groups at all. It is not immediately evident whether these findings confirm or reject Norlund's contestation that CBO development is fragmented (Norlund 2007: 79). However, overall the findings of the survey suggest that the groups do not engage in activities beyond their immediate group objectives and practical tasks, nor do they demonstrate the capacity to link up and develop into larger networks and engage in advocacy.

Conclusion

The profiles of, and trends in, water user and micro-credit groups in Can Tho City attest to the growing institutional diversity and emergence of CBOs, particularly in the Mekong Delta. It has been shown that CBO development accelerated from the mid-1990s and that rural production and micro-credit groups constitute an important subset of CBOs. Although some of these groups emerged from and replaced former collective groups and new-style cooperatives, the majority of CBOs were established through new initiatives. Seventy-six per cent of the surveyed groups were established prior to the promulgation of Decree 151 in 2007, but the survey shows that party-state agencies actively promoted the development of many of them. Research findings from other provinces in the Mekong Delta, however, show that a large number of farmers groups emerged without any state support (Fforde 2008, Wells-Dang 2011 oral communication).[12]

Many groups started with a clear scope of activity and with the intention of improving their livelihoods. Significant changes in the rural production system and agrarian modernization, for instance, raised the demand for joint irrigation management (Nguyen Duy Can *et al.* 2007: 77) and incentivizing the foundation of groups that would evolve to be an alternative to the new-style cooperatives designed by the state. The fact that people in rural communities preferred to organize outside official channels is a product of the negative experiences people had with state-imposed structures in the past (Fforde 2008). With the issuance of Decree 151, the government officially recognized this alternative type of farmers group and demonstrated an interest in engaging with these groups. This move represents a typical facet of the reform processes in Vietnam, whereby 'policy has tended to follow reality' (Fforde 2009: 28).

Kerkvliet (2003; 2005) understood the evolvement of *Đổi mới* as a state response to ongoing change processes initiated by peasants and other segments of the population. In this tradition, the progressive formalization and concomitant attempts to guide CBOs is considered a strategic step by the party-state to maintain control over civil society development in rural areas. In the context of top-down policy implementation, and perhaps owing to a certain continuity of central planning in the post-*Đổi mới* era, CBOs are considered convenient 'partners' for central agencies to promulgate and implement their policies. In agricultural production in the Mekong Delta, for instance, national directives have clear provisions on how water and land resources are to be used in order to achieve national output and growth targets. In this context, training and technology transfers are preferentially disseminated through CBOs. The groups are also involved in generating funds and mobilizing labour for local infrastructure development and maintenance in accordance with set plans (Benedikter and Waibel, forthcoming). Local agencies also actively promote micro-credit and production groups as part of an envisaged rural collective economy (which is also part of a market-oriented system) and follows the principles of socialization. The following summary illustrates this ideological linkage:

> Cooperative groups and clubs act as the groundwork for developing the collective economy and constitute one of the indispensable economic components of the national economy. The Sub-department of Cooperatives and Rural Development therefore intensified propaganda work and legal conditions for cooperative groups and enhanced the awareness of peasant households to engage in the sustainable development of cooperative groups.
>
> (DARD 2008)

A number of Vietnam scholars have identified potential socio-economic threats inherent to economic liberalization and socialization. This has not been directly confirmed by the data, but the rising number of micro-credit groups, functioning savings schemes, and initiatives striving for business and job development, actually points in the same direction: farmers have to engage in community-based groups in order to secure and possibly improve their livelihoods.

The research findings additionally demonstrate a clear tendency to formalize group management. This is achieved by standardized procedures of group registration, the establishment of a group leadership, and the administration of these formalities through mass organizations and local authorities (as prescribed in Decree 151). Moreover, when hamlet heads and mass organization leaders attend group meetings, act as facilitators for bank credits, and offer training opportunities, the collaboration between these authorities and the groups is enhanced through interpersonal interaction as well as formal links. Prescriptions for group registration and monitoring activities enable party-state agencies to keep records of CBO development and report the relevant data to higher levels of administration.

As it turns out, CBOs fit well into the current ideology of the socialist one-party state with regard to farming communities, as they represent a spirit of collective production and recruit their members among peasants and rural labourers. The mass organizations, namely the Women's Union and the Farmers' Association, are also strengthened through this process, since they benefit from increasing membership rates, income generation opportunities, and a broadening scope of activity. As a result, the party-state structure, at least at the local level, is even further reinforced.

Although the line between rural CBOs and the state has become more distinct after decollectivization, the boundaries remain permeable. The fact that the majority of the surveyed groups perceive themselves as closely linked or even part of either the Farmers' Association or Women's Union makes that point quite clear. Nevertheless, further research is needed to assess the daily practices of these relationships. The public discourse in Vietnam centres upon state support and promotion and negotiation processes, while some fieldwork observations revealed incidents of disagreement and a widespread phenomenon of group disbandment (not reflected in official statistics) (Nguyen Quy Hanh and Huynh Thi Phuong Linh, 2011 and 2012, personal communication). These accounts point to the following conclusion: the policy shift towards CBO promotion has apparently not been as effective as some government reports might suggest. Moreover, policy implementation practices and outcomes seem to largely depend on the daily interaction between local cadres and local people, on the one hand, and the vagaries of the local context, on the other. This finding suggests that national directives are being reinterpreted, sometimes ignored, or only partially implemented. In other words: at the grassroots, central state policies remain weak.

Another finding of this research is the apparent low potential for the development of CBO networks. In contrast to this, CBOs develop ties with state agencies and, even more importantly, the local branches of the mass organizations. With state organizations acting as the major contact point of CBOs, the representation of the interests of the rural population remains institutionalized through the mass organizations at intermediary and macro levels. In 1994, Nguyen Ngoc Truong (1994) stated, '[it is] illogical to view the recent emergence of formal and informal grassroots associations and societies as a separate and accidental event or phenomenon'. Almost 20 years after this statement was made, those words appear to have only gained in explanatory power. The number of CBOs in the rural areas of Can Tho City continues to grow, but, as has been shown, this process appears to be increasingly engineered through policies formulated by the party-state. Nevertheless, slippage in enforcement at the local level is perhaps higher than national or provincial policy-makers anticipated. The question must still critically be posed, To what extent can these CBOs truly be referred to as 'self-initiated' and/or 'voluntary'? From this answer emerges another question: which role do CBOs actually play in Vietnam's civil society landscape? Having asked these questions, it is nonetheless important to note that farmers reported having joined groups for strategic reasons of their own: for example, if they anticipate certain personal or material benefits, or because they might otherwise fail with an individual loan application if they lack membership iof a microcredit group. Improved access to state support systems, such as training, subsidies, relevant technical or market information, and other services seems to be another crucial factor for group mobilization. Further research on these strategic behaviours and the possible difficulties (as depicted by Wischermann 2010 in urban Vietnam) would help to throw more light on local governance and civil society development. Finally, an assessment of mutual cooperation and self-help initiatives beyond any of the described structures could also provide valuable information on social practices in a changing environment.

Notes

1 Wischermann and Nguyen Quang Vinh (2003: 186, 223) define civic organizations as 'non-state, voluntary, non-profit-oriented societal organizations'. The term 'civic organizations' is a literal translation of the Vietnamese *tổ chức xã hội* (Norlund *et al.* 2006: 25). These include four sub-groups, namely mass organizations, professional associations, associations of businesspeople, as well as so-called issue-oriented organizations. The latter includes social work, research and consulting as well as religious organizations.

2 As Painter (2005: 274) explains, socialization in Vietnam means that the state will maintain the principal role of exercising state management functions, while responsibility for delivery of and payment for services is increasingly passed on to the people, notably the clients and users of such services.

3 While the membership quota of households in northern Vietnam reached 96.7 per cent in 1979, the quota in the Mekong Delta remained rather low (24.5 per cent in 1980) (Ngo Vinh Long 1988). Farmers obviously resisted any enforcement of the collectivization policy (Hicks 2004: 293). However, in 1983, more than 27,000 collective production units were operating across the delta (Ngo Vinh Long 1988), although Porter (1993: 43) argues that a 'vast majority of cooperatives existed in name only'.

4 The Grassroots Democracy Decree 29/1998/ND-CP, later amended by Decree 79/2003/ND, provides directions for people's engagement in local governance affairs. The decree grants this to the community and not to the individual, which is often misunderstood (or intentionally misinterpreted) by foreign agencies. Inherent to the decree is a famous quotation of Ho Chi Minh: 'People know, people discuss, people execute and people supervise' [*Dân biết, dân bàn, dân làm, dân kiểm tra*].

5 The survey was conducted by the Center for Development Research (ZEF, University of Bonn, Germany) and the Mekong Delta Development Research Institute (MDI, Can Tho University) as part of the social science research agenda of the WISDOM project (www.wisdom.caf.dlr.de).

6 The identification of the groups captured by the survey was done in collaboration with the respective Commune People's Committees. Prior to this a number of field trips were organized during a first explorative phase of the research, during which the existence of so-called informal groups was categorically denied.

7 A large variety of clubs, comprising gardening, nutrition, population and HIV/AIDS clubs, sports, legal and culture clubs (poetry, traditional music), as well as charity associations, were identified in the pilot (interviews with representatives of various state agencies in four districts in 2009). As most of these clubs were not involved in water-related activities, they were excluded from the survey.

8 Membership is either defined on an individual basis or by household (44%). In exceptional cases, both the household head and spouse were registered individually as group members. Production groups have a membership ranging from ten to 145 members, while irrigation groups reported 14 to 47 members per group. Micro-credit group membership varied between 12 and 75.

9 Nguyen Quy Hanh and Huynh Thi Phuong Linh are junior researchers at ZEF; both conducted intensive field research in Can Tho City and provided very useful comments on the first draft of this chapter.

10 Loans are provided for various purposes, but the focus of the following will be kept on micro-credit groups operating in the field of water and sanitation. Since organizations other than the Women's Union facilitate credit delivery in the district, the following findings represent only a specific segment of such groups.

11 The Vietnam Bank for Social Policy, founded in 2003, is state-funded and disburses subsidized 'policy loans' to the poor. In the given example, loans were provided in the context of the national Rural Water Supply and Sanitation Strategy; by 2008 the total number of 15,000 households had benefited from such loans in the municipality (Vietnam Women's Union 2008).

12 Similarly, research findings from other parts of Vietnam detail the presence of registered and unregistered groups; in practice, these two categories have somewhat different patterns of activity (e.g. Dang Thi Viet Phuong and Bui Quang Dung 2011).

References

Benedikter, S. (2008) *Dezentralisierung und Demokratisierungstendenzen in Vietnam*, Saarbrücken: Verlag Dr Müller.
Benedikter, S. and Waibel, G. (2013) 'The Formation of Water User Groups in the Mekong Delta, Vietnam'. ZEF Working Paper 112, Bonn: University of Bonn. Online. Available at: www.zef.de/fileadmin/webfiles/downloads/zef_wp/wp112.pdf (accessed July 2013).
Biggs, D., Miller, F., Hoanh, C.T. and Molle, F. (2009) 'The Delta Machine: Water Management in the Vietnamese Mekong Delta in Historical and Contemporary Perspectives' in Molle, F., Foran T. and Käkönen, M. (eds), *Contested Waterscapes in the Mekong Region. Hydropower, Livelihoods and Governance*, London: Earthscan: 203–25.
Bloh, H.v. (2007) *Access to and Impact of Microcredit in Rural Northern Vietnam*, Diploma thesis, Passau: University of Passau.
Bui The Cuong (2005) 'Issue-Oriented Organizations in Hanoi: Some Findings from an Empirical Survey' in Heinrich Böll Foundation (ed.), *Towards Good Society: Civil Society Actors, the State, and the Business Class in Southeast Asia – Facilitators of or Impediments to a Strong, Democratic, and Fair Society?* Berlin: Heinrich Böll Foundation: 93–100.
CIDIN (Center for International Development Issues Nijmegen) (2006) *Vietnam: Working in Special Circumstances: Added Value of TMF*, Hanoi/Nijmegen: CIDIN.
CIVICUS. (2003) 'CIVICUS Civil Society Index. Summary of Conceptual Framework and Research Methodology'. Online. Available at: www.civicus.org/new/media/CSI_Methodology_and_conceptual_framework.pdf (accessed 15 May 2012).
Dang Kieu Nhan, Nguyen Van Be and Nguyen Hieu Trung (2007) 'Water Use and Competition in the Mekong Delta' in Tran Than Be, Bach Tan Sinh and Miller, F. (eds), *Challenges to Sustainable Development in the Mekong Delta: Regional and National Policy Issues and Research Needs*, Bangkok: Sustainable Mekong Research Network (sumernet), 143–88.
Dang Thi Viet Phuong and Bui Quang Dung (2011) 'Các tổ chức xã hội tự nguyện ở nông thôn đồng bằng sông Hồng: Liên kết và trao đổi xã hội. Tập chí Xã hội học số' [Voluntary-social organisations in the rural Red River Delta: associations and social exchange], 4 (116): 31–46.
DARD of Can Tho City (Department of Agriculture and Rural Development) (2008) 'Report on Collective Economy Situation of Can Tho City', Can Tho: Unpublished.
Evers, H.-D. and Benedikter, S. (2009) 'Hydraulic Bureaucracy in a Modern Hydraulic Society: Strategic Group Formation in the Mekong Delta' in *Water Alternatives*, 2 (3): 416–39.
Fforde, A. (2008) 'Vietnam's Informal Farmers' Groups: Narratives and Policy Implications' in *Südostasien Aktuell*, 2008 (1): 3–36.
Fforde, A. (2009) *Coping with Facts*, Sterling: Kumarian Press.
Government of Vietnam (2003) 'Providing for the Organization, Operation and Management of Associations', in *88/2003/ND-CP*.
Government of Vietnam (2007) 'On The Organization and Operation of Cooprative Groups' in 151/2007/ND-CP.

Gray, M. L. (2003) 'NGOs and Highland Development: A Case Study in Crafting New Roles' in Kerkvliet, B. J. T., Koh, D. W. H., and Heng, R. H.-k. (eds), *Getting Organized in Vietnam. Moving in and around the Socialist State*, Singapore: Institute of Southeast Asian Studies: 110–25.

Grossheim, M. (2004) 'Village Government in Pre-colonial and Colonial Vietnam' in B. J. T. Kerkvliet and D. G. Marr (eds), *Beyond Hanoi: Local Government in Vietnam*, Singapore: Institute of Southeast Asian Studies: 54–89.

Hannah, J. (2007) *Local Non-Government Organizations in Vietnam: Development, Civil Society and State-society Relations*, Seattle: University of Washington.

Heng, R. H.-k. (2004) 'Civil Society Effectiveness and the Vietnamese State – Despite or Because the Lack of Autonomy' in L. H. Guan (ed.), *Civil Society in Southeast Asia*, Singapore: ISEAS Publications: 144–66.

Hicks, N. (2004) 'Organisational Adventures in District Government in Long An Province: Central Regulation Versus Local Initiative' in *European Journal of East Asian Studies*, 3 (2): 279–306.

Hy V. Luong (2003) 'Wealth, Power, and Inequality: Global Market, the State, and Local Sociocultural Dynamics' in H. V. Luong (ed.), *Postwar Vietnam: Dynamics of a Transforming Society*, Oxford: Rowman & Littlefield: 81–106.

Hy V. Luong (2005) 'The State, Local Associations, and Alternate Civilities in Rural Northern Vietnam' in R.P. Weller (ed.), *Civil Life, Globalization, and Political Change in Asia. Organizing between Family and State*, London and New York: Routledge: 123–47.

ILO (2005) 'Towards a Viable Microfinance Sector in Vietnam: Issues and Challenges' in ILO (ed.), ILO Vietnam Working Paper Series No. 5, Hanoi.

Jamieson, N. L. (1995) *Understanding Vietnam*, Berkeley: University of California Press.

Kerkvliet, B. J. T. (2003) 'Authorities and the People: An Analysis of State-Society Relations in Vietnam' in H. V. Luong (ed.), *Postwar Vietnam: Dynamics of a Transforming Society*, Oxford: Rowman & Littlefield, 27–53.

Kerkvliet, B. J. T. (2005) *The Power of Everyday Politics: How Vietnamese Peasants Transformed National Policy*, Ithaca: Cornell University Press.

Kerkvliet, B. J. T., Nguyen Quang A. and Bach Tan Sinh (2008) *Forms of Engagement between State Agencies and Civil Society Organizations in Vietnam*, Hanoi: VUFO NGO Resource Center.

Kirsch, O. C. (1997) 'Vietnam: Agricultural Cooperatives in Transitional Economies', Discussion Paper 59, Heidelberg: Forschungsstelle für Internationale Wirtschafts- und Agrarentwicklung eV.

Kono, Y. (2001) 'Canal Development and Intensification of Rice Cultivation in the Mekong Delta: A Case Study in the Cantho Province, Vietnam' in *Southeast Asian Studies*, 39 (1): 70–85.

Le Meur, P.-Y., Hauswirth, D., Leurent, T. and Lienhard, P. (2005) *The Local Politics of Land and Water: Case Studies from the Mekong Delta*, Paris: GRET.

Marr, D. G. (2004) 'A Brief History of Local Government in Vietnam' in B. J. T. Kerkvliet and D.G. Marr (eds), *Beyond Hanoi: Local Government in Vietnam*, Singapore: Institute of Southeast Asian Studies: 28–53.

Menge, J. (2009) 'Zivilgesellschaft in Vietnam: Chancen und Grenzen zivilgesellschaftlichen Handelns im sozialistischen Einparteienstaat: Ein westlich-demokratisches Konzept auf dem Prüfstand' [Civil Society in Vietnam: Opportunities and limitations of civic engagement in the socialist one-party state: A Western-democratic concept under scrutiny], unpublished MA thesis, Faculty of Economics and Social Sciences, University of Potsdam.

Ngo Vinh Long (1988) 'Some Aspects of Cooperativization in the Mekong Delta' in D. G. Marr and C. P. White (eds), *Postwar Vietnam: Dilemmas in Socialist Development*, Ithaca: Cornell Southeast Asia Program: 163–77.

Nguyen Duy Can, Le Thanh Duong, Nguyen Van Sanh and Miller, F. (2007) 'Livelihoods and Resource Use Strategies of Farmers in the Mekong Delta' in Tran Than Be, Bach Tan Sinh and Miller, F. (eds), *Challenges to sustainable Development in the Mekong Delta: Regional and National Policy Issues and Research Needs*, Bangkok: The Sustainable Mekong Research Network (sumernet): 69–98.

Nguyen Ngoc De (2006) *Farmers, Agriculture and Rural Development in the Mekong Delta of Vietnam*, PhD thesis, Mie University.

Nguyen Ngoc Truong (1994) 'Grassroots Organizations in Rural and Urban Vietnam during Market Reform: An Overview of their Emergence and Relationship to the State', Vietnam Update 1994 conference, Doi moi, the State and Civil Society, Australian National University, Canberra.

Nguyen Xuan Tiep (2008) 'Nội dung hướng dẫn tành lập Tổ chức tác dùng nước' [Guideline on water user organization establishment] in Nguyen Xuan Tiep (ed.), *Nông dân Tham Gia Quản Lý Công Trình Thủy Lợi* [Participatory Irrigation Management and Emerging Issues], Hanoi: Nhà Xuấ Bản Nông Nghiệp: 372–95.

Norlund, I. (2007) 'Civil Society in Vietnam. Social Organisations and Approaches to New Concepts' in *Asien*, 105: 68–90.

Norlund, I., Dang Ngoc Dinh, Bach Tan Sinh, Chu Dung, Dang Ngoc Quang, Do Bich Diem, Nguyen Manh Cuong, Tang The Cuong and Vu Chi Mai (2006) *The Emerging Civil Society. An Initial Assessment of Civil Society in Vietnam*, Hanoi: Vietnam Institute of Development Studies (VIDS), UNDP Vietnam, SNV Vietnam and CIVICUS Civil Society Index.

Painter, M. (2005) 'Public Administrative Reform in Vietnam: Foreign Transplants or Local Hybrids?' in J. Gillespie and P. Nicholson (eds), *Asian Socialism and Legal Change: The Dynamics of Vietnamese and Chinese Reform*, Canberra: Pacific Press: 267–87.

People's Participation Working Group (PPWG) Vietnam (2007) 'Overview on Collaborative Groups CGs/CBOs', Workshop report, Hanoi, Vietnam.

Phan Dai Doan (2007) 'Traditional Institution of Vietnamese Villages in the Present Political System' in *Vietnam Social Science*, 2007 (2): 53–60.

Pike, D. (2000) 'Informal Politics in Vietnam' in Dittmer, L., Fukui, H. and Lee, P.N.S. (eds), *Informal Politics in East Asia*, Cambridge: Cambridge University Press: 269–89.

Porter, G. (1993) *Vietnam: The Politics of Bureaucratic Socialism*, Ithaca, London: Cornell University Press.

Reis, N. and Mollinga, P.P. (2009) 'Microcredit for Rural Water Supply and Sanitation in the Mekong Delta. Policy Implementation between the Needs for Clean Water and "Beautiful Latrines"', ZEF Working Paper Series 49, Bonn: Zentrum für Entwicklungsforschung. Online. Available at: www.zef.de/fileadmin/media/news/ac27_wp49_reis-mollinga.pdf.

Sabharwal, G. and Than Thi Thien Houng (2005) *Civil Society in Vietnam: Moving from the Margins to the Mainstream*, World Alliance for Citizen Participation (CIVICUS).

Salemink, O. (2006) 'Translating, Interpreting, and Practicing Civil Society in Vietnam: A Tale of Calculated Misunderstandings' in D. Lewis and D. Mosse (eds), *Development Brokers and Translators: The Ethnography of Aid and Agencies*, Bloomfield: Kumarian Press, Inc.: 101–26.

Seibel, H. D. (1992) *The Making of a Market Economy: Monetary Reform, Economic Transformation and Rural Finance in Vietnam*, Saarbrücken/Fort Lauderdale: Breitenbach.

Sidel, M. (1995) 'The Emergence of a Nonprofit Sector and Philanthropy in the Socialist Republic of Vietnam' in T. Yamamoto (ed.), *Emerging Civil Society in the Asia Pacific Community*, Singapore: Institute of Southeast Asian Studies. 293–304.

Taylor, P. (2004) 'Redressing Disadvantage or Re-arranging Inequality? Development Interventions and Local Responses in the Mekong Delta' in P. Taylor (ed.), *Social Inequality in Vietnam and the Challenges to Reform*, Singapore: Institute of Southeast Asian Studies: 236–69.

Thayer, C. A. (1995) 'Mono-Organizational Socialism and the State' in B. J. T. Kerkvliet and D. J. Porter (eds), *Vietnam's Rural Transformation*, Boulder: Westview Press: 39–64.

Thayer, C. A. (2009) 'Political Legitimacy of Vietnam's One Party-State: Challenges and Responses' in *Journal of Current Southeast Asian Affairs*, 4: 47–70.

UNDP (United Nations Development Programme) (2006) *Deepening Democracy and Increasing Popular Participation in Vietnam*, Hanoi: UNDP Vietnam.

Vasavakul, T. (2003) 'From Fence-Breaking to Networking: Interests, Popular Organizations, and Policy Influences in Post-Socialist Vietnam' in Kerkvliet, B. J. T., Koh, D. W. H. and Heng, R. H.-k. (eds), *Getting Organized in Vietnam. Moving in and around the Socialist State*, Singapore: Institute of Southeast Asian Studies: 25–61.

Vietnam Women's Union (2008) *Living Water and Sanitation Status of Can Tho Women's Union Management*, Unpublished report. Can Tho City.

Vietnam Women's Union and Social Bank for Policy (2003) Joint-document between Vietnam Women's Union and Social Bank for Policy, Ha Noi: Socialist Republic of Vietnam.

Vinh Thanh District Office of Agriculture and Rural Development (2009) 'Báo cáo sơ kết – Tình hình thực hiện kế hoạch phát triên nông nghiệp huyện Vĩnh Thạnh giai đoạn năm 2006–2008 và phương hướng thực hiện kế hoạch năm 2009' [Summary Report – Implementation of the Rural Development Plans in Vinh Thanh district in the period from 2006–2008 and Plan Implementation Directions for 2009], Unpublished report.

Wischermann, J. (2010) 'Civil Society Action and Governance in Vietnam: Selected Findings from an Empirical Survey' in *Journal of Current Southeast Asian Affairs*, 2: 3–40.

Wischermann, J. and Nguyen Quang Vinh (2003) 'The Relationship Between Civic and Governmental Organizations in Vietnam: Selected Findings of an Empirical Survey' in Kerkvliet, B. J. T., Koh, D. W. H. and Heng, R. H.-k. (eds), *Getting Organized in Vietnam: Moving in and around the Socialist State*, Singapore: Institute of Southeast Asian Studies, 185–233.

Woodside, A. B. (1976) 'Colonialism and the Vietnamese Community' in A. B. Woodside (ed.), *Community and Revolution in Modern Vietnam*, Boston: Houghton Mufflin Company: 1–25.

Wyatt, A. B. and Huynh Thi Ngoc Tuyet (2008) 'Participatory Community Development Project in An Giang and Soc Trang Provinces', unpublished report, Ho Chi Minh City.

14 Competitive discourses in civil society

Pluralism in Cambodia's agricultural development platform

Hart N. Feuer

The paradigmatic debates surrounding differing development goals and agendas occurring internationally are inevitably played out in developing countries. This chapter focuses on how socio-technical paradigms embodied in certain development discourses are instrumentalized in civil society initiatives and led to compete with each other on the ground for legitimation by both the public and the state. In Cambodia, the civil society 'representatives' of global movements or powerful international institutions are often large, charismatic organizations that follow externally provided archetypes of issues such as gender, agriculture, justice and the environment. Due to their international roots, these organizations typically view their respective initiative (i.e. their development discourse) as sufficiently universal and paradigmatic to be enshrined countrywide – a goal which is often only attainable through widespread endorsement or even absorption by the state. Civil society, in this case, is thus seeking to bridge the 'gap' in state–society relations (see Öjendal, this volume) by filling the political and technical space between the family and the state (following White 1994: 379) in order to develop into a national project.[1] As a suggestive case in this chapter, I focus on the paradigmatic contest between proponents of alternative and mainstream (or green revolution) agricultural development (see Beus and Dunlap 1990).

A stepping-off point of this chapter is that civil society groups, even the technically oriented development ones, are not apolitical in nature. On the contrary, they are often rooted in a development discourse that implies some socio-cultural or political arrangements (Fforde and Seidel 2010). To the degree that these arrangements are taken on board through the various processes of development, they alter the political landscape, often by privileging and building up institutional inertia behind certain worldviews (following Hughes 2010). Often, one worldview, such as 'productivist' agriculture,[2] becomes the officially sanctioned (or perhaps simply the de facto) framework for agriculture development in the state or civil apparatus, creating a path dependency that pre-empts the institutionalization of other development models. The comprehensiveness of this path dependency, however, is not inevitable. The agricultural and rural development policy of contemporary Cambodia, I will argue, is politically more neutral toward competing discourses. This is due to historical factors and because the selection of models for agricultural development is more contested by development agencies and other groups. In particular, I discuss how the state strategically arbitrates between civil society initiatives (and their underlying discourses), balancing their populist and technocratic merits as well as the response by international donors. In practice, this has created space for plurality in the legitimation of seemingly divergent development models, and drives competition between civil society agents with different worldviews.

Openness, deference or agency?

With competing discourses for development waxing and waning on their own time-frames, aid-receiving countries can be expected to respond strategically by striking a balance between maximizing aid flows and fixing a coherent and long-term development model of their own. As Hughes (2010: 46) describes,

> the space for contestation of donor policies depends upon the way that aid money and policies function in the context of the local political economy. In countries where there is high aid dependence, for example, this may lead to technocratic elites internalising donor models, as in contexts such as Rwanda and Tanzania. Alternatively, different local political economies of aid may see a variety of context-specific strategies of co-optation, negotiation, manipulation and outright resistance.

Subsequent to this quote, she specifically mentions Southeast Asia as a region in which these political economies of aid lead to more agency by national governments. However, in practice, doing so is challenged by the fact that various models of development tend to be embedded in more encompassing discourses that cannot easily be 'mixed and matched' by the state apparatus without muddying their discursive coherence. In a separate work, Hughes (2009: 168) describes how politicians often attempt to present themselves as being able to manage donor ideals (what she calls 'gatekeeping') while simultaneously supporting populist (or, as she calls, 'authentic') development practices that seem to run contrary to donor aims. I broaden this idea into a typology of three strategies for managing competing developing discourses.

1   Openness. In an effort to assert its sovereignty over the development process, the state absorbs and institutionalizes the myriad developmental functions carried out within its domain, often resulting in internal contradictions and haphazard development for a period of time (Guibernau 1999: 13).
2   Deference. The state can 'hover' for a while, allowing third-party development activities to compete with each other until a desirable configuration emerges or political pressure obliges the state to adopt a certain model.
3   Agency. The state can stay aloof of non-governmental and third-party activities by plying a middle path until it develops its own unique configuration, which may or may not resemble one of the dominant development models.

Although not using these terms, these scenarios are often used by academics and observers of Cambodia to explain the colourful mixture of developmental models coexisting in the country.

The first view, corresponding to the openness strategy, is that Cambodia, due to various conditions such as reconstruction, low human capital, and a desire to reassert its international credentials after the Vietnamese occupation, would officially embrace almost anything suggested by donors and carried out by non-governmental organizations (NGOs) if it served to bring in development aid or investment. According to Curtis (1998: 72), this view gained traction during the United Nations interventions in the early 1990s. To development veterans, Cambodia appeared 'unsullied by previous developmental mistakes' and open to applying all the new and fashionable development trends.

The second view is that Cambodia's ingrained culture of deference to authority provided space for a range of powerful donors and development agencies to compete with each other in an attempt to win over the state and the citizenry about the merits of various development models (Curtis 1998: 115; Landau 2008: 248). This occurs by simultaneously moulding the public sector through 'capacity building' projects while directly supporting civil society organizations (CSOs) that create a developmental reality (i.e. facts on the ground) around one model (see for example, SPM Consultants 2003: 25).

The third view explaining the mixture of development models in Cambodia, corresponding with the agency scenario above, regards the government as being more strategic in its encounter with donors and development agencies than many observers admit (see Hughes 2010: 46; Vickery 1984), allowing it to play various development models off against each other. Following this view, only a clear threat to state authority would prompt overt defensive reactions (Öjendal and Kim 2007: 510–11), while in the meantime the government would quietly enhance its legitimacy by claiming the achievements of NGOs as national achievements and, in doing so, crystallizing its own development model (Curtis 1998: 142).

Historical conditions of pluralism

The contemporary situation of civil society activity, as illustrated by Ou and Kim (this volume), is largely the result of a neo-liberal mode of development intervention, in which NGOs compete with each other and with the state to attract funding and gain legitimacy. However, due to constant changes in the funding whims of donors, support for NGOs is at risk unless they develop alternative models for sustaining themselves. Initiatives with broad appeal and politically palatable platforms, such as AMARA (see Öjendal, this volume) can leverage community support structures as well as tap into official government institutions to help ensure their existence. In agricultural development, the scale of the national project (i.e. infrastructure needs, extension, research and development, university training, etc.) practically necessitates state partnership in addition to grassroots appeal. NGOs attempting to influence policy to promote their initiatives, however, must contend with cultural inertia and other preconditions that are embedded in the broader historical narrative. Broadly speaking, agrarian change in Cambodia has largely mirrored historical fluctuations, resulting in periods of centralization and decentralization that have followed the rise and fall of various political regimes. During the height of the Khmer civilization in the twelfth to fourteenth centuries, one of the world's largest urban centres at Angkor thrived due to expansive irrigation and centrally coordinated rice cultivation.[3] The decline of Angkor from the fourteenth century led to the decay of waterworks and planned agricultural development for several centuries, but it proved that the ingenuity of Cambodian management could lead to agricultural achievement (particularly in rice cultivation). During the French protectorate and on through the limited agricultural modernization of King Norodom Sihanouk's *Sangkum Reastr Niyum* (Great Society) regime, few changes in rice agriculture took place (Ear 1995: 35–7; Samphan 1959: 23–5) before the spreading war in Vietnam began to eclipse development goals (Ear 1995: 67–8). In 1975 the Khmer Rouge under Pol Pot came into power; the ensuing upheaval led to the almost complete rearrangement of agricultural infrastructure and labour relations. Urban citizens were forced into the countryside and an agrarian social economy based on collective agriculture predominated until the Khmer Rouge was deposed by the Vietnamese in 1979 (Chandler 2000 [1983]; De Nike *et al.* 2000: 352–3).

During the 1980s, people were focused on returning to their land and rebuilding communities, while the government was focusing on reconstruction rather than assembling coherent agricultural policy. Although sporadic elements of 'productivist' agriculture began filtering into Cambodia during this period, this was not in the framework of a comprehensive agricultural policy. For example, throughout the 1980s, uncontrolled pesticide imports from Vietnam and use of subsidized mineral fertilizers became widespread (EJF 2002; McNaughton 2002; Yang Saing *et al.* 2000), causing severe health problems and compromising soil quality over the following decades. In this same period, the government initially endorsed and then abandoned the promotion of so-called high-yielding varieties (HYVs) of rice (Mak 2001). It was within this context that the first aid-funded projects focusing on agricultural development arrived in Cambodia. The most notable of these, the Cambodia-IRRI-Australia Project (CIAP), implemented by the International Rice Research Institute (IRRI) and funded by the Australian Agency for International Development (AusAID), began a pilot project in 1989 with government encouragement. The project initially focused on farmer practices and local soil conditions, subsequently implementing fertilizer banks, promoting HYVs and making policy recommendations (Nesbitt 2002). After the departure of the Vietnamese and the opening up of the country to development aid as a result of the Paris Peace Agreement in 1991, Cambodia was exposed to the less unified international discourse in agricultural development (Ellis and Biggs 2001; Pingali *et al.* 1995), including aspects that contrasted with the CIAP project, such as those focusing on food sovereignty and ecology (Altieri 1987; Vandermeer 1995).

Ultimately, this had the effect of broadening the scope of the development model for agricultural development and diminishing the CIAP project to one voice among many. And while the lasting physical influences of this project can only be seen in the pilot districts in the southern lowlands, there are two enduring national results of this project: (1) the adoption of HYVs for early and dry season cropping (around 30 per cent of the cultivation) (Agrifood Consulting International 2002), and (2) the eventual establishment in 1999 of CARDI, the Cambodian Agriculture Research and Development Institute (Nesbitt 2002) under the Ministry of Agriculture, Forestry and Fisheries (MAFF). In the meantime, a contrasting paradigm of agricultural development, embodied in alternative agriculture, found fertile ground in Cambodia. Many farmers were still 'organic' by default,[4] and others felt betrayed by the health impacts of pesticides and by the soil degradation resulting from fertilizer use (Sok Siphana in De Launey 2005; Keam 2007). Ecological agriculture was promoted as a more locally appropriate, neo-traditional form of agriculture for peasants in poor countries (Altieri 1987; Clarke *et al.* 2008; Goodman 1999; Singer 1974). This explains the rise of the main ecology-based rural development organization, the Cambodian Center for Research and Development in Agriculture (CEDAC),[5] founded in 1997. As the largest rural development NGO, its programmes had reached more than 140,000 families (approximately 8 per cent of Cambodian citizens) by the end of 2010.[6] Furthermore, in 2004, CEDAC's ecological rice farming system became officially integrated into the Department of Agronomy and Agricultural Land Improvement (DAALI) of the MAFF (Feuer 2007). Figure 14.1 anecdotally illustrates the relative degree of institutionalization of CEDAC and CARDI (including its predecessor the CIAP Project), indicating in which years these initiatives were officially promoted by the government.

While agricultural development in Cambodia has become more politically contested over time, and particularly since 2004, the practical face of agriculture change is influenced by global agricultural institutions and movements as well as by inertia in Cambodia's historical agro-social narrative. Alternative agriculture has made major inroads in academic, political and social spheres since the 1990s (Beus and Dunlap 1994), but mainstream industrial agriculture nonetheless commands the majority of research funding and is perpetuated internationally by multilateral agronomic institutions and private companies. The CIAP rural development project and CARDI are only individual instantiations of productivist agriculture discourse, which is reproduced by international agronomy research institutions, some development agencies, and the entire agribusiness complex. Perhaps more influential than its concrete institutions are the expectations of modernity and hopes for development that are linked with productivist agriculture. Indeed, during the *Sangkum Reastr Niyum* period between 1955 and 1970, King Norodom Sihanouk exhorted agricultural mechanization, infrastructure and external inputs, representing this as populist advancement toward modernity (Ear 1995: 51–3). This time is often nostalgically remembered by Khmers as the contemporary golden age of Cambodia, although it is also documented for urban bias, unjust land consolidation and rural displacement

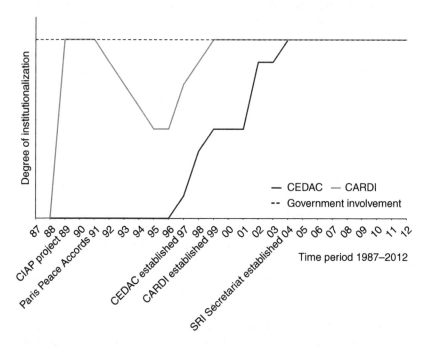

Figure 14.1 Institutionalization of CARDI and CEDAC over time (source: author).

(Ear 1995: 53–4). While typical of the rural development experience in many countries, the impacts of centralized agricultural change are more critically received in Cambodia, where socio-political and structural upheavals have long been associated with the decline of Angkorean productivity and the slow collapse of the fourteenth century Khmer civilization. Through the contemporary period, the Cambodian historical narrative contains recurring incidences of state-sponsored agrarian change, all of which have promised much, possibly succeeded for a time, but were ultimately unsustainable. The result is an enduring scepticism and conservatism regarding agricultural change, which has provided space for exploring the promises and realities of contemporary rural development.

Managed pluralism in civil society

Regardless of which view(s) – openness, deference, and/or agency – one uses as a lens to interpret the heterogeneity of civil society actors in Cambodia, it is increasingly clear that the government allows certain sectors to develop their own internal politics. Seemingly opposing organizations and viewpoints coexist and compete. Hughes (2010: 63) refers to these as 'controlling alliances', in which the government uses co-optation and contractualism to depolarize and integrate groups that would otherwise be in opposition. Looking to the agricultural sector, this accounts for how CARDI and CEDAC, which are ideologically opposed, can simultaneously receive official sanction from, and promotion by, the Council of Ministers and the MAFF. Practically speaking, both organizations inhabit different socio-technical regimes and have other paradigmatic differences in their methods and outlook (Beus and Dunlap 1990). CARDI is an outgrowth of a project implemented by the IRRI, the institute that developed many of the varieties responsible for the Green Revolution in rice. CEDAC was established in 1997 with French funding by a cadre of charismatic Cambodians passionate about alternative and ecological agriculture. From the government's perspective, however, both organizations (and their respective agricultural models) have a pedigree in development aid and both have worthy things to offer agricultural policy. Indeed, functionally speaking, the two organizations are not very different. CARDI is a semi-autonomous research wing at MAFF, while CEDAC's rice extension is internalized under the DAALI. CEDAC and CARDI both have independence in staff selection and funding (Mak 2001), yet both are beholden for funding to their respective international development institutions. In turn, both are affected by, and try to affect, agricultural policy and programming.

While CARDI and CEDAC do not independently cooperate with one another and often contradict each other in internal memoranda, a space of political pluralism created by the MAFF in this sector allows and requires both of them to coexist without open conflict. The government, which clearly values some developmental models underlying both organizations, even tries to encourage synergies between the two rivals. In a speech acknowledging CEDAC's work in 2009, the Minister of MAFF praised the high productivity and adoption rates of ecological rice intensification for smallholders, and then instructed CARDI to assist in improving its efficiency.[7] Although it is unlikely that CARDI will directly cooperate with CEDAC on this, the minister demonstrates that the government does not necessarily see the paradigmatic contradictions between their respective activities.[8] To observers accustomed to the adoption of more discrete development models, this might appear perplexing. Landau (2008: 249) highlights this, noting that, 'it is difficult in the Cambodian context to identify which ideology is the dominant one seeking hegemony and which are the subordinate ones'.

The equanimity with which the government of Cambodia and the MAFF treat the agriculture and rural development sector is likely the result of the political palatability of both models of agriculture and their respective utility in promoting the government or political party itself. On the one hand, the discourse and development model presented by CARDI embodies modernist expectations of rational scientific progress, with the focus on centralized intervention in water management, plant breeding and inputs. Looking to the past, particularly the Green Revolution and its emergent forms in South and Southeast Asia, this model has obvious entry points for government control. On the other hand, the alternative discourse, represented primarily by sustainable or ecological agriculture, also presents many advantages for government apparatuses. This is exemplified by the 2007–10 National Export Strategy of Cambodia, which featured organic products as one of five main focuses (and the only one in the agriculture sector). Embedded in the discourse of sustainable agriculture is also modernity, but of a post-industrial sort, which provides a strong populist dimension and valorization of productive smallholder agriculture and rural culture. This position also mirrors trends in international discourse in agricultural development, which has become increasingly critical of Green Revolution agriculture and open to alternative agriculture (e.g. Jacobs 1999; Lélé 1991; Tripp 2006; UNCED 1992a: Section II; 1992b). For the Cambodian state, both modernist and alternative agriculture offer legitimacy in the eyes of the world, productivity increases, and specific tools for enhancing government authority. Moreover, both forms of agriculture allow the government to make a presence in the countryside where most of the voters live. In the following, I analyse what each model of agriculture offers the political system, how the government seeks to assert itself, and which trade-offs each model presents for the state.

Modernist agriculture

CARDI, as the local representative of a sprawling scientific community and agrobusiness industry, is able to mobilize large-scale scientific research efforts regarding soil, hydrology, plant breeding and processing. This provides the government more transparency over the natural resource base for planning purposes while highlighting potential infrastructure interventions for the future (Sarun 2009). The breeding of new varieties (for now rice, but in the future, additional crops) assists in developing export-oriented agricultural commodities and, more generally, for evidencing Cambodia's progress toward modern agriculture, international trade and economic growth (IRRI 2007; James 2010; Sophal 2010). On a functional level, these new plant varieties provide the MAFF with an artefact that it can present to villagers during political ceremonies that reinforces the government's traditional position as caretaker and overlord (Landau 2008: 249; Öjendal and Kim 2007). These varieties, which are more standardized than traditional varieties, are also more easily processed and prepared for export. Export, in turn, promotes investment in high-tech rice milling infrastructure and presents Cambodia (and, by extension, the government) as a more important player and competitor in the region (*Rasmey Kampuchea* 2007). Processing improvements add value domestically, reduce imports, and allow the state to promote patriotism through food sovereignty.

The modernist agriculture system, however, is also understood by the MAFF as a victim of its own systematization. Each aspect of the modernist technology package can and might be abused if implemented without considering the farming system, the farmers themselves, and the existing economic relations. In the Cambodian People's Party magazine, *Pracheachun*, the Minister of the MAFF, H.E. Chan Sarun, frequently comments that agricultural inputs are largely uncontrollable and invasive to the environment and society. For example, in writing about the pest management in Cambodia, he concludes,

> Actually, pesticides are a double-edged sword. If used properly, they can
> help to manage pests and increase yields but used wrongly they can impact

health and other good animals and critters, as well as polluting the soil and environment. It also creates obstacles for exporting agricultural products to other countries and discourages tourism.... Furthermore, most pesticides sold in the market are illegal and are of low quality.

(Sarun 2005)

In the same article, Minister Sarun points out that even international efforts to control pesticides are challenging, and describes how Cambodia's latest efforts to ban and control problematic chemicals are limited in effectiveness. But his critique is rather neutral, namely that new technologies arise faster than we can develop the organizational capability to control their social and environmental side effects (Norgaard 1994: 56). The minister is echoing the views of many Cambodians farmers involved in natural production,[9] for whom one of the most salient philosophical desires is to maintain control over the process and pace of transformation (cf. Cleveland *et al.* 1994; Fitzgerald 1993). Farmers and the minister are, in a manner, admitting that the necessary technical and cultural conditions for systemic industrial agriculture are not present in Cambodia and that, furthermore, the nature of the industrial agriculture and the aggressive markets they accompany, are difficult for the government to control (Boyle and Chakrya 2010; Kampuchea Thmei 2008a; Koh Santepheap 2008b, 2008c). In a recent edition of *Pracheachun*, Minister Sarun (2009) describes in populist terms how the government supports the ecological system of rice intensification (SRI) because it provides an opportunity for farmers to begin adjusting their habits, particularly to prepare for climate change. The continuation of this article, which focuses on irrigation while critiquing synthetic fertilizer, is essentially an admission that a combination of factors including the timing, prevailing government capacity, and inherent problems in the technical package itself make deployment of the whole Green Revolution system problematic.

Alternative agriculture

Diverse in its expressions and forms, alternative agriculture is understood by the government as a form of rural development that speaks to sustainability, modernity, productivity, and populism and that, through these aspects, has complementary utility in promoting the legitimacy of the state. CEDAC, as the largest rural development NGO in Cambodia, monopolizes the discursive space as well as directly intervening in wide-ranging rural development initiatives. Its primary entry point into ecological agriculture has been to promote the now-famous SRI, which has been institutionalized by the government in the SRI Secretariat. By 2008, official statistics showed that Cambodia led Southeast Asia in share of produce that is organic (IFOAM and FiBL 2008, 2010).[10] As a result, both domestically and internationally, alternative agriculture has achieved notoriety and demonstrated benefit to the government. Through its autonomous activities, CEDAC serves many other important roles for the government, including training government extension workers, promoting a domestic market, championing sustainable development internationally, valorizing small farmers, and providing a populist model of agricultural development (Feuer 2007: 32–5; Muol 2008). Furthermore, farmer participation in training, small credit groups, or other programmes, increases their visibility to the government (cf. Scott 1998) and increases the bureaucratic interface. Emerging from CEDAC's work is also tangible evidence of the improvement of rural life, as symbolized by organic rice, vegetables, palm sugar and other ecological-oriented products that can be experienced and consumed in the city. Dimensions of alternative agriculture promoted by CEDAC, such as local and traditional, and organic, food, are useful for generating patriotic sentiment and supporting domestic market value-added initiatives (Vida and Reardon 2008). Internationally, support for ecological agriculture is increasingly viewed as a positive trait of progressive and modern developing countries (UNEP *et al.* 2011; UNESCAP 2002).

The main reservation on the part of the government concerning alternative agriculture is the indirect political involvement of rural people following agriculture training and empowerment programmes. Agricultural training, on its own, consists of rather basic gatherings that do not necessarily engender civic engagement. However, following international trends in alternative agriculture, CEDAC programmes are designed to draw rural people into continually higher levels of community engagement (Feuer 2007), beginning with savings groups and producer cooperatives, and ending in national-level farmer associations. The farmer-to-farmer training mechanism employed by CEDAC allows farmers to have technical encounters (Kampuchea Thmei 2008b), which the government appreciates, but these also lay the groundwork for increasingly differentiated engagement in civil society. Even small producer groups of ten families, which primarily focus on improving trading conditions in their villages, can become platforms for grassroots organization if threats to the village are faced, whether they be environmental (e.g. floods, crime, epidemics) or political (e.g. land grabbing, infrastructure projects, corruption, predatory traders). At higher levels of organization, such as the national Farmers' Association, the collective agency of the rural community is increased relative to the government. While the Farmers' Association has maintained very amicable relationships with the government (Koh Santepheap 2008a), the existence of large rural organizations is already an initial challenge to the monopoly of state authority in the countryside.

Spaces of plurality, spaces of innovation

Despite representing competing agricultural discourses in development, CARDI and CEDAC can be made to coexist in the same socio-technical landscape because of government intervention to create plural political space for them. This departs from the axiom in development policy that governments must eventually choose between discrete models; rather, it follows market logic, in which models are disaggregated and different parts appeal to different audiences. In a way, the peaceable coexistence of CARDI and CEDAC in Cambodia is a physical manifestation of the state of the (more neutral) international debate about agriculture and rural development among academics and policymakers. The debate within industrialized countries, in contrast, is largely between a structurally, politically and scientifically dominant school and a popular, but small, minority viewpoint. In Cambodia, this dichotomy has not emerged for two reasons. First, the government, as I have demonstrated above, has reasons to support and be suspicious of both schools of agricultural development and actively stays in the middle ground. Second, CEDAC and CARDI have so far largely followed complementary directions in agricultural development: CARDI focuses on dry season rice and export standardization whereas CEDAC focuses on wet season rice and productivity of farming systems and the organization of farming communities. In many ways the latter is the result of the government's ability to capture the strengths of each system and avoid some of the paradigmatic differences between them, though this may change over time.

This is demonstrated by the varying ways in which ecological and productivist agriculture are technically supported or politically leveraged in Cambodia (following the framework of Raynolds 2002). To start with, government planning documents and speeches carefully promote the organic sector and discourage agricultural chemicals while encouraging high-yielding varieties and irrigation infrastructure (MAFF 2006; Ministry of Commerce 2006). The media gives attention, air-time, and consistently favourable commentary to sustainable agricultural issues, training programmes and commentators.[11] CEDAC has a regular radio and television presence, and its director, Dr Koma Yang Saing, is interviewed for most reportages and newspaper articles concerning smallholder agricultural development. CARDI, in turn, is consistently interviewed in the context of agribusiness and export promotion, and their varieties are promoted by the MAFF. The current market itself is also evidence of the successful coexistence of both sides. Cambodia is the regional leader in organic production and the organic output is almost entirely consumed domestically, which is unusual for a less developed country. CEDAC, as quoted above, has reached around 8 per cent of Cambodia's farming population as well as having trained many extension agents in the provincial departments of agriculture. CARDI, in comparison, has developed varieties that are widely used for 30 per cent of rice cultivation (early and dry season), and has created some popular wet season varieties, some of which are even used for organic cultivation (e.g. Phkar Rumduol). They have helped improve agricultural processing, particularly milling quality, and have contributed extensively towards characterizing the soils across Cambodia.

However, due to paradigmatic differences in their respective development models (as elaborated in Beus and Dunlap 1990), it is only a matter of time before the discourses underlying both of these organizations come into open conflict. CARDI and its international supporters, for example, would likely prefer commanding or centralized government intervention in the distribution of its technological package in ways that bypass local populist conservativism. CEDAC, as a representative of the broader alternative agriculture movement, would likely prefer to improve the economic and political power of producers and promote decentralization through autonomous civil society, such as helping to empower farmers and valorize local (as opposed to expert) knowledge. Ultimately, the state and political parties will be the arbiters of this conflict but, in contrast to contemporary industrialized country governments, it will enter this conflict with less institutional and structural inertia. To the extent that this process does not fall prey to elite capture, business interests, or multilateral pressures, whether the government develops a novel middle ground or chooses a specific side will depend on the evolving merits of each development model.

Notes

1 This differs from other types of civil society initiatives, such as human rights and democracy organizations (Khus 2004 elaborates further on this delineation in Cambodia; Un 2006), whose motivations evolve with domestic conditions such that they maintain distance from the state (Landau 2008: 248–9).
2 Productivist agriculture is outlined by Wilson and Riggs (2003), referencing the package of agricultural practices (and often rounded out by certain policies) that rely on infrastructure and capital intensive cultivation. In this paper, and in general for development purposes, it is synonymous with the term green revolution agriculture.
3 Angkorean hydrological development has been studied by a series of researchers, most notably Bernard-Philippe Groslier, Christophe Pottier, and the team of the University of Sydney's Greater Angkor Project. See: http://acl.arts.usyd.edu.au/angkor/gap/.
4 Default organic is a term to describe farmers who minimally do not use (or have never used) agricultural chemicals such as inorganic fertilizer or pesticides. It can also include farmers who practice soil erosion control, crop rotation, use of natural fertilizers and manures, and mulching. Often it refers to farmers who do not intentionally practice natural agriculture, but lack resources (cash, credit, etc.) to purchase inputs (see the case study of Uganda in Källander and Rundgren 2008: 167–74).
5 The acronym CEDAC derives from the French name of the organization, the Centre d'Etude et de Développement Agricole Cambodgien.
6 Statistics are provided by CEDAC (2008; Yang Saing 2010).
7 Speech by His Excellency Dr Chan Sarun, Minister of Agriculture, Forestry and Fisheries at the closing ceremony of the meeting entitled 'Lessons Learnt and SRI Techniques Reflection from 2008–2009', April 2009. Translated by CEDAC. Accessed 13 December 2011. Online. Available at: www.cedac.org.kh/sri_pdf1.pdf.
8 In public speeches and ceremonial gift-givings, the Minister of MAFF often provides rice varieties from CARDI while instructing farmers to eliminate or reduce fertilizer and pesticide use and employ the ecological system of rice intensification.
9 Farmers in natural production include those engaged in the System of Rice Intensification as well as certified and non-certified organic production.
10 This is based on the percentage of organic agricultural output and excludes Timor Leste's coffee exports.
11 This is based on a six-year sampling of coverage of agricultural issues in three Khmer newspapers (*Koh Santepheap, Rasmey Thmei, Kampuchea Thmei*), two English-language dailies (*Phnom Penh Post* and the *Cambodia Daily*), two popular radio stations in rural areas (Radio France Internationale, Radio Bayon), and two television channels (Bayon TV and Cambodian Television Network).

References

Agrifood Consulting International (2002) *Rice Value Chain Study: Cambodia – a Report Prepared for the World Bank*, Phnom Penh: Agrifood Consulting International.

Altieri, M. A. (1987) *Agroecology: The Scientific Basis of Alternative Agriculture*, Boulder, Colorado: Westview.

Beus, C. E. and Dunlap, R. E. (1990) 'Conventional versus Alternative Agriculture: The Paradigmatic Roots of the Debate' in *Rural Sociology*, 55 (4): 590–616.

Beus, C. E. and Dunlap, R. E. (1994) 'Agricultural Paradigms and the Practice of Agriculture' in *Rural Sociology*, 59 (4): 620–35.

Boyle, D. and Chakrya, K. S. (2010) 'Govt to Push for Legislation on Chemicals' in *Phnom Penh Post*, Phnom Penh, 19 February.

CEDAC (2008) *Adoption and Non-adoption of System of Rice Intensification (SRI) in Cambodia*, Phnom Penh: Cambodian Center for Study and Development in Agriculture.

Chandler, D. (2000 [1983]) *A History of Cambodia*, Boulder, CO: Westview.

Clarke, N., Cloke, P., Barnett, C. and Malpass, A. (2008) 'The spaces and ethics of organic food' in *Journal of Rural Studies*, 24: 219–30.

Cleveland, D. A., Soleri, D. and Smith, S. E. (1994) 'Do Folk Crop Varieties have a Role in Sustainable Agriculture?' in *BioScience*, 44 (11): 740–51.

Curtis, G. (1998) *Cambodia Reborn? The Transition to Democracy and Development*, Washington, DC: Brookings Institution Press.

De Launey, G. (2005) 'Cambodia Targets Organic Market', BBC News. Online. Available at: http://news.bbc.co.uk/go/pr/fr/-/2/hi/asia-pacific/4350290.stm (accessed 12 September 2009).

De Nike, H. J., Quigley, J. and Robinson, K. J. (eds) (2000) *Genocide in Cambodia: Documents from the Trial of Pol Pot and Ieng Sary*, Philadelphia: University of Pennsylvania Press.

Ear, S. (1995) 'Cambodia's Economic Development in Historical Perspective: A Contribution to the Study of Cambodia's Economy', unpublished thesis, University of California.

EJF (2002) *Death in Small Doses: Cambodia's Pesticide Problems and Solutions*, London: Environmental Justice Foundation.

Ellis, F. and Biggs, S. D. (2001) 'Evolving Themes in Rural Development 1950s-2000s' in *Development Policy Review*, 19 (4): 437–48.

Feuer, H. N. (2007) 'Sustainable Agricultural Techniques and Performance Oriented Empowerment: An Actor-Network Theory Approach to CEDAC Agricultural and Empowerment Programmes in Cambodia', unpublished thesis, University of Oxford.

Fforde, A. and Seidel, K. (2010) *Donor Playground Cambodia? What a look at Aid and Development in Cambodia Confirms and What it May Imply*, Berlin: Heinrich Böll Foundation.

Fitzgerald, D. (1993) 'Farmers Deskilled: Hybrid Corn and Farmers' work' in *Technology and Culture*, 34 (2): 324–43.

Goodman, D. (1999) 'Agro-Food Studies in the "Age of Ecology": Nature, Corporeality, Biopolitics' in *Sociologia Ruralis*, 39 (1): 17–38.

Guibernau, M. (1999) *Nations without States: Political Communities in a Global Age*, Cambridge: Polity Press/Blackwell Publishers.

Hughes, C. (2009) *Dependent Communities: Aid and Politics in Cambodia and East Timor*, New York: Cornell University Press.

Hughes, C. (2010) 'Driving Development Effectiveness: Donors' politics without opposition' in Asia Research Centre (ed.), *The Elephant in the Room: Politics and the Development Problem*, Perth, 13–14 December: Murdoch University.

IFOAM and FiBL (2008) *Organic Agricultural Land Worldwide 2007*, Frick, Germany: International Federation of Organic Agriculture Movements, Research Institute for Organic Agriculture.

IFOAM and FiBL (2010) *Organic Agricultural Land Worldwide 2008*, Frick, Germany: International Federation of Organic Agriculture Movements, Research Institute for Organic Agriculture.

IRRI (2007) 'Busy week in the GMS' in *IRRI Bulletin*, 2007 (02).

Jacobs, M. (1999) 'Sustainable Development as a Contested Concept' in A. Dobson (ed.), *Fairness and Futurity: Essays on Environmental Sustainability and Social Justice*, Oxford: Oxford University Press: 21–45.

James, C. (2010) 'Agro-industry hurt by lack of processing' in *Phnom Penh Post*, Phnom Penh, 2 June.

Källander, I. and Rundgren, G. (2008) *Building Sustainable Organic Sectors*, Bonn, Germany: International Federation of Organic Agriculture Movements (IFOAM).

Kampuchea Thmei (2008a) 'Rice Export Business Still Not Profitable in 2007', Phnom Penh, 12 January.

Kampuchea Thmei (2008b) 'Why Farmers are Interested in SRI', Phnom Penh, 26 September.

Keam, M. (2007) 'Country Report on Organic Agriculture in Cambodia', paper presented at Regional Conference on Organic Agriculture in Asia, Bangkok, Thailand, 12–15 December.

Khus, T. (2004) 'Cambodian Civil Society Movement' in *Civil Society in Southeast Asia: Scope and Concepts*, Phnom Penh, 7–8 June: Heinrich Böll Foundation.

Koh Santepheap (2008a) 'Farmer and Nature Network makes Government Recommendations', Phnom Penh, 21 November.

Koh Santepheap (2008b) 'Japanese Authorities Recall 600,000 bottles of Rice Wine', Phnom Penh, 15 December.

Koh Santepheap (2008c) 'Worries About Chemical-laden Vegetables and Fruit from Thailand with no Oversight', Phnom Penh, 4 July.

Landau, I. (2008) 'Law and Civil Society in Cambodia and Vietnam: A Gramscian Perspective' in *Journal of Contemporary Asia*, 38 (2): 244–58.

Lélé, S. M. (1991) 'Sustainable Development: A Critical Review' in *World Development*, 19 (6): 607–21.

MAFF (2006) *Agricultural Sector Strategic Development Plan 2006–2010*, Phnom Penh: Ministry of Agriculture, Forestry and Fisheries.

Mak, S. (2001) 'Continued Innovation in a Cambodian Rice-based Farming System: Farmer Testing and Recombination of New Elements' in *Agricultural Systems*, 69 (1): 137–49.

McNaughton, A. (2002) 'Cambodia's Experience and Opportunities for Domestic and International Trade in Organic Agricultural Products', paper presented at Policy Dialogue on Promoting Production and Trading Opportunities for Organic Agricultural Products, Brussels, 21–2 February.

Ministry of Commerce (2006) *Cambodia National Export Strategy 2007–2010*, Phnom Penh: Ministry of Commerce.

Muol, S. (2008) 'Tramkok District is Number one for SRI' in *Rasmey Kampuchea*, Phnom Penh, 2 March.

Nesbitt, H. (2002) 'Developing Sustainable Rice Production Systems in Cambodia: An Australian contribution', paper presented at ATSE Crawford Fund Conference, Canberra, Australia.

Norgaard, R. B. (1994) *Development Betrayed: The End of Progress and a Coevolutionary Revisioning of the Future*, New York: Routledge.

Öjendal, J. and Kim, S. (2007) 'Korob, Kaud, Klach: In Search of Agency in Rural Cambodia' in *Journal of Southeast Asian Studies*, 37 (3): 507–26.

Pingali, P., Hossein, M. and Gerpacio, R. V. (1995) *Asian Rice Bowls: The Returning Crisis*, Wallingford, UK: Centre for Agricultural Bioscience International and International Rice Research Institute.

Rasmey Kampuchea (2007) 'Workshop on Agricultural Flows Between Cambodia and Other Countries', Phnom Penh, 14 September.

Raynolds, L. (2002) *Poverty Alleviation through Participation in Fair Trade Coffee Networks: Existing Research and Critical Issues*, New York: Ford Foundation.

Samphan, K. (1959) 'L'économie du Cambodge et ses problèmes d'industrialisation' [Cambodia's Economy and Industrial Development], trans. by Laura Summers, unpublished thesis: University of Paris.

Sarun, C. (2005) 'Situation of Pest Management and Pesticides in Cambodia', trans by Piseth Som, in *Pracheachun*, 47 (April).

Sarun, C. (2009) 'Agriculture in Cambodia', trans. by Piseth Som, in *Pracheachun*, 100 (September).

Scott, J. C. (1998) *Seeing Like a State*, New Haven, CT: Yale University Press.

Singer, P. (1974) 'All Animals Are Equal' in *Philosophical Exchange*, 1: 103–16.

Sophal, C. (2010) 'New Agreement Sets Target of 300,000 Tons to Sell Overseas' in *Phnom Penh Post*, Phnom Penh, 4 January.

SPM Consultants (2003) *Civil Society and Democracy in Cambodia: Changing roles and trends*, Stockholm and Phnom Penh: Swedish International Development Co-operation Agency.

Tripp, R. (2006) *Is Low External Input Technology Contributing to Sustainable Agricultural Development?* London: Overseas Development Institute (ODI).

Un, K. (2006) 'State, Society and Democratic Consolidation: The Case of Cambodia' in *Pacific Affairs*, 79 (2): 225–45.

UNCED (1992a) 'Agenda 21', Environment and Social Affairs, UN Conference on Environment and Development.

UNCED (1992b) 'Rio Declaration on Environment and Development', UN Conference on Environment and Development, UN General Assembly.

UNEP, UNCTAD and UN-OHRLLS (2011) *Green Economy: Why a Green Economy Matters for the Least Developed Countries*, New York, Nairobi and Geneva: United Nations Environmental Programme, United Nations Conference on Trade and Development, Office of the High Representative for the Least Developed Countries, Landlocked Developing Countries and Small Island Developing States.

UNESCAP (2002) *Organic Agriculture and Rural Poverty Alleviation: Potential and Best Practices in Asia*, Bangkok: United Nations Economic and Social Commission for Asia and the Pacific.

Vandermeer, J. (1995) 'The Ecological Basis of Alternative Agriculture' in *Annual Review of Ecology and Systematics*, 26: 201–24.

Vickery, M. (1984) *Cambodia: 1975–1982*, Boston: South End Press.

Vida, I. and Reardon, J. (2008) 'Domestic Consumption: Rational, Affective or Normative Choice?' in *Journal of Consumer Marketing*, 25 (1): 34–44.

White, G. (1994) 'Civil Society, Democratization and Development: Clearing the Analytical Ground' in *Democratization*, 1 (3): 375–90.

Wilson, G. A. and Rigg, J. (2003) '"Post-productivist" Agricultural Regimes and the South: Discordant Concepts?' in *Progress in Human Geography*, 27 (6): 681–707.

Yang Saing, K. (2010) *Building Experiences with SRI Development and Dissemination in Cambodia (2000–2010)*, Phnom Penh: Cambodian Center for Study and Development in Agriculture.

Yang Saing, K., Keam, M. and Lang Seng, H. (2000) *Pesticide Market in Cambodia: Pesticide Pollution in Tonle Sap Catchment*, Phnom Penh: Cambodian Center for Study and Development in Agriculture (CEDAC).

15 Conclusion

The civil society gaze

Hart N. Feuer, Phuong Le Trong and Judith Ehlert

The challenge we laid out as editors for this book was to assess, in a very functional sense, how practitioners, academics and other observers have defined, implemented, and evolved the concept of civil society over the past few decades. We did so in this collaborative book project by gathering together a diverse and interdisciplinary group of people either explicitly or implicitly working on civil society, who were tasked with exploring the ways in which the concept was applied in their (primarily empirical) work. While we do not ignore the lively debate about civil society that lies in the background of these efforts, we felt that the endogenous development of the theory of civil society, alongside its manifestations, often results in 'chicken or the egg' dilemmas that leave academics chasing their tails. What can at least be said is that the phenomenon of civil society, as a material object of study and as a conceptual sphere, is informed by temporally and spatially relevant factors. While theoretical conceptions of civil society are helpful and have proved salient in certain contexts, they may or may not prove particularly relevant in other contexts, except perhaps as a means for comparison. As a result, even if an encompassing definition for civil society could be found, applying it in any meaningful way would still require adaptation to match underlying characteristics of each setting, such as the composition of the state, historical trends, and influence of external discourses (all of these, incidentally, are discussed in various chapters in the book).

The individual authors in this volume complement and challenge many prevailing assumptions about the development, role, and persistence of civil society through their embedded research, much of which has focused on novel forms of civil society. Furthermore, as endogenous actors themselves (i.e. as researchers on the ground) in the ongoing conceptualization of civil society, the authors must reveal their personal views and theoretical comprehension of civil society through their selection of a topic, conceptual framing and methodology. The diverse frames and points of departure of the contributing authors' works suggest that civil society is often used as a lens (or an instrument) for studying associational activity a given domain. As some authors have suggested, this has also become the case for studies of what could be perceived as global civil society (Amoore and Langley 2004). More generally, however, we argue that observers often cast a civil society gaze on broader themes such as religion, HIV, human rights enforcement, or development programmes, which more often than not leads to explorations of the evolving types of associational activity generated in these areas.

The diversity of civil society

The original purpose of the book was to explore the bounds of the civil society debate by drawing inspiration from two neighbouring, but in many ways very different, countries. Many of the similarities and differences between Cambodia and Vietnam are reflected in the diverse regional and disciplinary backgrounds of the contributing authors, some of whom do not explicitly study civil society or even subjects typically encountered in civil society literature. Reflecting this, the resulting contributions are a collage of civil society that is both aligned with, and divergent from, contemporary research trends and theory. Some authors are well-steeped in contemporary civil society theory and chose to test the limits of various conceptions in practice. Others study phenomena that could readily be called civil society-like in the going debate, but they had not previously identified with nor applied the terminology of civil society in their work. Hiwasa, who had carried out an ethnography of women's groups and the engagement of women in local and national advocacy, primarily identified her work as contributing to feminist studies. Although her work empirically speaks to civil society, she had previously not elected to take on board the terminology or interface with normative definitions of civil society. In contrast, the civil society dimension in the contribution of Bourdier, who studied very similar associational activity in Cambodia, is very strongly pronounced. Feuer, similar to Hiwasa, identified his original research on large NGOs as a study of the environmental movement and social change, rather than on civil society. His contribution to this book, however, explicitly engages with debates in civil society and looks at typical subjects found in civil society literature, such as the relationship between government and NGOs. As a preliminary conclusion drawing from these cases in Cambodia, we suggest that, at least in empirical work, the civil society lens does not arise naturally from the subject matter but is rather a personal choice based on the orientation and goals of the author, which are, in turn, influenced and constrained by international and local conceptions of civil society.

In Cambodia, popular conceptions of civil society generally correspond to definitions and programmes that have been developed and implemented in the context of international aid and reconstruction. Indeed, in his survey of the evolution of civil society in Cambodia, Öjendal (this volume) suggests that development and advocacy activities are hegemonic in discussions of civil society. The civil society lens employed by many observers of Cambodia, therefore, tends to focus on formal organizations, human rights groups and other typical forms of civil society, such as unions. This emphasis comes through strongly in the contributions by Feuer, Hiwasa and Bourdier. Ehlert's work, in contrast, explicitly challenges this trend in her study of embedded religious-sphere associational activity. She argues that the predominance of development assistance in the conception of civil society has caused local institutions to slip between the cracks. Her work, like many from the authors writing on Vietnam in this book, takes the perspective that associational activities are inherent to society and that it is the task of observers to seek it out, highlight it, and thereby bring it into larger debates about civil society (including for foreign audiences). The contribution by Thim similarly tries to challenge dominant conceptions of civil society. In his chapter, what begins as a small local group of concerned citizens dealing with flooding becomes a significant and well-recognized civil society group through continual differentiation, formalization, and networking at multiple scales. Thim suggests that the actors themselves become aware of the legitimating power of being labelled 'civil society'. Wells-Dang, in his chapter on civil society networks in Cambodia and Vietnam, also seeks to uncover and legitimate informal associational activity. Through his comparison of meta-level associational activity and cooperation in Cambodia and Vietnam, he tests the boundaries of popular conceptions that have largely viewed civil society as diffuse groups acting unsystematically within bounded areas of interest. Like Ehlert, he argues that more (forms of) engagement, activism and coordination are undertaken by Cambodian and Vietnamese actors than is commonly recognized.

Many of the authors in this book writing about Vietnam similarly attempt to search for and identify emerging associational activities as civil society, or highlight the civil society content of well-established institutions and ideas. As presented in the discourse analysis by Phuong Le Trong, Vietnamese officials and academics are complicit in twisting around the concept of civil society in order to situate it in socialist historiography and in contemporary political-cultural ideology and social organization in Vietnam. Bach Tan Sinh's overview of the sprawling state and non-state associations demonstrates how this is, in practice, carried out. State-sponsored associational activity, such as the Vietnam Women's Union (elaborated in Pistor and Le Thi Quy), is officially seen as the core of civic participation in the Vietnamese conception of state–society interface. Pistor and Le Thi Quy, however, contend that breakdowns and evolving hybrid arrangements at the local level of implementation (in the case of gender advocacy) are evidence that top-down groups, in spite of their intentions to do so, are not fulfilling the diverse local aspirations for civic participation. And furthermore, as Waibel and Benedikter suggest, the growing and diversifying cohort of community-based organizations in southern Vietnam is indicative of expanding notions and relevance of alternative forms of civil society.

In contrast to authors in this volume seeking out and explaining existing associational activity in terms of civil society, two contributors take a critical stance against the aptitude of civil society explanations more generally. In her chapter, Reis questions whether turning the civil society lens on all types of associational activity in Vietnam is really just paying lip service to the core concept of civil society based on the division between state and society. She argues that many of the fundamental premises of civil society emerging from its historical manifestations in western Europe cannot naturally be merged with the cultural context and political economy in Vietnam. Even in Cambodia, where development aid has apparently transferred more Western conceptions of civil society, Ou and Kim argue that associations and organizations, which are popularly understood to constitute civil society, are often empty shells, bereft of the social orientation, volunteer spirit and grassroots focus that is hoped for in international civil society discourse. While the arguments made by Reis, and by Ou and Kim, may hold if one strictly compares the 'content' of civil society to various socially constructed ideals, most of the authors outlined above allowed the definition of civil society to emerge from empirical realities. In other chapters a middle course was taken, whereby the civil society lens was purposively applied, but the analysis ultimately shied away from normative comparisons concerning the content of civil society. This suggests that the civil society gaze is both a product of individual authors' thematic and conceptual points of departure, as well as a reflection of the contested discourse of civil society at the national level.

Micro themes, macro tendencies

While the backgrounds of the authors, their country of study, and their respective areas of expertise condition them to select certain 'micro themes', and investigate them in certain ways, their work often goes towards examining broader 'macro themes'. The authors gravitated toward two such macro themes: (1) analysing changes in political space, particularly through advocacy, and (2) teasing out the traces and tendencies in associational activity emerging from the political and cultural context as well as from foreign intervention. These macro themes are illustrative of two common ways the authors investigated civil society. Authors falling into macro theme 1 generally took an outward-orientation – looking at the goals and results of various activities. Authors falling into macro theme 2 had a more introspective orientation, looking at the structural and conceptual make-up of different activities. In short, some authors elected to look at what civil society tries to accomplish while the others looked at what underlies and influences civil society.

The predominance of these two macro themes is not surprising when one considers how the concept of civil society is commonly instrumentalized in development discourse. In mainstream development, 'civil society' is hoped to be a facilitator of liberal development goals such as good governance and decentralization, which leads to aid for advocacy and activism, and non-state service provision (Goetz and O'Brien 1995; White 1994). Historical conceptions of civil society also speak to the question of carving out political space for citizens in the public sphere. And with so much aid channelled to advocacy, thereby creating physical objects to study (usually formal organizations), it is to be expected that many observers tend to focus on advocacy and political space (macro theme 1). The discussions taking place as part of the authors' writeshop reflected this – with frequent, and often vigorously defended, references to the competitive, or even hostile, relationship between the state and civil society. However, when the dust settled after these debates, and the different experiences within and between

Cambodia and Vietnam had been represented, it was evident that the divide between public and private, and between state and society, does not manifest as a zero-sum relationship. One the one hand, although the state perceives that civil society plays a positive role in the governance of social welfare, poverty alleviation, public health, environmental protection, business administration and the organization of academic and cultural activities, the state is commonly prompted to act pre-emptively and reactively to control civil society because of its one-dimensional competitive view of local power. On the other hand, authors shared many instances of 'mutual' relationships between the state and civil society, in which emerging social groups and civil society organizations form a social space, even the infrastructure, for socio-economic development that both the state and civil society can also leverage to their own ends.

A corollary assumption coming out of historical views of civil society is that the growth of associational activity (often in the form of organizations) is a universal part of development (Lewis 1997; SustainAbility 2003; Tandon 1994) and helps to make transparent local people's needs and aspirations (Edwards *et al.* 1999; Farrington and Bebbington 1994; Sen 1999). This optimistic view of civil society was followed by critical perspectives concerning 'uncivil society' and the hijacking of civil society discourses in international development for political purposes (Boyd 2004; Monga 2009; Stewart 1997). One prominent strand of this critique warily views the directed support for non-state actors as a thinly veiled way of pushing a neo-liberal agenda (Gill 1998; Kamat 2004) and/or promoting Western political values using technocratic-oriented organizations (Ferguson 1994: 66; Judge 2003). It is therefore also not surprising that many observers, including those in macro theme 2 who are ostensibly investigating civil society, look at the underlying drivers and cultural roots of various associational activities.

Utility of the civil society lens

If, as in the case of this book, observers of civil society are already attached to various disciplines and well conceptualized subject areas, what is the purpose of, and intention behind, explicitly employing a civil society framework? Why not express the subject in simpler terms using traditional theoretical frameworks, such as 'the political economy of agriculture policy in Cambodia' (Feuer) or 'institutional analysis of the Vietnam Women's Union' (Pistor and Le Thi Quy)? Based on ideas suggested in the country overview chapters by Öjendal and Bach Tan Sinh, and drawing from the cohort of contributing authors to this volume, we have garnered a few cross-cutting rationales of researchers and practitioners for bringing the concept of civil society into empirical work, namely: claiming legitimacy; exploring the political dimension of civil society; and understanding the ethics of identifying civil society.

Claiming legitimacy

Due to its illustrious historical pedigree and its strong presence in contemporary nation-building and development discourses, the term civil society is more than just a conceptual container. For academics, governments, development agencies, and local people, civil society wraps a layer of meaning and significance around certain activities, elevating their relevance and legitimacy. For governments, civil society may be viewed as a threatening sector of activism, but it is also often viewed as a universal part of state–society relations and an integral partner in service provision. The entry by Phuong Le Trong elucidates how Vietnamese academics and officials transform and co-opt potentially destabilizing foreign concepts in order to render them politically palatable and useful in Party policy. In Cambodia, 'civil society' has been viewed by the state as a partner in service delivery and policy (see Öjendal and Feuer, respectively) as well as a challenge to state monopoly on power (see Thim). For contemporary researchers and practitioners, the aura of civil society can also be useful in branding one's own work. Appropriating the terminology of civil society to frame your research or development project can often bring legitimation and recognition from academic circles and donors. In this case, recognition would be largely a strategic endeavour relating to the availability of funding and popularity of certain definitions of civil society. Because international aid agencies have become increasingly interested in supporting certain types of initiative that they deem to be part of civil society (NGOs, human rights organizations, environmental groups, etc.), research or development projects that fit these descriptions are often more fundable. The contribution by Bourdier, which describes the mobilization of people living with HIV/AIDS and the growth in anti-retroviral treatment programmes, highlights how the identification with civil society is employed as a means to legitimize their activities and to conceptualize their growing institutionalization. Doing so makes individual initiatives seem to be part of an inevitable and socially relevant process in society. As Wells-Dang's overview of civil society networks highlights, the impacts of identification as civil society vary with the audience. On the one hand, popular civil society discourses in Cambodia bear connotations of grassroots resistance, as exemplified by an activist quoted in the chapter: 'We will rise up and speak for the people. We are Cambodia's civil society.' On the other hand, Wells-Dang also follows networks of activists that purposefully avoid formal registration as an organization because it would draw unwanted political scrutiny to local organizers. In general, however, the high profile of the civil society debate can provide incentive for academics to ostensibly study civil society, as well as for practitioners to promote activities that can be defined as civil society. The prominence of civil society in leading development agencies, in addition to academic discourse, sends a signal to practitioners that aligning with this conceptual space may lead to support.[1] In academia, as one scholar noted, civil society has become 'a growth industry in Chinese studies' (Nevitt 1996) and the same observation can be made elsewhere. In fact, this book itself contributes to this process.

Exploring the political dimension of civil society

If one distils many of the empirical chapters in this book (particularly those in the section 'Advocacy and Political Space') down to the core developmental themes being investigated, one often finds politically or socially controversial processes under way. These range from local people seeking justice and compensation in transnational diplomacy (Thim), to negotiating the role of women in decentralization (Pistor and Le Thi Quy; Hiwasa), to the evolving influence of independent scientists and ecological movements in natural resource management (Wells-Dang; Feuer). Often, however, the political controversies and debates inherent to these topics can become obscured by the focus on civil society. As Ferguson (1994: 253–65) wrote in his seminal work on Lesotho, international development agencies often seek to sequester the normative political dimension of their interventions in technocratic projects and jargon. Supporting various activities under the guise of civil society can be exploited as an indirect way of, among others, promoting liberal political regimes, interfering in national politics, or transferring social ideology such as feminism (Bui The Cuong 2005). In the programming of various agencies, these intentions are advertised with differing degrees of discretion. The United States Agency for International Development (USAID), for example, explicitly promotes civil society as an aspect of democratization and governance, while the World Bank more generally conceives of civil society as the respective activities of various organizations, movements and unions.[2] The governments of Cambodia and Vietnam are nonetheless becoming increasingly aware of the political nature of civil society but are forced to balance their responses. In Vietnam, as highlighted by Bach Tan Sinh and Phuong Le Trong, there is the sense that civil society is something of a moral imperative – a social concept to be adapted and included in ideology, albeit with modifications for the political and cultural context. This includes, as described by Waibel and Benedikter, decrees aimed at regulating, integrating and co-opting these developments. In Cambodia, in contrast, after initially being flooded by organizations and interventions from the early 1990s (see Öjendal; Ou and Kim), the government has recently taken legal steps to assert political control over civil society. Although undoubtedly responding to overtly political activities carried out by human rights organizations and unions, the attempt to pass an 'NGO Law' in Cambodia is likely also an acknowledgment that the government is increasingly aware of, and concerned with, the everyday politics of development initiatives (see Bratton 1989; Kerkvliet 2009). As evident in the contributions on Vietnam (with the exception of that of Reis), the government and Party have already subsumed much of the civic space of traditional practices and go further by attempting to co-opt Western civil society discourse (see Phuong Le Trong, this volume); official initiatives nevertheless struggles to match the dynamism of new civil society initiatives. In both the Cambodian and Vietnamese cases, the state is increasingly forced to control civil society from a distance by shaping (and restricting) the environment in which associational activity can emerge.

Understanding the ethics of identifying civil society

Although conceptions of civil society remain unsettled in theoretical debates, decisions are nevertheless made regarding who or what constitutes civil society in many publications, initiatives and policies. Because they are made within a context of contestation and uncertainty, the decisions themselves become interesting subjects of research. As discussed above, being labelled as civil society either through self-identification or by external parties, has political consequences and can influence a group's legitimacy. State–non-state boundaries can also be forged in this context, resulting in socially constructed conceptions of autonomy and the public/private divide. Scholars who write about various initiatives using a civil society lens, or publish in a book about civil society (particularly if they enumerate it), are thereby constituting a reality whether they intend to or not. This goes beyond Hann and Dunn's (1996) critique about judging local activities on the basis of Western models of civil society, and refers instead to judging local activities using any model of civil society. With a civil society lens, the object of research cannot be studied independently of various preconceptions and notions of civil society. Bourdier addresses this point in his chapter, arguing that assessments about the effectiveness of the HIV/AIDS interventions are interchanged with judgements about the grassroots and embedded nature of the attendant organizations and groups. Whether one eventually concludes that the objects of study are genuinely part of civil society or not, an a priori assumption has already been made that various social phenomena have something to do with civil society.

All of the contributions to this book speak to different aspects of this dynamic. A typical point of departure, which is critically discussed in the chapter by Ou and Kim and more generally elaborated upon by Bach Tan Sinh (2011), are reports that physically 'count' civil society, usually by tallying the numbers of certain organizations or the amount of funding received in various sectors. As Ou and Kim demonstrate, forcing a definition of civil society for the sake of tallying not only pays lip service to the diversity in institutional dynamics within various organizations, it also makes implicit judgements as to the legitimacy of various associational phenomena. Waibel and Benedikter, similarly, chronicle how official recognition (and registration) as CBOs often leads to integration into, or at least intervention from, the government. In other words, counting not only legitimizes, it also makes groups transparent, for better or worse. Another point of departure considers the agency of the actors in managing their identification as part of civil society. In this regard, the contributions by Ehlert, Hiwasa and Thim complement each other. Thim describes how a regional network of civic groups grows, differentiates their activities, and deliberately tries to gain official recognition so that they can be taken more seriously in national debates. Ehlert, in contrast, argues that many embedded and pagoda-based associational activities are not recognized as civil society by development agents and the state but that they nonetheless play a critical role in communal relations in Cambodia. Hiwasa complements this view, viewing village-level women's groups in

Cambodia as opportunistic platforms for communication, empowerment and civic participation *even when they dissolve as formal groups*. In sum, whether groups are perpetuated or dissolved, become registered or stay under the radar, announce their membership in civil society or keep to themselves, remains a contentious process that parallels other discussions about what civil society is or what it does.

Conclusion

The primordial attraction of scholars to the ideas surrounding civil society stretches back to Aristotle and Cicero, and weighs heavily on contemporary discourses on political transition and development. Co-editor Judith Ehlert once described the concept as having a certain 'charisma'. Indeed, this book is an attempt to draw together scholars and practitioners to write about Vietnam and Cambodia with the expectation that the concept of civil society would create a unified platform for academic exchange. The authors, who are mostly not experts in civil society per se, can nevertheless leverage the terminology and a general layman's familiarity of civil society to create dialogue with the other authors. Although the editors originally assumed that the contributors would write about civil society in a literal sense, it turned out that civil society became more of what Mollinga (2008) has termed a 'boundary concept'. In interdisciplinary studies, boundary concepts 'allow us to think, that is conceptually communicate about, the multidimensionality of the issues we study and address' (Mollinga 2008: 23). In the summary above we referred to this primarily as the 'civil society lens' – a shared set of concepts that, although defined by each author and in each empirical setting, facilitate interdisciplinary and cross-thematic dialogue about the respective associational activities we study. This is, however, not strictly an argument that civil society does not exist as such, but merely that it manifests through debate, contextual adaptation, and external influence. While certain manifestations may crystallize over time under specific circumstances, such as the NGO-dominant definitions popular in Cambodia, they also become destabilized and renegotiated as new authors and new cases test the boundaries of the concept.

This book is an experiment in testing the boundaries of civil society as they have been variously conceptualized and applied in Cambodia and Vietnam. We purposefully drew authors from a variety of national backgrounds and disciplines to write on their respective areas of expertise. When possible, we solicited works on themes or 'forms of civil society' that were relatively underserved in contemporary literature. Although some of these authors had not previously written using a civil society lens, their topic areas covered some part of the associational realm in Cambodia and Vietnam. The overviews written by Joakim Öjendal and Bach Tan Sinh are meant to serve as reference points, presenting the range of activities studied and the perspectives in use over various periods in the two countries. In their topics and in their analytical perspectives, however, the authors often diverged from, or expanded on, many of the national trends.

Their themes ranged from topics that are more routinely covered, such as state–society relations, organizations and associations, and political activism, to themes that emerged from the specific context, such as women's empowerment, associational activity embedded in the religious sphere, and health sector mobilization. More importantly, however, the authors studied what they knew, while framing the cases with a civil society perspective. Consolidating this range of perspectives, both in their diversity and in their commonality, is the primary goal of this volume.

Even contributions that outwardly appear to be investigating the concept of civil society itself are actually exploring more general social processes. The chapter by Reis, for example, characterizes the Vietnamese social imaginary and its openness to foreign concepts of social organization by looking at confrontation between Western and Vietnamese cultural precedents and political economy. The contributions can be largely clustered into two macro-level themes: advocacy and political space, and traces and tendencies in civil society. In the former, authors tended to focus on how people and their associational activities draw attention to their causes in the political sphere, while in the latter, authors described how culture, history and the political environment left an imprint on associational activities. However, while the collective focus on advocacy and political space is more clear-cut among chapters on this theme, a political dimension permeates almost all of the chapters. The activities studied are themselves often of a political nature, as are the mechanisms of development and international aid that incentivize, generate, or inspire them. The governments of Cambodia and Vietnam have also recognized this, taking measures to regulate, co-opt, or discursively nullify the activities of civil society that they view as undesirable. As many of the contributing authors demonstrate, this and other considerations shuffle the incentives for actors to formalize or officially announce their membership in civil society. On the one hand, transparency, i.e. 'being counted', allows for open political manoeuvering, legitimation and support from development agencies. On the other hand, this can lead to government intervention or draw unnecessary attention to local or embedded initiatives.

This last point raises the question of the academic's (or development agency's) ethical role in writing about and researching civil society. While civil society can be a useful boundary concept for interdisciplinary studies and collaboration, and naturally lends charisma to one's work, the act of carrying out research into civil society draws attention to, and often implies legitimacy of, certain activities. Regardless of which of the varied models of civil society researchers in a developing country context select, this book argues that civil society research, in itself, is a political act.

Notes

1 The World Bank publishes a biannual report on engagement with civil society, as well as providing a fund for civil society. Many bilateral agencies and foundations also provide specific programmes for civil society, such as the UK Department for

International Development (DFID), Irish Aid, the US Agency for International Development (USAID), the Global Fund and the Carnegie Endowment, to name a few.
2 Referenced from the following programme websites for USAID (http://transition.usaid. gov/our_work/democracy_and_governance/technical_areas/civil_society/) and the World Bank (http://go.worldbank.org/PWRRFJ2QH0) (accessed 24 August 2012).

References

Amoore, L. and Langley, P. (2004) 'Ambiguities of Global Civil Society' in *Review of International Studies*, 30 (1): 89–110.

Bach Tan Sin (2011) 'Civil Society in Vietnam' in S. Elies and T. Chong (eds), *An ASEAN Community for All: Exploring the Scope for Civil Society Engagement*, Singapore: Friedrich Ebert Stiftung: 138–47.

Boyd, R. (2004) *Uncivil Society: The Perils of Pluralism and the Making of Modern Liberalism*, Oxford: Lexington Books.

Bratton, M. (1989) 'The Politics of Government-NGO Relations in Africa' in *World Development*, 17 (4): 569–87.

Bui The Cuong (2005) 'Issue-Oriented Organizations in Hanoi: Some Findings from an Empirical Survey' in Heinrich Böll Foundation (ed.), *Towards good Society: Civil Society Actors, the State, and the Business Class in Southeast Asia – Facilitators of or Impediments to a Strong, Democratic, and Fair Society?* Berlin: Heinrich Böll Foundation: 93–100.

Edwards, M., Hulme, D. and Wallace, T. (1999) 'NGOs in a Global Future: Marrying Local Delivery to Worldwide Leverage' in *Public Administration and Development*, 19: 117–36.

Farrington, J. and Bebbington, A. J. (1994) 'From Research to Innovation: Getting the Most from Interaction with NGOs' in I. Scoones and J. Thompson (eds), *Beyond Farmer First*, London: Intermediate Technology Publications: 203–13.

Ferguson, J. (1994) *The Anti-Politics Machine: Development, Depoliticization and Bureaucratic Power in Lesotho*, Minneapolis: University of Minnesota Press.

Gill, S. (1998) 'New Constitutionalism, Democratisation and Global Political Economy' in *Pacifica Review*, 10 (1): 23–38.

Goetz, A. M. and O'Brien, R. (1995) 'Governing for the Common Wealth? The World Bank's Approach to Poverty and Governance' in *IDS Bulletin*, 26 (2): 17–26.

Hann, C. and Dunn, E. (1996) 'Introduction: Political Society and Civil Anthropology' in C. Hann and E. Dunn (eds), *Civil Society: Challenging Western Models*, London and New York: Routledge: 1–26.

Judge, A. (2003) *Framing NGOs in the Market for Change: Comment on a Report by SustainAbility, the United Nations Global Compact and the UN Environment Programme: Laetus in praesens*. Online. Available at: www.laetusinpraesens.org/docs00s/mktchan.php (accessed 17 April 2008).

Kamat, S. (2004) 'The Privatization of Public Interest: Theorizing NGO Discourse in a Neoliberal Era' in *Review of International Political Economy*, 11 (1): 155–76.

Kerkvliet, B. J. T. (2009) 'Everyday Politics in Peasant Societies (and Ours)' in *Journal of Peasant Studies*, 36 (1): 227–43.

Lewis, D. J. (1997) 'NGOs, Donors, and the State in Bangladesh' in *Annals of the American Academy of Political Science*, 554: 33–45.

Mollinga, P. P. (2008) 'The Rational Organisation of Dissent: Boundary Concepts, Boundary Objects and Boundary Settings in the Interdisciplinarity Study of Natural

Resources Management', *ZEF Working Paper Series 33*, Bonn: Zentrum für Entwicklungsforschung.

Monga, C. (2009) 'Uncivil Societies: A Theory of Sociopolitical Change' in *Policy Research Working Paper No. 4942*, Washington, DC: World Bank.

Nevitt, C. E. (1996) 'Private Business Associations in China: Evidence of Civil Society or Local State Power? in *The China Journal*, 36: 25–43.

Sen, S. (1999) 'Some Aspects of State-NGO Relationships in India in the Post-Independence Era' in *Development and Change*, 30 (2): 327–55.

Stewart, S. (1997) 'Happy Ever after in the Marketplace: Non-Government Organisations and Uncivil Society' in *Review of African Political Economy*, 24 (71): 11–34.

SustainAbility (2003) *The 21st Century NGO: In the Market for Change*, London, New York and Paris: SustainAbility, the UN Global Compact, United Nations Environment Programme.

Tandon, R. (1994) 'Civil society, the State and the Role of NGOs' in I. Serrano (ed.), *Civil Society in the Asia-Pacific Region*, Washington, DC: CIVICUS.

White, G. (1994) 'Civil Society, Democratization and Development: Clearing the Analytical Ground' in *Democratization*, 1 (3): 375–90.

Appendix 1
Country profiles: Cambodia and Vietnam

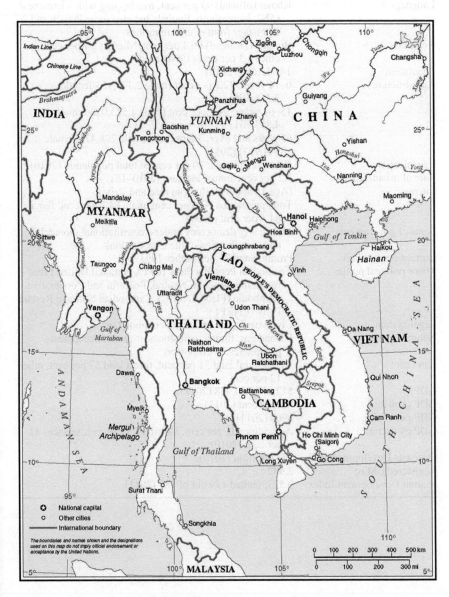

Figure A.1 The Greater Mekong Subregion.

Table A.1 Cambodia country profile

Official name:	Kingdom of Cambodia
Capital:	Phnom Penh
Major cities:	Seam Reap; Sihanoukville, Battambang
Area (total):	181,035 sq. km.
Ethnic groups:	Khmer 90 per cent, Vietnamese 5 per cent, Chinese 1 per cent, other 4 per cent
Languages:	Khmer (official) 95 per cent, overlapping with Vietnamese (5%), increasingly English, but also some French and languages from ethnic minorities
Religions:	Buddhist (official) 96.4 per cent, Muslim 2.1 per cent, other 1.3 per cent (1998 census)
Population:	14,952,665 (2012)
Age structure:	0–14 years: 32.2 per cent (male 2,375,155/female 2,356,305)
	15–64 years: 64.1 per cent (male 4,523,030/female 4,893,761)
	65 years and over: 3.8 per cent (male 208,473/female 344,993) (2011)
Urbanization:	Urban population: 20 per cent of total population (2010)
Rate of urbanization:	3.2 per cent annual increase (2010–15)
Literacy:	(Age 15 and over that can read and write)
	Total population 73.6 per cent, male 84.7 per cent, female 64.1 per cent (2004)
Form of government:	Multi-party democracy under a constitutional monarchy (since ratification of the Constitution)
Current constitution:	Promulgated 21 September 1993
Major political parties	Cambodian People's Party (CPP), National United Front for an Independent, Neutral, Peaceful and Cooperative Cambodia (FUNCINPEC), Cambodian National Rescue Party (CNRP)
Legal system:	Civil law system and some common law
Natural resources:	Oil and gas, timber, gemstones, iron ore, manganese, phosphates, hydropower
Land use:	Agricultural land 31 per cent, forest land 57 per cent, other 12 per cent
GDP:	$12,875,310,958 (2011)
GDP growth:	6.9 per cent (2011)
GDP per capita:	$900 (2011)
GDP by sector:	Agriculture 36 per cent, industry 23 per cent, services 41 per cent (2010)
Overseas Development Aid:	$737 million (2010)
Registered CSOs:	2,982
Human Development Index:	0.523, ranked 139 out of 187 (2011)

Table A.2 Vietnam country profile

Official name:	Socialist Republic of Viet Nam
Capital:	Hanoi
Major cities:	Ho Chi Minh City, Hanoi, Can Tho, Da Nang, Hai Phong
Area (total):	331,210 sq. km.
Ethnic groups:	Kinh (Viet) 85.7 per cent, Tay 1.9 per cent, Thai 1.8 per cent, Muong 1.5 per cent, Khmer 1.5 per cent, Mong 1.2 per cent, Nung 1.1 per cent, others 5.3 per cent (1999 census)
Languages:	Vietnamese (official), increasingly English, but also some French, Chinese, and Khmer, mountain area languages
Religions:	Non-religious 80.8 per cent, Buddhist 9.3 per cent, Catholic 6.7 per cent, Hoa Hao 1.5 per cent, Cao Dai 1.1 per cent, Protestant 0.5 per cent, Muslim 0.1 per cent (1999 census)
Population:	91,519,289 (2012)
Age structure:	0–14 years: 25.2 per cent (male 11,945,354/female 10,868,610)
	15–64 years: 69.3 per cent (male 31,301,879/female 31,419,306)
	65 years and over: 5.5 per cent (male 1,921,652/female 3,092,589) (2011)
Urbanization:	Urban population: 30 per cent of total population (2010)
Rate of urbanization:	3 per cent annual increase (2010–15)
Literacy:	(Age 15 and over can read and write)
	Total population 94 per cent, male 96 per cent, female 92 per cent (2002)
Form of government:	Communist state – single-party constitutional republic
Current constitution:	15 April 1992
Political party:	Communist Party of Vietnam
Legal system:	Civil law system
Natural resources:	Phosphates, coal, manganese, rare earth elements, bauxite, chromate, offshore oil and gas deposits, timber, hydropower
Land use:	Agricultural land 33 per cent, forest land 44 per cent, other 23 per cent (2010–11)
GDP:	$123,960,665,229 (2011)
GDP growth:	5.8 per cent (2011)
GDP per capita:	$1,411 (2011)
GDP by sector:	Agriculture 20 per cent, industry 41 per cent, services 40 per cent (2011)
Overseas Development Aid:	$2,945 million (2010)
Human Development Index:	0.572, ranked 116 out of 187 (2011)

Sources:
The World Factbook: https://www.cia.gov/library/publications/the-world-factbook/geos/cb.html
International Human Development Indicators: http://hdrstats.undp.org/en/countries/profiles/KHM.html
World Development Indicators: http://data.worldbank.org/indicator/

Appendix 2
Vietnamese legal documents on civil society (order of appearance in the book)

Table A.3 Vietnamese legal documents on civil society

Year	Name/Specification	Legal document number	Issuing organization
1946	1946 Constitution of the Democratic Republic of Vietnam		National Assembly of the Democratic Republic of Vietnam
1957	Law on the Establishment of Association	Law No. 102/SL/L004 of 5 May 1957	National Assembly
1957	Detailing the implementation of Law No. 102-SL/L004 of May 20, 1957 on Establishment of Association	Decree 258/TTg of 14 June 1957	Prime Minister
1992	Vietnamese Constitution		National Assembly of the Socialist Republic of Vietnam
1992	Decree on Science and Technology Management Task	Decree No. 35/HDBT of 28 January 1992	Council of Ministers
1996	Law on Cooperatives	Law No. 47/CTN of 20 March 1996	National Assembly
1998	Grassroots Democracy Decree	Decree No. 29/1998/ ND-CP of 11 May 1998 (later amended by Decree 79/2003/ND)	Government
1999	Law on Vietnam Fatherland Front	Law No. 14/1999/QH10 of 12 June 1999	National Assembly
1999	Law on Enterprises	Law No. 13/1999/QH10 of 12 June 1999	National Assembly
1999	Decree on the Organization and Operation of Social Funds and Charity Funds	Decree No. 177/1999/ ND-CP of 22 December 1999	Government
2000	Law on Science and Technology	Law No. 21/2000/QH10 of 9 June 2000	National Assembly

Year	Name/Specification	Legal document number	Issuing organization
2002	Decision on the Activities of Consultancy, Judgment and Social Expertise by the Vietnam Union of Science and Technology Associations	Decision No. 22/2002/ QD-TTg of 30 January 2002	Prime Minister
2003	Decree on Organization, Operation, and Management of Associations (Quy định tổ chức, hoạt động và quản lý Hội)	Decree No. 88/2003/ ND-CP of 30 July 2003	Government
2004	Guidance on Founding, Strengthening and Developing Water User Groups (Hướng dẫn việc thành lập, củng cố và phát triển tổ chức hợp tác dùng nước)	Circular No. 75/2004/ TT-BNN of 20 December 2004	MARD (Ministry of Agriculture and Rural Development)
2005	Civil Code	Civil Code No. 33/2005/QH11 of 14 June 2005	National Assembly
2007	Decree on the Organization and Operation of Cooperative Groups	Decree No. 151/2007/ ND-CP of 10 October 2007	Government
2008	Decision on NCFAW	Decision No. 114/2008/ QD-TTG of 22 August 2008	Prime Minister
2009	Decision on the List of domains in which individuals are allowed to establish science and technology organizations	Decision No. 97/2009/ QD-TTg of 24 July 2009	Prime Minister
2010	Decree on the Organization, Operation and Management of Associations (Quy định về tổ chức, hoạt động và quản lý hội)	Decree No. 45/2010/ ND-CP of 21 April 2010	Government

Glossary: Vietnamese and Khmer terms

Table G.1 Vietnamese terms

ấp văn hóa	'good hamlet'
hội	associations
bẩn	dirty
câu lạc bộ	club
Chỉ số hiệu quả hoạt động xây dựng và thi hành pháp luật kinh doanh	Ministerial Effectiveness Index
đoàn thể	mass organization
Chỉ số năng lực cạnh tranh cấp tỉnh	Provincial Competitiveness Index
chính nghĩa	exclusive righteousness
công	public (sphere)
công dân	citizen
Dân biết, dân bàn, dân làm, dân kiểm tra	people know, people discuss, people execute and people supervise
dân sự	civil/civic
Đổi mới	renovation
giáp	age groups/cohorts
hành chính hoá	administration policy
hương ước	village conventions/codes
hội đồng kỳ mục	(self-regulatory) village council (sixteenth century – 1945)
hội quần chúng	popular associations
hợp tác xã	cooperatives
cơ quan quản lý nhà nước	state-managed entity
kinh tế tập thể	collective economy
Liên hiệp các Hội Khoa học và Kỹ thuật Việt Nam	Vietnam Union of Science and Technology Association
kinh tế	economy, economic
kỳ dịch	executive (village) council (sixteenth century – 1921)
kỳ mục	legislative (village council) (sixteenth century – 1945)
kỳ lão	senior village advisory (sixteenth century – 1921)
Mạng lưới Sông ngòi Việt Nam	Vietnam Rivers Network
nhà nước hoá	nationalization policy
nhóm tín dụng	micro-credit groups
phản biện	critical feedback *continued*

phản biện, phản biện xã hội	advise, give critical feedback
phường	craft guilds
tập đoàn sản xuất	collective groups
tổ bơm tưới	irrigation groups
tổ chức phi chính phủ	organization not of the (main) government (NGO)
tổ chức chính trị xã hội, chuyên nghiệp	political, social, and professional organization
tổ chức xã hội tự nguyện	voluntary groups (Red River Delta)
tổ chức xã hội	civic organizations
tổ hợp tác sản xuất	production groups (Mekong Delta)
tư	family or private (sector)
quan	government officials (in ancient Vietnam)
văn hoá	culture
văn minh	civility, civilization
xã hội	society/social
xã hội công dân	civil society (society of citizens)
xã hội dân sự thông thái	knowledge-based civil society
xã hội dân sự	civil society (emphasizing the role of community)

Table G.2 Khmer terms

achar	Buddhist laymen, ritual specialists
angka (angkar)	organization – term often used for NGO; but historically different meaning
ataun oknia	indulgence
chbap srey	Women's Code of Conduct
chomnoh	dharma association fundraising group (for social welfare purposes)
devaraja	God – King
karma	accumulation of merit gained in current and former lives
kochorum robo sahakum	extended community, including administrators, families and monks; community participation
neak sahakum	member of the community/villagers
phdal amnach oy satrey	women's empowerment
Phka Rumduol	a modernized traditional rice variety
phum	village
pnort chas nouv dordeil	'old way of thinking'
punna	personal merit-making
sahakum	community: helping each other
samaki	solidarity
samakum	voluntary association of people
samakum prak	credit group (cash association)
samakum sraov	rice association
sangha (sanghka)	Buddhist order/Buddhist clergy
sangkat	downtown residential area (district)
sangkum	society (see also Sangkum Reastr Niyum)
sangkum civil	civil society
sangkum krusar	family matters
Sangkum Reastr Niyum	Great Society Period
srey kroup leakkh	a perfectly virtuous woman
wat	pagoda/temple

Index

Page numbers in *italics* denote tables.

Rouge 205–6; in Marxist-Leninist
ideology 82
associational forms, Vietnam 43–4
Australian Agency for International
Development (AusAID) 240
authoritarian regimes 3, 4, 10, 11;
deference to authority 239; one-party
state, Vietnam 39, 77, 84, 221, 230; *see
also* Khmer Rouge regime; Pol Pot
regime
authoritarian rule, within NGOs 196
auto-genocide, Cambodia 21, 26, 203
autonomy 41, 67, 126, 127, 173; and
community participation 117; as concept
62; financial 46; Gordan White on 22,
189; moral 82; from state 22, 50, 62, 72,
176, 178, 184, 189, 260; of Vietnam
Women's Union (VWU) 101; of women
143

Bach Tan Sinh 1, 9, 39–57, 255, 259, 260,
261
Baird, I. 66
Bajunid, O. F. 10
Bass, S. 66
Bebbington, A. J. 257
Benedikter, S. 62, 87, 218–36, 255, 259,
260
beneficiaries: accountability to 188, 189,
191, 196, 198; of development
intervention 6, 116, 118; NGOs
connection with 189, 194–5, 196;
participation 194
Bernader, B. 113
Beus, C. E. 237, 241, 243, 247
Biggs, D. 221
Biggs, S. D. 240
Bit, S. 206
Bloh, H. v. 222, 227
Blunt, P. 205
boat racing associations, Cambodia 210
Boeung Kak Lake campaign 69–70
boomerang strategy 69–70, 72
bottom-up development 26, 51, 123; critic
on NGOs 192; grassroots orientation of
NGOs 51
boundaries: between state and civil society
5, 6–7, 61, 219, 230, 260; and networks
61
Bourdier, F. 113–30, 254, 258, 260
Boyd, R. 257
Boyle, D. 245
Bratton, M. 259
Bridges across Borders 67

Brocheux, P. 83
Brown, D. 65
Brugha, R. 121
Buddhism 11; in Cambodia 26, 29–30,
189, 203, 204, 208–13; under the Khmer
Rouge 26, 208; merit-making 211–12,
213, 214; monks and nuns 208, 210,
212, 213, 215n1; pagodas *see* pagoda
associations; pagodas; in the People's
Republic of Kampuchea 208; political
co-optation of 212–13; politicization of
213; the *sangha* (clergy) 206, 208;
socially-engaged 214; in Vietnam 81, 85
Buddhism for Development 209
Buddhism for Social Development Action
(BSDA) 31, 32–3, 131, 209
Buddhism-oriented NGOs:
professionalization of 209; service
provision 209; social agendas 209; *see
also* Buddhism for Development;
Buddhism for Social Development
Action (BSDA)
Bui Quang Dung 172, 221, 222
Bui The Cuong 219, 259
Bukovansky, M. 78, 88
Bureau, E. 114, 124, 125
bureaucratization 118
Burnip, D. A. 190

Cambodia 1, 2, 10, 12, 13, 256, 259;
agricultural development 136, 237–52;
see also Cambodian Center for Research
and Development in Agriculture
(CEDAC); auto-genocide 21, 26, 203;
Buddhism 26, 29–30, 189, 203, 204,
208–13; civil society 1–2, 9, 12–13,
21–38, 61, 62, 63, 66–73, 113–30,
131–52, 157–66, 187–202, 190, 203–17,
237–52, 254–5, 256, 257, 258, 259,
260–1; civil war 21, 26, 30, 203, 205–6;
commune councils *see* commune
councils; community-based
organizations (CBOs) 2, 25, 27–8, 31,
33–4, 118, 131–52, 199n3, 204, 206–7;
community participation 23, 72, 115,
116–18, 120, 127, 135; decentralization
reform *see* decentralization reform;
democratization 13, 21, 24, 116, 203;
Department of Agronomy and
Agricultural Land Improvement
(DAALI) 241, 243; domestic violence
148; education 28, 205; fishing/fisheries
27, 28, 31, 33–4, 207, 209; gender
norms 131, 132–5, 147–8; health sector

discourse analysis: on civil society in
Vietnam by the media 171, 174, 183;
role of Vietnamese intellectuals 172–5,
177–82, 183–4
Dixon, C. 181
Đổi mới 13, 101, 177, 182; and
associational development 39, 179, 180,
220, 221, 229–30; and private business
219
domestic violence: in Cambodia 148;
donor policies 31, 100; state policies 99,
100; in Vietnam 94, 99, 100, 108n10;
and the Vietnam Women's Union
(VWU) 100; and women's rights 32; *see
also* International Convention on the
Elimination of all Forms of Violence
against Women (CEDAW)
Domestic Violence Prevention Network
(Dovipnet), Vietnam 94
donor policy: on agriculture 238, 239–40;
contestation 238; on domestic violence
31, 100; financial influence of 131,
191–2, 197; on gender 131; Global Fund
114, 120, 121, 122, 123, 124, 128n3; on
HIV/AIDS 118, 121–2; NGO promotion
5, 187
Downie, S. 205–6
Doyle, M. W. 24
Dunlap, R. E. 237, 241, 243, 247
Dunn, E. 6, 7, 9, 204, 260

Ear, S. 240, 242
Earth Summit (Rio de Janeiro, 1992) 5
East–West Management Institute (EWMI),
Program on Rights and Justice 68
Eastern Europe, political transformation in
1, 4, 77
Ebihara, M. 21, 23, 26, 132, 137, 188, 189,
206
Eckstein, H. 88
economic development 41, 53, 54, 179–80,
183, 226, 257; and gender relations 97,
99, 102, 132
economic liberalization/reform, Vietnam
39, 43, 45, 87, 94, 178, 219, 230; *see
also Đổi mới*
economy, privatized 79
education 61; Cambodia 28, 205; Vietnam
104
Edwards, B. 2
Edwards, M. 4, 5, 9, 21, 187, 189, 191,
197, 257
Ehlert, J. 203–17, 254–5, 260, 261
Ehrenberg, J. 3

elderly care, Cambodia 28
elitism 82
Ellis, F. 240
embedded advocacy 63, 65–6, 69, 72
employment: in NGOs 192–3; women and,
Cambodia 133–4
empowerment 117, 153, 155; Cambodian
women's groups as platform for 132,
136–46, 148–9; by CEDAC 136, 142;
and community participation 115, 117;
of farmers 136; of grassroots 51–2, 54,
67, 114, 125, 126, 127, 131, 163, 220;
NGOs and 192
Enlightenment 21; civil society concept 3;
European intellectual history 3
environment 9, 11, 61, 89; environmental
advocacy 63, 64–71, 157–66;
environmental impact assessment 65,
67, 164; and hydropower development
156–66; water and sanitation groups
84–7, 222, 227–8
equality 79, 81, 88, 89; *see also* gender
equality
ethics, of identifying civil society 260–1
European intellectual history: civil society
concept 3; Enlightenment 3
expert knowledge, and local knowledge
214

farmer associations, Cambodia 136, 143
farmer groups, Vietnam 51, 221–2, 223,
225, 229, 231; informal/formal 221;
producer cooperatives 221–2
Farmer and Nature Network, Cambodia
143
Farmer's Association, Vietnam 45, 224,
226, 227, *228*, 230, 231
Farmer's Association, Cambodia 246
Farrington, J. 257
Fatherland Front *see* Vietnam Fatherland
Front (VFF)
Federation of Labour, Vietnam 45
feminism: in Cambodia 131, 132, 149;
postmodern feminism 132, 149; in
Vietnam 95–6
Ferguson, A. 3
Ferguson, J. 257, 259
Feuer, H. 29, 237–52, 254
Fforde, A. 103, 221, 229, 237
Finlay, V. 11
fishing/fisheries, Cambodia 27, 28, 31,
33–4, 207, 209
Fitzgerald, D. 245
Foley, M. W. 2

For Product Safety Concerns and Information please contact our
EU representative GPSR@taylorandfrancis.com Taylor & Francis
Verlag GmbH, Kaufingerstraße 24, 80331 München, Germany